The Geography of China

An Annotated Bibliography
of pre-1974 English-Language
Journal Literature

In memory of
Howard F. Hirt, 1924–1987
and
Basheer K. Nijim, 1936–1991
who showed so many how to unlock the
excitement in the study of Asia's geography

The Geography of China

An Annotated Bibliography of pre-1974 English-Language Journal Literature

Roger Mark Selya

Published by the Association for Asian Studies, Inc.
Resources for Scholarship on Asia, Number 3.

© 2005 by the Association for Asian Studies, Inc.

All Rights Reserved. Written permission must be secured to use or reproduce any part of this book.

Published by:

Association for Asian Studies, Inc.
1021 East Huron Street
Ann Arbor, Michigan 48104 USA

www.aasianst.org

Cover Image: Photo courtesy of Imaginechina (www.imaginechina.com).

Library of Congress Cataloging-in-Publication Data

The Geography of China: An Annotated Bibliography of pre-1974 English-Language Journal Literature, edited by Roger Mark Selya.

p. cm.— (Resources for Scholarship on Asia; 3)
Includes bibliographical references and index.
ISBN 0-924304-46-4

1. China—Geography—Bibliography.
I. Selya, Roger Mark. II. Series.

Z3106.G46 2004
[DS706.7]
016.9151—dc22

2004057110

Acknowledgments

The completion and timely publication of this volume would not have been possible without the help of the many individuals. In particular I would like to thank the following:

The librarians and staff at the Baker, Biological Laboratories, Cabot Science, Comparative Zoology, Countway, Fairbank Center, Geology, Harvard-Yenching, Kennedy School, Lamont, Loeb, Pusey, Tozzer, and Widner Libraries at Harvard University for their assistance and kindness during the time I worked on this project while a visiting scholar at the John King Fairbank Center;

Rena Selya Cohen for retrieving materials I had overlooked, ignored, or was unaware of while working at Harvard;

Judy Moore, Hayfaa Wadih, Melissa Patterson, and Courtney Busemeyer of the Interlibrary Loan Department at the Langsam Library, University of Cincinnati, for their hard work, good cheer, and enthusiasm in obtaining photocopies of materials I had requested;

Sue Berry and the staff at the Southwest Ohio Depository Library for providing work space while I worked with materials in storage there;

The staff of the Lloyd Library, Cincinnati, for their interest in this project and assistance in accessing their resources;

Dr. Raymond Lum for guiding my proposal through the review process and advising me on technical details of the bibliography;

AAS Publications Manager Ann Beard, copyeditor Janet Opdyke, and designer Jonathan Wilson for their help in transforming my manuscript into a readable volume;

Of course, I am responsible for any omissions and misinterpretations of the content of the articles annotated.

Contents

Preface	ix
References Cited	xix
List of Journals Searched	xxiii
PART I: TOPICAL INDEX	1
1. Cartography and the History of Geography	3
2. Expeditions, Surveys, and Field Methods	23
3. Physical Geography: General	45
4. Climatology	49
5. Geomorphology	65
6. Biogeography, Soils, and Vegetation	73
7. Hydrology and Water Supply	83
8. Resources, Energy, and Minerals	97
9. Conservation and Environment	103
10. Human Geography: General	105
11. Population	159
12. Cultural and Historical Geography	173
13. Political Geography	191
14. Economic Geography: General	211
15. Agriculture	225
16. Industry	241
17. Transportation and Communications	255

Contents

18. Trade	271
19. Urban Geography	277
20. Regional Development and Planning	299
21. Tourism	303
PART II: AUTHOR INDEX	305
PART III: PLACE NAME INDEX	329

Preface

This volume is intended as a companion to my earlier bibliography devoted to the geography of China, which covered the period of Deng Xiaoping's influence (Selya 1992). As such, to the greatest extent possible I have followed the same methodology used to compile the materials included in the 1992 publication. Thus, an article was included if it was published in a geographical journal regardless of the disciplinary background of the author; if it was written by a geographer but published in a non-geographical journal; and if it was published in a non-geographical journal and fit into the four traditions of geography (spatial, area studies, man-land, and earth science) as identified by Pattison (1964), regardless of the disciplinary background of the author. One category in the 1992 volume—"Remote Sensing, Air Photo Interpretation, and Photogrammetry"—was eliminated, as no articles were found in this subject area.

The articles included here were identified by surveying the English-language geography journals listed in Harris and Fellmann 1971 and the English-language Asian studies journals available in the Harvard University Library system and at the University of Cincinnati. Access to the English-language geography materials was enhanced by the fact that the University of Cincinnati is the designated depository library for the exchange journal collection of the Association of American Geographers.

To ensure that the articles thus identified constituted a complete corpus of published work, they were then cross-checked with sources cited in the following:

1. Footnotes in the articles annotated

2. Bibliographies in the major English-language texts dealing with the geography of China (Buchanan 1970; Buxton 1929; Cressey 1934, 1955; deCrespigny 1971; Pannell and Ma 1983; Smith 1991; Treager 1980; Tuan 1969; Winfield 1948)

3. Items annotated in a previous bibliography of the geography of China by Herman (1967)

4. Materials in the *Bibliography of Asian Studies*, *Far Eastern Bibliography*, *Public Affairs Information Service*, and *Social Science Index*

5. The publications lists of major China geographers, as found in review articles, obituaries, the publication *Geographers: Biobibliographic Studies*, or curricula vitae

6. The *Research Catalogue of the American Geographical Society* (1962)

Items identified from these six types of sources were added to the original group. An occasional article published after 1975 was annotated if it was not included in the 1992 volume. Although the goal was to identify articles from the scholarly literature, materials from what appear to be more popular sources have been included. This was done for three reasons. First, in some cases, journals when first published were scholarly in orientation but at some point were deliberately changed to appeal to a broader audience (Freeman 1961; Rothenberg 1994). Second, geographers prior to the 1970s frequently published in a broad spectrum of journals. Yet it is often hard to discern any differences in content, style, or method between articles in professional and popular journals. Finally, standards of scholarship have changed radically over the years. What was an acceptable publication or presentation in the late nineteenth or early twentieth centuries would most likely not be publishable in 2004. Is it acceptable, therefore, to exclude older works that do not meet current standards? In the interest of providing as complete a record of the work of geographers as possible, articles from more popular journals have been included. The only materials not included from both types of journals are book reviews, abstracts of papers presented at professional meetings, news (the so-called "geographical record"), and editorials or opinion pieces if they were neither China nor geography related.

One major problem in preparing the bibliography was the issue of romanization of Chinese place names. Many of the articles were written before the publication of the first edition of Giles's *A Chinese-English Dictionary* (1892) or the development of the Wade-Giles romanization system. In addition, not every writer necessarily used the Wade-Giles system. Hence, the place names in the titles of articles often use very idiosyncratic romanization systems. Significantly, China geographers were well aware of the problems of romanization and the linguistic and professional obstacles of changing or modifying romanization systems. The reader will find numerous articles in both the "Cartography and the

Preface

History of Geography" and "Cultural and Historical Geography" sections of the bibliography, where the issue of romanization is debated and reviewed.

In order to ensure the maximum utility of the annotations and indices, I adopted the following romanization guidelines:

Original romanized spellings were kept in titles.

The annotations use the modern romanized spellings of the *pinyin* system, which has been adopted by the People's Republic of China.

In the place name index, original and Wade-Giles romanizations are included, with references to *pinyin* listings, which are considered the main listings.

The only exceptions to these guidelines are romanizations of non-Chinese names or Chinese names with well-known non-*pinyin* spellings such as Hong Kong or Canton. The main sources used to identify places with idiosyncratic romanizations were Playfair 1965 and Seltzer 1962. Proper *pinyin* spellings were drawn from Cohen 1998 and Zhao 1994.

The 1,280 articles annotated in this volume were written over a 141-year period from 1833 to 1974. During that time, geography as a discipline underwent major changes in the way data were collected, organized, analyzed, and interpreted. In order to appreciate how the changes in geography influenced both the content of the articles and my annotations, it is important to have a sense of the history of geography from around 1800 through 1974.

As with the other disciplines, modern geography emerged as part of a new "scientific" attempt to understand the earth in contrast to previous, religious forms of comprehension (Peet 1985). Yet delimiting the origins of modern geography is not an easy task, since the history and development of geography are closely tied not only to the scientific revolutions of the seventeenth and eighteenth centuries and the Enlightenment but to the development of imperialism and capitalism as well (Driver 1992). Attempts to clearly describe early modern geography are further clouded by the fact that academic geographers neither dealt adequately with new information generated by early explorers nor worked to advance the surveying and cartographic technologies so important to collecting and displaying data accurately (Freeman 1961). What is obvious, however, is that for each period in English and American social history, geography was linked to the ethos of the times. As such, geographers subscribed, for example, to the worldview of the early Victorians and generally assumed that Christianity and commerce were the two inseparable "pioneers" of civilization. Conversely, Victorians saw geography as the "science" of empire (Freeman 1980; Livingstone 1994). Early modern geography, then, was pragmatic and concerned with the commercial dangers associated with geographic ignorance of the crops and trade potential of foreign lands and infused with missionary zeal (Freeman 1961, 1980). However, geography during the age of empire was more than simply a tool of capitalism or cultural and political imperialism. Exploration for its own sake was equally important. Thus, the practitioners of early modern geography were a heterogeneous group of explorers, hunters, soldiers, missionaries, administrators, and gentlemen (Driver 1992). And, although tensions frequently developed between academic geographers and the practitioners of colonial geography, their vocabularies, worldviews, and methodologies frequently overlapped and intermingled (Claval 1994; Livingstone 1994). A set of parallel tensions and conflicts frequently developed between geographic learned societies over what ought to be the relative balance between exploration, geographic research, and geographic education (Freeman 1961, 1980). What is of interest is that tensions within and between geographic societies were frequently displayed in the topical emphasis found in the research or exploration projects that were funded, the papers presented at geographic meetings, and the articles published in journals and proceedings.

The intellectual roots of modern geography can be traced to two sets of influences. On the one hand, there are the writings and lectures of the philosopher Immanuel Kant, whose rejection of teleological explanations and the concern for final causes was clearly articulated in his concern for physical geography and in his descriptions of the features of the earth, human races, and landscapes as modified by human action, a theme developed early in the nineteenth century by George Perkins Marsh (James and Martin 1981). On the other hand, there were geographers, such as Alexander von Humboldt and Carl Ritter, who, while sharing with Kant the notion that geography was an emperical science and not merely a dull and lifeless summary of facts about places mingled with descriptions of curiosities, were concerned with achieving a synthesis of the new concepts and methods of study that had developed as a result of the Age of Exploration. As such, von Humboldt and Ritter mark the end of the classical period and the beginning of the modern period of geography. What set Ritter apart from modern geographers in particular was his search for meaning based on a deep belief in teleogical explanations.

Preface

Von Humboldt and Ritter nevertheless represent two important approaches to the practice of geography. Von Humboldt was an explorer who insisted on doing fieldwork, while Ritter was an academic who saw the advantages of fieldwork but also saw value in incorporating into his work the results of fieldwork conducted by others.

As the nineteenth century proceeded, the issues of defining geography and delimiting the relationships among generalizations or theory and knowledge of specific places were heavily debated. One China geographer, Baron Ferdinand von Richthofen, was especially influential. He saw the purpose of geography as focusing attention on the interrelationships among diverse phenomena that occur across space. According to von Richthofen, studies of specific places or regions provide the data necessary for deriving more general statements about processes operating on the earth's surface. Without question, however, for von Richthofen, the study of geography started with physical phenomena and processes.

In contrast, Friedrich Ratzel, who did fieldwork in the United States and Mexico, saw human activities as the appropriate focus of geography. It was Ratzel in the end who was the more influential in part because he saw the need to explore and include the methodological and social implications of Darwinism, and especially social Darwinism, in geography. The result was the introduction into geography of environmental determinism. In many ways, the development of environmental determinism incorporated the views of both von Richthofen and Ratzel. After all, according to environmental determinism human behavior could only be understood in the context of the environmental constraints imposed on human choices. The adoption of environmental determinism then can be seen both as an attempt to explain the important events of life in the late nineteenth and early twentieth centuries and as geography's attempt to integrate the findings of Darwin into its research (Peet 1985). There is no question that social Darwinism, with its emphasis on struggle, hierarchy, and the need for lebensraum, was incorporated into the assumptions and interpretations of geography. Although later geographers tried to distance themselves from strict determinism and social Darwinsim, for the better part of the late nineteenth and early twentieth centuries geographers assumed that human beings were passive objects subject to the direct impact and influence of the environment. A related corollary of environmental determinism was diffusionism, which postulated that all higher forms of civilization originated in the West and then diffused to the rest of the world (Blaut 1993). Missionaries commonly presented their materials through the lenses of both environmental determinism and diffusionism. By the first decades of the twentieth century, an alternative paradigm, regional geography, challenged the methodological hold of determinism. The goal of regional geography was to describe a region as fully as possible. A complete geography then included materials on an area's physical environment followed by a description of the population, culture, and economy of the area. Both the order of the topics and the explanatory framework of regional geography drew heavily on determinism but without the necessary causal links (Hartshorne 1961). By the 1940s, environmental determinism had been repudiated by geographers because of its incompleteness, erroneous assumptions, inductive leaps, and misuse by those in politics and the eugenics movement. In the 1960s, regional geography was rejected as being too descriptive. A more quantitative approach employing the assumptions of logical positivism then came to dominate geographic work.

Virtually all of the trends and issues in the development of modern geography are reflected in the materials covering the geography of China. The most noticeable of the influences on the changing nature of geography as a discipline is found in the high percentage of articles in the bibliography included in the categories of exploration (8.5 percent) and general human geography (15.2 percent). Almost one-quarter of the articles clearly reflect the fact that well into the nineteenth century there was literally no clear definition of what it meant to be a scientist (Huff 1993) let alone a geographer. As late as 1930, Sir Charles Close, exercising his rights as president the Royal Geographical Society, marked the centenary of his organization by claiming that the lack of a precise definition of either a geographer or proper geographical training was an asset to geography (Freeman 1980). Thus, for well over a century the publications of those claiming to be geographers were often rambling, somewhat disorganized, discursive, and laden with details. The details covered a wide range of physical, cultural, economic, and political topics. In contrast to geographers who wrote with a deterministic orientation, often there was no clear order to the explorers' reports. Rather, explorers appear to have adopted a form of presentation that I have labeled the itinerary format. Quite literally, the papers of explorers commonly provide an hour-by-hour and day-by-day description of virtually every detail of an expedition. Thus, information about what time the members of an expedition rose, what they ate at each meal, where they slept, what transportation or logistical challenges they met, how the expedition was received by local officials, or what the weather was like was commonly mixed in with the substantive or scientific findings of a trip. In contrast, soldiers and government officials, even when using the itinerary format, tended to stress practical issues such as trade and regional development potential, the importance of a military presence along major rivers and coasts to protect Western interests, or the need to continually survey areas to ensure that the navies had accurate maps.

The widespread use of an itinerary format, a determinist framework, or a diffusionism argument did present problems when deciding under which category to put an article. This was particularly true for the categories of exploration and general human geography. In deciding which of these two categories was most appropriate for any one article, I tended to look toward the intent of the report and the background of the writer. If the presentation was intended to quite literally provide a "scientific" report of an expedition that had been funded by the geographic society before which the paper was presented, then the article was placed under the category of exploration. If, however, the purpose of the report was to portray the general impressions of a trip, it was put in the general human geography category. Commonly, works by military personnel and explorers seemed to better fit the exploration category, while those of government officials or missionaries seemed better suited to the general human geography category.

In terms of the content and tone of China-related articles, with the exception of the diffusionism debate, in many ways China escaped the more extreme, and often racist, evaluations at the hands of determinists, in part because China and the Chinese were considered "honorary whites" (Rothenberg 1994). Because of this status, not only was China portrayed in a favorable light but pictures of Chinese women were respectful and did not reflect the over-eroticization of women so often seen in reports of other non-European cultures. However, with regard to pictures in general, China was treated as just another exotic area: frequently pictures accompanying an article had absolutely no link or relevance to the texts they accompanied.

Geographers practicing in the late-twentieth and early-twenty-first centuries often reject research findings from earlier periods since they were the products of now repudiated research methods or political ideologies. This being the case, it is reasonable to ask what the purpose or utility of an annotated bibliography of research published in the nineteenth and twentieth centuries could be. Several justifications can be offered. First, at one level each of the articles tells a story, apart from the actual

Preface

content. The story, in fact, is a very contemporary and universal one featuring the anxiety, confusion, and even terror of traveling to a strange place for the first time and making sense out of what is seen. An additional anxiety that underlies many articles is the fear of not being able to deliver a promised result to a sponsoring agency. In fact, no amount of background or competence in language, history, politics, sociology, literature, and even geography can truly prepare one for the shock of arrival in a new environment such as that of China. These concerns are as true today as they must have been in 1800 or 1900. So as we read the material included in these old reports we cannot help but marvel at the bravery of the authors, who struggled to interpret what they experienced for themselves and others. Recognizing this past struggle and the inclination of contemporary readers to reject an early report's perspective and contents should at a minimum provide a new scholar with a sense of the humility and caution that must accompany our work and its presentation. One future research area coming out of this observation would focus on the authors of the articles. Who were they? What were their educational and social backgrounds? How did they wind up in China? What type of careers did they have, especially once they left the China scene?

Second, the articles represent the locus classicus of our identification and understanding of numerous contemporary problems in China. Typical examples would include the questions: is China over-populated, can China feed itself, does China have sufficient resources, and is cross-cultural contact without sinification of the non-Han group possible? By reading these original papers, we can gain a better understanding of how past assumptions, methods, and perspectives have helped to shape contemporary understanding. This permits us to ask whether or not the original assumptions, methods of analysis, and conclusions are still valid. At worst, then, reading these old materials can help us to avoid some of the methodological mistakes of the past when addressing what appear to be new problems.

Third, the impact of politics on geographers and geographic research agendas can also be derived from a study of the articles. During the late nineteenth and early twentieth centuries, it is clear that there was a direct link between politics and geographic research and writing. However, this impact was not limited to empire and the priorities of colonialism. For example, in the post-1949 period the combination of a U.S.-sponsored political and economic embargo of the People's Republic of China and China's self-imposed isolation had direct and immediate effects on geographic research. No longer able to do fieldwork, geographers, once their store of field research was exhausted, instead debated the wisdom of five-year plans, attempted to evaluate their impact using the limited hard data available from China, or critiqued and rejected Chinese claims of success based on what were seen as faulty data. When a new generation of China geographers later sought field experience in a Chinese environment, the only possibilities were Hong Kong and Taiwan. Once China came out of its isolation and the United Nations and the United States recognized the People's Republic as the sole government of China, new opportunities for direct contact with China presented themselves. As a result, the numbers, content, and methodologies of geographical research on China shifted again.

Fourth, the current bibliography clearly provides a quantitative measure of how fully geographers have explored China. In reality, given China's size, population, and cultural, urban, and economic complexity, only a fraction of what could or should be studied by geographers actually has been. In all, the place name index contains entries for some 437 different places or features. Within this number, all but two of the pre-1949 provinces are listed. Yet provincial coverage is very uneven: material about Tibet (96 articles), Manuchuria (73), Yunnan (50), Taiwan (49), and Xinjiang (23) predominate. Similarly, while some 159 cities are listed in the index, 13—Hong Kong (70 articles), Beijing (41), Shanghai (27), Lhasa (18), Hankou (17), Canton (14), Macao (14), Tianjin (10), Hangzhou (7), Xian (7), Chongqing (5), and Nanjing (4)—account for 59 percent of the urban articles. The bias in studies of rivers or mountains is equally obvious. What is interesting is that fact that historically non-Chinese areas or areas under non-Chinese domination as well as non-Chinese cities predominate in the lists of places most heavily studied. While this may reflect political concerns or realities, the observation nevertheless leads to the conclusion that the geographical coverage of China was extremely uneven.

Finally, it appears that there is a renewed interest in, and greater appreciation of geography within Asian studies: witness the six articles that appeared in the August 2000 issue of the *Journal of Asian Studies* *(JAS)*—Elliott 2000; Oakes 2000; Ramaswamy 2000; Wigen 2000; Winichakul 2000; Yonemoto 2000; later articles by Agrawal (2001); Atwell (2002); Bello (2003); Colombijn (2003); Francks (2002); Li (2001); Ludden (2003); van Schendel (2003), and the entire spring 1998 issue of *Education About Asia* (Vol. 3:1) devoted to the teaching of the geography of Asia. This interest seems to be multidimensional, focusing on the facts of geography as well as the conceptual, methdological, and theoretical insights available from studying geographic research. Further, the six articles in the August 2000 *JAS* stress heavily what is termed historical geography. The annotated materials in this bibliography will provide a basis for researchers to access the very materials needed in order to extend for China this more general interest in geography.

In short, an annotated bibliography of the materials published up to 1974 can develop an appreciation of what has been studied and what is known as well as help frame the research that still needs to be done.

References Cited

AGRAWAL, ARUN. 2001. State Formation in Community Spaces? Recentralization of Controls over Forests in the Kuamon Himalaya, India, *Journal of Asian Studies* 60: 9–40.

ATWELL, WILLIAM S. 2002. Time, Money, and the Weather: Ming China and the "Great Depression" of the Mid-Fifteenth Century, *Journal of Asian Studies* 61: 83–114.

BELLO, DAVID. 2003. The Venemous Course of Southwestern Opium: Qing Prohibition in Yunnan, Sichuan, and Guizhou in the Early Ninteenth Century, *Journal of Asian Studies* 62: 1109–42.

BLAUT, J. M. 1993. *The Colonizer's Model of the World: Geographical Duffusionism and Eurocentric History*. New York: Guilford Press.

BUCHANAN, KEITH. 1970. *The Transformation of the Chinese Earth: Perspectives on Modern China*. London: G. Bell and Sons.

BUXTON, L. H. DUDLEY, ed. 1929. *China: The Land and the People*. Oxford: Oxford University Press.

CLAVAL, PAUL. 1994. Playing with Mirrors: The British Empire according to Albert Demangeon, 228–43. In *Geography and Empire*, edited by Anne Godlawska and Neil Smith. Malden, MA: Blackwells.

COHEN, SAUL B., ed. 1998. *Columbia Gazetteer of the World*. New York: Columbia University Press.

COLOMBIJN, FREEK. 2003. The Volotile State in Southeast Asia: Evidence from Sumatra, 1600–1860, *Journal of Asian Studies* 62: 497–530.

CRESSEY, GEORGE B. 1934. *China's Geographic Foundations: A Survey of the Land and the People*. New York: McGraw-Hill.

———. 1955. *Land of the 500 Million: A Geography of China*. New York: McGraw-Hill.

References Cited

DECRESPIGNY, R. R. C. 1971. *China: The Land and Its People*. New York: St Martin's Press.

DRIVER, FELIX. 1992. Geographic Empire: Histories of Geographical Knowledge, *Environment and Planning D* 10: 23–40.

ELLIOTT, MARK C. 2000. The Limits of Tartary: Manchuria in Imperial and National Geographies, *Journal of Asian Studies* 59: 603–46.

FRANCKS, PENELOPE. 2002. Rural Industry, Growth Links, and Economic Development of Ninteenth-Century Japan, *Journal of Asian Studies* 61: 33–56.

FREEMAN, T. W. 1961. *A Hundred Years of Geography*. Chicago: Aldine.

———. 1980. The Royal Geographical Society and the Development of Geography, 1–99. In *Geography Yesterday and Tomorrow*, edited by E. H. Brown. Oxford: Oxford University Press.

GILES, HERBERT A. 1892. *A Chinese-English Dictionary*. London: B. Quaritch.

HARRIS, CHAUNCY D., and JEROME FELLMANN. 1971. *International List of Geographical Serials*. 2nd ed. Research Papers, no. 138. Chicago: University of Chicago, Department of Geography.

HARTSHORNE, RICHARD. 1961. *The Nature of Geography: A Critical Survey of Current Thought in the Light of the Past*. Lancaster, PA: Association of American Geographers. Reprint of *Annals, Association of American Geographers* 19: 1–2, pp. 1–504 (1929).

HERMAN, THEODORE, ed. 1967. *The Geography of China: A Selected and Annotated Bibliography*. Occasional Publications, no. 7. New York: Foreign Area Materials Center, State University of New York, State Education Department.

HUFF, TOBY E. 1993. *The Rise of Early Modern Science: Islam, China, and the West*. New York: Cambridge University Press.

JAMES, PRESTON E., and GEOFFREY J. MARTIN. 1981. *All Possible Worlds: A History of Geographic Ideas*. 2nd edition. New York: John Wiley and Sons.

LI, TANIA MURRAY. 2001. Relational Histories and the Production of Differences in Sulawesi's Upland Frontier, *Journal of Asian Studies* 60: 41–66.

LIVINGSTONE, DAVID N. 1994. Climate's Moral Economy: Science, Race and Place in Post-Darwinian British and American Geography, 132–54. In *Geography and Empire*, edited by Anne Godlawska and Neil Smith. Malden, MA: Blackwells.

LUDDEN, DAVID. 2003. Presidential Address. Maps in the Mind and the Mobility of Asia, *Journal of Asian Studies* 62: 1057–78.

OAKES, TIM. 2000. China's Provincial Identities: Reviving Regionalism and Reinventing "Chineseness." *Journal of Asian Studies* 59: 667–92.

PANNELL, CLIFTON W., and LAURENCE J. C. MA. 1983. *China: The Geography of Development and Modernization*. London: Edward Arnold.

PEET, RICHARD. 1985. The Social Origins of Environmental Determinism. *Annals, Association of American Geographers* 75: 309–33.

PLAYFAIR, G. M. H. 1965. *The Cities and Towns of China: A Geographical Dictionary*. 2nd edition. Taipei: Literature House. Reprint of the 1910 edition bearing the imprint of Kelly and Walsh, Shanghai.

RAMASWAMY, SUMATHI. 2000. History at Land's End: Lemuria in Tamil Spatial Fables. *Journal of Asian Studies* 59: 575–602.

Research Catalogue of the American Geographical Society. 1992. Boston: G. K. Hall.

ROTHENBERG, TAMAR Y. 1994. Voyeurs of Imperialism: The National Geographic Magazine before World War II, 155–72. In *Geography and Empire*, edited by Anne Godlawska and Neil Smith. Malden, MA: Blackwells.

SELTZER, LEON E., ed. 1962. *The Columbia Lippincott Gazetteer of the World*. New York: Columbia University Press.

SELYA, ROGER MARK, ed. 1992. *The Geography of China, 1975–1991: An Annotated Bibliography*. East Lansing: Asian Studies Center, Michigan State University.

References Cited

SMITH, CHRISTOPHER, J. 1991. *China: People and Places in the Land of One Billion*. Boulder, CO: Westview Press.

TREAGER, T. R. 1980. *China: A Geographical Survey*. New York: Halsted Press.

TUAN, YI-FU. 1969. *China*. Chicago: Aldine.

VAN SCHENDEL, WILLIAM. 2002. Stateless in South Asia: The Making of the India-Bangladesh Enclaves, *Journal of Asian Studies* 61: 115–48.

WIGEN, KAREN. 2000. Teaching about Home: Geography at Work in the Prewar Nagano Classroom. *Journal of Asian Studies* 59: 550–74.

WINFIELD, GERALD F. 1948. *China: The Land and the People*. New York: W. Sloane Associates.

WINICHAKUL, THONGCHAI. 2000. The Quest for *"Siwilai"*: A Geographical Discourse of Civilization Thinking in Late-Nineteenth and Early-Twentieth-Century Siam. *Journal of Asian Studies* 59: 528–49.

YONEMOTO, MARCIA. 2000. The "Spatial Vernacular" in Early Modern Japan: Knowledge, Power, and Pleasure in the Form of a Map. *Journal of Asian Studies* 59: 647–66.

ZHAO, SONGQIAO. 1994. *Geography of China: Environment, Resources, Population, and Development*. New York: John Wiley and Sons.

List of Journals Searched

Amerasia
American Meteorological Society, Bulletin
Annals, American Academy of Political and Social Science
Annals, Association of American Geographers
Antipode
Asia and the Americas
Asian Affairs
Asian and African Studies
Asian Outlook
Asian Survey
Asiatic Journal, new series
Asiatic Review
Australian Geographer
Australian Geographic Magazine
British Columbia Geographical Series
Bulletin, American Geographical Society
Bulletin, American Geographical Society of New York
Bulletin, Geographical Society of Philadelphia
Canadian Geographer
Canadian Geographical Journal
Canadian Geographical Magazine
China Critic
China Journal
China Journal of Science and Arts
China Quarterly
China Review
Chinese Economic Journal
Current History

List of Journals Searched

East Midland Geographer
Economic Development and Cultural Change
Economic Geography
Ecumene
Ekistics
Far Eastern Quarterly
Far Eastern Review
Far Eastern Survey
Foreign Affairs
Focus
Geoforum
Geografia-Karachi
Geographia Polonia
Geographical Analysis
Geographical Digest
Geographical Journal
Geographical Magazine
Geographical Review
Geographical Reports of Tokyo Metropolitan University
Geography
Harvard Journal of Asiatic Studies
Imago Mundi
Indian Geographer
Indian Geographical Journal
Irish Geography
Journal of the American Geographical Society {of New York}
Journal of Asian and African Studies
Journal of Asian History
Journal of Asian Studies
Journal of Contemporary Asia
Journal of Developing Areas

List of Journals Searched

Journal of Geography
Journal of Historical Geography
Journal, Manchester Geographical Society
Journal of Meteorology
Journal, Royal Asiatic Society, Hong Kong Branch
Journal, Royal Asiatic Society, North China Branch
Journal, Royal Central Asiatic Society
Journal, Royal Geographical Society
Journal of Tropical Geography
Malaysian Journal of Tropical Geography
Modern Asian Studies
National Geographical Journal of India
National Geographic Magazine
New Zealand Geographer
New Zealand Geographical Society Record
Nigerian Geographical Journal
Norsk Geografisk Tidsskrift
Oriental Geographer
Pacific Affairs
Pacific Viewpoint
Proceedings, Association of American Geographers
Proceedings, International Geographical Union
Proceedings of the Royal Geographical Society and Monthly Record of Geography
Proceedings, Royal Geographical Society
Proceedings, Royal Geographical Society of London
Professional Geographer
Scottish Geographical Magazine
Singapore Journal of Tropical Geography
Soviet Geography: Review and Translation
Surveying and Mapping
The Geographer-Aligar University

List of Journals Searched

Tijdschrift voor economische en sociale geografie
T'oung Pao
Town Planning Review
Transactions, Institute of British Geographers
Transactions, Royal Asiatic Society, China Branch
Virginia Geographer
Weather
Yearbook of the Association of Pacific Coast Geographers
Yenching Journal of Social Science

Part I

Topical Index

1. Cartography and the History of Geography

0001. ANON. Mr. Fergusson's Map of the Lolo Country, *Geographical Journal* 36, 1910, 438–39. Map, p. 512.

> Describes map as complimentary to one published in *Geographical Journal* 32, 1908, 648. The first map plots the area south of the Tong River, while the current one includes the area in Sichuan west of the Min but north of the Tong. Criticizes earlier maps of area as being too small.

0002. ANON. Notes on Construction of the Karakorum Map to be Published in April [1940], *Geographical Journal* 95, 1940, 299.

> Describes the mapping and printing techniques used in preparing the map at a scale of 1:750,000 for elevations between 3,000 and 28,000 feet.

0003. ANON. The Story of a Chinese Map, *Imago Mundi* 6, 1965, 76–78.

> "Map" discussed is actually a set of twenty on one roll. Describes areas covered in each of the maps. Assumes map dates to circa 1746 and may be a rough copy of a 1744 map from a *Geography of the Empire* done by unnamed Jesuits. Provenance of map reviewed as well as the history of the map's critics.

0004. ANTE, Robert. JPRS: A Source for Geographic Literature on China, *Geographical Review* 52, 1962, 442–44.

> Describes joint publication research program, current contents, and how to access publications.

0005. AUROUSSEAU, M. Suggested Principles for the Use and Spelling of Geographical Names—Part II, *Geographical Journal* 100, 1942, 245–56.

> Broad linguistically and technically oriented discourse on history of Royal Geographical Society's consultations leading to the development of the preferred spelling system known as RGSII. Main focus of report is on Chinese place names, although other Asian countries are mentioned.

0006. BADDELEY, J. F. Father Matteo Ricci's Chinese World Maps, 1584–1608, *Geographical Journal* 50, 1917, 254–70.

> Reviews earlier studies of Ricci's maps. Describes the maps, including the Chinese annotations on them, such as place names, explanations, and descriptions. Contrasts the value of the maps to Europe and China.

0007. BELL, G. J. Father Ernesto Gherzi, S.J., 1886–1973: An Appreciation, *Weather* 29, 1974, 184–89.

Describes the life and work of Father Gherzi, a well-known scientist who worked along the China coast between 1910 and 1954. Between and 1930 and 1954 he was the director of the Zikawei Observatory in Shanghai. Father Gherzi was a practical meteorologist and insisted on fieldwork to collect data. International memberships and a publications list are included.

0008. BURRILL, Meredith F. Rejoinder to a Review of "Decisions on Names in China" by Erwin Raisz in the *Professional Geographer*, vol. IV, no. 5, p. 29, *Professional Geographer* 5:1, 1953, 5–7.

Contests Raisz's interpretation [item 0063 below] that changes made by the Board on Geographic Names regarding the spelling of Chinese place names is of limited use. Argues that it is incorrect to say, as Raisz did, that earlier versions of Chinese place names were misspelled, as China uses a character system; that many Chinese place names are actually not Chinese at all and rely on a system of transliteration first devised by Ariel Stein; and that there are long-standing name and spelling conventions that ought to be observed and preserved despite the rules of competing transliteration systems. Further criticizes Raisz for advocating use of spelling as found in the *China Postal Atlas* (Nanking: Ministry of Communications, Directorate-General of Posts, 1936), as it lacks a guide/index and for overlooking the disadvantages of using the Wade-Giles system of romanization. Concludes that to characterize the Board on Geographic Names action as radical, as Raisz did, is an overstatement, as there had been no revisions to recommended spellings for Chinese place names for over ten years.

0009. CARLES, W. R. Problems in Exploration II: Ordos, *Geographical Journal* 33, 1909, 668–79.

A comparison and contrast of the European literature from Marco Polo on regarding the agriculture, ethnography, geomorphology, hydrology, and need for irrigation of the Ordos.

0010. CARLES, W. R. Richthofen's China, *Geographical Journal* 41, 1913, 562–69.

Review of von Richthofen's three-volume study, published posthumously in 1912. Main focus of review is on volume 3, *South China*, which is defined as the territory south of the Qinling Mountains and their extensions. The South is then further subdivided into seven areas. Comments admiringly on von Richthofen's wide range of interests and cites his insights into physical and economic geography, especially manufacturing and agricultural practices.

0011. CARR, William K. Some Characteristics of Chinese Place Names, *Asian Survey* 1:6, 1961, 25–29.

Reviews general problems of romanization and provides some guidelines for interpreting names in the form of several vocabulary lists. Notes complications that can arise when no clear distinctions are made between official and colloquial names, when places are listed by dialects other than *guoyu*, and when a foreign presence creates yet another set of toponyms. Recommends that spellings adopted by the U.S. Department of the Interior Board on Geographic Names be used in scholarly reports.

0012. CHANG, Chi-yun. Geographic Research in China, *Annals, Association of American Geographers* 34, 1944, 47–62.

Surveys the twenty years of work by Ting Yen-kiang, Wong Wen-hao, and Chu Co-ching and their students. Description of works follows a sixteenfold topical classification.

0013. CHANG, Kuei-sheng. Geography of Contemporary China: Inventory and Prospect, *Professional Geographer* 27, 1975, 2–6.

Analysis based on 2,938 items available from the U.S. Joint Publications Research Service. Argues that there is no single explanation for why Chinese geographers appear to concentrate their efforts in the areas of physical and economic geography. Notes that the Great Leap Forward had little positive effect on geographic research, with the possible exception of physical geography. Urges readers to consult the publications of the U.S. Congress Joint Committee on Economics. Lists journals that may contain China geography materials. Awaits the fruits of the Nixon opening to China in the form of fieldwork by geographers in China.

0014. CHANG, Kuei-sheng. The Ming Maritime Enterprise and China's Knowledge of Africa prior to the Age of Great Discoveries, *Terrae Incognita* 3, 1971, 33–44.

Chronicles the 1405 to 1433 voyages of Cheng Ho and the reasons why they were undertaken. Includes detailed analysis of maps for voyages. Seeks to answer the question as to why the Chinese never circumnavigated Africa, as it was technically feasible. There appear to be three reasons: limited time before the expeditions were canceled, the successful discovery of a sea route to the ports with access to the Near East, and the fact that Cheng, being a Muslim, was not interested in the problem. Notes lack of interest in African areas that were discovered, as they had little to offer China in terms of trade potential.

0015. CHANG, Sen-dou. Manuscript Maps in Late Imperial China, *Canadian Cartographer* 11, 1974, 1–14.

Review based on materials in the oriental map collections at the Library of Congress and British Museum. Discusses map orientation, color selection, symbolization, purposes, and role of ideological distortion based on *fengshui* of Chinese maps. Notes that most maps reviewed were for administrative purposes and thus are based on a rigid geometric grid system.

0016. CHEN, Cheng-siang. Ups and Downs of "Acta Geographia Sinica:" Some Personal Observations, *Geographical Review* 57, 1967, 108–11.

Reviews impact of a wide range of historical events, including the Japanese invasion, the Chinese Civil War, and the Great Leap Forward on what is termed the leading Chinese geographical journal. Notes changes in number of issues per year as well as shifts in the number of articles published and their content. The latter is especially evident with more emphasis on the needs of economic development in general and the desire to increase agricultural production in particular. Overall, sees an improvement in style, originality, and critical attitudes in articles, although suggests that there is room for improvement in maps, photographs, and a livelier style.

0017. CH'EN, Kenneth. A Possible Source for Ricci's Notices on Regions Near China, *T'oung Pao*, ser. 2, 34, 1938, 179–90.

Assumed that Ricci used the following source maps when drafting maps in China: the 1569 Mercator, the 1570 Ortelius, and the 1592 Plancius. Chinese sources consist mainly of Ma tuan-lin's *Wen Hsien*.

0018. CH'EN, Kenneth. Early Expansion of Chinese Geographical Knowledge, *T'ien Hsia Monthly* 12, 1940–41, 53–63.

Seeks to refute notion that China's "splendid" isolation lasted for centuries, with no care or concern for foreign areas. Focuses on pre-Han, early Han, and later Buddhist explorers such as Chang Ch'ien, Pan Ch'ao, Fa Hsien, and Yuan Chwang. Identifies specific locations of geographic concepts in classicial literature. These references clearly indicate that China knew of Rome, India, and Southeast Asia, was concerned with nomenclature and transliteration of place names, and had a highly developed cartography. The major impact of the Jesuits on China's geographical knowledge was to increase the size of the body of knowledge and China's perception of the size of the world.

0019. CH'EN, Kenneth. Matteo Ricci's Contribution to and Influence on Geographical Knowledge in China, *Journal, American Oriental Society* 59, 1939, 325–59.

Focus of discussion is Ricci's 1584 map of the world done at Chaojing, Guangdong. Retells the history of Ricci and other Jesuits in China. Provides information on the actual location of the map in 1939. Analyzes Ricci's introduction to the maps. Describes the contributions of the map to Chinese geographical awareness, the map's errors, and the causes for the rapid decline of Ricci's influence on Chinese cartography and geography.

0020. COOPER, J. J. The Mapping of Hong Kong, *Journal, Hong Kong Branch, Royal Asiatic Society* 9, 1969, 131–40.

Describes process and progress of 1954 updating of 1899–1904 maps by the Indian Survey. Includes catalog of which maps are available, by source, data, and number of sheets.

0021. CRESSEY, George B. Some Recent Geographical Studies, *Geographical Review* 26, 1936, 504–7.

Describes Chinese publications dealing with climate, soils, agriculture, population, geomorphology, and regional geography.

0022. CRESSEY, George B. Source Material on Communist China, *Professional Geographer* 7:5, 1955, 3–4.

Covers four major topics: quantitative data on heavy industry output for prewar, 1954, and estimated 1957 periods; improvements in railroads; plans for damming the Huang He; and which Chinese and Western popular journals, such as *China Reconstructs* and the *Far Eastern Economic Review*, are useful sources of information.

0023. DARLEY, James M. The Society's New Map of China, *National Geographic Magazine* 87, 1945, 745–46.

Describes the Chinese, English, Japanese, Russian, and U.S. sources used in compiling the map. Touches on difficulties in deciding on the romanization of Chinese place names and indicates that the map relied on the Chinese postal guide spellings. Includes a bibliography of previous maps of the Society for China and East Asia. Concludes with an overview of Japanese aggression and Chinese resistance.

0024. D'ELLA, Pasquale M., S.J. Recent Discoveries and New Studies (1938–60) of the World Map in China of Father Matteo Ricci, S.J., *Monumenta Serica* 20, 1961, 82–164.

Reviews the history of the 1584, 1600, 1602, and 1603 editions of the maps and their reception in Rome. Argues that the first edition of the map was actually a prototype for smaller maps that followed. Explains the reasons for the various editions. Compares the prefaces of the various editions and their reprints. Identifies provenance of maps and their degree of completeness. Reviews and evaluates Kenneth Ch'en's works on topic. Argues that Ricci's work forced the Chinese to rethink their traditional views regarding the size and shape of the earth. Ends with an evaluation of Ricci's life and reputation as a scholar and human being.

0025. DRAKE, Fred W. A Mid-Nineteenth-Century Discovery of the Non-Chinese World, *Modern Asian Studies* 6, 1972, 205–44.

Analysis of works of Hsu Chi-yu and their impact on Chinese worldview and strategies for dealing with the West. Reviews Hsu's life and career. Focuses on Hsu's methodology and the content of his writing. Argues that despite errors in fact Hsu correctly described the strengths of the West and the weaknesses of China, suggested viable policy options for dealing with the West, and provided a basis for a Chinese understanding of the facts of the modern world.

0026. EBERHARD, Wolfram. Preliminary Note on Place Names in Medieval China, *Journal of the American Oriental Society* 74, 1954, 71–81.

Uses data from Dunhuang on 254 village (*li*) place names from Gansu, Henan, Hepei, Shandong, Shanxi, and Shaanxi to infer the political and social status of places. Categorizes places names as being either geographical or auspicious in meaning.

0027. FARQUHARSON, R. D. Some Pictures of Tibet, *Proceedings, Royal Geographical Society of Australasia, South Australian Branch* 51, 1949–50, 46–47.

Reports on twenty-seven pictures in the Royal Geographical collection taken between 1914 and 1918. Recounts the history of the pictures, including their apparent loss. Pleased to announce that slides of pictures were available for school use. In addition, two sets of the prints were available for view and study: one at the South Australian Branch Office and one at the Royal Geographical Society Library in London.

0028. FOLDI, Ervin. Conversion of Chinese Geographical Names, with Special Emphasis on Hungarian Cartographic Projects, *Special Libraries Association, Bulletin of the Geography and Map Division* 86, 1971, 31–43.

Provides basic information regarding Chinese dialects and writing system. Reviews history of development and use of the China Post Office, Wade-Giles, and *pinyin* systems of place name conversion (romanization). In Hungary cartographic projects aimed at school or local audiences use a Hungarian system of conversion; for more precise and scholarly work the *pinyin* system is used, based on the notion that cartographers should follow United Nations conventions and use the system favored by the controlling administrative authority in each country, in this case, the People's Republic of China.

0029. FUCHS, Walter. Development of Chinese Maps, *Korea Research Center, Seoul Seminar Series* 1, 1962, 7–10.

Argues that regardless of dynasty or intended use Chinese maps are accurate, practical, and simple, especially in comparison with European works. Describes measurement system used in Chinese maps. Notes the decline in mapping after the Chen Ho voyages.

0030. FUCHS, Walter. A Note on Father M. Boym's Atlas of China, *Imago Mundi* 9, 1952, 71–72.

Begins with a brief description of Boym's mission to China, which began in Macao in 1649 and finished in 1659. Concerned with history, provenance, and current location of maps. Argues that it is likely that Boym copied existing Ming dynasty maps and added lines of longitude and latitude and then transcribed Chinese names for places, mountains, and vegetation. The set of seventeen maps was never formally printed.

0031. FUCHS, W[alter]. The Peking Map Collection, *Imago Mundi* 2, 1964 reprint, 21–22.

Describes a set of maps made from copper plates ca. 1708–16, once thought destroyed. More generally deals with the history of the Imperial Collection. Provides a count of the number of maps in collection, a classification of maps, and an estimate of the number of still extant maps.

0032. GILES, L. Translations from the Chinese World Map of Father Ricci, *Geographical Journal* 52, 1918, 367–85; 53, 1919, 19–30.

Explicitly assumes that the reader knows the history of Ricci's maps. Provides full translation of notes and descriptions found on maps. Concludes that based on his translations the Amaborisian world map was not the work of Ricci.

0033. GINSBURG, Norton [S]. More about Chinese Place Names, *Professional Geographer* 5:2, 1953, 11–12.

In contrast to Raisz [item 0063], gives three reasons in defense of the Board on Geographic Names' use of the Wade-Giles system of romanization rather than the system found in the *China Postal Atlas*: the postal atlas is incomplete, its spellings give no hint as to the correct pronunciation of place names, and since no romanization system is perfect at least the Wade-Giles system is easy to use.

0034. GINSBURG, Norton S. Comments on Some Publications of the China Institute of Geography, *Annals, Association of American Geographers* 38, 1948, 147–50.

Survey of Chinese-language research. Includes the history of source institutions. Main focus is on memoirs, expedition reports, and atlases. Decries the poor quality of paper, printing, and maps. Questions the reliability of data found in the reports.

0035. GOODRICH, L. Carrington. Geographical Additions of the 14th and 15th Centuries, *Monuntica Serica* 15, 1956, 203–12.

Describes the text of the *Gazetteer of Chinese Empire* (*Ta-yuan Ta-i-t'ung-chih*) and the *Huan-yu-t'ung-chih*. Reviews the availability, history, size, areas covered, and sources of the two works. Includes a bibliography of research devoted to the two texts.

0036. GREGORY, J. W., and C. J. Gregory. Note on Map Illustrating the Journey of Percy Sladen Expedition in 1922 in Northwestern Yunnan, *Geographical Journal* 62, 1923, 202–5. Map, p. 240.

Describes the hydrology and geomorphology of the area. Raw data include measurements of rough prismatic computations along transverses as well as occasional latitudinal oberservations. Table of altitudes of selected sites also included. Makes explicit comparisons between map presented and earlier maps.

0037. HEAWOOD, E. The Relationships of the Ricci Maps, *Geographical Journal* 50, 1917, 271–76.

Attempts to explain the uneven coverage of the world in Ricci's maps. Concludes that a combination of Chinese needs and copyists' preferences account for variations in map content.

0038. H[ICKS], A[rthur]. R. Romanization of Place Names, *Geographical Journal* 102, 1943, 67–71.

Reviews the history, logic, and obstacles to romanization and notes how romanization and transliteration differ. Provides tables of alternative romanization systems and points out advantages of a system in which tones are indicated.

0039. HIRTH, F[rederick]. The Story of Chang K'ien, China's Pioneer in Western Asia, *Journal of the American Oriental Society* 37, 1916–17, 89–152.

Chinese text and English translation of chapter 123 of Ssu Ma-ch'ien's *Shi Ji*. Introductory material contains a critique of earlier translations and a description of the materials used in preparing the published translation and the author's magnum opus, *China and the Roman Orient* (1885).

0040. HOSIE, Lady. A Map of China in the Making, *Journal, North China Branch, Royal Asiatic Society* 57, 1926, 19–27.

Widow of Alexander Hosie describes his last work, the editing of the *Commercial Map of China*. The origin, method, and purpose of the work are described. One major reason for producing the map was for use by Chinese students, whose education was thought to be in a sorry state, as most Chinese citizens apparently did not know much about their own country.

0041. HOSIE, Lady. Mapping China, *Asia* 32, 1932, 640–45.

Personal history of Sir Alexander Hosie's work to create a modern, accurate map of China for commerical purposes. Provides details of personal sacrifices the work required, as Hosie had other, more official duties to perform in addition to compiling a map. Praises the work and efforts of past Chinese and Western cartographers.

0042. HSIEH, Chiao-min. Hsi-ke Hsu—Pioneer of Modern Geography in China, *Annals, Association of American Geographers* 48, 1958, 73–82.

Hsu is said to be the father of modern geography in China, as he introduced fieldwork as a methodology rather than relying on tradition or the reports of others. Hsu discovered the sources of many rivers and streams in Southwest China.

0043. HSIEH, Chiao-min. Status of Geography in Communist China, *Geographical Review* 49, 1959, 535–51.

Discusses the fate of the Institutes of Geography within Academia Sinica since 1950. The monographs and journals published have a greater stress on the regional geography of China, present the results of field surveys conducted in the context of implementing five-year plans, frequently include a denunciation of Western geographers, and show a preference for physical geography over human. Feels China geographers are modeling their work on Russian models in terms of both research and education.

0044. HSU, Ginn-Tze. Some Geographical Works during the War, *Scottish Geographical Magazine* 65:1, 1949, 54–58.

Update of Chang Chi-yun's survey in Chinese [*Journal of the Geographical Society of China* 2:3, 1935, 93–131; 2:4, 169–205; 3:1, 1936, 119–202] of literature produced from 1911 to 1935 for the period 1935 to 1948. Describes contents of forty-eight books on physical geography and fifty-three on human.

0045. HUTTMAN, William. On Chinese and European Maps of China, *Journal, Royal Geographical Society* 14, 1844, 117–26.

Describes Chinese maps produced from 1311 to 1711 in positive terms and notes their superiority to European equivalents. Maps from the Kangxi period on meet newer European standards thanks to help of Jesuits. Urges the government of Great Britain to assist in compilation of new maps so as to aid commerce.

0046. JEN, Mei-ngo. Progress of Geography in China during the Last 30 Years, *Professional Geographer,* old series, 8, 1948, 46–54.

Begins by describing the major twentieth-century Chinese geographers and their educational backgrounds, career paths, specializations, and current posts. Main body of article consists of an annotated bibliography of books, monographs, and journal articles for six subfields of physical geography, four subfields of human geography, and regional geography.

0047. KNIGHT, Thomas. Early Chinese Maps, *Hemisphere* 10, 1972, 30–35.

Overview of early Chinese cartography emphasizing the kinds of materials used in producing maps such as copper plates and bamboo. The development of paper led to a major expansion in the availability and use of maps. Dates earliest Chinese maps to ca. 1125 B.C., during the Early Zhou dynasty. Describes the accomplishments of P'ei Sieou, known as the Chinese Ptolemy. Suggests that Indian thought influenced how China came to conceive of the shape of the world. Similarly argues that Arab and Western cartographers contributed to the accuracy and quality of Chinese maps. Nevertheless, Chinese maps are said to have been superior to those of any other area. Maps were used for many purposes, including military and defense, trade, pilgrimage, tax collection, and hydrological studies.

0048. LAAI, Yi-faai, Michael FRANZ, and J. C. SHERMAN. The Use of Maps in Social Research: A Case Study in South China, *Geographical Review* 52, 1962, 92–111.

Describes the use of maps in the Modern Chinese History Project under way at the University of Washington. The main regional focus is on Guangdong and Guangxi, and the main time period is immediately before and during the Taiping Rebellion. Examples of findings include population and toponymy. Extensive review of types of questions that can arise out of studying maps of pawnshops and local dialects.

0049. LEE, A. O. Research Reports of the Fun-Min Geographical Institute of Economic Development, *Geographical Review* 49, 1959, 575–77.

Describes the history of the publication efforts of the institute, the venues of publication, languages of reports, and titles and content of most recent research.

0050. LESZCZYCKI, S. Development of Geography in the People's Republic of China, *Geography* 48, 1963, 139–54.

Provides overview of major centers of geographic research, including curricula and publications, a complete list of which is provided in an appendix. Characterizes research after 1961 as being focused, applied, and physically oriented. Provides examples of typical research projects including the economic utilization of the water resources of both the Huang and Chang river systems, dry area development, and transportation. Laments the political isolation under which Chinese geographers must work.

0051. MA, L. J. C. Serial Publications for Geographical Research on Communist China from Hong Kong, *Professional Geographer* 21, 1969, 38–39.

Lists publication details and samples of contents for *Survey of China Mainland Press, Current Backround, Extracts from China Mainland Magazines, University Research Service, China News Analysis*, and the *Far Eastern Economic Review*. Concludes that contrary to public opinion there is a considerable body of information regarding Mainland China available but that it is spread out over numerous short articles.

0052. MARKHAM, C. R. Travels in Great Tibet and Trade between Tibet and Bengal, *Journal, Royal Geographical Society* 45, 1875, 299–314.

Defines region based on 1708 Chinese and French maps as well as surveys by Jesuits. Compares and contrasts his observations with those of others.

0053. MASON, Kenneth. Karakorum Nomenclature, *Geographical Journal* 91, 1938, 123–28.

Report on conference called to establish rules and processes of surveying and mapping the Karakorum, especially in the context of working in areas with no local place names. Conference report, with all recommendations, included as appendix, pp. 129–52.

0054. McCOLL, Robert W. Geographic Material on Mainland China Available from the U.S. Joint Publication Research Service, *Professional Geographer* 20, 1968, 207–8.

Describes the Joint Publication Research Service, the contents of the materials it provides, and instructions for placing orders. Provides examples of materials available by both broad topics and specific geographic journals such as *Ti-li* (Geography) and *Tichih-lun-p'ing* (Geographical Review). Notes the best avenue for exploring JPRS holdings is the *Monthly Catalogue* of U.S. government publications.

0055. MEIJER, M. J. Map of the Great Wall of China, *Imago Mundi* 13, 1956, 110–15.

Report based on 1952 description of a set of eighteenth-century maps. Although the distances and locations of towns along the wall are highly accurate, the orientation and scale of the map change from one section of the wall to another. As the maps were intended for military purposes, any apparent inaccuracies may not be important. The map was highly decorated and contained numerous inscriptions describing the locations of barbarian intrusions and garrisons.

0056. MILLS, J. W. Three Chinese Maps, *British Museum Quarterly* 18:3, 1953, 65–67.

Describes two recent additions to the British Museum Map Room, a two-roll set of maps showing the coasts of China, and a copy of the so-called "Ch'ien Lung Map." Provides details regarding the age of the maps and their size, scale, content, provenance, coloring, and type of material used in the printing.

0057. MORSE, H. B. Lampacao: A Mystery of the Far East, *Journal, North China Branch, Royal Asiatic Society,* new series, 52, 1921, 137–38.

Argues that Portuguese place name Lampacao derives from the Chinese Langpehtsao (Lampienchau). Regardless of etymology of name, the place itself is a Ming-Ching pirate cove located some two miles from an earlier one at Outau.

0058. NAKAMURA, Hirosi. Old Chinese World Maps Preserved by the Koreans, *Imago Mundi* 4, 1965, 3–22.

Describes maps in terms of names, projections, and type of material excluded. Concludes that the set of maps examined dates from the Tang dynasty and arrived in Korea as a part of the diffusion of mapping technology from China to Korea during that time.

0059. NELSON, Howard. Chinese Maps: An Exhibition at the British Library, *China Quarterly* 58, 1974, 357–62.

Argues that a comprehensive catalog of Chinese maps is needed and feasible. Discusses three issues regarding Chinese maps: their accuracy, their relationship with scientific cartography and religious cosmology, and their role in indicating the status of geographical knowledge, administration, communications, networks, population, irrigation, and flood control in China over time.

0060. NELSON, Howard. Maps of Old Cathay: Two Millennia of Chinese Cartography, *Geographical Magazine* 47, 1975, 702–12.

Sketch of history of Chinese cartography using key personalities, such as P'ei Hsiuh and Chia Ta, and maps of Xian to demonstrate progress made in producing maps. Mentions problems in mapmaking and the contributions of Jesuits toward solving them. Notes that for China maps had dual purposes: they were administrative tools as well as works of art.

0061. NG, Ronald C. Y. The San On Map of Mgr. Volonteri, *Geographical Journal* 135, 1969, 231–35.

Discusses Volonteri's arrival in Hong Kong, his work, and his good relations with the local rice farmers. Feels that the true value of professional, accurate bilingual maps is underappreciated due to Volonteri's modesty. Article reprinted in *Journal, Hong Kong Branch, Royal Asiatic Society* 9, 1969, 141–48. Follow-up comment by James Hayes, *Journal, Hong Kong Branch, Royal Asiatic Society* 10, 1970, 193–94.

0062. QUIRINO, Carlos. The Lavezares Map of China, *Philippine Historical Review* 2, 1969, 269–74.

Describes second of two maps sent by the Governor-General of the Philippines to the Court of King Philip II in 1574. Map is still in the Archivo General de las Indies in Seville. Provides details regarding the size of the map, its reprint history, and a summary of previous studies on the map. Includes the complete English-language text of an article analyzing the map originally published in French in 1939 by Nakamura Hirosi. Speculates what the history of the area might have been had the Chinese invaded the Philippines in 1569.

0063. RAISZ, Erwin. Decisions on the Names in China, United States Board on Geographic Names, 1952, *Professional Geographer* 4:5, 1952, 29.

Describes changes made by Board on Geographic Names as radical, especially in its use of the Wade-Giles system to "respell" China place names, a move that he saw as useful only to scholars. Urges that the membership of the Board on Geographical Names be expanded to include a "practical" cartographer so as to avoid a split between government and private spellings.

0064. REYNOLDS, J. H. Place Names in Sinkiang, *Geographical Journal* 65, 1925, 242–47.

In his capacity as secretary of Permanent Committee on Geographcial Names, describes and defends a 1925 committee report using Turkic spellings for place names in Xinjiang.

0065. RUDNEV, Andrej. A Manchu Itinerary, *Imago Mundi* 12, 1955, 161–70.

Describes contents (including language, transcription of Chinese and Manchu terms, and orientation) of a Ching dynasty map of Shenyang's day and night stations discovered in 1919. The map, dating to ca. 1778, contains as a part of its extensive inscriptions an itinerary of a trip from Beijing to Shengyang in both Chinese and Manchu.

0066. SALTER, Christopher L. The Landscape of Contemporary Mainland China: A Review of Nine Educational Films, *Journal of Geography* 70, 1971, 337–46.

Review undertaken to demonstrate that sufficient materials were available to competently teach the regional geography of Mainland China and that use of film is an effective means of developing a sense of place and geographic process. Only films made between 1965 and 1969 are analyzed. Includes a table cross-listing topics and regions/provinces in China.

0067. SARGENT, R. H. First Modern Mapping in the Far Interior of China, *Surveying and Mapping* 9, 1949, 192–201.

Reports on a 1903 expedition to conduct geological surveys and topographic mapping of a 2,000 square mile area in China. Uses itinerary format. Describes the two methods, triangulation and plane table siting, of map compilation. Indicates that after the collection of maps is printed the originals will be placed in the Library of Congress, along with all available field notes.

0068. SHABAD, Theodore. More on the Treatment of Chinese Place Names, *Professional Geographer* 5:2, 1953, 12–13.

A positive reaction to Raisz [item 0063]. Explains why use of the Chinese Postal Service system of spelling is preferred. Reasons include the fact that these spellings are well known, especially for well-known places; that an alternative list of 13,000 places names is available; that the Board on Geographic Names has always used conventional spellings; and the fact that the *Columbia Lippincroft Gazetteer* cross-references both the Postal Service and Wade-Giles spellings.

0069. SHABAD, T[heodore]. Status of Geography in Communist China, *Professional Geographer* 6:4, 1954, 5–8.

Uses two articles from the Russian geographic literature to evaluate status of Chinese geography in the early 1950s. Describes research projects at major research centers. Analyzes contents of published monographs and journals and thus identifies the role of geographers in censuses, education, and economic development. Notes that Russians were concerned that "reactionary," bourgeois thinking may have started influencing Chinese geographic research.

0070. SOOTHILL, W. E. The Two Oldest Maps of China Extent, *Geographical Journal* 69, 1927, 532–55.

Talk in form of a eulogy for Sir Alexander Hosie. Reviews previous work on analyzing early Chinese maps. Maps under consideration are in fact engravings found in the Forest Tablets at Xian, Shaanxi. Evaluates provenance of maps. Concludes that Chia Tan was the author of the first map and that it is not possible to attribute the second one to any particular person. Includes a history of early Tang mapmaking and the impact of the invention of paper on mapmaking in general. Feels the maps under consideration are "truthful." Includes methodological discussions on dating maps, such as how to exploit the custom of a dynasty to change place names when it came to power when trying to date maps.

0071. STEIN, Sir {M.} Auriel. The Desert Crossing of Hsuan-tsang, *Geographical Journal* 54, 1919, 265–77.

Describes the route and hardships of the Buddhist pilgrim ca. 629 in the context of his own difficulty in traversing the area in 1907 and 1918. Judges narrative of Hsuan-tsang to be accurate.

0072. STEIN, {Sir} M. Auriel. Notes on Maps Illustrating Explorations in Chinese Turkestan and Kansu, *Geographical Journal* 37, 1911, 275–80.

As a result of his 1906–08 trip [described in item 0171 below] author is able to provide new maps of area. Describes technical aspects of data collection and map production, including difficulties in transcribing local place names of Turkiman-Iranian origin. Includes tables of locations, names, and observed latitudes of campsites used during course of work.

0073. STEVENS, H. The Mountains about Tatsienlu, *Geographical Journal* 75, 1930, 345–52.

Comparison and contrast of reports by nineteenth- and early-twentieth-century European explorers of study area. Heavily critcized by Edgar [see item 0285].

1. Cartography and the History of Geography

0074. SZCZESNIAK, Boleslaw. The Atlas and Geographic Description of China: A Manuscript of Michael Boym (1612–1659), *Journal of the American Oriental Society* 73, 1953, 65–77.

Describes the spatial content of the atlas and the special features of the map legends. Compares atlas to other works by Jesuits in China and notes particular influence of Boym's work on later French atlases. Argues that in general Boym was driven to his map work based on the belief that before he could diffuse European thinking to China he had to be knowledgeable about Chinese philosophies of science and life. Mapmaking provided a means for gaining such knowledge.

0075. SZCZESNIAK, Boleslaw. The Mappa Imperii Sinarium of Michael Boym, *Imago Mundi* 19, 1965, 113–15.

Describes three maps of China compiled by Boym between 1612 and 1653. Suspects that a fourth map was lost. Describes the history, provenance, location, content, and errors of the maps.

0076. SZCZESNIAK, Boleslaw. Matteo Ricci's Maps of China, *Imago Mundi* 11, 1954, 127–36.

Seeks to demonstrate that a set of French maps of China should be attributed to Matteo Ricci. Uses Jesuit archival material to describe Ricci's work in China. Assesses Ricci's role in both Western and Chinese geography and his importance in enlarging China's horizons by correctly placing China on a world map.

0077. SZCZESNIAK, Boleslaw. The Seventeenth-Century Maps of China, *Imago Mundi* 13, 1956, 116–36.

Analysis of achievements and contributions of Matteo Ricci, Michele Ruggieri, Samuel Purches, Martino Martini, Michael Boym, Alvarez Semedo, and Philippe Couplet as revealed in their maps of China. Concludes that the West was materially and culturally inferior to China when the maps were produced.

0078. TOWLE, Jerry. Jade: An Indicator of Trans-Pacific Contact, *Yearbook of the Association of Pacific Coast Geographers* 35, 1973, 165–72.

Argues for early Chinese-Mexican contacts based on chemistry, shapes, techniques of stonework and medicinal use of jade objects found on both sides of the Pacific.

0079. WALKER, J. J. Note on the Royal Geographical Society map of Tibet, *Geographical Journal* 4, 1894, 52–54.

    Describes sources of map, especially longitude and latitude measures and physical details.

0080. WALLIS, Helen [M]. Missionary Cartography in China: Jesuit Influence on Chinese Mapping, *Geographical Magazine* 47, 1975, 751–59.

    Jesuits conducted geographical surveys of China and their map work is seen as among their most impressive achievements.

0081. WALLIS, Helen M., and E. D. GRINSEAT. A Chinese Terrestrial Globe, A.D. 1623, *British Museum Quarterly* 25, 1962, 83–91.

    Concerned with a map made by two Jesuits, Father Manuel Dias the younger and Father Nicolo Longobardi. Reviews work of Ricci in China. Argues that all three Jesuits saw science as a means to an end—conversion of the Chinese—but found that China's needs for applied science detracted from their missionary work. Describes the size, materials, inscriptions, and provenance of globe. Evaluates the manner in which map shows Asia and the world more accurately.

0082. WANG, Ch'ien, and Jack F. WILLIAMS. The *Yu-kung*: A New Translation and Appraisal, *Chinese Culture* 11, 1970, 45–66.

    Describes the history and content of the text. Compares and evaluates older translations. Footnotes to actual translation contain alternative interpretations. Includes an English- and Chinese-langauge bibliography and map.

0083. WANG, Chih-cho. Surveying and Mapping Work in China, *Surveying and Mapping* 7, 1947, 150–54.

    Classifies mapping work into three broad categories: engineering, cadastral, and military. Describes political and logistical limits to mapping activities for each category. Notes the standards adopted regarding map projections and surveying methods. Argues that mapping in China is beset by a lack of coordination and long-range planning and by jurisdictional conflicts. Warns reader that topographic maps only available at 1:50,000 and 1:100,000 scales. Looks forward to improved maps when photogrammetry is added to tools available to cartographers.

0084. WIENS, Herold J. Recent Geographic Publications of Mainland China, *Professional Geographer* 15:2, 1963, 37–38.

Notes the difficulty in obtaining Chinese professional literature, in part due to a December 1959 export ban imposed by the Chinese. Reflects on content of nineteen volumes of *Acta Geographia Sinica* (1955–62) and twenty-six volumes of *Geographic Knowledge* (1957–61). Emphasizes changes in format, number of issues, and number of pages printed. Speculates that publication gaps may reflect the cost of publishing and the impact of the Great Leap Forward. Feels that the content of *Acta Geographia Sinica* has not changed, while that of *Geographic Knowledge* now seems to be more teacher oriented, with summaries of foreign regional texts.

0085. YULE, H[enry]. The Atlas Sinesis and Other Sinesiana, *Geographical Magazine* 1, 1874, 147–48.

Describes and evaluates the map of Martin Martini published ca. 1655. Speculates that Martini used Chinese sources and in so doing helped to correct errors in Western maps. Notes that all Jesuits ran afoul of their order's headquarters with their accommodation of Chinese culture and needs.

See also items 0285, 0443, 0445, 0729, 0732, 0761, 0766, 0768, 0775, 0788, 0800, 0809, and 0819.

2. Expeditions, Surveys, and Field Methods

0086. ABRAMOT, M. A. On Lake Nor Tsai-san and Its Neighborhood, *Proceedings, Royal Geographical Society of London* 9, 1865, 40–41.

Describes location of lake, quality of water, and abundance of fish such as sturgeon, salmon, and starled (*accipenser ruthenus*). Traces etymology of names of lake back to Kalmyk origins ca. 1650. Formally, lake was called Kun-bloth-Nor (lake of Bella) by the Mongols.

0087. AIMORE, Prince, of Savio-Aosta, Duke of Spoleto. The Italian Expedition to the Karakorum in 1929, *Geographical Journal* 75, 1930, 385–401.

Uses itinerary format. Presents geological and anthropometric data collected. Focus is on Baltoro glacier.

0088. ANDREWS, Roy Chapin. Explorations in the Gobi Desert, *National Geographic Magazine* 63, 1933, 653–716.

Provides extensive coverage of geological history of Central Asia. Includes a reconstruction of past climates based on physical evidence, including plants. When discussing non-technical material uses an abbreviated itinerary format to report on adventures along the way.

0089. ANON. Dr. Sven Hedin in Tibet, *Geographical Journal* 29, 1907, 539–45.

Extracts from letters sent by Hedin in 1907.

0090. ANON. Dr. Stein's Expedition in Central Asia, *Geographical Journal* 29, 1907, 31–35; 30, 1907, 503–7; 31, 1908, 509–14.

Interim reports emphasizing archaeological work on abandoned towns.

0091. ANON. Explorations by A-K in Great Tibet and Mongolia, *Scottish Geographical Magazine* 1, 1885, 352–72.

Describes and summarizes journeys taken by native employees of the Indian Survey Department to Tibet and Mongolia. Refers reader to Hennessey, *Proceedings of the Royal Geographical Society* 45, 1875, for more general information regarding the work of A-K, whose real name was Pandit Kishen Singh. For full details on Singh's life, see his obituary by Kenneth Mason in *Geographical Journal* 62, 1923, 429–40, where the work of Indian explorers is described in general.

0092. ANON. Exploration in West Tibet by the Trans-Himalayan Parties of the Indian Trigonometrical Survey, *Proceedings, Royal Geographical Society*, new series, 1, 1879, 444–52.

As a result of the survey of the Indian border, provides details of administration, ethnography, religion, economics, trade, and commerce on north side of boundary.

0093. ANON. Grueber and Dorville's Journey across Tibet, *Geographical Journal* 24, 1904, 663–69.

Summary of monograph by R. Tronnier, who seeks to vindicate the claims and work of two early (1661) German-Jesuit explorers Johannes Grueber and Albert de Dorville. Includes a brief description of the two explorers' lives and samples of letters they wrote.

0094. ANON. The Lushan District of Kiangshi, *Geographical Journal* 62, 1923, 424–29.

Uses secondary sources to describe Lushan and its surroundings. Focuses on geology, mountains, historic monuments, and Guling as a tourist destination.

0095. ANON. Mr. Cecil Celmenti's Journey across South China, *Geographical Journal* 30, 1907, 516–17. Map after p. 584.

Account of trip taken in October through December 1906 as a part of a route survey covering the area from Xunzhou at the confluence of the Baihua and Yu Rivers. Route actually follows that taken by Colquhoun in 1882 [item 0111]. Provides a list of previous explorations of branch streams.

0096. ANON. Mr. Fulford's Journey in Manchuria, *Scottish Geographical Magazine* 3, 1887, 421–24.

Excerpts of Parliamentary Paper, China, no. 2, 1887 [Command Paper number 5048]. Urges more government attention to accuracy of maps and place names.

0097. BABER, E. Colborne. Approximate Determinations of Positions in South-Western China, *Journal, Royal Geographical Society* 49, 1879, 421–33.

Describes how eight tables of latitude and longitude data for the area were derived and observed.

2. Expeditions, Surveys, and Field Methods

0098. BAILEY, F. M. Exploration on the Tsang-po or Upper Brahmaputra, *Geographical Journal* 44, 1914, 341–64. Map, p. 428.

Report of 1912–13 expedition. Begins by reviewing results of previous expeditions to area. Major question answered is whether or not there were falls along the river. Finds that there were no falls, just a 30 foot set of rapids. While mapping the Tsangpo and Nangong Chu, party discovered the Gyala Peri and upper reaches of the Subansir Rivers. Includes a description of flora and fauna found. Area was so remote that party frequently had to cut its own paths and roads. Notes that there was ample evidence of Chinese activities against the Tibetans, such as burned monuments.

0099. BAILEY, F. M. Journey through a Portion of Southeast Tibet and the Mishimi Hills, *Geographical Journal* 39, 1912, 334–47.

Report, using itinerary format, of 1911 trip undertaken to investigate the murder of two British nationals in study area. Considerable detail regarding the number of floral and faunal specimens collected. Includes a table with itinerary and miles and travel time between places; some measurements of latitudes included. Notes that goiter is endemic in area. Notes with concern the impact of Chinese schools and xenophobia on Tibetan youth.

0100. BAILEY, F. M. Note on a Portion of the Tsangpo, *Geographical Journal* 66, 1925, 519–22.

Reviews results of surveys of 1882, 1904, and 1913. Describes in detail flora and fauna found as well as the geological structure. Includes a description of Buddhism in the area and the monastaries found.

0101. BARTON, A{lfred}. On the Exploratory Expedition to the Western Borders of China and the Upper Waters of the Yang-tse-jiang, *Proceedings, Royal Geographical Society of London* 6, 1862, 85–95.

Focuses on impact of Taiping Rebellion on towns and the exploratory party that was attacked at Pingshan. Notes widespread cultivation of poppies. Comments on inability of Chinese and British officials to communicate so that addressing grievances or obtaining redress for either side very difficult.

0102. BENETT, Adrian. Rough Notes of a Visit to Daba in Thibet, August, 1865, *Proceedings, Royal Geographical Society of London* 10, 1866, 165–69.

Very general description of a hunting trip.

0103. BENZELEY, M. Formosa, Southern Part of, Notes of an Overland Journey, with Introductory Sketch of the Island, *Proceedings, Royal Geographical Society of London* 7, 1885, 1–22. Map, p. 64.

Trip, between June 18 and 26, 1884, was from Takow (Gaoxiong) to the South Cape. Reviews political geography of island and concludes that Chinese not well acquainted with island and that as a result modern order had not been established. Sees little prospect for economic development since island lacks good harbors.

0104. BLUE, A. D. European Navigation on the Yangtze, *Journal, Royal Asiatic Society, Hong Kong Branch* 3, 1963, 107–30.

Chronicles history of European and U.S. ships operating on the Chang Jiang from the time of the Macartney and Amherst expeditions through 1940. Notes continued need for trained pilots to guide ships.

0105. BORRADAILE, A. A. Notes of a Journey in Northern Mongolia in 1893, *Geographical Journal* 5, 1895, 562–72.

Sketches history of an area out of reach to British explorers but not to Russian or even Uighur ones. Main goal of trip was to explore archaeological sites. Additional notes at end by Ney Elias, pp. 572–75.

0106. BRINE, Lindsey. Expedition up the Si-kiang River, *Proceedings, Royal Geographical Society of London* 5, 1861, 238–41.

Describes physical features of area as well as identifying appropriate locations for military emplacements to enhance the area's security.

0107. BROWN, T. Graham. Masherbrum, 1938, *Geographical Journal* 95, 1940, 81–95.

Overview of climb of mountain 25,600 feet high. Reviews previous attempts (e.g., 1892) at assault.

0108. BRUCE, C. D. Journey across Asia from the Leh to Peking, *Geographical Journal* 29, 1907, 597–625.

Report characterized in opening paragraph as one of "length without breadth." Central focus is on physical features of route, but some material relating to fauna and minerals is included.

0109. BURDSALL, Richard L., and Terris MOORE. Climbing Mighty Minya Konka, *National Geographic Magazine* 83, 1943, 625–50.

Well-illustrated report on expedition to Xigang. Uses itinerary format when describing administrative and logistical problems of work and routes taken. Includes historical overview of other attempts to scale mountain, such as the 1879 Szechery Expedition. Notes importance of region as an area that pilots must fly over after the closing of the Burma Road. Concludes with posttrip disposition and occupations of participants in climb.

0110. CLEMENTI, Cecil. Positions Determined: Kashgar to Hong Kong, *Geographical Journal* 40, 1912, 624–28.

Includes tables and report of elevation measurements and barometric readings for fifty important places taken during a 1907–8 trip.

0111. COLQUHOUN, A. R. Exploration of the South China Borderlands from the Mouth of the Sikiang to the Banks of the Irrawadi, *Proceedings, Royal Geographical Society and Monthly Record of Geography*, new series 4, 1882, 713–29, 760–65.

Reports on three goals of trip: to collect geographical information useful to the Royal Society, to collect materials for a popular book on the region, and to explore Yunnan and the area to its southwest. Trip took place during 1881. Reviews reports of previous explorers. In section on Canton, focuses on crops, structure, and operation of the government and navigational limits. When discussing Yunnan, covers a long list of physical and human geography topics, but not in a deterministic order or framework. Concludes that Yunnan has great economic potential but that of four possible routes to it no one has the characteristics necessary to exploit all the trade potential.

0112. DeBEER, Dora H. Up a Yangtze Gorge, *Geographical Magazine* 14, 1942, 210–16.

Reports on trip made in November 1938 to the Kiaotou Valley, starting from Lijiang, Yunnan. Uses itinerary format. Describes the topography of the valley as well as the economy, settlement patterns, transportation, and religious practices of the non-Han tribes residing there.

0113. EDMUNDS, Charles Keyser. Thirty Thousand Miles in China, *Journal, Royal Asiatic Society, North China Branch,* new series 50, 1919, 191–25.

Describes efforts to survey China and establish precise measurements of longitude and latitude. Emphasis on five regions: Southeast Hainan, the salt margins of Inner Mongolia, Snow Mountain of Sungpang Pass, the southwest jungles of Laos, and the lakes of Yunnan.

0114. FARRER, Reginald. Kansu Marches of Tibet, *Geographical Journal* 49, 1917, 106–24.

Reports on botanical exploration of March 1914, which sought to collect alpine flora in a range called Chigla. Notes Tibetan dislike for both Chinese and Western missionaries, which leads to periodic local unrest.

0115. FARRER, Reginald. My Second Year's Journey on the Tibetan Border of Kansu, *Geographical Journal* 51, 1918, 341–59.

Continues material in item 0114. Comments on changes in ethnic mix of population. Describes cities and urban parks. Notes that Xining is an exception to traditional Chinese city planning traditions and rules. More explicit description of flora than in 1917 report. In describing ethnic mix of area, argues that Muslim population not Han Chinese in origin.

0116. FITZGERALD, C. Patrick. Northern Marches of Yunnan, *Geographical Journal* 102, 1943, 49–565.

Employs itinerary format to describe a trip undertaken in winter 1937 from Dali to Lijiang. Sees Yunnan as set of north-south contrasts and provides examples from climatology and ethnography. Notes potential difficulties in building modern roads.

0117. FITZGERALD, C. P[atrick]. The Tali District of Western Yunnan, *Geographical Journal* 99, 1942, 50–60.

In the course of describing accessibility, defense, ethnicity, and regional differences of district, questions the standard reports on geological origins of the plateau. Impressed with ancient irrigation and farming systems of area. Notes importance to economy of marble mining and woodcutting.

0118. FITZGERALD, C. P[atrick]. The Tiger's Leap, *Geographical Journal* 98, 1941, 147–53.

Reports on 1937 trip to western Lijiang, known as Hu Tiao Ching, or Tiger's Leap. Uses itinerary format. Notes that the geological features of the area are the result of downward cutting but with no terraces. Included in the ethnographic materials is a discussion of city design and village layout in the area.

0119. FORREST, George. Journey on the Upper Salween, *Geographical Journal* 32, 1908, 239–66.

Reports on expedition undertaken during December 1905 with two purposes: to discover whether or not the Salween and Irrawadi dividing range forms a distinct geographic/ethnographic boundary separating northwestern Yunnan and Upper Burma, and to explore the Salween Valley between 26 and 27 degrees north latitude. Uses itinerary format. Expedition was plagued by bad luck such as monsoons, an unreliable food supply, and civil war between Chinese troops and minority peoples, which was further complicated by intervillage hostilities and rivalries. Includes materials on Lisso tribe and its relations with the Chinese authorities.

0120. FOUNTAINE, Captain Eadric Clifford. The Haramosh Pass, *Geographical Journal* 99, 1942, 247–57.

Uses itinerary format to describe a trip undertaken between June 1940 and January 1941. Sees his report as accompanying and complimenting that of Shipton's 1939 trip [item 0163].

0121. GUIBAUT, Andre. Exploration in the Upper Tung Basin, Chinese-Tibetan Borderland, *Geographical Review* 34, 1944, 387–404.

Report on the second Guibaut-Liotard Expedition to Northeast Tibet. Uses itinerary format. Describes the general ethnicity of study area and especially the major ethnic group, the Golok Seta, as well as the hydrology. Describes Tong watershed characteristics, including valley types. Expedition was not able to solve the problem of the source of the Tong or the number and sources of its branches since the party was attacked by brigands and Liotard and several Chinese guards were killed, thus ending the expedition. Includes description of attack, the harrowing escape to a monastery in Dekho where they found refuge, and the trip back to safety.

0122. GUTZTAFF, Charles. Extracts from the Journal of a Resident in Siam and Voyages along the Coast of China to Mantchou Tartary, *Journal, Royal Geographical Society* 3, 1833, 291–310.

Most of article deals with Southeast Asia. Describes topography, travails of traveling, economy, and trade from Hainan Island to Tianjin and the Bohai area.

0123. HAMILTON, A. B. Notes of a Land Journey from Fuchau to Kiu-kiang, *Geographical Journal* 26, 1905, 69–74. Map, p. 128.

Describes 1902 trip along the upper reaches of the Min River, Sichuan.

Assumes that the reader is familiar with the general area.

0124. HAMMOND, C[aptain] Robert. Through Western Tibet in 1930, *Geographical Journal* 99, 1942, 1–15.

Uses itinerary format, but observations contain nothing new. Map at scale of 1:250,000 included.

0125. HANSON-LOWE, J. A Journey along the Chinese-Tibetan Border, *Geographical Journal* 95, 1940, 357–67. Map, p. 358.

Itinerary format report of expedition undertaken during the spring and summer of 1937 to study the Pleistocene glaciation of the area. Provides additional information on ethnography, flora, and fauna of area.

0126. HARRER, Heinrich. My Seven Years in Tibet, *Geographical Journal* 120, 1954, 146–55.

The tutor to the Dalai Lama describes the circumstances surrounding his arrival in 1944 in Tibet via India, including his imprisonment in POW camps and his subsequent escape. Reviews his work surveying Lhasa. Author fled Tibet when the Chinese invaded in 1950.

0127. HEDLEY, John. The Lao Ho in Inner Mongolia, *Geographical Journal* 29, 1907, 545–59.

Attempts to clear up uncertainties regarding the hydrology of the upper reaches of the Lao River. Provides sketch map to back up claims and to correct errors found in Turley's 1905 map [item 0403].

0128. HEDIN, Sven. Dr. Sven Hedin's Journey to Tibet, 1906–1908, *Geographical Journal* 33, 1909, 353–419. Discussion, pp. 419–40. Map, p. 516.

Reviews earlier records of expeditions but concentrates on eastern section of Tibet. Main issue explored is which geographical processes have operated in Tibet. Concerned with identifying the area's natural regions.

0129. HEDIN, Sven. Journeys in Tibet, 1906–8, *Scottish Geographical Magazine* 25, 1909, 169–95.

Argues that the stereotype that Tibet is a high plateau situated between the two highest mountain chains needs to be revised given the wealth of new materials available about Tibetan topography. Concludes with hope that his enduring great loneliness in Tibet will not have been in vain and that others will find his findings useful.

0130. HEDIN, Sven. Scientific Results of Dr. Sven Hedin's Last Journey, *Geographical Journal* 24, 1904, 524–45.

Outlines contents of projected six-volume report and atlas. Main focus is on volume 1, Tarim Basin.

0131. HEDLEY, John. Trip into Chihli Province, North China, *Geographical Journal* 25, 1905, 513–25.

Describes area as a sportsman's paradise. Praises lawfulness of region and reports that there is no need for arms. Favorably impressed by Mongols, although refers to them as primitive. Notes extensive market for animal skins and use of coal outcrops.

0132. HOU, Jen-chih. Topographical Setting and Geographical Relations of Peking, *Yenching Journal of Social Science* 5, 1950, 59–67.

Refers to Beijing region as the Bay of Peking and then makes comparisons with the Tigris-Euphrates Basin. Main concern is with the geology, sedimentology, and climate of area. Sees region as gateway to modern China. Includes toponyms for rivers and geological features.

0133. HUNTINGTON, Ellsworth. The Depression of Turfan, *Geographical Journal* 30, 1907, 54–73.

Reports on 1906 trip to area, whose main interest lies in the fact that it is below sea level. Describes climate, which features evening winds, vegetation, topography, hydrology, and geology of area. Argues that archaeological evidence supports hypothesis that there have been major climatic changes in the area during the Christian era. Notes use of *kariz* (*kariz* is a local variant of *karez*, syn. with *foggaras* and *qanat*), introduced from Persia, to support population settlements. Sees *kariz* as a good example of how man can overcome changes in physical environment.

0134. IMANISHI, Kinji. Ecological Observations on the Great Khingan Expedition, *Geographical Review* 40, 1950, 236–53.

Reviews the results of previous European and Japanese expeditions to area. Report is an account of a 1942 traverse from Haei Lar to Moho. Describes general route of trip, climatic conditions and measurements, and vegetation. Especially interested in placing the vegetation in the context of eastern Siberian classifications. Includes full description of types of taiga and steppe plants found, including growing characteristics. Some information about fauna included. Discusses question of past climatic change and reports on glacial topography. Contrasts cultural patterns of adaption to environment in western and eastern areas. Doubts whether area could be a true pioneer fringe given the dryness, which makes rice cultivation difficult if not impossible. However, dairy culture could succeed based on native hunter economy and native animal domesticants.

0135. JAMES, H. E., et al. Journey in Manchuria to the Pei-Shan Mountains and the Sources of the Sungari, *Proceedings, Royal Geographical Society*, new series 8, 1886, 779–80; 9, 1887, 235–39. Map, p. 594.

Preliminary report describing trip of James, Younghusband, and Fulord to the sources of the Sungari, an area not previously reached by Westerners. Trip continued on to northern and eastern Manchuria, an area well known for lawlessness and banditry. Extent of Chinese assimilation of Manchus described. Full report published in *Proceedings, Royal Geographical Society*, new series 9, 1887, pp. 531–67.

0136. KAULBACK, Ronald. The Assam Border of Tibet, *Geographical Journal* 83, 1934, 177–90.

Report by the cartographer on November 1932 trip led by L. Kingdon Ward to southeastern Tibet to search for new and rare plants. Access to area was via the Lohit Valley route. Found the Yarlung Zangbo Valley closed to them due to the hostile attitudes of natives. In contrast, the Dihang Valley was uninhabited and therefore difficult to explore. Comments on native peoples and fields of poppies.

0137. KAULBACK, Ronald. A Journey in the Salween and Tsangpo Basins, Southeastern Tibet, *Geographical Journal* 91, 1938, 99–122.

Expedition had five major goals: to see whether and where the Salween-Yarlung Zangbo divided, to explore the watershed between the Ngagong chu and Chindru chu, to survey the Salween from Shopando to its source, to transverse the Ngagong chu as far as it headwaters, and to collect plants and animals from all survey areas for the British Museum. Uses itinerary format. Mentions repeatedly the scarcity of transportation and the hostility of local governments to their work. Mixed ethnographic observations based on a combination of direct observation and hearsay.

0138. KELBURN, Viscount. Mother Yangtze, I, *Geographical Magazine* 6, 1937–38, 111–28.

Describes major cities along river, rural scenery, and local crafts such as boat building. Very well illustrated with black and white plates.

0139. KELBURN, Viscount. Mother Yangtze, II, *Geographical Magazine* 6, 1938, 181–90.

Describes fishing industry and attitude of rural residents toward river. Includes materials about climate, local flooding, and local technologies for using the river such as treadwheels and dikes.

0140. KROPOTKIN, P. Russian Explorations in Manchuria, *Geographical Journal* 11, 1898, 63–65.

Abridged version of paper by E. E. Amert, which appeared in volume 2, 1897, of *Izvestia*, the journal of the Russian Geographical Society. Records travels of Russian engineers, who were mainly concerned with structure of mountains and the possibility of finding exploitable minerals. Notes impact of monsoons on region's vegetation.

0141. LITTLE, Mrs. Archibald. Through the Yangtze Gorges, *Scottish Geographical Magazine* 18, 1902, 149–50.

Claims to be first to suggest that steamers could run in low water between Hankou and Ichang. Contrasts the good work and civilizing effects of missionaries with destruction visited upon North Cathedral in Beijing during Boxer Rebellion.

0142. MANIFOLD, C. C. Upper Yangtze Provinces and Their Communications, *Geographical Journal* 25, 1905, 589–620.

Argues that prosperity of the area guaranteed once a rapid and safe means of communication is brought in. Economic growth in upper Yangtze could be the catalyst for similar expansion in Yunnan, where the French were completing a railroad. The difficulties of building modern transportation in the Burma to Yunnan region described.

0143. MARGARY, Augustus Raymond. Notes of a Journey from Hankou to Ta-li fu, *Journal, Royal Geographical Society* 46, 1876, 172–97.

Extracts of diary of murdered member of China Consular Service, the first Westerner since the Jesuits to explore region. Contrasts high level of trade and commerce with lack of privacy and confidentiality when dealing with Chinese officials.

0144. MEARES, C. H. Mr. J. W. Brooke's Journey in Western Szechuan, *Geographical Journal* 34, 1909, 614–18.

Describes trip taken in March 1908 from Chengdu, to map and explore as well as collect plants and butterflies, an area known as Land of

Eighteen Tribes. According to notice in *Geographical Journal* 34, 1909, p. 340, Brooke was murdered during expedition while on the way to Lolo country.

0145. MERZBACHER, Gottfried. Further Exploration in the Tian-Shan Mountains, *Geographical Journal* 31, 1908, 395–400; 33, 1909, 278–88.

Describes third trip to area starting in Yining. Goal was to collect more data on the Tianshan, especially on the eastern fringes. Provides history of earlier expeditions. Major finds include two mountain rivers, the Koksu and Agias, whose hydrology and sources are described. Notes that data collected do not contradict earlier findings on the area.

0146. MONTGOMERIE, T. G. On the Geographic Position of Yarkund and Some Other Places in Central Asia, *Journal, Royal Geographical Society* 36, 1866, 157–72.

Left Kashmir on June 12, 1863, with a detachment of the Great Trigonometric Survey to work in Xinjiang. Uses modified itinerary format, especially when dealing with daily administrative and logistical issues. Describes towns visited and includes tables of measures taken.

0147. MONTGOMERIE, T. G. Report on the Trans-Himalayan Explorations in Connection with the Great Trigonometric Survey of India during 1865–7. Routes Survey Made by Pundit [*sic*], from Nepal to Lhasa, and Thence through the Upper Valley of Brahmaputra to Its Source, *Proceedings, Royal Geographical Society* 12, 1868, 146–73.

Reports on use of local informats and memoirs to establish the source of the Brahmaputra.

0148. MORGAN, E. Delmar. Expedition of the Brothers Grijimailo to the Tienshan Oasis and Lob Nor, *Proceedings, Royal Geographical Society*, new series 13, 1891, 208–26. Map after p. 248.

Translation with notes and introductory remarks of the Grijimailo report, which emphasizes surface geology and economy.

0149. OLIVER, Lieutenent. Notes on the Country to the West of Canton, *Proceedings, Royal Geographical Society of London* 6, 1862, 85.

Reports on trip to Xinjiang and Tenfoo Mountains. Pleased to note that treatment of foreigners had improved. Extract of additional letter published in *Proceedings, Royal Geographical Society of London* 6, 1869, 227–31.

0150. PELLER, C. S. du Richi. Chinese Turkestan, *Scottish Geographical Magazine* 41, 1925, 164–76.

Describes the organization, purposes, itinerary, and progress of the De Flippi expedition to trans-Himalaya, the Karakorum, and Xinjiang in 1913–14. Praises highly the published reports of the expedition, which focus mainly on physical geography.

0151. PEREIRA, Cecil. Peking to Lhasa, from the Diaries of the Late Brig.-Gen. George Pereira, *Geographical Journal* 64, 1924, 97–120.

Outlines his brother's twenty years of travels in China. Main focus is on a trip undertaken between February and October 1921 from Beijing to Lhasa. Uses itinerary format, just as found in the diaries. Touches on famine, rebellions, physical hardships on the trip resulting in frostbite, and hunting successes. Describes traditional system, "*ula*," which obligated village headmen to provide transportation at a fixed rate.

0152. RAWLING, C. C. Explorations of Western Tibet and Rudock, *Geographical Journal* 25, 1905, 414–28.

Report on 1903 expedition, the first exploration of the A-Li Tso area by Europeans.

0153. ROCK, Joseph F. The Glories of Minya Konka, *National Geographic Magazine* 58, 1930, 385–437.

Reports on 1928 expedition undertaken to locate definitively the Minya Konka Mountains. Uses modified itinerary format, especially when dealing with start of trip, obtaining equipment, and stops along the way. Trip began at Daxian, northeast of Chengdu, and proceeded south to just north of Lijiang, Yunnan. Covers issues such as threats of bandits, local religious practices, and transportation, including native bridge-building techniques. Includes pictures of flora and daily life of natives.

0154. ROCK, Joseph F. Seeking the Mountains of Mystery, *National Geographic Magazine* 57, 1930, 131–85.

Reports on trip said to be first undertaken by Westerners approaching the Amnyi Machen Mountains, located between the Kunlun and Koko Mountains, from the east. Comments on the state of relations between the Chinese, Tibetan, and Muslim populations. Estimates that the highest peak is some 28,000 feet. When discussing religious practices, notes role of mountains in Tibetan worship and location of monasteries.

0155. RYDER, C. H. D. Exploration and Survey with the Tibet Frontier Commission and from Gyangste to Simla via Gartok, *Geographical Journal* 26, 1905, 369–94.

Describes the accomplishments of the 1903 trip: triangulation of some 45,000 miles; a topographical survey of 17,000 square miles; and the drafting of a large-scale (four miles to the inch) plan of Lhasa.

0156. RYDER, [C.] H. D. Dr. Sven Hedin's Exploration in Tibet, *Geographical Journal* 32, 1908, 585–90.

Report on two years' fieldwork. Major accomplishments include discovery and careful exploration of the Trans-Himalayn Range, discovery and exploration of the main branch of the Indus, and survey of true source of the Brahmaputra River. Hedin's visit there and and report seen as superior to previous reports by Nain Singh and Rawling and Ryder because he actually visited the source and compiled more accurate maps.

0157. SAREL, Lt.-Col. [Henry Andrew]. Expedition up the Yang-tse-jiang, *Proceedings, Royal Geographical Society of London* 6, 1861, 2–4.

Reports on expedition of February 1861, which sought to get to Lhasa and then on to India via the Himalayas. Only got as far as Pingshan, a few miles beyond Suzhow, due to the civilian unrest associated with the Taiping Rebellion. Emphasizes hydrology of the river as well as extent of trade between Ichang and Chongqing. Remarks that it was necessary to show force and threaten physical violence in order to get local officials to cooperate.

0158. SCHOMBERG, R[eginald]. C. F. North Karakorum: A Journey in the Muztagh-Shaksgam Area, *Geographical Journal* 109, 1947, 94–98.

Includes a history of Western exploration of area, including the 1889 Younghusband expedition, in this report on a May 1945 trip. Uses itinerary format. Emphasizes the dangers of traversing glaciers.

0159. SEMENOFF, P. P. First Ascent of the Tien-Shan, or Celestial Mountains, and Visit to the Upper Reaches of the Jaxarites or Syr-Daria in 1857, *Journal, Royal Geographical Society* 31, 1861, 356–65.

Translation of Russia report. Reviews general topographic structure of four mountian ranges with emphasis on geology, climate, and vegetation found.

0160. SHAW, Earl B. Early American Exploration of Lop Nor, *Military Review* 47, 1967, 24–31.

Describes the location, topography, and climate of the Chinese nuclear testing area using indirect quotations from the work of Ellsworth Huntington, who explored the area on foot and by animal in 1905–6.

0161. SHIH, Chan-chun. An Ascent of Minya Konka, *Canadian Geographical Journal* 58, 1959, 20–29.

Reports on ascent of peak 24,895 feet above sea level in Garze Tibetan Autonomous Zhou, Sichuan, begun May 14, 1957, and completed on June 13. Lists sponsors and participants. Sketches earlier attempts at ascent. Retells myths about the geological origins of the mountain and its features. Describes stages of ascent, difficulties with changing weather conditions, loss of four lives due to weather and avalanches, and the descent. Very rich descriptions of flora passed on way up.

0162. SHIH, Chan-chun. The Second Ascent of Minya Konka, *Alpine Journal* 63, 1958, 194–202.

Verbatim reprint of article that appeared in *Canadian Geographical Journal* 58, 1959 [item 0161].

0163. SHIPTON, Eric. Karakorum, 1939, *Geographical Journal* 95, 1940, 409–27.

Using itinerary format, provides details surrounding the exploration of the Aghil Range in a mountainous area northeast of the Shimshal Pass. Object of expedition was to provide data to permit completion of a map showing the major features of the Greater Karakorum Range. Appendix, pp. 421–24, by R. Scott Russell, gives botanical results of expedition. See also item 0120.

0164. SHIPTON, Eric. The Shaksgam Expedition, *Geographical Journal* 91, 1938, 313–39.

Reports the results of an assignment designed to explore frontier features of Ladakh, Hunza, and Xinjiang. Reviews alternative routes to the study area and reasons for using routes over glaciers. Describes tribulations involved in surveying. Uses itinerary format.

0165. SMITH, A. Donaldson. A Journey through the Khingan Mountains, *Geographical Journal* 11, 1898, 498–509.

Describes trip taken in 1897 enroute from Beijing to Mongolia and

Xinjiang. Notes seasonal variations in river regimes. Critical of Chinese demographic policies that aim at suppressing the Mongols and their traditional occupations of military service or priesthood and their replacement with Han Chinese settlers. Expresses disappointment at inability to collect butterfly and moth samples.

0166. SMITH, H. U. A Trip to Thibet, Kylas, Source of the Sutlaj and the Mansurwur [Manasarowar] and Rakhas [Rakshas or Landak Tso] Lakes, *Proceedings, Royal Geographical Society of London* 11, 1867, 119–22.

Report of boating trip clearly shows heavy-handedness of Great Britain in dealing with local Chinese and Tibetan authorities who sought to restrain European movements in the area. Comments focus on the debate regarding the differences regarding the size of Lake Mansurwur and its surrounding hydrology. Attributes differences in reports to field conditions at different times of the year and season of visit.

0167. SOLTAU, Henry. Across China from Bhamo to Shanghai, *Scottish Geographical Magazine* 4, 1888, 83–98.

Describes first European trip from Bhamo to western China in 1868 and subsequent trips in 1874–75 and 1879–80. Provides detailed ethnographic data on non-Han peoples. Notes the impact of the Taiping Rebellion on economy and people. Skimps on details of eastern end of trips since these areas better known than western extremes.

0168. SPICER, Eva D. A Journey over the Burma Road, *Scottish Geographical Magazine* 57, 1941, 29–34.

Uses itinerary format to describe trip taken from Madras to Kunming, 18–27 January 1939. Argues that construction and maintenance of road demonstrate that man can master nature. Impressed by the speed of construction of the road, the ease of mobility, and the scenery. Notes presence of goiter among road and construction workers and urges a government-sponsored iodized salt distribution program.

0169. SPRYE, R. H. F. Communication with the Southwest Province of China from Rangoon in British Pegu, *Proceedings, Royal Geographical Society of London* 5, 1860, 45–47.

Description of Yunnan and Sichuan based on literary sources, not field reports. Notes presence of mineral resources such as gold, copper, zinc, stones, and marble. Questions whether Yunnan rich enough in trade goods to make the establishment of a trade route practical.

0170. STEIN, Sir {M.} Aurel. A Third Journey of Exploration in Central Asia, 1913–16, *Geographical Journal* 48, 1916, 97–130, 193–229.

Expedition began July 31, 1913, in Srinagar and ended on May 15, 1916, after covering some 10,000 miles. Uses modified Itinerary Format. Presents the history and logistics of the expedition. Main topics touched on include the discovery and excavation of abandoned cities, the weather, and the ethnic makeup of the peoples encountered during the trip.

0171. STEIN {Sir} M. Aurel. Explorations in Central Asia, 1906–8, *Geographical Journal* 34, 1909, 241–71.

Discursive history of settlement of Turkestan, which he claims is the result of joint Sino-Indian and classical influences.

0172. STEIN, Sir {M.} Aurel. Explorations in the Lop Nor Desert, *Geographical Review* 9, 1920, 1–34.

Final report of trip undertaken from 1913 to 1916. Uses itinerary format. A major goal of the expedition was to find evidence that might support the desiccation theory advocated by Huntington. Feels that evidence from sites in and around Lou-an give credence to the theory. Assumes that the expedition was able to establish the ancient Chinese trade routes based on old daggers, coins, arrowheads, and watchtowers. Reports that part of the route is now a wild camel trail. Also comments that remnants of canals to bring water into desert from Su-lo River were excavated.

0173. STEVENS, H. Sketches of the Tatsien Lu Peaks, *Geographical Journal* 75, 1930, 353–56.

Provides daily itinerary of Kelley-Roosevelt 1928 expedition to Yunnan and Sichuan.

0174. SWINHOE, R{obert}. Additional Notes on Formosa, *Proceedings, Royal Geographical Society of London* 10, 1866, 122–28.

Formally an update on the progress of a naval survey. Praises completed maps of Takow (Gaoxiong) harbor. Describes exploration of northeastern and southwestern Taiwan. Notes Chinese origin of residents as evidenced by the economy, crops, social organization, and dress.

0175. TEICHMAN, Eric. Journeys through Kam (Eastern Tibet), *Geographical Journal* 59, 1922, 1–19. Map, p. 80.

Describes the hydrology and climate of the Salween, Mekong, Changjiang, and Yalung Basins. Includes routes of travel.

0176. **TEICHMAN, Eric.** Routes in Kan-su, *Geographical Journal* 48, 1916, 475–79. Map, p. 520.

Notes accompanying a map based on prismatic compass traverse. By the author's own admission, his map is not "geographically accurate" but is an improvement over existing ones. Prefers Chinese maps for their accruacy over those of Western explorers and especially Russian ones. Divides his route into segments based on cities visited; as such, provides travel times between cities and catalog of difficulties of transportation. Includes information about the geology, hydrology, and general agricultural economy for each route segment.

0177. **TRINKLER, Emil.** Explorations in the Eastern Karakorum and in the Western Kunlun, *Geographical Journal* 75, 1930, 505–17.

Reports on expedition undertaken during 1927–28 in two caravan traverses of the area. When in Aksai Chin region, retraces routes of explorations undertaken in 1865 and 1908. Uses itinerary format. Speculates on the reasons for the shrinkage of lakes in Tibet. Expresses preference of the Kadahis over the Turkis. Describes plans to publish more detailed observations on the morphology and geology of the study area.

0178. **WALKER, General J. T.** The Lu River: Is It the Source of the Irawadi [*sic*] or the Salween? *Proceedings, Royal Geographical Society*, new series 9, 1887, 352–77. Maps after p. 398.

Revisits the Anglo-French controversy regarding the lower course of the Yaro-Stanpo River within the general hydrology of the area.

0179. **WARD, F. Kingdon.** Botanical and Geographical Explorations in Tibet, 1935, *Geographical Journal* 88, 1936, 385–413.

Describes extent and value of vegetation. Coverage includes forests, scrub, and grasses as well as desert and tundra vegetation. Uses itinerary format and includes ethnography for each village visited. Concludes with list of twenty-five general accomplishments associated with the explorations undertaken by the British.

0180. **WARD, F. Kingdon.** Explorations on the Burma-Tibet Frontier, *Geographical Journal* 80, 1932, 465–77.

Report on 1930 Cranbrook-Ward expedition, which had three main objectives: to collect hardy flora and fauna specimens to be introduced to Great Britain, to cross the pass at the head of the Nam Tami Valley directly into Tibet with hopes of meeting any other travelers, and to observe whether or not glaciers were advancing or retreating. Found that glaciers were retreating and were a major source of Irrawady stream water, discovered small streams along headwaters of Irrawady, and postulated that mountains inhibit east-west spread of flora and fauna but they advance the north-south movements. Appendix, pp. 477–83, contains notes on actual natural history collections amassed for shipping to Britain.

0181. **WARD, F. Kingdon.** Explorations in Southeastern Tibet, *Geographical Journal* 67, 1926, 97–123.

Report on 1923 botanical expedition of eastern Tibet. Reviews findings of earlier explorations. Special emphasis given to evidence of deglaciation and vertical differences in flora. Notes seven distinct accomplishments of research, such as discovering new routes of access to study areas, and the exploration of Transumkake, Nam La, and the Tsangpo Gorge. Uses itinerary format.

0182. **WARD, F. Kingdon.** From the Yangtze to the Irrawady, *Geographical Journal* 62, 1923, 6–20.

Reports on 1922 excursion. Describes climate, glaciers, recent flooding, and flora in context of theories of climate change and deglaciation. Some ethnographic details included. Confirms that the Mekong-Salween dividing-point extends to the twenty-eighth parallel and forms a rough border between Chinese and Indo-Malayan flora.

0183. **WARD, F. Kingdon.** Notes on a Journey across Tsa-rung, *Geographical Journal* 47, 1916, 45–51.

Based on trip in 1913 from northwestern Yunnan. Attempts to explain patterns of topography amnd hydrology based on uplift and crustal movements. Argues that poor roads inhibit both trade and exploitation of local resources. Describes two patterns of villages: diffuse and concentrated. Also describes building styles and difficulties in securing water supplies.

0184. **WARD, F. Kingdon.** The Himalaya East of the Tsangpo, *Geographical Journal* 84, 1934, 369–97.

Report of field trip to "botanize in Zayul" as result of an invitation extended in 1913 by the Tibetan government. Uses itinerary format. Reviews previous explorations and reports on area. Touches on climate, flora, hydrology, towns, and religious shrines in region. Proposes a solution to the alignment of the Himalaya and Ladakh Ranges. Pages 393–94 contain an appendix by Malcolm Smith dealing with amphibians and reptiles in the area.

0185. WARD, F. Kingdon. The Mekong-Salween Divide as a Geographical Barrier, *Geographical Journal* 58, 1921, 49–56.

A refutation of Prince Kropotkins' assertions that the Himalayan System and Da Hinggan Mountains are now structurally connected and that there are no north-south trending ranges between the eastern Himalayas and the mountains of western China. Bases arguments on geological structure, petrology, and flora and fauna of area.

0186. WARD, F. Kingdon. The Snow Mountains of Yunnan, *Geographical Journal* 64, 1924, 222–31. Map, after p. 272.

Notes that there should be no surprise that earlier travelers missed the mountains because the snow peaks are veiled with clouds in the summer and trade routes do not skirt the mountains. Attempts to estimate heights of peaks. Describes the structure of the Lijiang and Kakarpo Ranges and their peaks. Mentions active and remnant glaciers.

0187. WELLBY, M. S. Through Tibet to China, *Geographical Journal* 12, 1898, 262–80.

Describes trip made in 1896. Enumerates the physical and political obstacles to full exploitation of Tibet. Notes that even in remote areas such as Tibet the impact of Japanese hostilities against China can be felt.

0188. WILLIS, Bailey. Among the Mountains of Shensi, *Bulletin, American Geographical Society* 38, 1906, 412–24.

Describes the course of the Wei River, starting from Xian. Relates the history of Western exploration of the area. Comments on transportation and communications of region, security, and reception by local officials. Some sections use itinerary format. Feels it would be easy to build a railroad in the area.

0189. WINGATE, A. W. S. Nine Year's Survey and Exploration in North and Central China, *Geographical Journal* 29, 1907, 174–208, 273–306.

Broad review of surveys, including those of the author. Major accomplishments of all expeditions include surveying and mapping of major rivers, locating mineral deposits, surveying disputed boundaries, solving geographic "mysteries," and accurately measuring the longitude and latitude of major places.

0190. WOLLASTAN, A. F. R. The Natural History of Southwest Tibet, *Geographical Journal* 60, 1922, 5–20.

Entered Tibet via Jelep La from Sikkim. Goal of trip was to collect hardy plants and seeds for use in England. Reports that areas visited are virtual flora and fauna sanctuaries, although there are conflicts among local groups over use of resources. Set in a mixed geographic travelogue.

0191. VISSER, Ph. C. The Karakorum and Turkestan Expeditions of 1929–30, *Geographical Journal* 84, 1934, 281–95.

Overview of botanical, geological, glaciological, meteorological, and zoological questions explored. Especially good section on glaciers, including photographs. Complete list of expedition personnel included. Trip was author's third to area.

0192. YATE, A. C. F. M. Bailey's Latest Exploration (of Tibet), *Scottish Geographical Magazine* 30, 1914, 191–97.

Reprint of article from *Journal of the Central Asian Society* 1, 1914. Evaluates eight of Bailey's papers that had appeared in various issues of the *Journal of the Royal Geographical Society* against the reports of other explorers. Notes difficulty in comparisons and evaluations due to no one standard for transcribing place names.

0193. YOUNG, E. C. A Journey from Yunnan to Assam, *Geographical Journal* 30, 1907, 152–80.

Trip via the Salween Valley in 1905 designed to "explore the country which lies between the empires of India and China south of the Tibetan frontier." Uses itinerary format. Provides details about ethnography and housing in Salween and Mekong river valleys. Estimates the size and discharge of rivers. Notes that the area has a bad reputation due to the presence of malaria and that this, along with the climate in general, has inhibited Chinese intrusions. Mentions poor state of transportation.

0194. YOUNG, E. C. Journey among the Highlands of Chili, *Geographical Journal* 26, 1905, 307–18.

Reports on four goals of 1904 field trip: to explore the area north of Chozhou, a large provincial town on the Franco-Belgium railroad concession; to survey the route for the benefit of the British Intelligence Branch of the North China Command; to trace the course of the Chu-ma River; and to visit the Great Wall.

0195. YOUNGHUSBAND, Sir Francis [E]. In the Heart of Asia: A Summary of the Record of the Expedition to the Forbidden City of Lhasa, *Canadian Geographical Journal* 1:1, 1930, 53–59.

> Report of summer-fall 1903 expedition sent by Lord Curzon to negotiate with the Dalai Lama permitting the English to enter Tibet. The Tibetans had refused to negotiate with the British after Tibet had invaded parts of India in 1888; a treaty ending the dispute then was negotiated by the Chinese for the Tibetans. Britain was anxious to short-circuit Tibetan overtures to Czarist Russia. Negotiations successfully concluded after British threatened an invasion the Tibetans knew they could not withstand.

0196. YULE, H[enry]. Notices of Cathay, *Proceedings, Royal Geographical Society of London* 10, 1866, 270–78.

> Describes and contrasts papers about European visits to China scheduled to appear in the Hakluyt Society collection of medieval reports on China.

3. Physical Geography: General

0197. BARBOUR, George B. Physiographic History of the Yangtze, *Geographical Journal* 87, 1936, 17–34.

Reviews the various theories of the origins of the Changjiang by classifying the authors of other studies by their occupations. Notes that the most striking feature of the river is how it responds to changes in bedrock and rock structure in its various sections. Full description of river by sections: upper, middle, lower, and delta.

0198. CARLES, W. R. The Emperor Kang Hsi's Edict on Mountains and Rivers of China, *Geographical Journal* 59, 1922, 258–69.

The edict, which describes the sources and headwaters of the major Chinese rivers, was issued ca. 1720–21 in conjunction with a Jesuit mission to Tibet to map that area. The edict itself includes a mix of firsthand reports and historical tracts of dubious accuracy and therefore adds nothing to the basic knowledge of the area but does give insight into what was known by the Chinese at the time.

0199. CRESSEY, G[eorge]. B. Fenghsien Landscape: A Fragment of the Yangtse Delta, *Geographical Review* 26, 1936, 396–413.

Study area is some twenty miles southeast of Shanghai. No part of the area is more than twelve feet above sea level, and tides in the area often exceed twenty feet in height. Descibes how population has survived by building and maintaining a system of dikes and canals. Reviews economy of area, including fishing, farming, and salt production. Provides some details into nature of communal and social activities of area in this subtropical settlement.

0200. GODWIN, Austen H. H. On the District of Lake Pangong in Tibet, *Proceedings, Royal Geographical Society of London* 11, 1866, 32–33.

Survey of lakeshore shows evidence of prior occupation based on fishing. Water is now too salty for molluscs, suggesting that the climate has changed. Full version of paper in *Journal, Royal Geographical Society* 37, 1867, 343–63.

0201. GREGORY, J. W., and C. J. GREGORY. The Geology and Physical Geography of Chinese Tibet, *Philosophical Transactions, Royal Society of London*, series B 213, 1925, 171–298.

Describes geological origins of area based on seventeen transits of Tibet.

Physiography described based on division of Tibet into seven regions. Concludes with a comparison and contrast of Tibet with Yunnan and East Africa. Appendices describe large collection of fossils collected during fieldwork.

0202. HU, Huan-yong. A Geographical Sketch of Kiangsu Province, *Geographical Review* 37, 1947, 609–17.

Describes climate, drainage, hydrology (including floods and navigable waterways), minerals, crops, and population density in one of China's most productive regions for rice, cotton, and silk. Notes need to engage in reclamation programs along Huai and Huang Rivers if rice output is to be increased. Feels the foremost geographical problems of the postwar era will be the reconstruction of the area and dealing with soil salinity. Includes fifteen maps.

0203. KIKOLSKI, Bohdan. Contemporary Research in Physical Geography in the Chinese People's Republic, *Annals, Association of American Geographers* 54, 1964, 181–89.

In general, contemporary geographic research is organized to implement state economic plans. This is demonstrated by the creation of a branch of geography known as chemical geography, which investigates the chemical processes that take place as landscapes, especially ones in dry environments, develop. Land use is linked to climatology in a deterministic framework. To progress further, Chinese physical geography needs to develop a more independent theoretical framework and structure.

0204. LIU, En-lan. The Physical Setting of China, *Journal of Geography* 45, 1946, 1–9.

Argues that to know a culture one must know its environment. Describes area, topography, patterns of precipitation, and cultivation. Provides numerous points of comparison between China and the United States for each topic covered.

0205. STRAHEY, H. Physical Geography of Tibet, *Journal, Royal Geographical Society* 23, 1853, 1–68.

In addition to a detailed description of topography, climate, and geology of area, notes how local terms and place names can be used as indicators of physical geography. Includes chart of administrative divisions of the study area.

3. Physical Geography: General

0206. TATOR, Benjamin A. Physical Geography of Kunming Basin, Yunnan Province, China, *Journal of Geography* 49, 1950, 103–13.

Uses deterministic format to present topics. Feels that Roman Catholic missionaries to region had generally positive influence. Predicts that Kunming will be a focal point of economic activity given the mineral wealth of the province and its good start on the development of transportation infrastructure.

0207. TSOU, Pao-chun. The Physical Environment of Shantung and Its Natural Regions, *Ts'e Fu, the Depository* 36:7–8, 1964, 69–77.

Describes the location, size, strategic importance, geology, topography, soils, flora and fauna, and climate of area. Provides ample climatic analogues for the United States and Europe. Does not consider Shandong to be a natural region since it has no natural boundaries and shares many physical features with surrounding provinces. Does divide area into at least three sets of subregions, including mountains, hilly areas, and alluvial plains.

4. Climatology

0208. BLUMEN, William, and Warren M. WASHINGTON. Atmospheric Dynamics and Numerical Weather Prediction in the People's Republic of China, *Bulletin, American Meteorological Society* 54, 1973, 503–18.

Presents survey of Chinese research in six basic areas: theoretical structure of circulation patterns, numerical weather prediction, seasonal changes in the stratosphere and troposphere, the influence of solar activity on the atmosphere, theoretical and practical work on artificial stimulation of precipitation, and atmospheric electricity and radar meteorology. Bibliography divided between Chinese publications in Chinese language and other languages. Optimistic regarding the contributions of Chinese meteorologists to the understanding of world weather patterns.

0209. BORCHERT, John R. A New Map of Climate of China, *Annals, Association of American Geographers* 37, 1947, 169–76.

Presents Koppen maps of China based on Chinese data and methods of Biel. Explains regions by referring to interaction between convergence zones, cyclones, and frontal activities. Describes each climate type.

0210. BROOKS, C. E. P. A Contribution to the Climatology of Western China, *Quarterly Journal of the Royal Meteorological Society* 56:232, 1929, 399–404.

Report based on data collected between 1920 and 1926 at the Friends Mission Hospital, Tongchuan, Sichuan. Provides technical details regarding instrumentation and location of weather station. Includes tables of mean, maximum, and minimum temperatures by month. Notes that the greatest weather hazard is heavy rainfall that results in flooding. Weather station abandoned in 1926 when the hospital had to be evacuated due to local unrest.

0211. CHANG, Chi-yun. Climate and Man in China, *Annals, Association of American Geographers* 36, 1946, 44–73.

After describing six major themes (seasons, humidity regions, agricultural belts, droughts and floods, mountain climates, and climatic change) concludes that there is no evidence of climatic change in China and that climate expresses itself explicitly in the landscape of the country and the modes of human occupation and livelihoods. Includes twenty-six figures, including vertical distribution of population in Yunnan Province, an area subject to frequent floods.

0212. CHANG, Jen-hu. Air Mass Maps of China Proper and Manchuria, *Geography* 42, 1957, 142–48.

Begins with a history of attempts to produce air mass maps for all of China. Provides maps and descriptions, including extent and origins, for winter and summer air masses. Notes important role of mountains in general, and the Hinggan Mountains in particular, in limiting the impact of the summer monsoons.

0213. CHANG, Jen-hu. The Chinese Monsoon, *Geographical Review* 61, 1971, 370–95.

Reviews history of Chinese interest in the phenomenon. Compares and contrasts winter and summer circulation patterns. Includes details regarding rainfall, synoptic systems, and typhoons. Refers to Tu [item 0269].

0214. CHANG Jen-hu. Climate of China according to the New Thorntwaite Classification, *Annals, Association of American Geographers* 45, 1955, 392–403.

Uses 1948 Thorntwaite classification to map data for eastern half of country at the scale of 1:5 million. After comparing his maps to the soil maps of Thorp, concludes that it is not possible to use the Thorntwaite system to delimit Chinese climatic regions.

0215. CHATLEY, Herbert. Floods and Flood Prevention, *Far Eastern Review* 14, 1918, 99–103.

Article based on a review of records available for what were northern Chihli, southern Anhui, and southwestern Jiangsu Provinces. Provides estimates of discharge rates during floods. Attributes flooding to insufficient runoff storage and low discharge capacity of canals as well as a rise in the levels of streams and channels. Deals with floods of typhoon origin separately. Notes that the obvious solution to flooding, channel deepening, is not so much a technical as a political problem.

0216. CHEN, Cheng-siang. The Climate and Climatic Regions of Taiwan, *Journal of Tropical Geography* 5, 1955, 26–38.

The rationale for the article is that despite the beginning of industrialization, the economy of Taiwan will be highly dependent upon agricultural output and raw materials. Thus, it is necessary to understand the climate of Taiwan. Beyond general patterns, describes in detail exceptions to main seasonal and regional patterns and the negative results of extremes of precipitation and drought. Includes extensive tables for major weather stations across Taiwan.

0217. CHIN, P. C. Dirunal Variation of Winds over Hong Kong, *Journal of Tropical Geography* 17, 1963, 46–56.

Seeks to describe the significance, form, and magnitude of diurnal shifts in winds at elevations ranging from 0.3 to 10.8 kilometers over Hong Kong. Data were collected daily at 00, 06, 12, and 18 hours GMT from 1957 to 1961. Uses January and July as examples. Feels wind shifts are related to the correolis effect and pressure oscillations. Links wind changes to those in precipitation. For full understanding of the presentation, a knowledge of calculus and Fourrier analysis is necessary.

0218. CHU, Co-ching. The Aridity of North China, *Pacific Affairs* 8, 1935, 207–17.

Using U.S. climatic analogies by latitude, concludes that North China is drier than expected, despite similarities between the United States and China in terms of ocean currents and topography. Finds lack of offshore winds, the irregular coastline, the Qinling Mountains, and the effect of the Siberian anticyclone as best explanations for dryness. One consequence of aridity is the need for irrigation. Maps include rainfall variability, tectonic structure, and precipitation (the latter borrowed from George B. Cressey's *China's Geographic Foundations*).

0219. CHU, Co-ching. Climatic Changes during Historic Time in China, *Beitrage zur Geophysik* 32, 1931, 29–37.

Enumerates the four basic sources for the study of historical climatic patterns in China: phenological records from Chinese classics, accounts of floods and droughts in court records, dates of earliest and last frost in old gazetteers, and meteorological instrument readings.

0220. CHU, Co-ching. Climatic Changes during Historic Time in China, *Journal, Royal Asiatic Society, North China Branch*, new series 62, 1931, 32–40.

Describes and reviews sources of climatological data: phenological records; reports of floods and droughts in Chinese annals; data on first and last frosts, snow, and severe winters in old chronicles; and instrument and meteorological records. Disputes claim of Aurel Stein [in his *Innermost Asia*, vol. 1 (Oxford: Oxford University Press, 1928) 459–60] of progressive desiccation in North Gansu since late medieval times. Yao [item 0275] feels this article contains no new information, in contrast to Chu's 1926 *Geographical Review* article [item 0221].

0221. CHU, Co-ching. Climatic Pulsations during Historic Time in China, *Geographical Review* 16, 1926, 274–82.

Includes in analysis tables of location and dynastic period of floods and droughts. Notes that not all floods and droughts were equal in their intensity or areal extent, yet they were treated as such in the dynastic records. Also includes materials on severe winds, late frosts, and snowfalls. Based on a comparison with European data, concludes that unusual climatic conditions in China are related to sunspot cycles. Makes frequent reference to works of Hosie [items 0236 and 0376].

0222. CHU, Co-ching. Distribution of Precipitation in China during the Typhoon of 1911, *Monthly Weather Review* 44, 1916, 446–50.

Of the seventeen typhoons that developed over the Pacific Ocean in 1911, seven approached the China coast, but only four actually made landfall. Discusses which areas were actually affected by these four typhoons, including the path of the storms and the amount of rainfall. Concludes that the heaviest rain occurred at the point of landfall, that there was no decline in the velocity of the storm as it passed over land, and that the heaviest rainfall occurred along the trajectory of the storm. Compares China's 1911 experiences with those of Georgia and the hurricane of August 13–23, 1915.

0223. CHU, Co-ching. A Preliminary Study on the Weather Types of Eastern China, *Geography* 14, 1928, 507–10.

Data cover period from January 1924 through June 1926 for Shanghai, Hong Kong, Nanjing, Qingtao, and Beijing. Defines four "centers of action" influencing weather changes in China. Identifies six weather patterns for winter and five for summer. Notes that well-developed cyclones are rarely seen in China. Includes U.S. weather analogues.

0224. CHU, Co-ching, Some Chinese Contributions to Meteorology, *Geographical Review* 5, 1918, 136–39.

Argues that before the introduction of Western science meteorology in China never advanced beyond prediction by proverbs, some of which are offered as examples. Nevertheless, the Chinese invented a number of scientfic instruments helpful in meteorology, including the kite, seismometer, wind vanes, rain gauges, the magnetic needle, thermometers, and hygroscopes. In addition, Chinese sunspot obeservations have been used by Western scientists to understand past climates.

0225. deTERRA, H., and G. Evelyn HUTCHINSON. Evidence of Recent Climatic Changes Shown by Tibetan Highland Lakes, *Geographical Journal* 84, 1934, 311–20.

Presents field evidence gathered to test Huntington's 1905 desiccation hypothesis about climatic change in Asia. Team visited five lakes northeast of Ladakh along the Kashmiri-Tibetan border. Concludes that there is evidence of slight changes in climate but that this was due to normal oscillations in precipitation, not to desiccation.

0226. DWYER, D. J. China's Natural Calamities and Their Consequences, *Geography* 47, 1962, 301–5.

Main focus is on the 1960 food crisis, which resulted from a poor harvest. Describes regional patterns of droughts, floods, and typhoons and the role of Communist ideology in managing the crisis. The crisis forced the government to reevaluate the management of communes, to increase food imports, to develop transportation that would permit transshipment of food across China, and to refocus planners' attention on agricultural needs.

0227. EBDON, R. A. Periodic Fluctuations in Equitorial Stratospheric Temperatures and Winds, *Meteorological Magazine* 100, 1971, 84–90.

Analyzes data for period January 1955 through December 1966 for wind and temperature at 30 and 50 millibar levels. Finds quasi-biennial oscillation pattern as dominant feature accounting for 46 and 33 percent of the variation at the 30 and 50 millibar levels, respectively. For wind, the quasi-biennial pattern is important, whereas annual variations are increasingly important for temperatures. One deviation from this pattern apparently occurred during the 1964–66 period and may be related to the March 17, 1963, volcanic eruption at Mount Agung, Bali.

0228. ELGAR, J. Huston. Notes on Temperatures in High Altitudes on the Thibetan Border, *Journal, Royal Asiatic Society, North China Branch*, new series 45, 1914, 57–64.

Reports on data collected between 8,500 and 17,000 feet during winter 1910–11 along 30 degrees north latitude by himslf and others. Remarks on higher than expected temperatures. Reports on lack of rainfall, absence of clouds, and high albedo. Snow season is late, March through May, so that it melts quickly.

0229. ENGLANDER, A. L. On the Origin and Growth of Deserts and the Environment of the Desert in North China, *Journal, Royal Asiatic Society, North China Branch* 59, 1929, 146–68.

Compares the desert of North China to that of the Sahara, Syrian-Arabian, Gobi, and Taklamakan Deserts and concludes that they are all manmade due to deforestation.

0230. FREEBERNE, Michael. Natural Calamities in China, 1949–1961, *Pacific Viewpoint* 3, 1962, 33–72.

Asserts that a China historically at harmony with its environment is a myth. Evaluates sources of Chinese natural disasters for study period and finds that reporting has become more accurate and detailed. Feels that the best indicator for early problems can be found in the revision of agricultural production statistics. Impressed that Chinese display a willingness to acknowledge calamities and their role in not meeting the goals of five-year plans. Provides maps of incidence of calamity at provincial level. Concludes that Chinese sources are adequate for measuring the extent and impact of natural disasters.

0231. GHERZI, S.J., Rev. W. Ionospheric Reflection and Weather Forecasting for Eastern China, *Bulletin, American Meteorological Society* 27, 1946, 164–66.

Describes how radio soundings of ionosphere were used to predict the weather, and especially typhoons, from 1941 to 1946. Notes that technique is still new and that data from soundings are still being analyzed, especially the so-called fading effect.

0232. HANSON-LOWE, J. Notes on the Climate of the South Chinese-Tibetan Borderland, *Geographical Review* 31, 1941, 444–53.

Notes that there are no precise borders for study area. Gives a general overview of climate in region, citing a two-season year. Provides more details and data for specific places such as Chanhua, Kanzi, Lidang, and Daofu. Seeks to characterize temperature and precipitation regimes that are felt to be related to monsoonal and not orographic forces. Speculates on the microclimatology of gorges using vegetation as a marker.

4. Climatology

0233. HENRY, Alfred J. Father E. Gherzi, S.J., on a Study of the Rainfall of China, *Monthly Weather Review* 57, 1929, 12–17.

Discusses and explicates a 1928 two-part work by Gherzi. Part one is a summary of the rainfall data and a discussion of the extratropical and tropical causal forces that lead to rainfall in China. Part two contains the actual barometric and precipitation data.

0234. HEYWOOD, G. S. P. Meteorology in Hong Kong, *Weather* 10, 1955, 413–16.

Recalls history of weather reporting and prediction, beginning with the opening of the Hong Kong observatory in 1884. Since then, there have been continuous weather observations with the exception of the 1941–45 period of Japanese occupation. Notes difficulty in predicting weather since data for Mainland China conditions are not readily available. Fortunately, the major weather hazard, typhoons, approach from the sea so that tracking these storms is easier. Describes basic seasonal variations in weather and their causal mechanisms.

0235. HIRTH, Frederick. The Word "Typhoon": Its History and Origins, *Journal, Royal Geographical Society* 50, 1880, 260–67.

First use of term in Western literature is found in a 1560 report of Plinto's journey. Suspects that etymology of the word is not Chinese and that the term was corrupted by Chinese usage.

0236. HOSIE, Alexander. Drought in China, A.D. 620–1643, *Journal, Royal Asiatic Society, North China Branch*, new series 12, 1878, 51–98.

Article inspired by data on Indian famines. Uses Chinese text (*T'u Shu Tsih Ch'eng, Ch'eng Tien*) and derives thirty-four tables of years, seasons, and locations of droughts. Sees main cause of drought as excessive northern extension of summer monsoon, which causes both floods and droughts. Drought particularly frequent in Chihli, Henan, Shanxi. Yao [item 0276] feels this article is mainly descriptive, not analytical.

0237. HSIEH, Chiao-min. Typhoons and Rice Cultivation in Taiwan, *Proceedings, International Geographical Union Regional Conference in Japan* 1957, 326–31.

Lists the factors, including high precipitation levels, long growing seasons, and ample alluvial plains, which would lead one to expect Taiwan to be a rice bowl of East Asia. Describes rice planting and cultivation schedules. Data suggest that in a multiple cropping cycle, where

Ponlai strains are grown, typhoons have little effect on a first rice crop but do considerable damage to a second crop. Argues that ways be found to begin the multiple-cropping season earlier so as to shorten the time needed to grow a second crop.

0238. HSU, Gin-tze. A Note on the Climatc Conditions of Lhasa, *Bulletin, American Meteorological Society* 22, 1941, 68–70.

Recommends Lu's 1939 article [item 0249]. Argues that Lhasa has a simple two-season regime: from May to September it is rainy and from October through April dry and cold. City is protected from cold by mountains. Prefers Cw, not Df or ET classification of climate. Cites Huntington, *Civilization and Climate*, to argue that nomads are successful due to climate and location.

0239. HSU, Jen. The Climatic Condition of China during the Time of Sinathropus, *Scientia Sinica* 15, 1966, 410–16.

Palynological investigation of deposits located near the Beijing suburb of Choukoutien. Argues that the flora and climate of China in the interglacial period not much different from conditions found during the mid-twentieth century.

0240. HU, Huan-yong. Some Remarks on the Climate of Omeishan, *Journal of Meteorology* 3:2, 1946, 50–52.

Data for both weather and climate for the periods 1932–33 and 1939–42 for a mountain in western Sichuan Basin some 3,093 meters above sea level. Compares readings with those for Sungpan Mountain, at 2,856 meters above sea level, Xian at 2,295 meters, and Lhasa at 3,732 meters. Concludes that the high variability in precipitation at Omeishan and Lhasa shows the relative strength of the monsoon.

0241. HUNTINGTON, Ellsworth. The Rivers of Chinese Turkestan and the Desiccation of Asia, *Geographical Journal* 28, 1906, 352–67.

Presents field evidence, in the form of data on old river channels and abandoned towns, for the desiccation of Central Asia. Argues that climate change was the main force behind major emigration from region. For the Tarim Basin, the evidence for change is less clear since the rivers do not appear to have changed, are large, and support major oases. However, some terminal lakes, such as the Lop Nor, are shrinking, suggesting a desiccation process here as well.

0242. JACOT, Arthur Paul. Life Zones and Temperature Conditions in Shantung, China, *China Journal of Science and Arts* 2, 1924, 550–55.

Explores problems of classifying climate of Shandong through climatic analogues with the Carolinas in the United States.

0243. KOEPPE, C. E., and N. H. BANGS. The Climate of China, *Monthly Weather Review* 56, 1928, 1–7.

Despite a weak data base, an attempt to describe basic weather-producing mechanisms and patterns is made. Mentions floods and droughts. Sees urgent need for reforestation since the other sources of floods, erratic rainfall and flat topography, are not subject to human changes or control.

0244. LEE, John. Precipitation on the Islands along the Chinese Coast, *Monthly Weather Review* 64, 1936, 287–91.

Explains the lower than expected levels of precipitation on a series of offshore islands by discussing different wind patterns and how they develop over land and sea areas. Notes a rainfall continuum: rainfall increases as one goes from north to south along the islands. Provides two tables of data that include place names with Chinese characters and romanizations and a comparison with Spanish islands.

0245. LIN, Gong-yuh. Secular Variation of Rainfall over the Island of Taiwan, *Proceedings, Association of American Geographers* 5, 1973, 143–47.

Uses Kraus and Lamb's theory of Ferrel westerlies to explain secular changes in precipitation between 1960 and 1968. Four types of variations are identified. Identifies secular trends by region and relates these to weather systems and topography.

0246. LIU, En-lan. Climate and China's Agricultural Industry, *Journal of Geography* 45, 1946, 90–96.

Essay is written in context of how people must adapt to environmental changes. Reviews the history of Chinese government efforts to expand irrigation and other waterworks. Describes landholding systems and compares and contrasts different forms of traditional and modern agricultural systems, including nomadism. Argues that to ensure the future development of agriculture the central government, in addition to its traditional concern for assisting after floods and droughts, needs to invest in transportation and develop the use of rivers in order to increase the demand for agricultural products.

0247. LIU, En-lan. The Climates of China, *Calcutta Geographical Review* 7, 1945, 27–31.

In describing the climates of China, makes frequent use of climatic analogues in the United States and Australia. Specific variables described are monsoons, typhoons, rainfall distribution and reliability, and temperature. Typhoon data for April through December 1944 for six coastal provinces are included.

0248. LOWDERMILK, W[alter]. C. Changing Evaporation-Precipitation Cycles of North China, *Proceedings, Engineering Society of China* 25, 1925, 97–128.

Research set against theories relating to locational origins of moisture for precipitation. Although research was conducted in three *hsien* in Shanxi (Jinyuan, Fanshan, and Ningwu), also includes comparative data for Changjiang Basin as well as United States and Europe. Feels that Chinese runoff/precipitation cycles are unique due to the removal of the original vegetation cover and the presence of communal forest reserves. Concludes that runoff is higher in denuded areas but that cultivation practices in fact increase runoff, leading to increased river discharges, floods, and decreased precipitation. Includes twelve plates of study areas.

0249. LU, Alfred. A Brief Survey of the Climate of Lhasa, *Quarterly Journal of the Royal Meteorological Society* 65, 1939, 297–302.

Uses four years of data from observatory the author helped to found. Notes winds calm 49 percent of time and that the temperature is warmer than expected for latitude due to isolation and protection from mountains. Classifies climate as ETH or EF (Cwb in Koppen system), despite Chinese perception that weather is cold and arid.

0250. LU, A[lfred]. Precipitation in the South Chinese–Tibetan Borderland, *Geographical Review* 37, 1947, 88–93.

Study area includes Jinsha, Min, and Yalong river valleys as well as the headwaters of the Lancang River. While the area is in the reach of the southeastern monsoons, the role of distance from the sea as well as topographic controls on precipitation patterns are described. Plum rains (*pai yu*) and frontal activity effects observed in area. The precipitation regime features 75 to 90 percent of annual rainfall occurring from May through September.

0251. LU, A[lfred]. The Weather Frontology of China, *Bulletin, American Meterological Society* 26, 1945, 307–14.

Describes the shifts in the polar Siberian air mass over North China between March and October. The air mass is cold, dry, and stable and associated with frequent inversions. Impact of air mass on North China compared with weather in Manila and Japan.

0252. MOYER, Raymond T. The Aridity of North China, *Journal, Royal Asiatic Society, North China Branch*, new series 63, 1932, 65–80.

Reviews data regarding whether or not China is gradually drying up. Concludes that there is no evidence of short-term aridity. Uses historical and contemporary records to conclude that dryness is the result of abuse of forest resources, especially logging.

0253. NORIN, Erik. Quaternary Climatic Changes in the Tarim Basin, *Geographical Review* 22, 1932, 591–98.

Reports on reconnaissance survey taken in 1930 at direction of Sven Hedin. Major goal was to determine the rate of recession of late Quaternary glaciers as part of a test of the desiccation hypothesis regarding Central Asian climates. Describes the moraines of the Duwa region, the topography of the high Karakorum, the extent of glaciers, and glacial sediments. Concludes that his data support the desiccation hypothesis.

0254. RAMAGE, C. S. Analysis and Forecasting of Summer Weather over and in the Neighborhood of South China, *Journal of Meteorology* 8, 1951, 289–99.

Summer, from May to September, in South China is said to be affected by three major circulation patterns: a southerly monsoon flow, occasional westward extensions of the North Pacific High, and tropical storms. Attempts in Hong Kong to use models based on this classification and temperate latitude air mass and frontal analysis to predict weather in South China have not met with success. Reclassifying available data and adding pressure waves to the above three patterns leads to the conclusion that the best predictor of South China weather is air flow at 10,000 feet.

0255. RAMAGE, C. S. Non-frontal Crachin and the Cool Season of Clouds of the China Seas, *Bulletin, American Meteorological Society* 35, 1954, 404–11.

Crachin, a humid period of fog, drizzle, and light rain, interrupts otherwise normally dry periods in January. By describing the synoptic conditions producing the *crachin*, and seasonal and diurnal variations in *crachin*, it is possible to define a *crachin* zone and postulate that the phenomenon is non-frontal but rather due to surface crossing of warm, moist air masses.

0256. RAMAGE, C. S. Variation of Rainfall over South China through the Wet Season, *Bulletin, American Meteorological Society* 33, 1952, 308–11.

Paper establishes that a secondary minimum in precipitation in Hong Kong is also found in all of South China. Describes data used in analysis and divides summer wet season into five subperiods. Concludes that five-day mean values of precipitation can be used to describe and explain the stability of rainfall patterns.

0257. SANDER, E. M. The Climate of Japan and Formosa, *Journal of Geography* 20, 1921, 201–16.

Section on Taiwan is found on pp. 213–15. Climate seen as influenced by geographical position, presence of ocean currents, and frequency of storm tracks. Describes precipitation patterns and provides classification and zonation of climate.

0258. SCHOMBERG R[eginald]. C. F. Alleged Changes in the Climate of South Turkestan, *Geographical Journal* 80, 1932, 132–44.

Argues against Huntington's hypothesis and states that no climatic changes ever occurred in study area and that fieldwork does not provide any evidence or indication of past or present changes. Rejects and refutes all assumptions of desiccation that are based on the notion that the Lop Nor region is more arid or that the Keriya River has disappeared. Alternative interpretations and explanations of place abandonment include diseases, salt in soil, floods, and natural meandering of rivers in sandy areas. Comments after talk suggest that presentation was very well received.

0259. SCHOMBERG, R[eginald]. C. F. Aridity of the Turfan Area, *Geographical Journal* 72, 1928, 357–59.

Reviews the debate and evidence regarding the desiccation of Xinjiang. Concludes that human activity is now the main cause of microclimatic changes. In particular, focuses on the collapse and blocking of *karez* (*qanats*), which were introduced to the area some two hundred years earlier. Compares climatic changes in Xinjiang to those in Punjab.

4. *Climatology*

0260. SCHOMBERG, Reginald C. F. The Climatic Conditions of the Tarim Basin, *Geographical Journal* 75, 1930, 313–23.

Reviews theories regarding desiccation of the area. Rejects the notion that the Lop Nor and lowland areas east of Keriya are drying up. Sees snowfall as best indicator of moisture as it is main source of river water. Notes that the hydrology of Tarim is so complex that it is probably unexplorable even by air.

0261. SHOVE, D. Justin. Chinese "Raininess" through the Centuries, *Meteorological Magazine* 77, 1949, 11–16.

Seeks to refine understanding of degrees of raininess by regraphing the data of Chu [item 0223] and Yao [item 0276]. Notes the impact of the invention of paper and civil strife on record keeping and bias in data. Argues that the discovery and analysis of early Chinese weather records led Europeans to do the same for Europe. Suggests that Chinese data do not support Huntington's desiccation hypothesis in terms of either space or time. Feels that a more accurate understanding of raininess in China must await pollen and tree ring studies.

0262. SOWERBY, Arthur de C[arle]. Famine and Flood Control in China, *China Journal* 21, 1934, 70–75.

Sees famine as resulting from destructive land use practices of Chinese farmers that have led to the spread of desert conditions. Government programs for land remediation and flood control not well coordinated.

0263. SOWERBY, Arthur de Carle. Approaching Desert Conditions in North China, *China Journal of Science and Arts* 2, 1924, 199–203.

Recent aridity in North China is due to denudation of forests, loss of vegetation due to drought and fire, and the expansion of desert conditions in Central Asia. Uses data and findings of Aurel Stein, along with his own fieldwork. Calls for wholesale reforestation and careful conservation of water resources to improve situation.

0264. TODD, O[liver]. J[ulian]. Flood and Famine, *Asia and the Americas* 35, 1935, 352–57.

Deals with Huang and Chang Rivers and the causes, problems, and impacts of flooding. Provides list of remedial programs and estimates total cost of their implementation. Notes hydroelectric potential of flood control. Compares Chinese flooding problems to those in India and the United States.

0265. TRINKLER, Emil. The Ice Age on the Tibetan Plateau and the Adjacent Areas, *Geographical Journal* 75, 1930, 225–32.

Focuses on extent of glaciers during ice ages based on his own fieldwork and use of Royal Geographical Society collection of photographs. Includes a comparison and contrast of his work with that of others for Karakorum, Kunlun, and Tibet.

0266. TSUKADA, Matsuo. Late Pleistocene Vegetation and Climate in Taiwan (Formosa), *Proceedings, National Academy of Sciences* 55, 1966, 543–48.

Traces the vegetational and climatic history of Sun Moon Lake in west central Taiwan from the beginning of the last glacial age. As background, provides a description of contemporary vegetation. Based on core samples, reconstructs a climatic sequence for the lake area. Concludes that preglacial climate was a moderate subtropical one. During the maximal Tali glacial age, there were three climate changes. Since Taiwan was probably not an island at the time, concludes that the weather was dominated by a winter monsoon pattern. Lists what plants grew around lake during Pleistocene. Relates findings to European and U.S. data and concludes climatic depression of Asiatic subtropics not as great as in other glaciated areas.

0267. TU, Chang-wang. A Note on the Constitution of Typhoons, *Bulletin, American Meteorological Society* 29, 1939, 117–19.

Compares and contrasts the different hypotheses regarding the air mass origins of typhoons, especially the mT (tropical maritime) versus mE (equitorial maritime) air mass debate.

0268. TU, Chang-wang. China Rainfall and World Weather, *Memoirs of the Royal Meteorological Society* 4, no. 38, 1934, 99–117.

Concerned with low correlation between Chinese precipitation and three of the major world circulation and oscillation patterns. Notes that since China is not climatically homogeneous, a way must be found to divide China into meaningful climatic regions. Best match between world weather patterns and those in China are for North China, the Changjiang Delta, and southeast coastal areas in the summer. Anticipates that this type of analysis will improve foreshadowing and forecasting techniques based on probabilities calculated.

0269. TU, Chang-wang. Chinese Air Mass Properties, *Quarterly Journal, Royal Meteorological Society* 65, 1939, 33–51.

Report based on soundings from four stations, which author admits is an inadequate and incomplete number. Compares his findings to those of Bergeron.

0270. TU, Chang-wang, and Sze-sung HWANG. The Advance and Retreat of the Summer Monsoon in China, *Bulletin, American Meteorological Society* 26, 1945, 9–22.

> Since summer weather in China is to a large extent controlled by the summer monsoon, it would be desirable to define a method to find the average date of arrival and retreat of the monsoon for different parts of China. This can be done by extrapolating wet bulb temperatures from Neuhalf diagrams. This method suggests that the true monsoon does not begin early in April but rather starts in the Nanling Mountains toward the end of April and progresses north and northeast at roughly two-week intervals. There is a rapid retreat from the end of August to the end of September, resulting in a secondary precipitation maximum in the southeast and west.

0271. TURNER, F. B. Flood and Famine in North China, *Journal, Royal Asiatic Society, North China Branch* 57, 1926, 1–18.

> Focus is on the flood of 1924 and especially on those *hsien* left destitute by it. In contrast to the popular explanation for the floods—Vicissitudes of Heaven—author argues that the floods and famine were avoidable since they were the outcome of man's foolishness. Major specific causes of flooding include manmade restrictions on outlets for streams, the denudation of hills, and continued building of dikes, which are no longer effective, if they ever were. Recommends that to avoid future problems the river channels be deepened, the hills reforested, and a flood channel from Duliu to the sea dug. Includes a description of relief measures of labor paid in kind and cash.

0272. WILLIAMS, John. The Day Typhoon Elsie Visited Taiwan, *Geographical Magazine* 43, 1970, 108–11.

> Despite tracking and early warnings, Taiwan sustained heavy damage due to Typhoon Elsie. Predicting the course of typhoons is especially difficult for Taiwan due to its topography.

0273. WITTVOGEL, Karl. Meteorological Records from Divination Inscriptions of the Shang, *Geographical Review* 30, 1940, 110–33.

> Uses Shang inscriptions to test whether the hypothesis of recent climatic change in China is viable. Concludes that data do support the idea of a

change to a slightly warmer climate. Reaches no conclusions regarding world climatic change.

0274. YAO, Augustine Y. M. Climatic Hazards to the Agricultural Potential in the North China Plain, *Agricultural Meteorology* 6, 1969, 33–40.

Estimates that there is a 10 to 40 percent chance of spring drought and a 30 to 50 percent chance of summer floods or drought in North China. Therefore recommends that government programs focus on flood control and irrigation so that the region can reach its full potential.

0275. YAO, C. S. On the Origin of the Depression in Southern China, *Bulletin, American Meteorological Society* 21, 1940, 351–55.

In general, this topic has been ignored due to the lack of data, but a number of studies have been completed. Reviews these studies and speculates on whether or not cyclones in southern China are due to the "western disturbances" from India or if tropical cyclones could carry their temperature and humidity characteristics all the way from the Bay of Bengal.

0276. YAO, Shan-yu. The Chronological and Seasonal Distribution of Floods and Droughts in Chinese History, 206 B.C.–A.D. 1911, *Harvard Journal of Asiatic Studies* 6, February 1942, 273–312.

Includes list of floods and droughts by location and dynasty. Analytical studies of data included. Emphasizes subjective problems of definition in trying to determine frequency of drought, given that there are many ways to interpret little rain in a dry season. Maximum periods of flooding occur within two months of maximum rainfall, while maximum drought occurs within one month after inadequate rainfall.

0277. YAO, Shan-yu. The Geographical Distribution of Floods and Droughts in Chinese History, *Far Eastern Quarterly* 2, 1943, 357–78.

Although the size of a province is related to the number of floods and droughts, the relationship does not hold for the rates of these catastrophies. Postulates that floods and droughts may be related to internal Chinese migration, although they are also associated with the construction of canals, ditches, and flood control measures. Companion piece to author's 1942 work in the *Harvard Journal of Asiatic Studies* [item 0276].

See also items 0134, 0281, and 0406.

5. Geomorphology

0278. BERRY, L., and B. F. BUXTON. The Evolution of Hong Kong Harbour, *Zeitschrift fur Geomorphologie–Annals of Geomorphology* 4:2, 1960, 97–115.

> Argues that Hong Kong was formed from a drowned, denuded center of a granite copula, which has subsequently become a zone of dominant deposition. Includes materials about climate, vegetation, chronology, specific erosional and depositional processes, and landscape evolution.

0279. BOURNE, F[rederick]. S. A. The New Rapid on the Yang-tse, *Geographical Journal* 10, 1897, 101–6.

> Describes impact of a landslide that occurred on September 30, 1896, after forty days of incessant rain. An area 700 x 300 yards intruded on the river, reducing its width from 300 to 80 yards and rendering all navigation impossible. Sees feature as an example of a rapid that is really a millrace since water levels in channel are due to constrictions by boulders and not by differences in river bottom levels.

0280. BURDSALL, Richard L. The Altitude and Location of Minya Konka, *Geographical Review* 24, 1934, 118–28.

> Describes a trip taken to the highest peak in the range of mountains some thirty miles south of Tatsienlu. Refers to earlier attempts to explore and measure elevations, especially that of Stevenson [item 0627]. Presents full description of trek to site, including logistics of establishing base and advance camps. Includes tables of some seventy barometric measurements. Origins of the name, Minya Konka, presented.

0281. BURRARD, S. G., and H. H. HAYDEN. The Geography of the Himalaya Mountains and Tibet, *Scottish Geographical Magazine* 25:1, 1909, 18–23.

> Abstract of book of same title, with special attention to geomorphology and hydrology. Argues that there are insufficient data to arrive at a final conclusion regarding desiccation of Central Asia.

0282. CLOSE, Upton, and Elsie McCORMICK. "Where the Mountain Walked": An Account of the Recent Earthquake in Kansu Province, China, Which Destroyed 100,000 Lives, *National Geographic Magazine* 41, 1922, 445–64.

> The earthquake occurred on December 16, 1920, beginning around 9:30

P.M. Some 60 percent of the dead were Muslims. There are two local interpretations of the disproportionately heavy death toll among this group. From the Muslim perspective, the deaths are seen as a visitation from Heaven for offenses against Islam. The Chinese see it as a blessing from Heaven, since their population and property were relatively untouched. Includes a map of areas by degree of damage. The major impacts of the earthquake include loess slides, damming of creeks, and the creation of new lakes. Poor communciations and transportation inhibited the spread of news of the incident and the arrival of relief. Uses itinerary format in describing visits to damaged areas. Includes an unrelated eight-page set of colored pictures entitled "In the Land of Kublai Khan."

0283. CRESSEY, George B. Landforms of Chekiang, *Annals, Association of American Geographers* 28, 1938, 259–76.

Based on fieldwork completed during 1934. Describes the location, surface geology, petrology, and geomorphological processes of study area. Reviews availability and nature of topographic maps available in China. Divides the area into five regions. Refers to Fengxian, designated as a model province between 1933 and 1937, its location, land use, and regional specialization in agriculture.

0284. DAVIS, William Morrison. Drainage Evolution on the Yunnan-Tibet Frontier, *Geographical Review* 12, 1919, 413–15.

Critique of Ward's work [item 0406]. Argues that Ward disregarded the reuplift history of the region and therefore his deductions regarding the landscape are incorrect. Notes the probability of earlier cycles of erosion, as evidenced by hanging valleys and incised meanders. Notes possibility of renewal of uplift.

0285. EDGAR, J. H[uston]. Notes on the Mountains about Tatsienlu, *Geographical Journal* 82, 1933, 264–67.

Heavily criticizes Stevens' 1930 *Geographical Journal* article [item 0073] for not including the more accurate work of others. Notes difference between written and spoken Tibetan place names. Corrects place names found in 1930 article.

0286. FRIEDERISCHEN, Max. Tien Shan: Ground Plan, *Scottish Geographical Magazine* 15, 1899, 403–16.

Abstract and translation of paper that appeared in *Zeitschrift der Gesell fur*

Erdkunde zu Berlin 1, 1899. Notes impact of climate on geomorphological processes. Divides area into three subranges. Describes rock types and notes extensive coal deposits, which are estimated to last three hundred years at 1899 rates of use.

0287. FULLER, Myron L. Some Unusual Erosion Features in the Loess of China, *Geographical Review* 12, 1922, 570–84.

Features include natural bridges, dikes, wall divides, pinnacles, and wells. After describing the variations within each feature, their geographical distributions are presented. Argues that no one cause can account for the presence or absence of the features.

0288. GREGORY, J. W., and C. J. GREGORY. The Alps of Chinese Tibet and Their Geographical Relatives, *Geographical Journal* 61, 1923, 153–79.

Seeks to show the relationships between the European and Asian alpine systems by exploring the Yunnan/Tibet area. Includes a comparison of mountain ranges of Southeast Asia and southern Africa in the context of geological uplifting and faulting. Admits material overly geological and that final conclusions await the results of analysis of collected fossils. Includes description of hydrology of Yunnan/Tibet.

0289. HANSON-LOWE, J. Notes on the Pleistocene Glaciation of the South Chinese-Tibetan Borderland, *Geographical Review* 37, 1947, 70–87.

Study area is just west of the Daxue mountains. Uses itinerary format to describe area traversed from Kangding to Lihua (Lidang) and on to Kansteo (Guangdong). Defines limits of glaciation and concludes that glaciation was active at levels lower than at present. Cites and agrees with other works on the same subject. Regrets that the position of the present-day snow line could not be established.

0290. HANSON-LOWE, J. The Structure of Lower Yangtze Terraces, *Geographical Journal* 93, 1939, 54–67.

Report of 1936 trip to examine the terrace features between Ichang and the delta. Expedition undertaken to help clarify questions regarding climatic change in area, the location of the southernmost extent of loess, and changes in the mean annual sea level at Changjiang Delta. Provides details on morphologcial appearance of terraces as well as their lithology and spatial structure. Although very critical of the work of Barbour, author is hesitant about drawing conclusions regarding the Tertiary period of the Yangtze.

0291. HEDIN, Dr. Sven. The Lakes beside the Lower Tarim, *Bulletin, American Geographical Society of New York* 37, 1905, 78–83.

Report on results of fieldwork undertaken on December 6–7, 1899. Attempts to explain the origins and characteristics of lakes Tus-alghutch-kol and Segt-kol. Reviews Russian research on topic up to 1890. Concludes that the lakes are artificial and the result of canal building gone bad. Describes local fishing techniques used to exploit lakes.

0292. HEIM, Arnold. The Glaciation and Solifluction of Minya Gongkar, *Geographical Journal* 87, 1936, 444–54.

Reviews exploration history of the area in the nineteenth century. Goal is to present a general view of the glaciation of the area. Describes the location, size, ice type, drainage, and extent of glaciers.

0293. HUNTINGTON, Ellsworth. Lop-Nor: A Chinese Lake, *Bulletin, American Geographical Society* 31, 1907, 65–77, 137–46.

Uses itinerary format. Much detail on the hardships of access, assembling pack animals, and travel. First part describes the unexplored salt desert, the second part the historic lake. Includes Western and Chinese materials as historical background and when possible reports on visits to famous sites mentioned in these sources. Notes that the area in the past supported a flourishing [Buddhist] culture but that it was and is subject to desiccation.

0294. HUNTINGTON, Ellsworth. Pangong: A Glacial Lake in the Tibetan Plateau, *Journal of Geology* 14, 1906, 599–617.

Pangong is the lowest and largest of the five lakes known as Tso-mogualari in western Tibet. Lake is saline and has no outlet. Provides data on quality and temperature of water. Analyzes diagrams of cross sections of lake against background of hydrology, lithology, and soils of the region. Assumes lakes glacial in origin but recognizes that data insufficient to construct a chronology of area. Fieldwork completed May 1–6, 1905.

0295. KOWALSKI, K. Cave Studies in China Today, *Studies in Speleology* 1, 1965, 75–81.

Based on 1962 fieldwork in karst cave areas. Describes the location and signifiance of caves in Choukoutien, Hebei, Hubei, Hankou, and the southwest (Yunnan, Guangxi, Guizhou, and Guangdong). Explains how fossils found in caves made their way to traditional Chinese medicine shops under the guise of "dragon bones." Reports that the formal, scientific study of karst caves was just beginning in China, that there was no formal Chinese organization of speleologists, and that visits by foreign speleologists were being discouraged.

0296. LONGSTAFF, T. G. Glacier Exploration in the Eastern Karakorum, *Geographical Journal* 35, 1910, 622–58. Map, p. 744.

Describes previous visitors and their results. Main emphasis is on Indian side of the border.

0297. SO, Chak-Lam. Effect of Typhoons on Beaches in Hong Kong, *International Geography* 1, 1972, 101–9.

Argues that typhoons level beaches under the surf zone at the expense of preexisting ridges. Typhoons also bring about changes in beach materials. Nevertheless, beaches apparently adjust to the wash and backwash effects of typhoons and recovery takes place through the processes of cut and fill.

0298. WARD, F. Kingdon. Aftermath of the Great Assam Earthquake of 1950, *Geographical Journal* 121, 1955, 290–303.

Earthquake struck April 15, 1950, with the epicenter located some twenty miles northwest of the Rong Thu Chu branch of the Lohit River. Notes that there was little direct loss of life but that geomorphological changes to Brahmaputra River and its banks will create flooding and irrigation problems in the near future due to the movement of tons of rock and debris. While remediation may be possible, floods are endemic to the region. Given the fact that the Brahmaputra is an exotic stream, argues that there is not much a government can do to control flooding. Explores the climatology of region, including the sources of precipitation.

0299. WARD, F. Kingdon. Caught in the Assam-Tibet Earthquake, *National Geographic Magazine* 101, 1952, 403–16.

While on a trip in 1950 to survey the flora of Asia and collect seeds of plants for potential use in Western gardens, the author and his company were trapped in the field for three months by an earthquake that registered 8.6 on the Richter Scale. Describes the impact of the earthquake on geomorphology, vegetation, hydrology, local economy, and transportation. Includes details regarding avalanches, floods, and burst dams.

0300. WARD, F. Kingdon. Glacial Phenomena on the Yunnan-Tibet Frontier, *Geographical Journal* 48, 1916, 55–58.

Describes the distribution and extent of glaciers in area of the Mekong-Yangtze divide and the variety of valley types resulting from glaciation. Argues that heavy precipitation in area is also a major causal process contributing to the geomorphological forms.

0301. WARD, F. Kingdon. Glaciation of Chinese Tibet, *Geographical Journal* 59, 1922, 363–69.

Continuation of discussion of evidence of glaciation found in author's work on the valleys of Kam [item 0303]. Includes materials about deglaciation, desiccation, and uplifting. Concludes that ranges in Tibet are post-Himalayan in origin.

0302. WARD, F. Kingdon. On the Possible Prolongation of the Himalayan Axis beyond the Dihang, *Geographical Journal* 54, 1919, 231–41.

Based on the similarities in the flora in the Himalayas and western China, postulates a geographical connection between the eastern Himalayas and the mountain system extending out of Tibet into the maritime plains. Notes that before the connection can be established more data are needed regarding hydrological changes in past periods.

0303. WARD, F. Kingdon. The Valleys of Kham, *Geographical Journal* 56, 1920, 183–95.

Compares the Changjiang and Taron Valleys with regard to climate, geomorphology, hydrology, topography, vegetation, and transportation. Notes roles of mountains in creating isolation that has preserved unique sets of flora and fauna not subject to exchange. Bases discussion on Mekong-Changjiang, Mekong-Salween, and Salween-Irrawaddy divides. Sees Yunnan as link between China and India and the Mekong-Salween divide as separating the Tibeto-Burman from the Siamese-Chinese cultural realms.

0304. WILLIAMS, A. T. Beach Morphology and Tidal Cyclical Fluctuations around Hong Kong Island, *Journal of Tropical Geography* 32, 1971, 62–68.

Seeks to describe micromorphological changes to parts of Repulse Bay, Stanley Bay, and Shek O Bay during 1969 as tides rise and fall. Describes experimental design and equipment used. Concludes that retreating tides increase scouring while rising tides minimize it and provide some aggregation of sand. No net changes reported.

0305. WILLIAMS, A. T. Seasonal Short-Term Beach Changes at Repulse Bay, Hong Kong, *Indian Geographical Journal* 48, 1973, 10–17.

Although the beach appears to be in equilibrium, the research projects described sought to establish impact of erosional and depositional processes. Describes methodology of study, which was undertaken during the months of January, June, and September 1971. Concludes that by themselves high windspeeds are not reflected in increased sediment movements. Rather, wind direction and tidal range are more important determinants of morphological changes. Notes that seasonal reversal of wind and currents results in reversal of geological processes. Includes medium-scale map of study area.

0306. WILLIAMS, A. T. Short-Term Beach Changes in Hong Kong: The Examples of Shek O and Stanley Bays, *Journal of Tropical Geography* 36, 1973, 66–77.

Describes the experimental design and equipment used. Provides information regarding location of beaches, direction of water approaches, beach height, fetch, and median grain size. Finds that falling tides are associated with deposition, while rising ones are linked to erosion. Seasonal differences in depositional rates are different only at Stanley Bay.

0307. WILSON, R. C. Note on the Channel Connecting the Lakes Manasarowar and Rakas, *Geographical Journal* 71, 1928, 439–40.

Report of 1926 trip. Explores various explanations for water transfers between the two lakes, including seepage, feeder drainage, and seasonal melts.

See also items 0554 and 0751.

6. Biogeography, Soils, and Vegetation

0308. ANDREWS, Roy Chapman. Traveling in China's Southland, *Geographical Review* 6, 1918, 133–46.

Describes findings on the second half of the Asiatic Zoological Expedition sponsored by the American Museum of Natural History in 1917 along the route from Dali to Ma-li-pa. Although there are comments regarding roads, footbinding, climatic gradients, interactions with local officials, and the opium trade, the main emphasis is on the 2,100 mammals, 800 birds, 200 reptiles, 150 Paget natural color prints, and 10,000 feet of motion picture film that were shipped back to New York for cataloging and study.

0309. ANDREWS, Roy Chapman. Zoological Explorations in Yunnan Province, China, *Geographical Review* 6, 1918, 1–18.

After traveling across six mountain ranges in Yunnan, concludes that neither mountains nor deep, swift rivers are effective barriers to the migration of flora.

0310. BARBOUR, George D. The Loess Problem of China, *Geological Magazine* 67:796, 1930, 458–75.

Article deliberately written to be a part of fifty-year debate regarding the age, origins, and mode of accumulation of Chinese loess. Argues that Chinese loess is aeolian in origin, dating to the Gunz-Mindel and Riis-Wurm interglacial periods. Describes variations in deposits and evolution of landscape.

0311. BARBOUR, George D. Recent Observations on the Loess of North China, *Geographical Journal* 86, 1935, 54–64.

Survey of progress into questions about the origins and value of Chinese loess. Notes the failures of others to properly measure the structures underlying the loess as well as the difficulties in applying a common nomenclature. Includes details regarding erosion, chemical and mechanical analyses of loess, and climatic inferences that can be made from proper analyses and measurements.

0312. CHENG, Tso-hsin. On the Geographic Distribution of Birds in China, *Peking Natural History Bulletin* 18, September 1949, 45–57.

Groups 1,087 species of birds in China into three geographic regions: a Mongolian zone, the North China zone, and the South China zone.

Describes the environmental impact on migration patterns across zones. Notes that some intermingling of foreign (Palaeartic and Oriental) species may occur along the coast and in the Trans-Himalayas in Yunnan.

0313. COBB, Collier. The Loess Deposits of China, with Special Reference to the Hwang Ho Valley, *Journal of the Elisha Mitchel Scientific Society* 40, 1924, 191–96.

Defines loess, its characteristics, and geographic distribution. Notes special features of Chinese loess and the environmental stresses it is under due to Chinese cultural practices such as terracing and cutting structures into its sides. Alludes to controversy regarding the origins of loess, but refuses to take a position within the debate. Concludes with a mini tour of streams in loess area in order to describe land use and landscape.

0314. DORESETT, P. H., and J. H. DORESETT. Peacetime Plant Hunting about Peiping, *National Geographic Magazine* 72, 1937, 509–34.

On the serious side, describes how by scouring food markets in Beijing it is possible to discover new plants and then by tracing the routes of food distribution locate the precise sources of new plants. Also describes Chinese methods of food storage. On the more lighthearted side, includes descriptions of adventures in the capital, especially involving eating.

0315. FAIRCHILD, David. Hunter of Plants, *National Geographic Magazine* 36, 1919, 57–77.

Describes the accomplishments of Frank N. Meyer, plant hunter for the U.S. Department of Agriculture, who drowned in 1918 in the Yangtze River. Meyer started working in China in 1905. Quotations from Meyer's letters vividly describe his field methods and the trials and hardships of fieldwork, especially his feelings of loneliness. A list of plants Meyer discovered in China is included.

0316. HOWARTH, H. H. Traces of a Great Post-Glacial Flood: Evidence of the Loess, *Geological Magazine* 9, 1882, 9–18, 69–81.

Rejects the freshwater and saltwater and aeolian hypotheses regarding the origins of loess in favor of a volcanic model. Assumes that in addition to the mud generated in volcanoes, there were climatic changes that increased precipitation; the combination of volcanic mud and rain created materials for the development of loess.

0317. **JOHNSON, Ray G.** Exploring a Grass Wonderland of Wild West China, *National Geographic Magazine* 85, 1944, 713–42.

Reports on trip taken in May 1943 to grasslands just west of Kangding [Tatsienlu] in Xigang Province. Includes an overview of Western attempts to upgrade Chinese livestock. Provides a positive evaluation of ecological status of grasslands but indicates that they are not fully utilized. Suggests ways in which areas could be more efficiently used in order to both preserve the ecosystem and increase output. Does not anticipate a thriving dairy industry since the growing season is too short and the area too remote from any major markets. Notes the importance of developing a network of markets connected by modern transportation as well as providing an education to all if area is to reach its full potential.

0318. **LEPPIK, E. E.** Assumed Gene Centers of Peanuts and Soybeans, *Economic Botony* 25, 1971, 188–94.

Shows the danger of assuming that contemporary distribution of crops is related to areas of original domestication. Argues that peanuts came to China from Peru, either directly or via Portuguese use in Macao; in contrast, the *glycine* species of soy was most assuredly domesticated in Manchuria.

0319. **LI, Hui-lin.** The Phytogeographic Division of China, with Special Reference to the Araliaceos, *Proceedings of the Academy of Natural Science of Philadelphia* 96, 1944, 249–77.

Reviews the history of modern botanical studies on China and the attempts at regional divisions. Uses Araliaceae to divide China into fourteen regions and to test the validity of other divisions. Includes a description of the number, origins, and diffusion of araliaceous plants.

0320. **LOWDERMILK, W[alter]. C.** A Forester's Search for Forests in North China, *American Forester and Forest Life* 31:379, 1925, 387–90, 427, 444–46.

Uses an earth as modified by human activity framework to report on a two-thousand-mile trip that started in Kaifeng to Henan, Shanxi and Shaanxi, taken in 1924 with O. J. Todd. Uses modified itinerary format. Describes mix of vegetation and how it has been modified by the planting of domestic and foreign crops. Attributes the loss of trees to the brick industry and the need to fire kilns. Bemoans the negative impact of deforestation, especially erosion, fires, and silting of rivers. Argues that the future of China is tied to the proper use of its mountains and that this will require reforestation.

0321. LOWDERMILK, Walter C. China Fights Erosion with U.S. Aid, *National Geographic Magazine* 87, 1945, 641–80.

Begins with the assumption that famines in China are not related to climate but rather to the "suicidal agricultural practice" of plowing up steep-sloped hills with no compensating soil erosion measures. Reports on a 1942–43 mission to collaborate with officials and farmers in reclaiming farmland and increasing agricultural output as a part of the war effort. Reviews and enumerates the long history of flood control going as far back of Li Ping as well as traditional Chinese means of maintaining soil fertility. In addition to recommending improved transportation and education, notes the practical measures taken to introduce contour plowing and reforestation. Provides a province by province summary of problems, activities, and accomplishments.

0322. LOWDERMILK, W[alter]. C. Forest Destruction and Slope Denudation in the Province of Shensi, *China Journal of Science and Arts* 7, 1925, 127–35.

Explains reasons behind the choice of study areas and provides names of study team members. Argues that erosion on Shaanxi is related to long-term deforestation due to pressure to produce more food. In turn, postulates that cycles of drought and erosion are due to torrential rains generated by convection.

0323. LOWDERMILK, W[alter]. C., and D. R. WICKES. China and America against Soil Erosion, *Scientific Monthly* 61, 1945, 393–413, 505–20.

Attributes heavy silt load in Chinese rivers to deforestation, cultivation on slopes, and overgrazing, none of which are particularly new to China.

0324. MOYER, Raymond T. Agricultural Soils in a Loess Region of North China, *Geographical Review* 26, 1936, 414–25.

Main geographical focus is on Shanxi. After describing the general characteristics of the topography, climate, and vegetation, the location, classification, and characteristics of the loess soils are described. Notes that only some 20 percent of the area is tillable and that full use depends of irrigation, fertilizers, and appropriate seeds. Disagrees with Huntington's hypothesis regarding desiccation of the area.

0325. PANFILOV, D. V. The Location of the Boundary between the Tropical and Subtropical Landscapes in Eastern Asia (Based on Material from a Field Study of Yunnan), *Soviet Geography: Review and Translation* 1:5, 1960, 24–36.

> Reviews prior Russian and Soviet divisions of the flora and fauna realms of East Asia. Notes that setting natural boundaries is complicated by the extent to which culture has modified the natural landscape. In the end, relies on relief, especially valleys, and watersheds to divide area. Despite some invasion of tropical organisms into subtropical areas, it is assumed that natural boundaries are barriers to such diffusions.

0326. PENNINSTON, John B. The Origin of Loess, *Journal, Royal Asiatic Society, North China Branch*, new series 64, 1933, 106–11.

> Argues that loess of North China Plain is meteoritic in origin, not aeolian or aqueous.

0327. ROOSEVELT, Theodore. Lessons from China, *National Geographic Magazine* 20, 1909, 18–29.

> Reprint of message to Congress delivered on December 8, 1908, in which the example of China's experiences with floods, droughts, and siltation of rivers is used as a rationale for a strong U.S. Forest Service.

0328. SCHWEINFURTH, Ulrich. Distribution of Vegetation in the Tsangpo Gorge, *Oriental Geographer* 1, 1957, 59–73.

> Begins with a history of the exploration of the gorge. Detailed description follows an elevation-based division of area into microclimates. Relates observations to more general relationships between climate and vegetation found in rest of Himalayas.

0329. SHALLEY, I. J., and C. VITA-FINZI. Formation of Fine Particles in Sandy Deserts and the Nature of "Desert" Loess, *Journal of Sedimentary Petrology* 38, 1968, 766–74.

> Argues that Chinese loess is the product of widespread Pleistocene glaciations, in contrast to the wind-deposited loess of deserts such as the Negev, Israel.

0330. SOWERBY, A[rthur]. de C[arle]. By the Waters of the Min, *China Journal* 10, 1929, 21–28.

> Concerned with the Min River in Fujian Province. Describes the headwaters, rapids, tributaries, and commercial use of the river. Comments that there is no complete ethnography of the region. Main focus is on describing especially the fauna, and to a lesser extent the flora, of the Min Valley.

0331. SOWERBY, A[rthur] de C[arle]. Famine, Afforestation, and Conservancy in China, *China Journal of Science and Arts* 11, 1929, 303–6.

Denudation and deforestation of landscape assumed to be of recent origin based on early-nineteenth-century Jesuit reports on vegetation and presence of recently sand-buried towns. Improvements in runoff do not require extensive reforestation; planting and maintenance of grasses and bushes would accomplish much the same.

0332. SOWERBY, Arthur de C[arle]. Forestry in China, *China Journal of Science and Arts* 2, 1924, 299–303.

Argues that forests were protected until the end of the Qingu period. After 1911, however, absent laws to the contrary, forests were cut with devastating results, including floods and climatic change.

0333. SOWERBY, Arthur de C[lare]. The Menace of Locusts in China, *China Journal* 14, 1932, 75–79.

General description of the impact of locusts on affected areas. Concerned with identifying which species of locusts affect which specific areas. Questions whether any control of problem is possible.

0334. SOWERBY, Arthur de Carle. The Natural History of China, *Journal, Royal Asiatic Society, North China Branch* 53, 1922, 1–20. Reprinted in *Smithsonian Institution Annual Report*, 1923, 351–68.

While acknowledging both the enormity of the task and the need for further research, provides an overview of the more prominent and interesting orders, families, genera, and species of plants and animals in China. Speculates on the geological, topographic, climatic, and cultural reasons for plant and animal diversity in China. Especially interested in the role barriers and corridors play in floral and faunal intrusions and diffusions. Discussion is based on extensive fieldwork, although an annotated bibliography of Western works on the subject is included.

0335. STEWARD, Albert N., and Shu-yuen CHEO. Geographic and Ecological Notes on Botanical Explorations in Kwangsi Province, China, *Nanking Journal* [*Chin-ling Hsueh-pao*] 5, 1935, 173–95.

Report on field studies in Ling Yuin [*sic*], Sanjiang, and Yung Hsien near Guizhou border. Description of the outstanding topographic features (*t'u shan*—earthy mountains with deciduous and evergreen forests—and *shih shan*—rugged, sharp, conical peaks) included. Provides alternative explanations for forest burning. Technical details in tables regarding domestic crops grown, types of wild plants, soil analyses, and weather measurements by broad site types.

0336. THORP, James. Notes on Soils and Human Geography in China, *American Soil Survey Association Report of the 15th Annual Meeting and Weekly Bulletin* 16, 1935, 18–24.

> Begins by highlighting the uneven coverage of soil surveys in China. Comments that with the possible exceptions of Mongolia, Xinjiang, and Tibet there are virtually no virgin soils in China. Reviews most important natural factors in soil formation and then describes soil types by location and use. In terms of human geography, points out that most food in China is produced on floodplains or low hills; that rice does best on pedalfer soils; that erosion is widespread; that China is a "Good Earth" as long as the government engages in preventative measures against floods, droughts, and famines; and that there is a constant conflict over use of grasslands.

0337. TIEH, T. Min. Soil Erosion in China, *Geographical Review* 31, 1941, 570–90.

> Begins by describing distribution of topographic forms, climate, soils, and vegetation cover in China. Attempts to describe the extent of soil erosion based on qualitative records, silt records, and the spread of deserts. Presents a tentative map of erosion in Southeast China. Argues that reforestation is the single most important government program that could halt and reverse the erosion of China's most important resource.

0338. von RICHTHOFEN, [Baron] F[rederick]. On the Mode of Origin of the Loess, *Geological Magazine* 9, 1882, 293–305.

> A refutation of the work of Howarth [item 0316]. Argues that the desiccation of parts of Central Asia created the raw materials and climatic conditions for aeolian processes, termed subaerial, to deposit loess in North China.

0339. WALKER, Egbert H. The Plants of China and Their Usefulness to Man, *Annual Report, Smithsonian Institution, 1943*, 1944, 325–62.

> Describes the history and status of botany in China as studied by both westerners and Chinese. Divides China into ten flora regions and catalogs by region the major plants, the soils they grow on, and their major uses. In the section on economic botany, decries deforestation. Also touches on the food, medicinal, and industrial uses of plants in China. Notes how

China imports *kaoliang*, wheat, and rice and has exported ornamental plants and the knowledge of plant diseases and their cures.

0340. WANG, Shou-chun, and Tsung-ju MU. Cotton and Wheat from Silica Soils of North Henan, *Outlook on Agriculture* 5:2, 1966, 85–89.

Report on 1963 efforts of the Agricultural Reserach Station in Hungmen Commune, Xinxiang, Henan, to coordinate programs aimed at reducing the saline built up on 25 percent of a 2,500 acre farm area. Outlines five major steps taken and provides data on soluble salts in soils and salt tolerances of cotton and wheat.

0341. WARD, F. Kingdon. The Chinese Coffin Tree, *Geographical Magazine* 25, 1952, 381–89.

Describes the richness of China's flora and fauna in contrast to that of Europe. Main focus is on aromatic and coniferous woods used to make coffins.

0342. WARD, F. Kingdon. Notes on the Flora of the West Ssuch'uan Mountains, *Journal, Royal Asiatic Society, North China Branch*, 47, 1916, 39–48.

Begins with a theoretical discussion regarding the impact of different climatic variables on the distribution and characteristics of vegetation. Remarks how plant communities change with elevation and availability of moisture. Notes presence of alien species and wonders how and when they were introduced into Sichuan. Makes frequent comparisons with alpine vegetation complexes found in Europe. Uses itinerary format.

0343. WARD, F. Kingdon. On the Sino-Himalaya Flora, *Transactions and Proceedings of the Botanical Society of Edinburgh* 27, 1916, 13–53.

Attempts to extend the understanding of the well-recognized relationship between the alpine flora found in the Himalayas and western China. Reviews the reasons for expecting both similarities and differences in the two areas. Main focus is on the areas between Tibet and Yunnan and Burma and Yunnan, proceeding by latitude and climatic and geological evidence. Notes the impact of climatic changes on flora and remnant flora. Speculates on the mechanisms of seed dispersal. Arrives at no definitive conclusions regarding alternative working hypotheses about the origins of alpine flora.

0344. WARD, F. Kingdon. Sino-Himalayan Flora, *Proceedings, Linnaean Society of London* 139, 1926–27, 67–74.

Basic hypothesis is that the flora of Tibet is similar to that found in the Burma-Yunnan ranges. Includes data on specific plant species by elevation. Makes frequent reference to European alpine flora and its similarities to the Tibetan complexes.

0345. WARD, F. Kingdon. A Sketch of the Geography and Botany of Tibet, *Journal of the Linnaean Society, Botany* 50, 1935, 239–65.

Seeks to extend and reinforce two hypotheses: that Tibetan flora is derivative and dates back to the Tertiary period, and that the flora is largely Himalayan and thus part of a complex found over a broad area in Sikkim, western China, the eastern Himalayas, southeastern Tibet, and Sichuan. Reviews the differences between political and geological boundaries for Tibet. Provides a detailed analysis and comparison between the Himalayan complex and Central Asian flora. Adamant that Tibetan plants are not part of the Central Asian complex. Specific plants are described within a fourfold regional breakdown of Tibet: Chang Tang and Tsidam, Outer Plateau, River Gorge, and Chinese Tibet. Speculates on the role of geological uplift and glaciation on the distribution of flora across Central Asia, Tibet, and Southeast Asia.

0346. WARD, F. Kingdon. Some Plant Associations of Northwest Yunnan, *Transactions and Proceedings of the Botanical Society of Edinburgh* 27, 1916, 1–12.

Provides an analysis of the plants in study area against a conceptual background that divides the determinants of flora into dominant (climatic) and incidental (all other) factors. Main remarks focus on the flora of the Mekong-Salween and Mekong-Changjiang divides. Includes a list of plants, using Latin names, by location and climatic features of location.

0347. WARD, F. Kingdon. Some Plant Formations from the Arid Regions of West China, *Annals of Botany* 26, 1912, 1105–10.

Study area, which includes Gansu, Sichuan, and Yunnan, is referred to as Chinese Tibet. Describes hydrology, geomorphology, climatology, and lithology of region. Lists specific plants found, their origins, uses, and growth patterns. Notes that flora is of greater interest to the geologist than the botanist. Urges a complete survey of desert valleys of Himalayas and western China.

0348. WESTOBY, Jack C. Growth Industry from Chinese Firs, *Geographical Magazine* 47, 1975, 567–71.

Reports on successes in 1964 planting of an estimated 1 million hectares with Chinese fir in Juding *hsien*, Hunan.

0349. YANG, Han-yung. Forest Shelter Belts in China, *Nigerian Geographical Journal* 13:1, 1970, 85–86.

Describes the plans and progress in reforestation. Compares and contrasts programs and progress under Chinese Nationalist and Communist governments. Labor for projects is supplied by local communes, while technical services are provided by local and national research institutes. Pleased with results in controlling pests and diseases. Describes three main areas: the western section of the northeastern provinces and the eastern part of Inner Mongolia [termed the Great Green Wall], the fringe of the Maowusu Desert in Shaanxi, and the sand dunes of Tinpak *hsien*, Guangdong.

See also items 0099, 0100, 0114, 0125, 0134, 0163, 0179, 0180, 0181, 0190, 0232, 0239, 0270, 0302, 0593, 0647, and 0751.

7. Hydrology and Water Supply

0350. ANDERSON, J. The Irawady [*sic*] and Its Sources, *Journal, Royal Geographical Society* 50, 1870, 286–302.

Comparison and contrast of existing views on subject and plea for more fieldwork to settle issue of the source of the Irrawady.

0351. ANON. Storing Water for Dry Summers in Hong Kong, *New Scientist* 31, 1966, 476–77.

Description of the construction of the 1.25 mile long dam across Plover Cove and the canals and conduits needed to deliver the water. Once filled, the new reservoir will add some 30,000 million gallons of water to Hong Kong's resources.

0352. BAILEY, F. M. Exploration on the Tsangpo or Upper Brahmaputra, *Scottish Geographical Magazine* 30, 1914, 561–82.

Report of 1912–13 survey of the Dibang river basin. In addition to extending the work of the Morshed survey, cites five major accomplishments: professionally mapped some 380 miles of the Yarlung Zangbo, mapped the lower course of the Nangong Chu River, discovered at 23,460 feet the Gyala Peri snowpack and its glaciers and the associated peak at Namcha Barwa, made more accurate measurements of the river, and discovered the upper reaches and branches of the Sabansir. Describes the collection of wildflowers, birds, and butterflies.

0353. BAILEY, F. M. Falls on the Tsangpo, *Scottish Geographical Magazine* 30, 1914, 90–92.

Describes hydrologic features and estimates of heights of the falls. Unable to conduct a complete survey due to the lack of bridges and access roads.

0354. BAILEY, F. M. The Source of the Irrawady, *Geographical Journal* 84, 1934, 73–74.

Brief note comparing and contrasting author's work with that of Ward [see item 0180]. Tries to reconcile the different names of tribes and rivers used in different reports on the headwaters of the Irrawady.

0355. BARBOUR, George B. The Springs of Tsinanfu, *Journal, Royal Asiatic Society, North China Branch* 56, 1927, 72–77.

Springs were an important part of the life of Jinan, the capital of Shandong, before the Huang He shifted its course and settled in a new course two miles away. Provides technical data on rates of flow, chemical analyses of water, contrasing theories of spring sources, and the reason why the springs appeared to emit steam.

0356. BLACKNEY, William. Ascent of the Yangtze-Kiang, *Journal, Royal Geographical Society* 30, 1860, 92–99.

Describes challenges and results of surveying the river from a boat traveling at five to seven knots an hour.

0357. BLACKWELDER, Eliot. The World's Great Rivers: The Yangtze-kiang, *Journal of Geography* 9, 1910, 101–2.

Main focus is course of river in Sichuan. Notes hydrological constraints to shipping and topographic limitations to building an alternative rail system along the river.

0358. CAMERON, Nigel. Taming the Yellow River, *Geographical Magazine* 33, 1960, 147–58.

Based on a 1957 visit to the San Men Dam site, author attributes the calamities associated with the Huang He to geographical and climatic origins and predicts improvements once the dam is completed.

0359. CHAPMAN, Frederick G. The Hwang Ho, the Yellow River, *Geographical Review* 11, 1922, 1–18.

Reviews the historical importance of the river. Traces the sources of the river through the history of Western exploration of the headwaters. Describes the tributaries on a province by province basis, noting the impact of the river on the local economy. Also provides an overview of ethnic makeup of each province discussed. Analyzes river, and especially changes in course, by four broad sectors: Great Falls, Ordos Loop, Lowland portion, and lower course.

0360. CHAPMAN, Herman H. Forests and Floods in China, *American Forestry* 25, 1919, 835–43.

Paraphrase of material published in China by Lin Dau-yang of the Chinese Forestry Association. Main cause of flooding, especially in North China, is deforestation. Only solutions to flooding are barrier dams, reservoirs, and reforestation. The building of more dikes will only worsen flooding in the long run.

0361. CHARLES, W. R. The Yangtze-Chiang, *Geographical Journal* 12, 1898, 225–40.

General description based on historical and contemporary Chinese sources of riverine activities emphasizing the location of the main headwaters of the river and the fact that the actual length of the river is unknown. This must be discovered in order to fully promote navigation and trade on the river.

0362. CHATLEY, Herbert. The Hangchow Bore, *Asiatic Review* 45, 1949, 811–22.

Presents details of bore, including mechanisms, timing, and height. Argues that Chinese had a longer history of interests in tides and the influence of the phases of the moon on them. Discounts any notion that the tidal bore has any hydroelectric potential.

0363. CHATLEY, Herbert. River Problems in China, *Journal, Royal Asiatic Society, North China Branch*, new series 49, 1918, 1–12.

Survey of seven main rivers (Liao, Hai, Hung, Chang, Min, Xi, and Red) in terms of irrigation and water supply, navigation, flood prevention, and power supply potential. Optimistic that waterpower can be developed to supplement coal-fired plants, especially in areas lacking coal reserves.

0364. CLUBB, Edmund. Floods of China, a National Disaster, *Journal of Geography* 31, 1932, 199–206.

Refers to floods in the Changjiang and Huai river systems in 1931, which were characterized by unusually high levels of flooding. Surprised that the Chinese appeared to have done nothing to prevent the flood. Describes the economy of the area as bare subsistence. Includes details regarding the extent of the flooding, the plight of refugees as they endured exposure to the elements, and the outbreaks of dysentery and cholera. Predicts that the flood would have serious, long-term, negative impacts on the social structure and economy of affected areas.

0365. COLCHESTER, Lord, and Capt COLLINSON. On the Yangtsze-kiang, *Journal, Royal Geographical Society* 17, 1847, 130–44.

Reports on British efforts in 1840 and 1842 to conduct surveys along the Changjiang. Especially good material on latitude, longitude, and elevations at strategic points along the river as well as depth soundings of river and distances between ports and landings.

0366. COVILLE, Lilian Grosvenor. Here in Manchuria: Many Thousand Lives Were Lost and More Than Half the Crops Destroyed by the Floods of 1932, *National Geographic Magazine* 63, 1933, 233–56.

Report by resident of Harbin. Describes life in Harbin before and after the floods, with special attention to the cost of living, health and infectious disease prevention, and transportation. Notes past role of Russians and new role of Japanese in life of city and area. Despite the heavy hand of the Japanese administration, banditry is common. The Chinese appear to be at a loss as to how to cope with both political and natural disasters.

0367. EDKINS, Joseph. On Chinese Notices of Their Own Great Rivers, *Proceedings, Royal Geographical Society* 3, 1858–59, 375–76.

Focuses on recent changes in the courses in the *thalweg* [navigable channel] of the Changjiang and Huang He. Refers to a large corpus of classical and historical Chinese literature on the topic of river changes. Argues that a knowledge of physical geography is necessary to ensure commercial and military successes in China.

0368. EDMUNDS, Charles K[eyser]. Taming the Yellow River, *Asia Magazine, Journal of the American Asiatic Association* 21, 1921, 538–39, 567.

Reports on projects undertaken by the American Red Cross and the American International Corporation to reconstruct the Grand Canal and Huang He dikes and canals.

0369. ELIAS, Ney. A Visit to the Valley of the Shuili in Western Yunnan, February, 1875, *Journal, Royal Geographical Society* 46, 1876, 198–227.

Appendix to report on ill-fated expedition to Yunnan. Outlines circumstances of trip and causes of termination. Ethnographic detail focuses on economy and material culture. Reports that there is little trade among non-Han groups and that taxes are paid to central government.

0370. ELIAS, Ney. Notes of a Journey to the New Course of the Yellow River in 1868, *Journal, Royal Geographical Society* 40, 1870, 1–32.

Assesses the impact of the new course of the river on shipping and especially whether vessels of "sufficiently light draught" can navigate the sharp bends. Makes specific recommendations regarding the rehabilitation of the old course and regional economy.

0371. ELIASSEN, Sig. Topographic Maps and Related River Questions of the North China Plain, *Norsk Geografisk Tidsskrift* 15, 1955, 99–124.

Written in response to the floods of summer 1917, which inundated Tianjin for several months. Reviews the history of Chihli River and Hai Ho Conservancy Commissions and their programs. Provides details of fieldwork to survey and map the flood-affected areas as well as recommendations for dealing with the changing courses of the river tributaries around Tianjin.

0372. ELIASSEN, S[ig]., and O[liver]. J[ulian]. TODD. The Wei Pei Irrigation Project in Shensi Province, *China Journal* 17, 1932, 170–80.

The location, soil, and precipitation patterns of area are not ideal for growing crops. Nevertheless, a successful agricultural economy has emerged due to irrigation systems. After describing the long-term history of irrigation projects in the area, the focus turns more narrowly to the work of the China International Famine Relief Commission, which began its work in reaction to the 1920–24 famines. Evaluates the construction, technology, and financing of projects.

0373. FREEBERNE, J. D. M. The Haiho River Basin Project, *Geography* 57, 1972, 217–25.

Uses Haiho as an example to describe state-sponsored water conservancy projects. The food crisis of 1960 and flooding in 1963 in the Haiho Valley are seen as the main stimuli to government action. Describes generally what water conservation projects were possible. Includes details regarding the hydrology of the Haiho, including the incidence of floods and droughts. Relates government projects to Mao's retelling of the tale of the foolish old man who moved the mountain.

0374. FREEBERNE, Michael. Glacial Meltwater Resources in China, *Geographical Journal* 131, 1965, 57–60.

China has 44,000 square kilometers of glacial and perennial snow areas containing a total water reserve of 240,000 million cubic meters. Fully one-half of these reserves are in the northwest. Glacial meltwater has great potential in China's efforts to meet the challenges of population growth. Reviews location of areas where these waters could be used in irrigation and the attempts, such as spreading coal dust on the surface of some glaciers, to increase the runoff.

0375. HEIDENSTANN, H. von. Growth of the Yangtze Delta, *Journal, Royal Asiatic Society, North China Branch*, new series 53, 1922, 21–36.

Comprehensive report on Changjiang discusses the following topics: headwaters, tides, growth of delta, geology, subsidence, Chinese records of mouths of the river, and land use along the river going back as far as 200 B.C.E.

0376. HOSIE, Alexander. Floods in China, 630–1630, *China Review* 7, 1879, 371–72.

Contains abridged table of four hundred instances of floods in China based on information in *T'u Shu Tsih Ch'eng* (Encyclopedia of Literature), complied during reign of the Kangxi emperor. Data listed by province and time but notes that an entire province is not always affected. Mean interval between floods calculated as 21.7 years.

0377. HUBBARD, George D. Min River Sections between Kuan-hsien and Wei-chou, Szechuan, China, *Bulletin, Geological Society of America* 48, 1937, 123–51.

Comprehensive description of structure and petrology of area with special emphasis on geologically derived economic products of area. Outlines future research needs, including a catalog of fossils, and the correlation of mineral deposits of economic significance and determination of the ages of various strata.

0378. HUBBARD, George D. The Pearl River Delta, *Lingnan Science Journal* 7, 1928, 23–36.

Catalog of geological forms and processes that contributed to development and use of delta. These include tributaries, islands, drowned topography, recent subsidence, erosion, and submergence.

0379. HUBBARD, James Mascarene. The Tsang Po, *National Geographic Magazine* 12, 1901, 32–35.

Describes the location and nature of river headwaters in Southwest Tibet. Provides details regarding the course of the Yarlung Zangbo River. Sketches the history of exploration in the area by westerners. Notes that 150 miles of the river are still not explored due to the reluctance of the Tibetan government. Hopes that as relations between the governments of India and Tibet improve the unexplored areas will be surveyed.

0380. JONES, Fred O. Tukiangyien: China's Ancient Irrigation System, *Geographical Review* 44, 1954, 543–59.

Provides the hydrologic background necessary for understanding the Min River diversion projects devised by Li Ping ca. 250 B.C.E. Describes the digging of channels, construction of temporary diversion dams and suspension bridges, and length of all engineering works.

0381. JIRO, Yonekura. Geographical Comparison between the Bengal Plain and the Lower Yangtze Plain, *National Geographical Journal of India* 17, 1971, 161–64.

Eight-point comparison of the two river basins concludes that both were exploited under colonialism and redeveloped after independence.

0382. KIRBY, John. Managing Water Resources in Taipei, Taiwan, *Iowa Geographer* 28, 1971, 15–21.

Claims no modern city planner would choose Taipei Basin as a site for a city. Describes the site, population, and propensity for flooding in area. Hard data involve the 1969 typhoon and its consequences, which included difficulty in accessibility and increased food costs. Notes how city, provincial, and national flood control plans exist and can be in conflict and lead to confusion over who is ultimately responsible for flooding and implementing flood prevention measures. Not optimistic that either adequate flood prevention measures or securing water supplies will occur since such activities are low on the list of priorities of the North Taiwan Regional Planning Commission.

0383. LITTLE, Archibald [J]. The Crux of the Upper Yangtse, *Geographical Journal* 18, 1901, 498–508.

Describes trip to flooded upper reaches of Changjiang taken in 1910 despite the perils of travel. Argues that a permanent steam service would be profitable if appropriate, shallow draft, steam-powered craft could be employed. Sees no reason why the British could not supply craft and therefore control trade.

0384. LOCKHART, William. The Yang-tse-kiang and the Hwang-Ho, or Yellow River, *Journal, Royal Geographical Society* 28, 1858, 288–97.

Seeks to demonstrate the importance of rivers as inlets to China. Traces routes of rivers and their tributaries. Notes the administrative costs to the Chinese government of maintaining dikes. Adverse impact of Taiping Rebellion on livelihoods described.

0385. LOCKWOOD, Edward T. Floods and Flood Prevention in China, *Far Eastern Survey* 4, 1935, 164–68.

Main focus is on the 1935 floods at Hankou. Describes on a region by region basis for all of China main causes of flooding in general, including underlying hydrological situation, changes in river channels, and siltation. Notes that there is agreement on the part of all experts on solutions to the problem.

0386. MEAD, Daniel W. Floods and Famine in China, *Journal of Geography* 14, 1916, 261–64.

Notes that farmers in China recognize the dangers of flooding, which are due mainly to heavy rains associated with typhoons. Main focus is on consequences of flooding along the Huai River in 1910. Describes humanitarian efforts by Red Cross and American businessmen who raised money for long-term solutions. The reclamation of Hongzi Lake is seen as the type of project that should be supported, yet feels that the Chinese and their government are not up to the type of massive work required for large-scale, widespread reclamation. Argues that if the Chinese could muster the will to work they could succeed as they did in the past and as the Japanese were doing to modernize their country.

0387. MOSSMAN, Samuel. Double Delta on the Whang Ho, or Yellow River, in China, *Geographical Magazine* 5, 1876, 92–97, 152–54.

Describes the development of channels by referring to the underlying geology and discharge rates of the river. Speculates on the geological history of the Shandong Peninsula and the hydrology of the Huang He. Includes a comparison and contrast of Western reports about the Huang He. Praises the work of the public works departments in their conservancy of the river.

0388. MOULE, A. C. The Bore on the Ch'ien-t'ang River in China, *T'oung Pao*, series 2, 22, 1923, 135–88.

Chinese text and translation of description of the bore recorded between 1241 and 1252. Supplements translation with modern observations of the bore and a Western-language bibliography on subject.

0389. OLIPHANT, Laurence. Notes of a Voyage up the Yang-tze or Ta-Kiang, from Wusung to Hankow, *Proceedings, Royal Geographical Society* 3, 1858–59, 162–64; *Journal, Royal Geographical Society* 30, 1860, 75–92.

Notes how rapidly the river course has changed, thus rendering

Admiralty charts obsolete. Describes landscapes and topography along route. Includes abstract of travel dates and distances covered.

0390. OXENHAM, E. L. On the Inundations of the Yang-tse-Kiang, *Journal, Royal Geographical Society* 45, 1875, 170–83.

Based on three years' residency in Hankou, describes impact of three successive floods on population and area. Indicates how floods and drought conditions can coexist in close geographic proximity. Catalogs general causes of flooding and classifies floods by number, type, and sources.

0391. PRATT, Sir John. The Yellow River: China's Sorrow, *Geographical Magazine* 21, 1948, 217–25.

Describes the history of river use, including the 1938 decision to blow up the dike at Huakuankou to stop the Japanese invasion. Rehabilitation of affected region hurt by continuing conflict between the Kuomintang and the Chinese Communist Party.

0392. RHYNSBURGER, Willert. Ground Water Supply Problems of Taiwan, *Proceedings, International Geographical Union Regional Conference in Japan* 1957, 170–73.

Despite being rich in well- and groundwater resources due to high levels of precipitation, Taiwan must still deal with the supply of adequate water supplies for the complex demands of a modern economic system. Two-thirds of urban water supplies are derived from surface sources. Sees groundwater as an excellent way to meet future water needs due to the extent and quality of aquifers for both storing and transporting water. Provides maps and tables of regions according to potential to draw water. In the end, concludes that only some 5,500 square kilometers, or some 15.3 pecent of area evaluated, are underlain by good to abundant aquifers.

0393. ROCK, Joseph F. Through the Great River Trenches of Asia, *National Geographic Magazine* 50, 1926, 133–86.

Describes the headwaters and courses of the Changjiang, Mekong, Salween, and eastern branch of the Irrawaddy river systems. Includes a description of process of exploration. Nonphysical topics covered include religious practices, such as burials and pilgrimages, and rope bridges, including their use, hazards, design, history, and construction. General goal of report is said to be to provide National Geographic Society members with pictures; therefore thirty-eight pages of pictures included.

0394. RYDER, C. H. D. Exploration in Western China, *Geographical Journal* 21, 1903, 109–26.

Describes 1898 survey of hydrology of Yunnan aimed at providing accurate maps (printed on p. 220) and assistance in possible reconstruction of area. The latter is seen as a political rather than an economic issue.

0395. SHIH, Ya-feng. Making Glacial Ice Serve China's Socialist Construction, *National Geographical Journal of India* 5:1, 1959, 34–37.

Describes first attempts at assessing use of glacial runoff in Chilian Range. One local technique, blackening the top of the glacier, while improving available supplies by extending the runoff season, may not be practical on a large regional scale. Feels use of glaciers is justified for their economic value as well as the scientific benefits that will accrue by their use, including the development of a model of general atmopsheric and water circulation in dry regions.

0396. SOWERBY, Arthur de C[arle]. Famine, Floods, and Folly, *China Journal of Science and Arts* 2, 1924, 395–99.

Reports on 1917 and 1924 floods of Tianjin. Blames inept, corrupt government that did nothing after the 1917 floods to ameliorate the problem as well as local practices of Chinese such as cutting bushes and grass for fuel.

0397. TODD, O[liver]. J[ulian]. Four Rivers of Shansi, *Far Eastern Review* 31, 1935, 62–69.

Actually the draft of a preliminary report of the China International Famine Relief Commission. Goal of report was to suggest possible improvements in irrigation and to follow up on the commission's Fen River Report [item 0399]. Describes the commission's work, organization, financing, and proposals for the Hu To, Sang San, Jang, and Jin Rivers. Argues that silt is needed to maintain soil fertility; therefore any construction must ensure that silt gets to soils. To ensure this, emphasis is placed on constructing small-scale dams. Richly illustrated with large-scale maps and pictures of fieldwork.

0398. TODD, O[liver]. J[ulian]. Irrigation Work, *Far Eastern Review* 29, 1933, 60–71.

Describes history of irrigation in North China. Includes hard data on hydrometrics, including discharge rates. Compares progress made by various governmental agencies and the China International Famine Relief Commission in constructing new bridges, dams, and tunnels and remodeling old canals. Notes how construction projects aid in relief work. Richly illustrated with large-scale maps and pictures of construction.

0399. TODD, O[liver]. J[ulian]. Regulation of the Fen Ho for Flood Protection and Conservancy of Winter Flows as an Aid to Irrigation, *Far Eastern Survey* 30, 1934, 165–77, 221–30.

Article is based on a 1933 survey of canals and diversion dams for the Shanxi Water Conservancy Commission. Describes the organization, personnel, and financing of surveys. Provides a history of water regulation and specific proposals for new dams, reservoirs, and irrigation projects. Includes projected costs and benefits. Argues that Fen river basin an ideal place to start conservation work since the area is relatively peaceful, with no bandits. Furthermore, the proposals fit well into other plans for irrigation and conservation. Richly illustrated with large-scale maps and pictures.

0400. TODD, Oliver J[ulian]. Taming "Flood Dragons" along China's Hwang Ho, *National Geographic Magazine* 81, 1942, 205–34.

Notes inherent tension in two physical phenomena, China's Good Earth, and China's Sorrow, the Yellow River. Describes the floods, loss of crops, refugee streams, and banditry that resulted from the political decision to breach the river's dams to halt the Japanese invasion in 1938. Recommends long-term emphasis on repairing breaches and reforestation. Excellent pictures of breaches being repaired with traditional materials and technology.

0401. TODD, O[liver]. J[ulian]. Yellow River Reharnessed, *Geographical Review* 39, 1949, 38–56.

Report of 1946–47 UNRRA (Relief and Rehabilitation Administration) to restore the Huang He to its pre-1938 course. Includes effects of the 1938 diversion on population and especially refugee flows. Includes a history of past Yellow River channel locations as well as the precipitation regime and silt loads of the river. Technical topics covered included plans, materials and equipment, transportation issues, efforts at reclamation, and a comprehensive seven-point program of river control. Concludes with notion that in the world's food-population nexus the Huang He is a world problem unto itself.

0402. TREAGAR, T. R. Dig the Beds Deep, Keep the Dykes Low, *Geographical Magazine* 38, 1966, 787–88.

Uses quotations from Li Ping to show how the "walking on two legs" policy is a viable option in controlling flooding along the Min River, which drops 9,000 feet in 200 miles.

0403. TURLEY, Robert T. Notes of the Upper Liao, Manchuria, *Geographical Journal* 25, 1905, 297–99.

Describes river tributaries. Notes which of these are navigable by small junks. Remarks on the lack of bridges and poor quality and variety of fishing stocks. See item 0127.

0404. VENIUKOF, M. The Pamir and the Sources of the Amu-Daria, *Journal, Royal Geographical Society* 36, 1866, 248–65.

Translation of paper published in the *Journal of the Imperial Geographical Society* of St. Petersburg. Consists of a compilation of literary sources on the topic.

0405. WALKER, {General} J. T. The Hydrography of South-Eastern Tibet, *Proceedings, Royal Geographical Society* 10, 1888, 577–83. Map after p. 612.

Summarizes 1887 trip on Lu River to determine whether it is a possible source of the Irrawaddy. Criticizes reports by others on same subject.

0406. WARD, F. Kingdon. The Hydrography of the Yunnan-Tibet Frontier, *Geographical Journal* 52, 1918, 288–99.

Sees precipitation patterns as main explanation for stream patterns and river beheading. Notes impact of topography on distribution of and communication between different ethnic groups.

0407. WIENS, H{erold}. J. Regional and Seasonal Water Supply in the Tarim Basin and Its Relation to Cultivated Land Potentials, *Annals, Association of American Geographers* 57, 1967, 350–66.

Material presented in context of Chinese concern for a growing population. Describes the origins of water supplies, including glaciers, streams, and meltwater, in order to establish the characteristics and seasonality of water flow and losses. Describes oasis production and history of agriculture in scattered places. Notes that not all water resources are used well and that important hydrological data have not yet been collected. As such, warns against the dangers of overdrawing groundwater and overexploitation of surface water.

0408. WINGATE, A. W. S. Further Notes Concerning the Liao Ho, *Geographical Journal* 26, 1905, 421–29.

Corrects maps and notes of Turley [item 0403] for five broad topics: nomenclature, headwaters, course of streams and places they pass, the source of the Liao, and the impact of the Boxer Rebellion. Agrees with Turley that area needs more bridges.

See also items 0127, 0180, 0193, 0215, 0241, 0452, and 0477.

8. Resources, Energy, and Minerals

0409. BAIN, H. Foster. China's Coal Reserves, *Foreign Affairs* 6, 1928, 498–500.

Pessimistic review about the possibility of development in China based on assumption that coal reserves will last only one-hundred years were China to use coal at the rate the United States did in 1928. Refers readers to his 1927 publication, *Ores and Industry in the Far East*, for details of argument.

0410. BARBOUR, George B. The Iron Mines of Hsuan Hua, Chihli, China, *China Journal of Science and Arts* 2, 1924, 478–85.

Concerned that von Richthofen's estimates of mineral reserves in Shandong are too high, as evidenced by more up-to-date surveys, since industry is beginning to develop. Describes geological history and structure of area, methods of mining, varieties of ore, and modes of formation.

0411. BELDEN, W., and M. SALTER. Coal Resources of China, *Economic Geography* 11, 1935, 304–6.

Uses data from the *1933 China Yearbook* to describe extent and distribution of coal. Coal is widely, but spottily, distributed. Reserves are subject to considerable controversy. Focuses on Shanxi-Shaanxi, Fuxin, and Kailan fields.

0412. BELDEN, W., and M. SALTER. The Iron Ore Resources of China, *Economic Geography* 11, 1935, 426–30.

Promotes the idea that China's iron ore reserves are more limited than generally supposed. Notes that Japan controls 90 percent of Chinese and Manchurian iron ore reserves. Chinese mining operations tend to be small scale, although the government does have a ten-year development plan, about which the authors are doubtful. In addition to a limited supply of ore, impediments to development include inadequate transportation, high production costs, lack of capital and technical personnel, lack of political stability, and Chinese opposition to foreign exploration and exploitation. Maps of location of ore and ore-producing areas, as well as a table of reserves, are included.

0413. BROCK, R. W. China and Its Mineral Resources, *Economic Geology* 23, 1928, 209–13.

Editorial based on limited fieldwork in China in 1927 argues that China is deficient in all essential minerals except coal. Sees geology of China as being suggestive of western America, albeit with less mineralization. Concludes that the Chinese economy should be agriculturally based and should rely on imported mineral and industrial products. Pessimistic about predictions that a democratic revolution can or will succeed in modernizing the Chinese economy to the extent that it would be able to overtake the West.

0414. CHEN, Cheng-siang, and Kam-nin AU. The Petroleum Industry of China, *Die Erde* 103, 1972, 316–33.

Against historical background of low use of petroleum products, argues that the People's Republic of China has four goals in developing its petroleum industry: to accelerate prosperity, to maximize the potential of existing oil-exploiting infrastructure, to expedite the development of Yumen fields and the construction of an oil refinery in Lanzhou, and to develop synthetic fuels based on resources in the northeastern part of the country. Describes major production areas. Notes the potential of oil shales. Expects China to become a net importer of oil as internal demand grows.

0415. DWYER, D. J. The Coal Industry in Mainland China since 1949, *Geographical Journal* 129, 1963, 329–38.

Uses 1936 data as a basis for evaluating Chinese claims of having restored coal production under its five-year plans and during the Great Leap Forward period. Describes locations of large, small, and new mines. Major problems in the coal industry include poor quality of the final product, with the delivered product being frequently mixed with stones, regional and temporal shortages, a weak transportation system, and the conflicts over coal versus coke production and use.

0416. ErSELCUIK, Muzaffer. Japan's Oil Resources, *Economic Geography* 22, 1946, 14–28.

Includes discussion and production data for period 1932–36 on oil in Formosa, North China, and Manchuria. Notes the discovery in 1940 of the Fuxin fields. Crude oil is extracted from the Taihofu fields in northern Taiwan. Doubts that large fields will ever be found in Taiwan due to the high rate of geological faulting. Similarly, although Standard Oil Company surveyed parts of North China, including Shangdong, Hebei, and Henan, this region is not expected to be a major oil-producing region. Were large reserves of oil to be found, production would depend on maintaining political stability.

0417. FREY, John W. Economic Significance of the Mineral Wealth of China, *Annals, American Academy of Political and Social Science* 152, 1930, 116–26.

Notes that China observers from Marco Polo on have overestimated China's mineral wealth. Feels China has weak raw material base and using the example of surface mines notes how historically there has been little done to develop resources. Sees China's industrial future as dependent on coal production.

0418. GINSBURG, Norton S. Taiwan: A Resource Analysis of an Oriental Economy, Part I, *Economic Development and Cultural Change* 1, 1952, 37–56; Part II, 1, 1952, 110–31.

Sees Taiwan as a "fortunate accident" for those interested in problems of resources and economic development. Evaluates agricultural and industrial potential against background of Japanese heritage. Predicts that economy will stagnate if political economy of area permits only expansion of political and military strength at the expense of other developments.

0419. HEENAN, L. D. B. The Chinese Petroleum Industry, *Tijdschrift voor economische en sociale geografie* 57, 1966, 149–59.

Reviews post-1949 progress in developing a sector of the economy that was small, poorly equipped, and technically backward. Major factors influencing petroleum production include the size and nature of the technical resource base, the withdrawal of Soviet aid, the indigenous manufacturing of refining equipment, and the identification of newfound physical resources. Doubts that in the long run China will be self-sufficient even though production and refining capacities have increased. Notes role of transportation in petroleum development.

0420. JUAN, V[ei] C[how]. Mineral resources of China, *Economic Geology* 41, 1946, 399–474.

Article is a U.S. Geological Survey report. Sees a fully industrialized China within twenty-five years as a real possibility given the size and extent of its mineral resources. Argues that China will surpass Japan as an industrial power and absorb all the Far Eastern markets. Describes geological data on thirty-three individual minerals and a catchall category of "other minerals." Provides data on location and production of raw materials for selected years in 1930s and 1940s. Bibliography arranged by specific mineral.

0421. KAMBARA, Tatsu. The Petroleum Industry in China, *China Quarterly* 60, 1974, 699–719.

Asks whether projections of production levels of 100 million metric tons are possible and if so what are the implications. Argues that there was little development of the petroleum industry before 1949 because of the lack of political stability, of knowledge of the geology of China, and of interest by the major international oil companies. Notes two exceptions: in 1907 the Yenchang field was developed in Shaanxi, and in 1914 Standard Oil began exploration.

0422. LOCKHART, Jack. Two Trips to the North of Cheng-tu, *Geographical Journal* 21, 1903, 282–88.

Goal of survey was to ascertain what mineral resources were available for commercial exploitation in Sichuan. Notes the lack of wheeled traffic outside the main cities and the Chinese aversion to cold drinks. Praises achievements in irrigation that are seen as the basis for a large, well-fed population.

0423. NORIN, E[rik]. Notes on the Coal and Iron Ore Deposits of Central Shansi, *Journal, Royal Asiatic Society, North China Branch*, new series 53, 1922, 95–104.

Describes origins and characteristics of southern Shanxi coal formation. Describes extent of exploration and exploitation of shale and coal deposits.

0424. NYSTROM, Erik T. Geophysical Prospecting for Gold, Metallic Ores, and Petroleum and Its Possible Application in China, *Journal, Royal Asiatic Society, North China Branch*, new series 67, 1936, 131–46.

Argues that the Chinese Geological Survey, founded around 1916, should use most modern exploration methods since mineral seams are often discontinuous, erratic, and thin. China cannot industrialize as long as it must import lead and zinc and has inadequate iron and coal reserves.

0425. SHIMAN, Russell G. The Iron Reserves of Chahar, *Far Eastern Survey* 4, 1935, 17–21.

Argues that the common perception that Chahar is devoid of any economic significance save trade is incorrect. Notes that since the area has rich iron deposits and good transportation linking it to Beijing it could become a major mining center. Presents estimates of iron reserves and China's iron consumption. Comments on the Japanese role in Chinese international trade and predicts that the area will fall under Japanese domination.

8. Resources, Energy, and Minerals

0426. **SMYTH, Helen.** China's Petroleum Industry, *Far Eastern Survey* 15, 1946, 187–90.

Describes the impact of war damage on the industry, including the development of synthetic gasoline, increased alcohol production, the use of vegetable oils for lighting, and increased imports. Provides an estimate of reserves, especially for Xinjiang and Shaanxi. Argues that the main obstacles to full development of petroleum include a poor transportation system and lack of modern production and storage facilities. Predicts that China will need to continue imports until such time as geological surveys are completed and new industries develop that could provide machinery and transportation.

0427. **STEWART, John R.** The Resources of Manchuria, *Journal of Geography* 31, 1932, 45–57.

Manchuria is subject to conflicting national rivalries due to its rich resource base and strategic location. After describing political divisions of Manchuria, its agricultural and mineral resources are treated separately. Sees region's major future role as a supplier of raw materials to industry elsewhere and as such predicts Manchuria will not develop into a major industrial center.

0428. **SUTULOV, Alexander.** The Mineral Potentials of Russia and China, *Mining Congress Journal* 58:10, 1972, 36–41.

Highly polemical evaluation of differences between Russia and China in terms of resource base and need and ability to exploit the environment. Attempts to explain the reasons why China is not self-sufficient, focusing on inadequate transportation and the use of old-fashioned, inefficient technology. China's major handicap in developing its resource base is the lack of capital for investment. Both Russia and China need to adjust their economic planning concepts so they can fully participate in world trade in resources.

0429. **WANG, Kung-ping.** Mineral Resources of China with Special Reference to the Non-ferrous Metals, *Geographical Review* 34, 1944, 621–35.

Provides estimates of reserves for coal, iron, petroleum, and nine other major nonferrous minerals, based on 1936 and 1941 data. Includes tables and maps of major mines by individual mineral type. Assumes that nonferrous minerals will be of greater value in a postwar China.

0430. WILLIS, Bailey. The Mineral Resources of China, *Economic Geology* 3, 1908, 1–36, 118–33.

Begins with an overview of traditional mining and metallurgical activities in China. Argues that present data do not permit a definitive statement regarding China's mineral potential but is quite sure that superficial deposits have already been depleted. Notes that the lack of capital, wood, transportation, and labor along with taxes and graft act as impediments to foreign investment in Chinese mines. Concerned that Chinese not open to foreign investment or assistance in developing their mineral wealth. Provides estimates of exploitable resources on a provincial basis.

9. Conservation and Environment

0431. MURPHEY, Rhoads. Man and Nature in China, *Modern Asian Studies* 1, 1967, 313–33.

Using literary and landscape evidence, reviews the traditional, orthodox attitudes and views held by the Chinese toward man-nature relationships and argues that Chinese views were not static. Sees the environmental policies being enunciated and implemented by the Chinese Communist Party as radically different and new. Traces the origins, rationales, and policy tools for new attitudes and policies. Questions whether the risks and costs to the environment are balanced by the benefits.

0432. ORLEANS, Leo A., and Richard SUTTMEIER. Maoist Ethic and Environmental Quality, *Science* 170: 3063, 1970, 1173–76.

As the leadership of the Chinese Communist Party sought to reconstruct and develop the Chinese economy, it adodpted an environmental ethic/strategy stressing frugality, mass mobilization, recovery, and relocation. It is not clear that such approaches to problems such as sanitation, public health, and pollution are in the long run beneficial or economically efficient. The ethic is appropriate in an environment featuring low levels of consumption and poverty but may not be if consumption is to be increased.

0433. ROLLERSTON, George. Modifications of the External Aspects of Organic Nature Produced by Man's Interference, *Journal, Royal Geographical Society* 49, 1879, 320–92.

Chinese example of type of conservation work done by George Perkins Marsh in Europe.

0434. TUAN, Yi-fu. Discrepencies between Environmental Attitude and Behavior: Examples from Europe and China, *Canadian Geographer* 12, 1968, 176–91.

Takes issue with three assumptions regarding man-nature relations in China: that Europeans see man as superior to nature while the Chinese seen man as a part of nature; that Western contacts were the source of antienvironmental attitudes that led to pollution in Asia, as suggested by the White hypothesis (The Historical Roots of Our Ecologcial Crisis, *Science* 67, 1967, 1203–7); and that the only Chinese sources governing attitudes toward the environment were Taoist and Buddhist. Describes large- and small-scale manmade landscapes in both China and Europe.

Using classical Chinese texts, argues that the Chinese had an adaptive attitude toward nature. Points out that in both Europe and China there were clashes between theory and practice, and between attitudes and behavior, with regard to man-nature interactions.

0435. WHITNEY, J. B. R. Ecology and Environmental Conflict, *Proceedings, Academy of Political Science* 31, 1973, 95–109.

Argues that China's leaders do not see themselves as players in the vanguard of worldwide environmental movements, although their foreign supporters do. This attitude stands in stark contrast to the Chinese belief that they are the rightful spokesmen for Third World opposition to imperialism, capitalism, and moral and social problems. Notes that the Chinese attitude toward the environment, based on Marxist theory and Soviet practice, assumes that nature must be subdued and controlled at any cost. Since the Maoist development model does not provide any solution to environmental problems, given Chinese development programs and slogans, any observed improvements in environmental conditions therefore must be indirect and inadvertent. Urges the Chinese leadership to reexamine its anthropocentric view of the environment.

10. Human Geography: General

0436. AGASSIZ, A. R. From Haiphong in Tongking to Canton Overland, *Proceedings, Royal Geographical Society*, new series 13, 1891, 249–64. Map follows p. 312.

Report of trip started on February 17, 1890. Emphasizes state of urban places, local administration, and transportation. Expansion of Western inland navigation inhibited due to popular disapproval, nationalism, and dislike of competition. Concludes with cautionary note about concerns regarding when and whether Europeans will really win the allegiance of the Chinese.

0437. ALLEN, Nellie B. Tibet: A Geographical Essay for Teachers, *Journal of Geography* 19, 1920, 185–96.

Suggests using Tibet as an example to show U.S. students the range of humanity we must appreciate and how similar all cultures really are. Covers a wide range of topics, including population, political dominance, physical geography, agriculture, occupations, and male and female roles in Tibetan society. Concludes that if correctly done such a study would make students less judgmental, especially in terms of the physical appearance of people. Urges educators to ask students how they would fare and behave if they were put in the place of the Tibetans.

0438. AMUNDSEN, Edward E. A Journey through Southwest Szechuan, *Geographical Journal* 15, 1900, 620–26; 16, 1900, 531–37.

Trip in 1898 not taken for "scientific purposes." Traces route through territory nominally considered to be independent Tibetan "kingdoms." Describes poverty of region and his impression of repression of the local population.

0439. ANON. Borderlands of Soviet Central Asia: Sinkiang, *Central Asian Review* 4, 1956, 432–47.

Abridged translation, with analysis, of materials on ethnography, and administrative and social change that appeared in Soviet periodicals in 1956. Specific topics discussed include agriculture and land reform, industry, language and literature, magazines and newspapers, and health. Doubts that life or standard of living have improved for the non-Han population.

0440. ANON. Changing China, *New Zealand Geographical Society Record* 27, 1959, 8–10.

Optimistic assessment of the social and economic progress made in the People's Republic of China. Notes the challenges confronting the Chinese, including the limitations of the physical environment and unequal landownership. Blames West for Chinese industrial backwardness and argues that five-year plans will improve the lives of the Chinese by ensuring enough raw materials, cut down on transportation, and balance the roles of agriculture and industry in each province. Expects an end to regional economic disparities and rapid rise in standard of living so that China will emerge as a regional and world power.

0441. ANON. The Great Wall of China, *Bulletin, American Geographical Society* 42, 1910, 438–41.

Sees Great Wall as a metaphor for Chinese isolation and rebirth. Places heavy emphasis on role of railroads in revitalizing and reuniting China.

0442. ANON. Hong Kong Restored, *National Geographic Magazine* 91, 1947, 483–90.

Photo essay showing daily life after restoration of British rule.

0443. ANON. New Look of Changing China, *National Geographic Magazine* 126, 1964, 641–42.

Overview of general developments in China since 1949. Notes that secrecy of the Chinese hinders mapmakers and makes the production of a new map of China more difficult. An inset is devoted to Taiwan and the extent of transportation development there.

0444. ANON. Shantung, *Journal of Geography* 18, 1919, 312–16.

Refers to Shandong as the cradle of Chinese civilization. Describes the people, resources, and strategic position of province. Notes impact of floods and droughts. Wonders whether Japanese will restore former German Concessions in province to China.

0445. ANON. The Tribes of Western Szechuan, *Geographical Journal* 32, 1908, 594–97.

Brief description of map compiled by W. N. Fergusson during 1906–7, when he was the British and Foreign Bible Society agent in Chengdu. Describes non-Han groups that live along northern reaches of Min River and operate as independent or semi-independent tribes. These groups are categorized by Chinese officials as rebels or barbarians. Notes that inaccessibility of area has been a major factor in the preservation of the groups.

0446. ATWOOD, Wallace W. The Background of the Turmoil in China, *Journal of Geography* 26, 1927, 247–54.

Feels that despite a civil war China has made progress in education and economic and political organization. Provides a sketch of then current Chinese cultural developments keyed to major events in European history. Feels China is at a disadvantage since it lacks a lingua franca, a mass education movement, modern Western institutions, and modern industry. Sees a positive role for foreign trade in fostering change. Doubts that China will adopt a socialist ideology but rather will adopt elements of Western European and American thought, as the Japanese have successfully done.

0447. BABER, E. Colborne. China in Some of Its Physical and Social Aspects, *Proceedings, Royal Geographical Society* [of London], new series 5, 1883, 441–58.

Early attempt to correct myths held by Europeans regarding China and its people. In particular, emphasizes degree of physiographic and ethnic diversity to be found in China. But still argues that all common Chinese persons in some vulgar sense are Buddhist. Notes tendency of European observers to overestimate the size of the Chinese population.

0448. BAILEY, F. M. South East Tibet and the Mishani Hills, *Scottish Geographical Magazine* 28, 1912, 189–203.

Notes early attempts to sinify Tibet by using Chinese place and surnames instead of Tibetan ones. Remarks on extent of endemic goiter. Indicates that some two thousand species of butterflies and two hundred species of moths collected for cataloging and future study.

0449. BALLANTINE, Joseph W. I Lived on Formosa, *National Geographic Magazine* 87, 1945, 1–21.

Report by a U.S. foreign service officer who served in East Asia for some twenty-five years. Describes the ethnic breakdowns and origins of the Taiwanese population, including aborigines, and the attempts at Japanization by the colonial government. Places Japanese accomplishments in developing the island against the history of Western experiences on Taiwan. Sees Taiwan's location and self-sufficiency in food as important strategic advantages to any power holding the island. Includes dramatic air photographs showing the results of Allied bombing of strategic targets.

0450. BANKS, Mike. Europe's Side-Door to China, *Geographical Magazine* 39, 1967, 887–98.

Tells the history of Portuguese in Macao, with major focus on the mainstays of the economy—tourism and gambling. Predicts that relations with China will be less tense than for Hong Kong because the Portuguese have maintained rapport with the government in Beijing and because no formal treaty specifies the end of Portuguese control.

0451. BARRETT, John. China: Her Development and History, *National Geographic Magazine* 12, 1901, 209–18, 266–71.

Narrative of Chinese history from mythological period to well into written history. Describes Golden Age of Past, the development of Confucian thinking, the introduction of Buddhism, and Sino-Roman relations. Warns against underrating or underestimating China and the possibility of war. Questions the validity of any policy of "firmness" against China.

0452. BARTON, Alfred. Notes on the Yang-tsze-kiang, etc. [*sic*], *Journal, Royal Geographical Society* 32, 1862, 26–41.

Describes course of river from headwaters to sea. Reports that in addition to local officials not being receptive to British visits the central government is not effective in maintaining law and order or the economic functions of cities.

0453. BEECH, Joseph. Eden of the Flowery Republic, *National Geographic Magazine* 38, 1920, 355–90.

To get to China's interior, one must travel along the Changjiang from the coast to Sichuan. Impressed with improvements in passage. Notes that the further inland one goes the more likely there will still be heavy reliance on traditional, non-Western means of transporation such as sedan chairs. Touches on the importance of rice cultivation and salt production in provincial economy. Postulates a four-stage history of Sichuan's development: retreat of the aborigines, ruthless wars of the Chinese, Chinese immigration/repopulation movements, and contact with missionaries. As a result, the area is seen as a "museum of races." Notes with pride the role of U.S. educational institutions, whether in the form of YMCA or missionary schools, in the bringing about important economic and social changes.

0454. BELL, Sir Charles. A Year in Lhasa, *Geographical Journal* 63, 1924, 89–105.

Report based on nineteen years in India-Tibet areas. Includes history of 1910 Chinese invasion of Tibet and the subsequent two-year departure of the Dalai Lama. Similarly describes reform programs started by the Dalai Lama upon his return after 1912. Actual trip by author in 1920. Most concerned with transportation, diet, and religious literature of Tibet.

0455. BICKMORE, Albert S. Sketch of a Journey from Canton to Hankou, *Journal, Royal Geographical Society* 38, 1868, 50–68.

Report of trip during April 1866. Notes economic potential of degraded landscapes once proper reforestation is instituted. Comments on the juxtaposition of low yields, multiple cropping, and use of all types of manures and silt from flooding. Heavy emphasis on geology. Records mixed reception British receive from Chinese local officials as they travel from place to place.

0456. BILLARD, Jules B. Macau Clings to the Bamboo Curtain, *National Geographic Magazine* 135, 1969, 521–39.

Despite riots by pro-Communist citizens, Macao continues to be a working society continuing to bridge the gap between East and West. Describes the history of the colony and its economic relations with China as well as its place in the total Portuguese empire. Notes recent accomplishments in economic development, the elimination of drugs as a social problem, and the securing of a dependable water supply. Critical of the role of gambling in the economy.

0457. BISCH, Jorgen. This Is the China I Saw, *National Geographic Magazine* 126, 1964, 591–641.

Report of return trip of a Danish writer to ten major cities. Compares the China of 1958 to that of 1964 and finds the people more prosperous, with more goods available but few luxuries. Food supplies appear to be adequate, demonstrating that the government took to heart the lessons of the Great Leap Forward and the associated crop failures. Impressed with the incentives offered to farmers to grow more as well as attempts to use modern, appropriate farm machines and chemicals. Frequently complains about seemingly arbitrary restrictions on his mobility and ability to take the photographs he sought to take.

0458. BISHOP, Carl Whiting. The Beginnings of North and South in China, *Pacific Affairs* 7, 1934, 297–325.

Sees regional differences in China as part of broader Eurasian patterns. Given existing archaeological evidence, argues that Chinese civilization could not have developed without borrowing many domesticated plants and animals, including rice, sheep, goats, and the water buffalo. Traces settlement and culture from Paleolithic though Bronze Age and finds long-standing regional differences within China.

0459. BISHOP, Carl Whiting. The Geographical Factor in the Development of Chinese Civilization, *Geographical Review* 12, 1922, 19–41.

Opens with the hypothesis that the Far Eastern Question exists and cannot be solved due to the lack of nationalistic spirit on the part of the Chinese people. Notes an inherent tendency in China to periodically break apart, beyond the obvious division of China into a north and south. Reviews evidence of earliest settlement and civilization and speculates on the nature and diffusion of early Chinese culture. Sees the areal division of China as extending back to earliest history. Ends discussion with policies of Qin Shihuang, which may be the end of the era when occidental elements diffused to China via a land route. Thereafter, Western influences arrived via sea.

0460. BISHOP, C[arl]. W[hiting]. The Rise of Civilization in China with Reference to Its Geographic Aspects, *Geographical Review* 22, 1938, 617–34.

Extends conclusions presented in earlier article on same subject [item 0459]. Concludes that new archaeological evidence from the Neolithic period supports hypothesis that Chinese civilization borrowed heavily from Indian and Central Asian civilizations, especially with regard to rice, tools, and the water buffalo. Sees subsequent diffusion of Chinese civilization as slow and incomplete.

0461. BISHOP, Mrs. Isabella L. A Journey to Western Sze-chuan, *Geographical Journal* 10, 1897, 19–50.

Describes 1896 trip as a major accomplishment since it was able to visit places not explored by westerners before. Includes excellent pictures. Uses itinerary format, with careful attention to geomorphology and hydrology. Abstract of paper appeared in *Scottish Geographical Magazine* 13, 1897, 252–55.

0462. BOURNE, Frederick S. A. Imperial Mausoleum, East of Peking, *Proceedings, Royal Geographical Society*, new series 5, 1883, 23–31.

Reports on trip taken in January 1880. Compares churches and tombs of the U.K. royalty to Chinese royal tombs that are perceived to be remote and inaccessible. Includes a generalized model sketch map of tombs. Enumerates known locations of specific tombs. Includes local folklore material.

0463. BROWN, Josephine A. 6,000 Miles over the Roads of Free China, *National Geographic Magazine* 85, 1944, 355–84.

Uses itinerary format to report on trip between Kunming and Lanzhou, a route the author had previously traversed in 1936. Emphasis is on coping skills of Chinese and their inventiveness in finding substitutes for daily needs such as petroleum products. Shows the impact of cooperative movement and the role of women in the war economy.

0464. BRYCE, E. J. Yunnan: Southwestern China, *Australian Geographer* 2:7, 1935, 23–27.

Uses itinerary format to describe a trip from Hong Kong to Haiphong to Yunnan. Notes that area really only accessible after the 1910 opening of a rail link from Haiphong and that previously it would take six weeks to journey up the Changjiang from Shanghai. Comments that province is a recent addition to Chinese territory. Includes materials about the origin of the provincial name, climate, elevation, hydrology, religion, towns, extent of opium production, and ethnic mix. Argues that full development of the area's resources requires peace and investment in transportation.

0465. BUCHANAN, Sir Walter. A Recent Trip into the Chumbi Valley, Tibet, *Geographical Journal* 53, 1919, 403–10.

Trip made during harvest of 1919. Compares his findings to those of 1903–4 Musa expedition. Finds that major change is disappearance of any Chinese influence. Comments that roads generally bad and settlements dirty.

0466. BURKI, H. K. Ladakh: Roof of World, *Canadian Geographical Journal* 44:1, 1952, 38–41.

Photo essay of religious and nomadic life of area now included in India but claimed by China as a former part of Tibet.

0467. BUSHELL, S. W. Notes of a Journey Outside the Great Wall of China, *Journal, Royal Geographical Society* 44, 1874, 73–96.

Describes a trip from Beijing to Shangdu, site of Yuan tombs. Empasizes impact of Buddhism on landscape. Details regarding what fruit trees cultivated and state of walls. Includes particulars about the city form and population of Jehol.

0468. BUXTON, L. H. Dudley. Present Condition in Inner Mongolia, *Geographical Journal* 61, 1923, 393–413.

Uses itinerary format for trip begun on April 29, 1922. Refers to visits of other Russian and English explorers between 1875 and 1893. Alludes to Huntington's theory of climatic change and argues that Mongol movements out of the area are evidence that desiccation is occurring. Topics described include ethnicity, use of tobacco, massacres of local Christians, village types, state of transportation and communications, vegetation, and landscapes. Notes that there was no evidence of Chinese penetration but that Chinese trade goods were readily available and Chinese was widely spoken.

0469. CAMPBELL, W[illiam]. Formosa under the Japanese, Being Notes of a Visit to Taichu Prefecture, *Scottish Geographical Magazine* 18, 1906, 561–76.

Presents positive evaluation of Japanese administration, especially regarding public works and efforts to control crime such as prisons. Optimistic that Taizhong will be an important center despite lack of a good harbor. Generally optimistic regarding future of entire island despite presence of opium addiction and prostitution.

0470. CAMPBELL, W[illiam]. The Island of Formosa: Its Past and Future, *Scottish Geographical Magazine* 12, 1896, 385–99.

Reviews the history of administration and trade for the island. Notes that Chinese sources are vague on these issues. Predicts that the Japanese takeover of the area will have positive impacts, especially in the areas of transportation development, the replacement of Chinese personnel with Japanese, and pacification of the aborigines.

10. Human Geography: General

0471. CAREY, A. D. Journey Round Chinese Turkestan and along the Northern Frontier of Tibet, *Proceedings, Royal Geographical Society*, new series 9, 1887, 175-76, 731-52. Map, p. 790.

Describes an 1885 trip that started in Simla and Lhasa via the Kulu and Lahoul Valleys. Emphasis is on economic geography, especialy crops, and urban places. Pleased with good reception expedition given; notes absence of Chinese troops. Fuller report is found on pp. 731-52.

0472. CASELLA, Alexandro. A Visit to Inner Mongolia, *Royal Central Asiatic Society Journal* 55, 1968, 152-57.

Report on visit to area in autumn 1965. Uses itinerary format. Comments on the impact of the Cultural Revolution, Han migration, and the administrative status of area. Concludes that to develop Inner Mongolia the Chinese first need to extend and expand the railroad so that resources can be accessed.

0473. CHAMBERLIN, Rollin T. Populous and Beautiful Szechuan: A Visit to the Restless Province of China, in Which the Present Revolution Began, *National Geographic Magazine* 22, 1911, 1094-1119.

Notes the expansion of the province at the expense of Tibetan territory. Divides attention between Chengdu Plateau and Chengdu City. For both areas, describes climate, irrigation systems, architecture, and reliance on backpacks and wheelbarrows for transporting goods and people. In describing the city, focus is on the walls, quarters, and university. Lapses occasionally into itinerary format, as when describing a side trip to the alpine area.

0474. CHANG, Chi-yun. Taiwan, China's Lost Province, *Asia and the Americas* 45, 1945, 428-30.

Written on eve of expected return of Taiwan to Chinese administration. Argues that Taiwan should be seen as a giant sitting aircraft carrier in terms of its strategic value. Describes the Chinese history of the island from Ming times on as well as the distribution of the population by ethnic groups and the role of Taiwan in Japan's strategic planning. Acknowledges Japan's contribution to the development of Taiwan's agriculture, resource base, and infrastructure.

0475. CHAPIN, William W. Glimpses of Korea and China, *National Geographic Magazine* 21, 1910, 895-934.

Section on China found on pp. 928-34. Photographs in color. After describing the difficulties in taking pictures (especially of women), the travails of travel, the Great Wall, funerals, and the justice system, warns that China is so big that it is dangerous to generalize about the country since customs vary from place to place.

0476. CHAPMAN, F. Spencer. Lhasa in 1937, *Geographical Journal* 91, 1938, 497–507.

Report on activities as secretary to a Mr. Gould, political officer in Sikkim, who had been invited to Lhasa, as had Younghusband in 1904, as part of an occasional local government program to invite political officers for consultations. Provides details regarding the interior of Potala monastery, local housing conditions, vegetable gardens, and lack of infrastructure. Promises to provide notes on flora and fauna of area in a future publication.

0477. CHATLEY, Herbert. The Yellow River as a Factor in the Development of China, *Asiatic Review* 35, 1939, 134–41.

Although the Changjiang and Xi Jiang are popularly associated with modern China, rice, and canals, it is actually the Huang He that is the area where China developed. Describes the headwater locations, watersheds, soils, and climate of the river basin. Contrasts Chinese experience in cultural development with other areas featuring major river plains. Argues that in contrast to the Middle East/Fertile Crescent area, China was isolated and therefore was an active innovator and inventor of agriculture and writing systems. Major physical problems in exploiting the Huang He include the buildup of silt and climatic change. Traditional Chinese remedies for these problems, as well as flooding, are reviewed and praised.

0478. CHEN, Cheng-siang. Geographic Regions of Taiwan, *Studia Taiwanica* 1, 1956, 21–30.

Argues that the major geographic factor determining regional differences in Taiwan is topographic diversity. Notes that Taiwan has twenty peaks in excess of 3,500 meters. Major regions defined are northern hills, marsh plain, southeastern valley, and central mountains. These are in turn divided into a total of twenty-eight subdivisions.

0479. CHEN, Cheng-siang. The Pescadores, *Geographical Review* 43, 1953, 77–88.

After describing the physical characteristics of the islands, including size, vegetation, climate, and soils, concludes that the population is ten times the actual carrying capacity of the islands. As such, main focus of report is on land use, population, food supply, and the role of the fishing industry in maintaining the local economy and population.

0480. CHEN, Chang-siang. Taiwan, *Focus* 17:4, 1966, 1–6.

General review of economic history emphasizing agriculture, land use, and industry. Although future economic growth will depend on an adequate supply of trained labor and capital, there is reason to be generally optimistic about likely improvements in per capita income and quality of life.

0481. CHENGTUNG, Liang-cheng. China and the United States, *National Geographic Magazine* 16, 1905, 554–57.

China sees the United States in a good light since it never engaged in the unfair, unequal practices the European countries did. Therefore, there is a great potential for Sino-U.S. economic and commercial cooperation. There are nevertheless two sore points in Sino-U.S. relations: China is unhappy about the Chinese exclusion policy; and the government of China, while apologizing for the murders of U.S. missionaries, cannot assume responsibility since the perpetrators were beyond the control of the central government.

0482. CLAPP, F[rederick]. G. Along and across the Great Wall of China, *Geographical Review* 9, 1920, 221–49.

Describes trip taken by three Americans (the author; Myron Fuller, a geologist; and Kenneth T. McKoy) starting on February 17, 1914. Started at Shanhaikwan and proceeded three miles along base of Great Wall. Explored the Manchurian extension, which they found not well preserved. Each section of wall, and all the bifurcations, are fully described. Notes that the original wall did not keep the nomads out of China. Now there is a need for a "green" wall to protect the north from the desert. Expects with the establishment of democracy investments will be made in irrigation and reforestation.

0483. CLARK, F. R. H. Colonel Sosnoffsky's Expedition to China, 1874–5, *Journal, Royal Geographical Society* 47, 1877, 150–87.

Abridged translation of original Russian report. Since goal of trip was to find ways to expand Sino-Russian trade, focus is on cities, transportation, and what specific goods are traded.

0484. CLARKE, F. C. M. Kuldja, *Proceedings, Royal Geographical Society* 2, 1880, 489–99.

Uses deterministic format. Concerned with the strategic and historic prominence of Yining in the context of migration and trade. Traces times when area was in and out of Chinese realm. Describes the religions and ethnic groups in area as well as place names. Notes the role of Russia after the eighteenth century as part of a general survey of Russian influence in Asia. Argues that Yining is important node in route to southeast for the Russians in their search for the El Dorado of Asia.

0485. COALES, Oliver. Eastern Tibet, *Geographical Journal* 53, 1919, 228–53.

Heavily historical description of area with emphasis on Sino-Tibetan (Kham State) relations, which ended as such with the civil war of 1910 and subsequent Chinese intervention. Provides both Chinese and Tibetan names of sites visited in 1916 and corrects Western misspellings. Especially impressed with local architecture and state of buildings.

0486. COLLINGWOOD, Dr. A. A Boat Journey across the Northern End of Formosa from Tamsuy Northwest to Kee-lung on the East, with Notices of Hoo-wai, Mangka, and Keelung, *Proceedings, Royal Geographical Society of London* 11, 1867, 167–73.

General description of population and economy of area. Includes some details regarding hydrology and biogeography.

0487. CRESSEY, George B. China, the Middle Kingdom, *Home Geographic Monthly* 2:2, 1932, 31–36.

Compares China's perception of itself to that of the United States. To understand China, one needs to appreciate its large areal extent, limited accessibility and mobility, climate and topography, food differences, and language. Urges the United States to be patient with and sympathetic to the Chinese in their attempts at modernization.

0488. CRESSEY, George B. How the Chinese Dress, *Home Geographic Monthly* 2:4, 1933, 31–36.

Given the unheated houses of the Chinese and diurnal changes in daily temperatures, the Chinese tend to dress in layers. Notes that the materials used to make clothing in China do not include wool. Most clothing is custom made. There are color preferences by age for each type of cloth.

0489. CRESSEY, George B. The Chinese of Celestial Cathay, *Home Geographic Monthly* 1:3, 1931, 8–14.

Relates the variety of ethnicity in China to the five stripes on the Chinese flag. Focuses on the misconceptions held by the United States regarding China, such as the stereotype that all Chinese migrants from the south are engaged in laundry activities. Notes the variety in physical traits displayed by the Chinese. Provides evidence for the early development of China. Argues that the major problem confronting the Chinese is the small average size of plots farmed and how to diffuse Westernization to rural areas to relieve this situation.

0490. CRESSEY, George B. Ordos Desert of Inner Mongolia, *Denison University Bulletin, Journal of Scientific Laboratories* 28, 1933, 155–248.

Report based on fieldwork conducted between 1923 and 1929. Conceived of as a study using the notion of human adjustments to the environment. Describes climate, settlement history, Western opinions, and Mongol and Chinese ethnography of area. Concludes that in contrast to Manchuria the area cannot act as a demographic safety valve for surplus Chinese population.

0491. CRESSEY, George B. Who Are the Chinese? *Home Geographic Monthly* 2:1, 1932, 31–36.

History of China as a country, and its early political organization. Identifies the spatial origin of Chinese civilization, migration patterns, and Han and non-Han interactions. Despite a plethora of dialects, the Chinese have a cultural unity based on a rural, friendly, genuine population. Warns reader not to take urban Chinese behavior as the cultural norm.

0492. CROSBY, Oscar T. From Tiflis to Tibet, *Bulletin of the American Geographical Society* 37, 1905, 703–6.

Argues that Tibetan history starts circa 710. Expresses disdain for Tibetan property relations and polyandry, both of which author feels can be done away with following proper "Westernization." Notes that native repulsion of Western attempts to forge relations with area led to British forced treaties, and ultimate supremacy over the area, starting in 1716. Sees potential for mischief by Great Britian and Russia in interior areas.

0493. CROSBY, Oscar T. Turkestan and a Corner of Tibet, *Geographical Journal* 23, 1904, 705–22.

While enamoured of scenery, concludes that area has nothing to offer Western civilization and may be an effective barrier to any exchange between China and the West.

0494. CUTSHALL, Alden. Taiwan (Formosa): Japan's South Base, *Journal of Geography* 43, 1944, 247–57.

Provides information on a wide range of topics, including location, strategic importance, land surface, hydrology, climate, flora and fauna, ethnic mix of the population, and urbanization. Reports that Japanese policies had resulted in the loss of food self-sufficiency for the island, as farmers abandoned subsistence practices for a more market-oriented agriculture. Notes industrial development on island. Japan has used the island as a commercial base and a training ground for military expansion. Senses that the mountain peoples have still not been fully integrated into the transformed Chinese society.

0495. DAVIDSON, Basil. China's Farthest West, *Geographical Magazine* 30, 1957, 119–30.

Describes trip to Kashgar and outlying oases in 1956. Remarks that there were no visible hints of sinification programs or impact of Chinese economic reforms on traditional daily life.

0496. DAVIES, Llewellyn James. The Chinese "Boxers," *National Geographic Magazine* 11, 1900, 281–87.

Describes the origins, organization, and goals of the Boxers as a political and anti-Western movement. Attributes the roots of Chinese xenophobia to contempt, fear, and a sense of injustice. Sees no evidence in China of religious animosity. Reviews ways in which the Chinese goverment has tried to deal with the Boxer movement.

0497. DAVIS, John Francis. Memoir on the Neighborhood of Canton and Hong Kong and the East Coast of China, *Proceedings, Royal Geographical Society* 1, 1855–57, 330–41.

Written in the context of the Opium Wars. Describes the destruction of Canton and subsequent decline in trade. Enumerates the number and location of defenses for Canton. Provides details regarding the development of Amoy, Ningbo, Tinghao, and Shanghai. Comments on problems of overpopulation, resulting in the need of the Chinese to emigrate to Southeast Asia and engage in piracy.

0498. DAVIS, J[ohn]. F[rancis]. View of the Great Valley of the Yang-tse-Kiang before and since Its Occupation by the Rebels, *Proceedings, Royal Geographical Society* 3, 1858–59, 164–68.

Remarks on contrast between his impressions of the Changjiang area and those of Lord Elgin in 1816, who described the area as rich and prosperous. Argues that earlier estimates of the population of Hankou and surrounding towns were overestimated by at least a factor of two. Sees value in trips along the Changjiang by British naval forces, as they act as a deterrent against rebel attacks on British interests.

0499. deBUNSEN, E. H. Formosa, *Geographical Journal* 70, 1927, 266–87.

Bases review of early history of Taiwan on Davidson's 1903 [*The Island of Formosa: Historical View from 1430 to 1900*] and Campbell's 1915 [*Formosa under the Dutch and Sketches from Formosa*] works. Argues that between 1662 and 1862 Taiwan was a part of China in name rather than in fact. Praises Japanese for restoring the law and order absent under Chinese rule. Rich ethnographic description of trip taken in December 1925. Includes maps of tribes and tribal boundaries.

0500. DODD, John. Formosa, *Scottish Geographical Magazine* 11, 1895, 553–70.

Abstract of paper read at the British Association, 1895. History of occupation and exchange especially after 1842. Describes places in terms of accessibility. Includes details of material culture of inhabitants but omits references to marriage or religion. Ethnic conflicts, including Hakka dislike of Mainland Chinese, reviewed. Anticipates development of economy under Japanese rule and expansion of trade with Britain. Notes history of rice exports, especially to Mainland China.

0501. DOERR, Arthur H., and Gershom CHAN. The Impact of Man on Land: The Example of Hong Kong, *Ecumene* 6, 1974, 14–18.

Qualitatively attributes changes in natural vegetation, landforms, and hydrology to human behavior and especially population growth. Argues that diffusing the population to centers in the New Territories could ameliorate some environmental problems but notes that such a population transfer may be politically difficult.

0502. DRAKAKIS-SMITH, D. W. Portugal on the Chinese Frontier, Development in Macao, *Geographical Magazine* 47, 1975, 676–80.

In contrast to Hong Kong, Macao's economy has been hurt by the United Nations' embargoes imposed after the Korean and Vietnam Wars. Funds for industrial investment come from personal savings and the merchant marine. Some landscape changes have developed as a result of modernization, but residential areas are still needed, since a land shortage has driven prices up. All such changes require approval from the People's Republic of China, and that government is mainly concerned with preserving stability and the status quo.

0503. DUNCAN, Marion H. Through a Side Door into Inner Tibet, *Canadian Geographic Journal* 10:5, 1935, 226–38.

Describes one-month journey starting in Batang, capital of Xigang, Sichuan, following Batang River, with stops at Leh, Drubalong, Lhamdu, Pula, Gartok, and Tsongshe. In addition to photographs, map of trip provided.

0504. EDGAR, J. H[uston]. Through the Land of Deep Corrosion, from Batang to Mekong, *Journal, Royal Asiatic Society, North China Branch*, new series 45, 1914, 32–45.

Describes travels in Tibet and in areas of headwaters of the Changjiang, Mekong, and Salween in particular. Especially interested in etymology of place names and how the Chinese have adopted Tibetan ones. Touches on major population centers and describes economy and transportation.

0505. EDMUNDS, Charles K[eyser]. Shantung: China's Holy Land, *National Geographic Magazine* 36, 1919, 231–52.

Uses itinerary format to describe travels, which start in Jinan. Disturbed by what he considers the cruel justice system in place yet feels that traditional Chinese philosophies can be the basis for the modernization of China. Describes attempts to cure "China's Sorrow," the Huang He. Title derived from observation that Shandong is home to a number of shrines and temples that are pilgrimage destinations for Confucianists and Buddhists.

0506. ELIAS, Ney. Narrative of a Journey through Western Mongolia, July 1872 to January 1873, *Journal, Royal Geographical Society* 43, 1873, 108–55.

Reports on exploration of area previously closed due to civil unrest. Goals of trip include locating the ruins of the ancient Tartar capital city and reaching, by any route possible, the former Chinese colony of Ili, which for two years had been occupied by a Russian force.

0507. FENNENMAN, N[eville]. M. Geography of Manchuria, *Journal of Geography* 4, 1905, 6–11.

Analysis of maps of population, topography, climate, and vegetation to show that the nature and direction of army movements were in fact controlled by the surface features of the area. Makes comparisons with Japanese military expeditions and successes elsewhere in 1895 and 1905.

0508. FITZGERALD, [C.] Patrick. The Yunnan-Burma Road, *Geographical Journal* 95, 1940, 161–74.

Focuses on the war-driven economic development of the western provinces of China. Notes both the natural and human obstacles to be overcome, including the lack of roads, machinery, and trained personnel. Uses itinerary format.

0509. FISCHER, Emil S. Through the Silk and Tea Districts of Kiangnan and Che-kiang Province, *Journal of the American Geographical Society of New York* 32, 1900, 334–66.

Uses itinerary format. Very discursive, especially in discussion of local economies. Begins by describing the internal political stresses confronting the government of China up to 1900. Comments on the widespread use of opium. Main observations concern the Ping-shui Valley. Concludes that expeditions to this area are rare and difficult due to constraints of transportation.

0510. FORREST, George. The Land of the Crossbow, *National Geographic Magazine* 21, 1910, 132–56.

Describes a trip charged with surveying the Salween Valley [item 0119]. Reports on related visits to Lissoo villages. After commenting on the difficulties in traveling, describes the goverment, clothing and decorations, and economy of Lissoo. Provides names of articles used in hunting. Describes the flora and fauna of the area, with special concern for insects.

0511. FOSTER, John W. China, *National Geographic Magazine* 15, 1904, 463–78.

Attempts to provide an answer to the question: How can such an ancient people have reached such a state of helplessness? Enumerates the major characteristics of China, including its longevity, large population, market orientation, and Great Wall. Sees the Chinese as handicapped by blind conservatism and conceit, accompanied by low levels of social and public morality. Sees hope in the adoption of modernizing programs such as the rehabilitation of the postal and customs services, the growth of newspapers, and the improvement in material standards of living. Since Britain is the dominant world power, its presence in East Asia will assist China.

0512. FOSTER, John W. Present Conditions in China, *National Geographic Magazine* 17, 1906, 651–72, 709–11.

Sympathetic to the Chinese irritation with Europeans. Optimistic that China can modernize given its reforms of girls' schooling, religious affairs, legal systems, and diplomatic relations as well as the adoption of Western ways such as smoking and sending students abroad for study. Sees Japanese development and reform as a model for China.

0513. FRESHFIELD, Douglas W. Notes from Tibet, *Geographical Journal* 23, 1904, 361–66, 420.

Analysis, using explorer reports, of thirteen photographs sent to the Royal Geographical Society by Lord Curzon. Includes a map of Lhasa compiled by L. A. Waddell said to be comparable to Rockhill's map, which was based on Chinese sources and published in the *Journal, Royal Asiatic Society of Great Britain and Ireland*, vol. 23, new series.

0514. FRESHFIELD, Douglas W. The Roads to Tibet, *Geographical Journal* 23, 1904, 79–92.

Based on cited secondary sources and limited fieldwork, report describes precisely the region and roads available for use by British soldiers seeking access to and in Tibet.

0515. FUSON, Chester G. The Geography of Kwangtung, *Lingnan Science Journal* 6, 1928, 241–56.

Form of plea for the citizens of China to know their country. Uses Guangdong as an example of how this can be accomplished. Includes materials on size, site, location, climate, vegetation, natural divisions, earth history, mineral resources, out-migration, ethnic communities, and agriculture. Argues that compared to the rest of China Guangdong historically has had a good system of communications based on waterways. Since the ease and abundance of communications is the secret of prosperity, Guangdong needs to further develop a road and railroad system to remain an example for China. Material for Hainan included.

10. *Human Geography: General*

0516. GARDNER, Chr. T. Notes on a Journey from Ningpo to Shanghai, *Proceedings, Royal Geographical Society of London* 13, 1869, 170–82, 249–51.

Very general report of 1868 trip.

0517. GATZLAFF, Charles. Tibet and Sefan, *Journal, Royal Geographical Society* 20, 1850–51, 191–27.

Indicates that boundaries of region ill-defined and that in areas outside of eastern Tibet Chinese influence is minimal.

0518. GILL, W. J. Travels in Western China and in the Eastern Borders of Tibet, *Journal, Royal Geographical Society* 48, 1878, 57–172.

In addition to general description of trip, provides tables of temperature and precipitation of sites visited. Itinerary format used.

0519. GINSBURG, Norton S. Hong Kong, *Focus* 4:3, 1953, 1–6.

Compares negative site characteristics, especially water shortages, to strength of situational attributes. Notes the potentially unsettling issue of Hong Kong's future after 1997 in economic and social development.

0520. GOFORTH, W. W. Jehol: Twilight Land of Nomadism, *Canadian Geographical Journal* 6, March 1933, 107–18.

Describes area's ambiguous political status over time and notes that unless area is under Chinese control it would be a threat to China. Describes hydrology, climate, ethnography, and commerce in area. Some discussion of Chinese place names.

0521. GOODCHILD, Thomas. Northeastern Chehkiang, China: Notes on Human Adaption to the Environment, *Bulletin of the American Geographical Society* 43, 1911, 801–26.

Uses deterimistic format to provide a comprehensive regional geography. Notes failures in adaptation: overcutting of forests, superstition as evidenced by use of *fengshui* concepts, and misuse of water resulting in either floods or disease due to standing water. Attributes failures to ignorance.

0522. GRIEG, James A. A Journey from Kirin Overland to Moscow, *Scottish Geographical Magazine* 14, 1898, 241–54.

Only first five pages deal with Manchuria, the remainder with Russian part of trip. Notes availability of excellent roads in Manchuria but that bridges are lacking. Reports on meeting with Russians exploring for coal near Kirin. Notes evidence of recent floods on Manchurian-Korean border.

0523. GRINNELL, Walton. Journey through Eastern Mantchouria and Korea, *Journal of the American Geographical Society of New York* 3, 1873, 283–99.

Main focus is on activities in Korea. Goal of trip: to reach Samarkand via Manchuria and Mongolia. Claims Manchuria originally Korean and describes archaeological evidence to support that. Notes presence of Russians in Manchuria and argues that these settlers represent a forced military migration and that the resulting settlements are not self-sufficient. Presumes that most changes in vegetation are due to clearing of land by Western settlers. Compares area to California due to the presence of gold. Sees Manchuria as long-standing demographic safety valve for China proper.

0524. GROFF, G. Weidman, and T. C. LAU. Landscaped Kwangsi, China's Province of Pictorial Art, *National Geographic Magazine* 72, 1937, 671–86, 695–726.

Describes return trip to Guangxi, but using motorcars, boats, and airplanes instead of more traditional Chinese means of transportation. Includes materials on site and topography of Guangxi. Extended coverage of cormorant fishing included. Describes specific changes observed in Canton, Guilin, Wuzhou, Guiyang, and the Grand Canal.

0525. GROSVENOR, Gilbert [H]. The National Geographic Society's Yunnan Province Expedition, *National Geographic Magazine* 48, 1925, 493–98.

Describes goals of expedition, which was led by Jospeh F. Rock. In 1923, the National Geographic Society took over the operations of a U.S. Department of Agriculture expedition to collect samples of flora and fauna of possible economic value in Yunnan. Among the 60,000 specimens of plants, 16,000 birds, and 60 mammals collected were blight resistant chestnuts, coniferous trees, and new varieties of rhododendron.

0526. GROSVENOR, W. Clayton. The Province of Hunan: Some Characteristics and Peculiarities, *Scottish Geographical Magazine* 44, 1928, 144–50.

Major focus is on Dongting Lake, which was already silting up and therefore of reduced value as a flood control mechanism. Describes religious activities and cultural events such as the Dragon Boat Festival. Expects exports of coal to increase given potential of mines. Urban flavor and orientation to report.

0527. **HANBURY-TENISON, Euphan.** In China Today: Sian, *Geographical Magazine* 29, 1966, 139–48.

Impressions of an escorted tour of Xian, including a visit to a kindergarten. Author concludes that "life for the worker in Shenshi is not only monotonous and wearing but full of hardships unknown even to the poor of Southeast Asia." Assumes that life in Xian is typical of life in an average provincial town in China.

0528. **HARRINGTON, Lyn.** China Digs into Its Past, *Canadian Geographical Journal* 88:6, 1974, 12–19.

Overview of archaeological treasures found recently in China. Ends with a one-paragraph summary of the state of archaeology after 1949.

0529. **HARRINGTON, Lyn.** The New Territories of Hong Kong, *Canadian Geographical Journal* 58:1, 1964, 22–27.

Explores area and reports on major problems of inadequate water supply and transportation.

0530. **HOSIE, Alex[ander].** A Journey in Southwest China from SsuChuan to Western Yunnan, *Proceedings, Royal Geographical Society* 8, 1886, 371–84.

Notes how previous attempts at survey were not successful due to the distraction of other places and goals. Remarks on the presence of a goiter belt in the Jianchang Valley and the difficulty of tracing the causes. Rich details about mining, mineral resources, vegetation, and general economy. In addition to route traversed, four other possible routes with trade potential are identified.

0531. **HSIEH, Chiao-min.** Formosa: A Rich Island of the Far East, *Journal of Geography* 51, 1952, 45–54.

Reviews basic information regarding location, history, strategic importance, climate, agriculture, raw materials and energy base, and transportation system of island. Optimistic regarding Taiwan's future because of its location relative to Asia and the Western Hemisphere. Argues that island is destined to play an important, but unpredictable, role in postwar world.

0532. HSIEH, Chiao-min. Sequent Occupance of Formosa, *Proceedings, 8th General Assembly and 17th International Congress, International Geographical Union*, 1972, 481–85.

> Application of Whittlesey's 1929 (*Annals, Association of American Geographers* 19, 162–65) model of settlement changes. Divides settlement history of Taiwan into three stages: aboriginal, Chinese agricultural settlement, and Japanese industrial development. As required by the model, relies heavily on relics on landscape of economic activities, settlement patterns, and house types as evidence for stages.

0533. HSIEH, Chiao-min, and Alice TAYLOR. Formosa, *Focus* 5:8, 1955, 1–6.

> General overview of island with emphasis on climate and agriculture. Two constraints to development are population pressure and inadequate transport. Nevertheless, prospects for development assessed as good due to the youthful population and the programs of the Joint Commission on Rural Reconstruction.

0534. HUBBARD, George D. Geographic Significance of the Min Valley, above Chengtu, West China, *Bulletin, Geographical Society of Philadelphia* 33, 1935, 76–87.

> Discussion based on fieldwork conducted in 1923. Argues that area has military, commercial, ethnic, and religious significance. As such, juxtaposes role of Chinese and Tibetan cultures in area. Comments on fact that local transportation carried out despite a lack of roads. Postulates that villages are clusters of houses grouped for protection against bandits. Area could flourish if proper roads and a railroad were to be built but doubts whether a railroad will be built. Expects air service to be instituted before the development of ground transportation.

0535. HUBBARD, James M[ascarene]. Problems in China, *National Geographic Magazine* 11, 1900, 297–308.

> Sees Chinese as anxious to resolve conflicts with West over religion, law, and the impact of religious conversion on Chinese independence. Outlines rise of Boxers, Taipings, and Reform parties in general. Questions the wisdom of forcing China to interact with the West. Argues that it is inevitable that China will be a world power, given its potential resources.

0536. HUGHES, R. H. Hong Kong: Far Eastern Meeting Point, *Geographical Journal* 129, 1963, 450–65.

Stresses problems and planned solutions regarding water supply, land shortages, squatters, and viable agriculture in the context of a broad discussion involving population and manufacturing. Agnostic as to whether a Malthusian nightmare or a balanced society the likely outcome.

0537. HUNTINGTON, Ellsworth. The Mountain and Kibitkas of Tien Shan, *Bulletin of the American Geographical Society* 37, 1905, 513–50.

Divides discussion into six parts: the geomorphology of the area; the migration of the Kirghiz, who live in *kibitkas* (round felt tents) and who are seen as lazy; the effect of glaciation on physiographic forms; the effects of glacial period on human life; the salt lake of Shor Kul; and the lake and associated buildings of Issik-kul. All material presented against the background of questions relating to whether the area has undergone climatic change in historical times.

0538. JOHNSTON, A. R. Note on the Island of Hong Kong, *Journal, Royal Geographical Society* 14, 1844, 112–16.

Argues that there was no real settlement on the island before the British established one in 1841. Estimates that cultivated area of island was less than 1,500 mou (227 acres). Notes native plants and the cultivation of the potato, imported from Canton and Macao. Detailed description of rock types.

0539. JUDGE, Joseph. Hong Kong, Saturday's Child, *National Geographic Magazine* 140, 1971, 54–73.

Seeks to explain economic success of Hong Kong by noting the work ethic displayed by the Chinese in the context of political uncertainty regarding the possible end of the British lease on the New Territories. Describes the official and unofficial presence of the Communists and their economic, political, and social impact, which has been limited due to strong government reaction to illegal activities. Praises accomplishments of British in creating what is termed the "Switzerland of Asia."

0540. JUNOR, Kenneth F. Curious and Characteristic Customs of China, *National Geographic Magazine* 21, 1910, 791–806.

Expresses regret for the manner in which the West has treated China for over 150 years. Argues that it is in the best interests of the West to go beyond trade in its relations with China. Main purpose of the article is to demonstrate how the West can learn from China, especially in the areas of philosophy and literature, government, letters as a means of communication, food, and Chinese inventions. Impressed with the concept of the "superior man" in Confucianism. Devotes some space to the role of women in Chinese society and Chinese attitudes toward women.

0541. KEENLEYSIDE, Katherine, and Hugh KEENLEYSIDE. Changing China, *Canadian Geographical Journal* 73:1, 1966, 28–37.

Explicit comparison of earlier trips with a fifteen-day, nine-hundred-mile journey made during October 1965. Specific topics covered include population, population policies, urban landscapes, and transportation. Concludes that the Chinese are not interested in events outside their realm and only interested in trade if it is to their advantage.

0542. KEMP, Emily G. The Highways and Byways of Kweichow, *Journal, Royal Asiatic Society, North China Branch*, new series 52, 1921, 158–85.

General description of extended trip taken in 1920 covering the following subjects: vegetation, transportation, and non-Han peoples. Actual anthropometry taken of these groups. Notes important role of opium cultivation in local economy. Favorably compares non-Han peoples with Chinese. Argues that strong local military personalities play an important role in determining degree of development and wealth.

0543. KING, F. H. The Wonderful Canals of China, *National Geographic Magazine* 23, 1912, 931–58.

Text is abstracted from author's *Farmers of Forty Centuries*. In the description of the Grand Canal, Zhejiang, and the area between Shanghai and Nanjing, makes use of frequent comparisons with the United States. Main focus is the extent, construction, and use of canals in agriculture, especially for irrigation, flood control, conservation, and the collection and transport of human and animal wastes for fertilizers.

0544. KIRBY, E. Stuart. Anatomy of Hong Kong, *Far Eastern Survey* 18, 1949, 114–16.

Attributes Hong Kong's economic potential to the regional origins of Hong Kong residents, who see themselves as open, adventurous "men of T'ang" rather than the more conservative northern "men of Han." Describes postwar changes in trade patterns, including diversions to Macao. Notes, however, that China is still a major trading partner. Assumes Hong Kong will be immune to the turmoil of China.

10. Human Geography: General

0545. KIRBY, E. Stuart. Hong Kong Looks Ahead, *Pacific Affairs* 22, 1949, 173–78.

Argues that Hong Kong citizenry optimistic about the future, especially since it now has a lessened sense of dependency upon the People's Republic of China. This is so because trade links for Hong Kong and China have changed and Hong Kong is no longer seen as just a gateway to China. Internal challenges to be met include the need to control population growth, reduce housing shortages, eliminate beggars, and upgrade infrastructure.

0546. KIRJASSOFF, Alice Ballantine. Formosa the Beautiful, *National Geographic Magazine* 37, 1920, 246–92.

Reviews key components of Taiwan's topography, climate, and vegetation. Describes the impact of the Japanese on the architecture of buildings and more generally sees the Japanese administration as having strengthened old industries and developed new ones such that foreign trade and the standard of living have both gone up. Touches on religion, the economy of the aborigines, and the export crops of tea and camphor.

0547. KOZLOFF, P. K. The Mongolian Szechuan Expedition of the Imperial Geological Society, *Geographical Journal* 34, 1909, 384–408; 36, 1910, 288–310.

Report on expedition started in summer 1907. Uses itinerary format. Notes hazards of traveling at different times of the year. Observations touch on ethnicity and interethnic relations, economy, religion, and religious architecture. Investigated upper course of Huang He while in Kokonor area of Mongolia. Includes a list of the geological, botanical, ethnographic, and zoological objects collected for future study.

0548. KOZLOFF, P. K. Through Eastern Tibet and Karn, *Geographical Journal* 31, 1908, 402–15, 522–34, 649–61. Map, p. 405.

Translation of Russian report of 1899–1901 expedition. Describes living with Mongols and provides details about their clothing, animals, and lifestyle. Includes particulars regarding the logistics of the trip, the collection of flora and fauna, and hunting.

0549. KORKER, Bruno. A Brief Study of the Geography of China, *China Journal* 34, 1941, 203–8, 253–58.

Uses a deterministic format and is concerned with showing how farmers depend upon nature in order to earn a livelihood. Main geographic focus is on the Huang, Xi, and Changjiang Rivers, although a table comparing North and South China is included and analyzed. Includes frequent comparisons with the United States.

0550. LACY, Walter N. Chinese Items, *Journal of Geography* 16, 1917, 114–15.

Presents population data derived from 1916 returns of trade reports. Estimates population to be around 445 million, including data for cities larger than 500,000 and foreigners. Mentions that Chinese diet is changing, with more dairy, especially butter, being consumed.

0551. LATTIMORE, Owen. After 4 Years, *Pacific Affairs* 14, 1941, 141–53.

Argues that the failure of the major powers to deal with Japanese aggression led to the outbreak of war in Europe. Feels that the Chinese situation is not appreciated in the goal to defeat Hitler. Compared to Germany, Japan is a second-degree aggressor. Explores reasons for Japanese aggression, including the problems of a dual economy and the need for Japan to have a diversion for its anger and energy. Similarly tries to account for Chinese weaknesses, especially the difficulties of fighting a two-front war. While questioning the concept of a "good" war, nevertheless concludes with a plea for colonial powers to fight for local democracies.

0552. LATTIMORE, Owen. Byroads and Backwoods of Manchuria, *National Geographic Magazine* 61, 1932, 101–30.

Personal account of a year spent in Manchuria doing fieldwork among non-Han groups and learning languages. Reflects on cultural clashes that develop due to Han migrations and modernization. Reviews history of Mongols and Manchus in region. Comments on how opium producers become bandits in the nongrowing seasons.

0553. LATTIMORE, Owen. China Opens Her Wild West, *National Geographic Magazine* 82, 1942, 37–48, 357–67.

Describes the impact of war on the economy, population, and transportation of Yunnan. Describes history of Chinese encounters with the West. Sees China's size as providing a position from which it can withstand Japanese aggression. Pages 349–56 are a photo supplement entitled "South of the Clouds, Yunnan."

0554. LATTIMORE, Owen. The Geography of Chingis Khan, *Geographical Journal* 129, 1963, 1–7.

Emphasizes that past Chinese-Mongol interactions have been along an east-west axis, whereas future interactions will be along a north-south axis.

0555. LATTIMORE, Owen. Mongols of the Chinese Border, *Geography* 6, 1938, 327–44.

Describes landscapes created by Chinese despite close proximity of Mongols. Landscapes seen as part of dynamic interaction between the two groups over time. Sinification has been accelerated due to the extension of the railroad. Sympathetic toward Mongols and their way of life, especially their system of marking borders, religion, sports, and economy. Particularly critical of Chinese agricultural practices, which will lead to soil exhaustion.

0556. LATTIMORE, Owen. Return to China's Northern Frontier, *Geographical Journal* 139, 1973, 233–42.

Report on two-month visit from September through October 1972 at invitation of the Chinese government. Trip a return visit to areas worked in during 1927. Focuses on the following changes: new modes of Chinese-Mongol interaction, sedentarization of the Mongols, use of Chinese as language for educational purposes, and the emphasis on Maoist theory and practice in the educational curriculum. Sees improvements in infrastructure, especially irrigation and drainage. Some discussion of proper terminology for the area: the Chinese prefer North East China, not Manchuria, the name used by the Soviet Union.

0557. LEE, Shu-tan. Demarcation of Geographical Regions of China, *Annals, Association of American Geographers* 27, 1947, 155–68.

Derives "boundary girdles" from seven other attempts to divide China into regions. Finds results better than previous attempts because the regions were derived in a more objective manner. All contain at least four common physical and cultural features, are easily subdivided, and can be used as planning units.

0558. LESLIE, L. A. D. Notes on a Journey to the Burman-Yunnan Frontier, *Scottish Geographical Magazine* 59, 1943, 28–31.

Report based on fieldwork in late fall 1926. Uses itinerary format. Comments on diet, economy, religion, marriage customs, and personalities of groups he encounters. Notes that Burma-China border is not demarcated and that no Chinese customs posts were seen. Given difficulty of terrain and lack of transportation, reiterates that the completion of a modern road would enhance Burma-Yunnan trade and provide a link to the Western world and a way around the Japanese blockade. Further outlets will develop when the railroad under construction is completed.

0559. LIU, En-lan. Forgotten Land of the Szechuan Border, *Geographical Magazine* 17, 1945, 438–56.

Describes trip, taken in July 1943, to area known as Lifan Zidu, some two hundred miles northwest of Chengdu. Residents of area are nomads of Tibetan descent. Uses determinist format to describe cultural landscape and economy. Special emphasis on how physical isolation has influenced a wide range of political, religious, and social customs, especially marriage. Reports that women are seen as equals to men in rights and responsibilities.

0560. LIU, En-lan. The Ho-shi Corridor, *Economic Geography* 28, 1952, 51–56.

Notes that corridor, located in Gansu, west of the Huang He, is very inaccessible. Since the area is an important political and demographic safety valve, the population is quite heterogeneous and includes Fan (Tibetan shepherds), Mongols, Han Chinese, Hussacks, and Uighurs, who are described as Buddhist converts to Islam. Sees area as a study in varied adaptation to harsh climatic settings. Divides area into an economically active southeast and empty northwest. Describes resources and crops grown, especially the coarse grains. Since the geology of the area is not well known, little can be said about what resources are available. Argues that with proper management area could safely support up to three million people.

0561. LLEWELLYN, Bernard. Life on Chinese Waterways, *Geographical Magazine* 24, 1952, 547–51.

Describes life of permanent residents on the waterways across a variety of boat and watercraft types. Part of a three-article series focusing on waterways in China, the Netherlands, and the United Kingdom.

0562. LONG, George W. Macau: A Hole in the Bamboo Curtain, *National Geographic Magazine* 103, 1953, 679–88.

Provides a sketch history of colony. Describes urban structure and nature of economy, whose major industry is regulated gambling. Argues that the Portuguese have been on good terms with every Chinese government since the Ming and that there is no reason to suppose that they will not have good relations with the People's Republic. Major problem for the area is limited mobility: the only place to visit is Hong Kong.

0563. MARKHAM, J. Notes on a Journey through Shantung, *Journal, Royal Geographical Society* 40, 1870, 207–27.

Describes tour in 1869 of recently opened area. Topics surveyed include cities, seaports, markets, and growing areas. These notes are seen as supplement to official reports to the government.

0564. McCARTHY, J. Across China, from Chin-kiang to Bhamo, 1877, *Proceedings, Royal Geographical Society* 1, 1879, 489–509.

Reports on trip via Hankou. Describes towns and commercial activity along the way. Notes that part of missionary travel is to engage in "free and happy" interviews with people. Expresses hope that firsthand geographical and geological impressions were gained and then transmitted via the article.

0565. McCORMICK, Frederic. Present Conditions in China, *National Geographic Magazine* 22, 1911, 1120–38.

Sets out to correct Western misconceptions about China, especially those dealing with food habits, honesty, clothing, and hairstyles. Describes current events as he understands palace politics. Sees the dislike of a corrupt central goverment, and not Western unequal loans, as the main cause of civil unrest. Sees Western education and modernization as best hopes for China reestablishing any sense of stability. Argues against any attempt at Western intervention.

0566. MENG, C. Y. W. Sikang: China's "Baby Province," *China Journal* 35, 1941, 32–41.

Describes 1936 decision to establish Xigang as a province. Includes a list of six rationales for such a decision. Optimistic about both agricultural and mining potential of province and especially the Ning District. Feels area could provide China with a model of development and provide materials necessary to successfully resist Japanese aggression.

0567. METCALF, Franklin P. Formosa, the Beautiful Island, *China Journal* 10, 1929, 312–24.

Based on an environmental determinist format. Concludes that Japan has transformed the island economically and that the area will be a major tourist destination.

0568. MICHIE, A. Narrative of a Journey from Tientsin to Moukden in Manchuria in July 1861, *Proceedings, Royal Geographical Society* 7, 1862–63, 25–26; and *Journal, Royal Geographical Society* 33, 1863, 153–66.

Focuses on rural economy, state of Great Wall, and status of walled towns. Notes that the notion that the Qing government has established a strong military presence in the area is a myth. Economy underdeveloped and trade limited due to inadequate transportation facilities. Compares Shenyang to Edinburgh, Tianjin to Glasgow, and Suzhou, Hangzhow, and Canton to London. More favorably disposed toward the Manchus than the "enervated race" of central China.

0569. MICHIE, Mr. [A]. China: Notes of a Cruise in the Gulf of Pe-che-li and Leotung in 1859, *Proceedings, Royal Geographical Society of London* 4:2, 1860, 58–62.

Describes climate, soil, and vegetation along with major imports and exports. Comments by members of Royal Geographical Society take issue with report since it is seen as based on personal adventures.

0570. MONTGOMERIE, T. G. Journey to Shigatze in Tibet and Return by Dingri-maiden into Nepal in 1871 by the Native Explorer no. 9, *Journal, Royal Geographical Society* 45, 1875, 330–69.

Describes findings of unnamed Indian explorer in employ of Topographical Survey. Includes measures of latitude, longitude, and elevation for every major site visited.

0571. MONTGOMERIE, T. G. Narrative of an Exploration of the Namcho, or Tengri Nur Lake, in Great Tibet, Made by a Native Explorer during 1871–2, *Journal, Royal Geographical Society* 45, 1875, 315–24.

Reports on hired explorer who attempted to explore watershed of upper Brahmaputra. Comments on politics of explorations as well as number and type of field measurements taken.

0572. MOORE, W. Robert. Along the Yangtze, Main Street of China, *National Geographic Magazine* 93, 1948, 325–56.

Describes agricultural production and changes in the urban-economic structure of places along the river. Emphasizes need to continually maintain dikes in order to prevent flooding. Evaluates positively the Yangtze Gorge Project to control future flooding and extend irrigation.

0573. MOORE, W. Robert. In Manchuria Now, *National Geographic Magazine* 91, 1947, 389–414.

Despite the passing of V-J Day, the area was still in turmoil. Sees area as a perennial cradle of conflict. Outlines history of Japanese conflict and the extent of Japanese impact on the economy and urban structure of Manchuria. Freely reports on how the Soviet Union stripped the area of industrial plants. This, along with the continued fighting between the Communist and Nationalist armies, has paralyzed the area.

0574. MOORE, W. Robert. Life along the Central China Coast, *National Geographic Magazine* 62, 1932, 316–24.

Photo essay of fourteen pictures of life in and around Ningbo.

0575. MORGAN E. D[elmar]., translator. Northwest China and Eastern Tibet, Potanin's Journey in, *Proceedings, Royal Geographical Society*, new series 9, 1887, 233–35.

Abstract of paper by M. Potanin given before the Eastern Siberian Section of the Russian Geographical Society, December 1886. Expedition started in Beijing and was expected to cross the Ordos Desert to Lanzhou, capital of Gansu. Includes overview of function of settlements along travel route and a history of the Mongols in the area. In fact, expedition was confined to Sichuan and Tibet.

0576. MORRISON, G. J. Journeys in the Interior of China, *Proceedings, Royal Geographical Society* 2, 1880, 145–66. Map, p. 208.

Paper and subsequent discussion of 1878 journey to the Grand Canal and on to the Huang He and from Hankou to Canton. Describes hydrological features and the state of repairs of canal and its locks. Sees possibility of a railroad along the Huang He ultimately ending in Canton. Surprised at changes in customs and manners as he went from province to province. Predicts that coal will be an important element in Chinese development.

0577. MORRISON, Hedda [M]. The Chinese Artist, *Geographical Magazine* 20, 1947, 150–51.

Report on visit to the home and studio of Wang Ching-wang, a woodcutter on the faculty of Beijing University. Describes topics artist prefers to portray and his unusual method of creating works based on imagination without preliminary sketches. Includes pictures of artist at home and work.

0578. MORRISON, Hedda [M]. Chinese Harmony, *Geographical Magazine* 21, 1948, 151–54.

Uses seven examples of how Chinese craftsman have created harmony in landscapes.

0579. MORRISON, Hedda [M]. Street Life in China, I: Made for Children, *Geographical Magazine* 21, 1947, 34–37.

Focus is on street traders in Chinese towns, especially candy and toy makers, as well as puppet shows.

0580. MORRISON, Hedda [M]. A Visit to the Lost Tribe, *Geographical Magazine* 21, 1947, 253–60.

"Lost Tribe" is actually a village made up of exiles from Li Tzu-ch'eng's rebellious army who were permitted to subject themselves to Manchu rule on the condition that they live several hundred miles to the west of Beijing. After telling the history of the group, uses itinerary format to describe her 1936 trip. Notes that Chinese are curious about westerners' physical appearance and clothing but mean no harm or discourtesy in staring. Comments on Lost Tribe's habit of pseudo-foot binding, which they began after 1911, when the rest of China was abandoning the real practice. Older women have their feet bound to give the appearance of full and early binding.

0581. MORRISON, Ian. Lama Twilight, *Geographical Magazine* 22, 1949, 222–32.

Describes trip to western China where lama-monastic way of life is declining in the face of increasing suppression. Compares his observations to those of Owen Lattimore for Mongolia in the same issue.

0582. O'CONNOR, Sir Frederick. Tibet in the Modern World, *Geographical Magazine* 6, 1937, 93–107.

Firsthand report by member of the Younghusband expedition to Lhasa (1903–4). Focus is on the political history of the area from 1903 through 1937. Emphasizes the Chinese encroachment into the area and the conflict between the Tashi and Dalai Lamas. Impressed at attempts at modernization in administration, infrastructure, and foreign relations as well as the internal debate regarding the theological basis of government. Includes black and white and color photographs.

0583. ODELL, N. E. A Picture of Tibet, *New Zealand Geographical Society Record* 11, 1951, 3–7.

Report is a condensed version of a November 1950 radio broadcast. Describes Tibet as an ideally secluded country. Includes material regarding climate, feudal social and economic structure, diet and food, and acculturation, which takes place mainly through trade with China. Notes in this regard that, although Chinese may be the nominal suzerains, the Tibetans maintain their independence to the extent that they refer to themselves and their country using the Tibetan, not Chinese, names (i.e., Bhotias and Boht).

0584. OLIPHANT, Laurence. Notes of a Voyage up the Yangtse-Keang from Wosung to Han-Kow, *Proceedings, Royal Geographical Society* 3, 1858–59, 162–64.

Describes a five-hundred-mile trip started on November 9, 1858, and ending in mid-January 1859 by five naval vessels. Notes changes in the geomorphology of the river, and especially the disappearance of shoals, since the last survey. Such changes make the use of Chinese pilots for eighty- to ninety-mile stretches of the river necessary. Reports that the convoy was subject to weapons fire from forts along the river and that there was a lack of life and human activity along the riverbanks and in the cities due to the Taiping Rebellion. Sees great trade potential for Wusung.

0585. OSBORN, Sherard. Notes, Geographical and Commercial, Made during the Passage of *HMS Furious* in 1858 from Shanghai to the Gulf of Pecheli and Back, *Proceedings, Royal Geographical Society* 3, 1858–59, 55–87.

Reports on a trip made by Lord Elgin in an attempt to force the Chinese to accept Franco-British demands for changes in trade. For cities passed, describes the size, form, layout, and function. Includes data regarding weather, sailing conditions, sounding results, and channel changes. Stresses need to update navigational charts with regular surveys. Includes tables of British and Russian tidal observations, as well as sailing directions, provided by the Royal Navy.

0586. OUTHWAITE, Alison. China's Struggle, *Geographical Magazine* 15, 1942–43, 10–17.

Traces evolution of struggle against Japan, which started in 1931 and led to China's alliance with the Western powers. Tone of article is favorable to Kuomintang and Chiang Kai-shek.

0586. PANNELL, Clifton W. Time, Territory, and Man: A Geographic Instructional Approach to Growth and Change in China, *Journal of Geography* 73, 1974, 35–43.

Set against the background of the question of why China did not develop along Western lines, provides a catalog of Chinese and geographic terms that allow Chinese history to be divided into three periods: traditional, transitional, and modern. Specific geographic concepts include economic conditions, spatial arrangements and linkages, and environmental circumstances. Concludes with questions regarding how China can or might deal with its Malthusian dilemma.

0587. PARSONS, William Barclay. From the Yang-tse Kiang to the China Sea, *Geographical Journal* 19, 1902, 711–35.

In addition to commonplace observations regarding the people and landscape of the Changjiang, emphasizes the negative impact of the Boxer Rebellion on the trade and mineral production potential of the area, especially for Hunan.

0588. PARSONS, William Barclay. Hunan: The Closed Province of China, *National Geographic Magazine* 11, 1900, 393–400.

Reports on a 742-mile trip taken in 1898–99 as chief engineer for the U.S. syndicate holding the Hankou to Canton railroad concession. Describes the location of Hunan and its exploration by westerners. Outlines the flooding, topographic, and geological problems of building a railroad in an area that is one of China's most important trade and commercial centers. Reviews traditional modes of transporation along the Changjiang River and Tongting Lake. Envisions region developing into a prosperous base for China's modernization given its large population and substantial mineral riches.

0589. PEARCY, G. Etzel. Mainland China: Geographical Strengths and Weaknesses, *Department of State Bulletin* 55:1418, 1966, 294–303.

Attempts to assess China's potential as a world power without referring to the political prowess of the Communist regime. Rather, focuses on the differential impact of landscape, climate, population, mineral resources, and transportation on both internal and international Chinese needs and policies. Concludes that the planned economy, when supported by political strength and military might, can succeed in improving the lot of the Chinese people.

10. Human Geography: General

0590. PENNELL, W. V. Hong Kong Looks to a Greater Future, *Canadian Geographical Journal* 47:1, 1953, 2–13.

Hong Kong will succeed for positive reasons: it is a trade center for China and a link between China and the West. In contrast, Macao is too small to survive and thrive.

0591. PEREIRA, George. Across the Ordos, *Geographical Journal* 37, 1911, 260–64.

Very precise report of mileage distances traveled during a 1910 trip. Updates and corrects maps of area, especially for location of monasteries and villages. Comments on recent changes in political boundaries that extended the area of Shaanxi to the west. Expresses concern regarding Chinese incursions into Mongol areas. Reports that, in contrast to Gansu, there was no poppy cultivation in Shaanxi.

0592. POWELL, John B. Today on the China Coast, *National Geographic Magazine* 87, 1945, 217–38.

Reflections on twenty-seven years of experience in China. Describes the area of Japanese control, style of Japanese administration, and history of U.S. and British trade with China. Touches on role of missionaries and impressions of Manchuria, Tianjin, Chefoo, Shanghai, and Ningbo.

0593. PRATT, A. E. Two Journeys to Ta-tsien-lu on the Eastern Borders of Tibet, *Proceedings, Royal Geographical Society*, new series 13, 1891, 329–43.

Describes visits to a mountain village at an elevation of 8,400 feet in Sichuan in 1889 and 1890. Informs reader of types of transportation used to get to village, the impact of a succession of missionaries in area, and the ethnic mix. Provides a detailed enumeration of vegetation found in area.

0594. PRICE, M. Philips. A Journey on the Upper Yenesei Basin, Outer Mongolia, and Chinese Turkestan in 1910, *Geographical Journal* 134, 1968, 181–93.

Uses itinerary format. Major conclusion is that the use of horses as the major means of transportation is out of date yet given the absence of roads really the only practical way to visit villages. Sees his visit as the last of the old type of expedition for exploration of villages.

0595. PRICE, Willard. Grand Canal Panorama, *National Geographic Magazine* 71, 1937, 486–514.

Sees the Grand Canal and the Great Wall as the lasting, universally recognized features of China. Relates adventures of sailing along the Grand Canal. Includes observations about the hydrology and reconstruction of the canal, barge traffic, trade and fairs, daily life, social and religious customs and practices, and the security situation.

0596. RAVENSTEIN, E[rnst]. G. Formosa, *Geographical Magazine* 1, 1874, 292–97.

Written in reaction to the occupation of southern Taiwan by a Japanese military force. Describes the history of Chinese administration of the island as well as Chinese knowledge of the area. Provides information for general reader on topography, ethnicity, trade items, domesticated animals, and mineral potential. Explains the reasons for the Japanese invasion and questions the true extent of the Chinese government's concern for the island. Nevertheless, hopes that Japan will evacuate the island soon.

0597. RAWDEN, Fisk N. The Rise of Agriculture and the State in Ancient China, *Monadnock of the Clark University Geographical Society* 33, 1959, 4–8.

Exploratory essay, with appeals for corrections and suggestions. Defines the center of Chinese civilization and describes protoagricultural practices found there. Speculates on the extent of influences of India and Southeast Asia on Chinese agriculture. As such, alludes to the debates regarding diffusionism and the Wittvogel hypothesis. Argues that the real rise of Chinese civilization was tied to the development of food surpluses. Although Chinese civilization is a great one, it also is insular and contains the seeds of its own destruction.

0598. REITLINGER, Gerald. The Snow Mountain Gorge on the Yangtze in Northern Yunnan, *Journal, Royal Central Asiatic Society* 28, 1941, 413–22.

Compares the Snow Mountain Gorges with the more famous Yangtze Gorges at Wushan as well as those along the Indus in Kashmir. Terms the Snow Mountain gorges mysterious because of the circuitous route they take and their relative obscurity despite their proximity to areas explored by westerners. Reviews the history of Western exploration. Uses itinerary format. Main comments deal with logistical problems and

10. Human Geography: General 141

accessibility, local food, manners, clothing, and the interplay of local religious practices and Western missionary activitiues. Comments that central government is providing educational facilities to aboriginal peoples. Notes impact of earthquakes on local landscape and economy, and the need, therefore, to carry one's own food. Not impressed with local inn accommodations.

0599. RICHARDSON, Ralph. The Expedition to Lhasa, *Scottish Geographical Magazine* 21, 1905, 246–49.

Comparsion and contrast of reports by Francis Younghusband and Douglas Freshfield with books by Perceval Landon, Edmond Candler, and Powell Millington.

0600. ROCK, Joseph F. Konka Risumgongba, the Holy Mountain of the Outlaws, *National Geographic Magazine* 60, 1931, 1–65.

Article, in a modified itinerary format, is based on a 1928 trip from Kunming to Muli and the Konkaling Peaks. Claims to have been the first westerner to visit the area: others have only seen it from a distance. Describes ethnic makeup of area and notes the poor relationships between the Han and minority populations that led first to anarachy and then to the rise of banditry. Main resource of area is gold. Reports that he was forced by local bandits to end the trip earlier than wanted due to reports that the gods were angry with his presence in the region, as evidenced by hailstorms that destroyed the barley crop in areas he had recently visited.

0601. ROCK, Joseph F. The Land of the Tebbus, *Geographical Journal* 81, 1933, 108–27.

General description of trip taken in 1920 to an area west of Minshan, Gansu Province. Describes ethnography and origins of people. Mentions flora found along way. Elaborates upon the role of monasteries in local economic and political life.

0602. ROCK, Joseph F. The Land of the Yellow Lama: National Geographic Explorer Visits the Strange Kingdom of Muli, Beyond the Likiang Snow Range of Yunnan Province, China, *National Geographic Magazine* 48, 1925, 447–92.

Explains that an earlier attempt in 1919 to visit the area was postponed when the king refused permission to enter, presumably due to poor security situations. Trip actually completed in 1921. Material presented in itinerary format. Refers to Muli as "a land of babel" due to presence of numerous minorities such as the Lolo, the Nashi, and the Lushi. Touches on the role of religion in the political and daily life of the kingdom, the scenery, and the lives of minorities. Long description of planning and events leading up to an audience, including a photographer's session, with the king. Notes that the area is ignored by the local Chinese administrators, who are posted at various settlements between seventy and ninety miles away. Kingdom covers some nine thousand square miles and has a population of some twenty-two thousand. Major economic resource is gold.

0603. ROCKHILL, Mr. Travels in Northeast Tibet, *Proceedings, Royal Geographical Society*, new series 11, 1890, 730–34; 14, 1892, 777–78.

Describes trip from Beijing to Lhasa. Able to travel and enjoy local hospitality since he speaks both Chinese and Tibetan. Notes hostility of local government officials to his trip as evidenced by their refusal to permit local residents to assist author or sell him anything. Purpose of trip was to correct incomplete and biased Russian ethnographic descriptions of Mongols. Material in volume 14 also includes an extract of a letter, dated April 19, 1892, sent to one E. Delman Morgan, which describes in detail the physical characteristics of the region as well as names of the hydrological features in Chinese and Mongolian.

0604. ROORBACK, G. B. Some Significant Facts in the Geography of China, *Journal of Geography* 12, 1913, 45–51.

Notes problems resulting from China being isolated by both sea and land. Presents material about China's physical geography and climate with U.S. analogues. Describes the distribution of resources and emphasizes which province most important for each. Optimistic regarding China's prospects for economic development.

0605. ROSS, E. A. Notes on China, *Journal of Geography* 12, 1913–14, 55–58.

Covers five major topics: transportation, loess, the Great Wall, coal, and money. For each, describes some history and use.

0606. ROSS, John. Manchuria, *Scottish Geographical Magazine* 11, 1895, 217–31.

General survey, including ethnography of area and government system of administration. Details on lithology and stone trade, mineral deposits and their exploitation, and trade. Some historical material on native dynasties and administration under Ming and Qing.

0607. ROXBY, Percy Maude. China as an Entity: The Comparison with Europe, *Geography* 19, 1934, 1–20.

Sees Chinese civilization as having developed from a single area, with some assimilation of minority groups early on. Argues that, in contrast to Europe, China has a higher degree of cultural unity and is best understood as a living personality with territorial extent. Sees old Chinese unity as having been upset by European intrusions and civil wars. The great challenge to the Chinese is to restore their old unity.

0608. ROXBY, Percy M[aude]. Changing Structure of Chinese Society, *Geography* 26, 1941, 53–61.

An evenhanded presentation of the effects and impact of the Western economic system and prolonged struggle against Japan on the traditional Chinese social structure. Argues that Chinese society actually more dynamic than most westerners assume. Western economic institutions influencing China include treaty ports and transportation development. Describes Chinese attempts to use traditional coping policies to deal with both the West and Japan.

0609. ROXBY, Percy M[aude]. The Terrain of Early Chinese Civilisation [*sic*], *Geography* 23, 1938, 225–36.

Describes the physical geography of the North China Plain, including the latest in fossil finds. Concludes that Chinese civilization was an indigenous development located on the North China Plain, not in the Shanxi-Shaanxi area. Does not deny the existence of either a Western corridor or outside influences on Chinese development.

0610. RUSSELL, Claude. Journeys from Peking to Tsitsihar, *Geographical Journal* 23, 1904, 613–23.

Notes how little has changed in the Beijing to Jehol area since the 1794 visit of Lord Macartney. Pessimistic about potential for area: not seen as attractive for hunting, European colonization, or railroad investment. Doubts if region is rich in undiscovered minerals. Notes with disdain the negative impact that Western colonization has had on area, especially weapons and railroads.

0611. RUTTER, Owen. Awakening of Formosa, *Scottish Geographical Magazine* 41, 1925, 158–64.

Positive evaluation of impact of Japanese rule on economy, especially in building up old industries and establishing new ones. Major failure of

Japanese is inability to control aboriginal population. Urges that the Japanese should emulate the British and their handling of native peoples. Finds rural areas beautiful, cities anything but; feels public buildings especially hideous.

0612. RUTTLEDGE, Hugh. Notes on a Visit to Western Tibet in 1926, *Geographical Journal* 71, 1928, 432–40.

Description of trip undertaken at the initiative of Indian government to investigate conditions of Tibetan trade. Reviews trips of previous missions. Notes how retreat of glaciers has improved accessibility. Uses internary format.

0613. SAREL, Henry Andrew. Notes on the Yang-tsze-Kiang from Hankou to Ping-shan, *Journal, Royal Geographical Society* 32, 1862, 1–25.

Emphasizes military potential of sites along the river. Describes climate, topography, hydrology, crops, and trade patterns. Includes tables of locations, sunrise, and three daily temperature readings of selected places. Notes difficulty of completing mission due to presence of Taiping rebels. Indicates that rebellion has led to village abandonment.

0614. SCHOMBERG, Reginald [C. F.]. Chinese Turkestan, *Scottish Geographical Magazine* 49, 1933, 154–61.

Positive evaluation of Xinjiang, its peoples, and its mineral resources. Warns that place names often misnomers, with no visible relationship between names and environment or history.

0615. SCHOMBERG, R[eginald]. C. F. The Habitability of Chinese Turkestan: A Fourth Journey in the Tien Shan, *Geographical Journal* 79, 1932, 368–78.

Uses itinerary format to describe trip to Xinjiang taken between May 31 and August 16, 1931, starting from Qara Shahr. Very uneven description of transportation and communications, vegetation, religions and religious practices, and geomorphology.

0616. SCHREIDER, Helen, and Frank SCHREIDER. Taiwan: The Watchful Dragon, *National Geographic Magazine* 135, 1969, 1–45.

Despite the need to maintain a large defense force, Taiwan is not merely a battleship. The economy is thriving due to the entrepreneurial spirit of the Taiwanese and foreign investment. Despite the increase in per capita income, disparities between rural and urban places, aborigines and the Chinese, and modern industry and traditional agriculture still exist.

0617. SCIDMORE, Eliza R. Mukden, the Manchu Home, and Its Great Art Museum, *National Geographic Magazine* 21, 1910, 289–320.

Real focus is on Manchuria generally, not the city of Shenyang. Main themes include the apparent lack of any Chinese attempts to develop Manchuria, the comparative and contrasting roles of the Japanese and Russians in the area's economy, the centrality of the soybean to economic prosperity, the role of foreigners in railroad construction, and the climate. Impressed with the large number of foreign tourists and the cityscape but decries the neglect of Manchu dynasty palaces and homes. Tends to minimize the impact of war on the life and economy of area.

0618. SHIELDS, E. T. Omei San, *Journal, Royal Asiatic Society, North China Branch*, new series 44, 1923, 100–109.

Describes trip from Shanghai to Omei San in Sichuan. Includes legends of area, especially the Great Flood and Jointed Snake.

0619. SIMPICH, Frederick, Jr. Changing Formosa: Green Island of Refuge, *National Geographic Magazine* 111, 1957, 327–64.

Describes the impact of retrocession on the economic and educational systems. Notes the continuing need of the programs of the Joint Commission on Rural Reconstruction. Attempts to assess the impact of Chinese culture on the aboriginal population and the continuity of aboriginal traditions, such as food, even in the face of rural-urban migration. Touches on life of military recruits and recreational opportunities for the entire population. Remarks that the government's main goal in fostering economic development is food self-sufficiency. Notes decline of mining and general impact of industrialization on southern part of island.

0620. SLADEN, E. B. Exploration via the Irrawaddy and Bhamo to Southwestern China, *Journal, Royal Geographical Society* 41, 1871, 257–80.

Describes topography, ethnic groups, and economy seen during an 1868 steamer trip. Special emphasis on non-Han economy and social practices. Complains of interference by local Chinese government officials in his exploration work.

0621. SOWERBY, Arthur de C[arle]. The Exploration of Manchuria, *Geographical Journal* 54, 1919, 73–92.

Report by practicing field naturalist for the Smithsonian Institution on trips made in 1913, 1914, and 1915 to areas previously closed to westerners except for Russians. Provides a rapid survey of drainage, communications, resources, and agricultural practices. Argues that Japan failed to use Manchuria as a demographic safety value. Notes that absent a complete geological survey there is no way to assess mineral wealth, although deposits of gold, coal, and iron had been identified in the south.

0622. SOWERBY, Arthur de C[arle]. Manchuria, Land of Promise, *China Journal* 9, 1928, 235–38.

Argues that Manchurian grasslands similar to those of the United States, except that Manchuria is more thickly populated. Discusses exploitation of forests along northwestern periphery. Notes the conflicts between Manchus and Han Chinese migrants. Sees title "land of opportunity and promise" as related to the number and amount of resources that can be easily secured and exploited.

0623. SPENCER, Joseph E[arle]. Ancient China under Modern Communism, *California Geographer* 3, 1962, 1–27.

Argues that the government of the People's Republic of China is making major changes in the six fundamental foundations of ancient China, namely, family, village settlements, walled cities, social organization, egocentric worldview, and agrarian orientation. Feels that such a reorganization was long overdue since by 1900 China had outgrown its landscape of the past civilization complex. Provides ample examples of ancient complex and manner in which current policies are changing it.

0624. SPENCER, J[oseph]. E[arle]. Down the Wu Kiang by Crooked Stern Junk, *China Journal* 32, 1940, 55–61.

Reports on a trip taken in May 1940 from Sichuan and northeastern Guizhou near the head of navigation of the Wu. Divides the river into four sections, each of which requires a different type of boat in order to continue transporting goods. Notes that main commodity carried by crooked stern vessels is salt. Reviews debate regarding how to power boats—steam or oar. Offers alternative folk explanations for the shape of the boats and concludes best answer relates to the ease of navigating rapids. Includes a discussion of repairs made to boats due to damage sustained while in rapids. Includes six pages of photographs.

0625. SPENCER, J[oseph]. E[arle]. The Prospects of Communist China Today, *Journal of Geography* 66, 1967, 364–71.

Quotes works evaluating the prospects for the United States published between 1870 and 1900 and shows how they could easily be mistaken for evaluations being published for China during the 1960s. Feels that there is no effective way to measure or judge China's performance since 1949. Concludes that China is making progress in feeding, housing, and maintaining its population. Argues that Chinese are seriously engaged in programs of development in the context of contending political and social theories within Marxist-Maoist thought. At a minimum, China can expect to see modest rises in the standard of living regardless of which social theory of change comes to dominate. Concludes with a note from a U.S. Department of State bulletin estimating the size and rate of natural increase for the population of China.

0626. SPENCER, J[oseph]. E[arle]. Resurgence of Modern China, *Iowa Geographer* 32, 1973, 3–12.

Not concerned with either the political direction of post-1949 China or the nature of the political-economic constitution. Rather, focuses on the fact that since 1949 China has displayed a vital creativeness that will result in the rebuilding of its culture such that it can participate as an equal in world affairs. Points out that resurgence implies return to a former status. Describes China during the eighteenth century, when it reached a peak. Attributes decline to cultural egocentrism, population pressure, and missionary activities. Impressed with the ability of the leadership of China to rebuild and reestablish Chinese confidence.

0627. STEVENSON, Paul Huston. Notes on the Human Geography of the Chinese-Tibetan Borderland, *Geographical Review* 22, 1932, 599–616.

Report of an anthropological reconnaissance taken during the spring and summer of 1926. In describing the distribution of the Chinese and their settlements, notes importance of large-scale water management. The description of the non-Han population focuses on the independent Lolos and their subgroups. Their distribution, origins, culture, languages, and social-psychological adaptations are described. Non-Han populations are assumed to be related to Southeast Asian populations. Comments that the major urban center, Daxian, is the Shanghai of Tibet.

0628. STONE, John. A Fragment of China, *Canadian Geographical Journal* 1:2, 1930, 152–64.

Reports on train travel between Beijing and Shenyang. Includes author's and Chinese reactions to Japanese occupation of area. Well illustrated with pictures of prime historical tourist sites.

0629. STOUT, Arthur Purdy. Penetration of Yunnan, *Bulletin, Geographical Society of Philadelphia* 10, 1912, 1–35.

Designed to provide a general introduction of area for Americans. Based on European sources, especially English and French, written between 1890 and 1911. Feels that the light of European civilization has shown in a dark corner of the world but that much remains to be done to bring civilization to Yunnan, an area isolated by Mother Nature.

0630. SWINHOE, Robert. Notes on the Island of Formosa, *Journal, Royal Geographical Society* 34, 1864, 6–18.

Begins with the Chinese mythology regarding the origins of the island. Reports on trip designed to establish trading post for British. Explains why Tainan (Taiwan-fu) not a viable location. Main focus on Tamshui River and history of settlement, including difficulties in procuring a safe water supply.

0631. TAYLOR, Annie R. Experiences in Tibet, *Scottish Geographical Magazine* 10, 1894, 1–8.

Describes three routes to Tibet: the official one from Sichuan, the so-called Tea Road from Sichuan, and one via Siuning, Gansu. Emphasizes trade patterns and ethnic diversity. Concludes with warning that those anticipating such trips should learn either Chinese or Arabic [*sic*] to ensure a meaningful trip.

0632. TAYLOR, George. Formosa: Characteristic Traits of the Island and Its Aboriginal Inhabitants, *Proceedings, Royal Geographical Society*, new series 11, 1889, 224–38.

Remarks that the Imperial Customs Service was able to establish a lighthouse in 1881 on the South Cape of Formosa after negotiating with hitherto unruly aborigines. Notes hydrological features of rivers (i.e., short and steep). Points out the displacement of the aboriginal population by Chinese migrants. Compares the economies of the aborigines and the Chinese. Sees great potential for island given its forests and mineral base. Evaluates ports and prefers Gaoxiong (Takao).

10. Human Geography: General

0633. TEICHMAN, Eric. Notes on a Journey through Shenshi, *Geographical Journal* 52, 1918, 333–51. Map, p. 402.

Report of four-month journey to Shaanxi starting in Dongguan and ending in Chengdu. Describes the unsettling impact of the 1911 Revolution on the landscape and economy.

0634. THOMPSON, H. Gordon. From Yunnan-fu to Peking along the Tibetan and Mongolian Borders, Including the Last Journey of Gen. [*sic*] G. E. Pereira, *Geographical Journal* 67, 1926, 2–26.

Report on six-stage trip during summer 1923. Emphasizes ethnography of areas, especially local industries such as salt wells. Mentions medical assistance expedition received. Leader, Gen. Pereira, apparently died at Kantse after having been captured by brigands outside of Paotou. Author managed to save maps, but all other equipment lost.

0635. THOMPSON, J. Notes of a Journey in South Formosa, *Journal, Royal Geographical Society* 43, 1873, 97–107.

Full notes of abstract published in *Proceedings, Royal Geographical Society* 17:3, 1873, 144–48. Describes trade in Gaoxiong and speculates on the Malay origins of the aborigines.

0636. TIPTON, C. E. Into China's Northwest, *Geographical Magazine*, 2, 1935–36, 1–9, 199–202.

Photos of business trip to borders of Xinjiang via Shaanxi, Gansu, Qinghai, and Suiyuan.

0637. TOLSTOY, Lt. Col. Ilin. Across Tibet from India to China, *National Geographic Magazine* 90, 1946, 169–222.

Report, using itinerary format, of Australian officer's 1942 trip to deliver a letter to the Dalai Lama. Describes the potential of the area for development, especially given Tibet's reputation as a spectacular paradise. Provides details of city life for monks and common people. Recounts meeting with the Dalai Lama.

0638. TOPPING, Audrey. Return to Changing China, *National Geographic Magazine* 140, 1971, 800–834.

Describes reactions to a 7,000-mile return trip to China by two sisters who had lived there during the period 1946–48. Favorably impressed with changes in cities, which are now much cleaner and more orderly, health, education, and pollution control. Notes that the evidence of ravages by imperialism have disappeared. Urges adherence to a One China Policy.

0639. TOURS, B. G. Notes on the Overland Journey from Chungking to Haiphong, *Geographical Journal* 62, 1923, 117–32.

Report on 4,000-mile journey made over 113 days. Major by-product of tour was ability to describe in detail the opium trade as a part of the agricultural system. Presents general conditions of climate, ethnography, and government-aborigine relations. Has very negative impressions of Guizhou, which is seen as poor, and Yunnan, which was nothing more than a wilderness.

0640. TREWARTHA, Glenn T. Field Observations on the Canton Delta of South China, *Economic Geography* 15, 1939, 1–10.

Part of an issue devoted to deltas around the world. Article not intended to be a systematic or detailed analysis. Canton's ability to survive is compromised by poor transportation, threat of flooding, and political instability. Yet it has potential based on weather, soil, occupance history, and its silk-mulberry industry.

0641. TROTTER, H. Account of the Pundit's Journey in Great Tibet from Leh in Ladakh to Lhasa and His Return to India via Assam, *Journal, Royal Geographical Society* 47, 1877, 86–136.

Report of trip made by Nain Singh in 1867 in itinerary format. Given trials and tribulations of travel, the Pundit was anxious to retire since trips had had an adverse impact on his health.

0642. TSYBIKOFF, G. G. Journey to Lhasa, *Geographical Journal* 23, 1904, 92–97.

Abstract of paper published in *Izvestia*, the journal of the Russian Geographical Society, in 1903. Contains detailed estimates of population, standard of living, and governance structure.

0643. VENBT, Herbert J. A Brief Geographical, Historical, and Political Evaluation of Formosa, *Philippine Geographical Journal* 6:1, 1958, 39–41.

Very diffuse description of Taiwan. Japanese given due credit for developing the island and achieving a higher standard of living than found on Mainland China. Suggests that there are four solutions to the political uncertainty over Taiwan's future: conquest by the People's Republic, surrender to the People's Republic, remaining under Kuomintang/Chiang Kai-shek administration, or a United Nations' plebiscite.

0644. von ENGELN, O. D. In a Chinese Harbor, *Journal of Geography* 32, 1933, 218–20.

Uses Hong Kong to demonstrate the contrast between the liveliness of Chinese ports and the dullness of Japanese docks. Includes details about Chinese ship design and decorations.

0645. WALKER, Gen. J. T. Chinese Turkestan, Notes on M. Dauvergne's Travels in, *Proceedings, Royal Geographical Society*, new series 14, 1892, 779–84.

Summarizes work by the French geographer Henri Dauvergne that appeared in the 1892 issue of the *Bulletin of the French Geographical Society*. Report analyzes the differences among French, Russian, and English travelers.

0646. WALKER, Gen. J. T. Four Years' Journey through Tibet by a Native Explorer, *Proceedings, Royal Geographical Society*, new series, 7, 1885, 65–92. Map after p. 136.

Report on expedition undertaken by an unnamed Asian working for Indian Survey in spring 1878. Traces route from Tibet to Mongolia. While in Lhasa, twenty-two measurements of longitude and latitude were made and recorded. Expresses concern for low level of education found in survey employees; calls for further training. Bemoans fact that westerners no longer have access to Tibet for exploration and therefore the need to send in Asians.

0647. WALTON, W. H. Murray. Among the Mountains and Headhunters of Formosa, *Geographical Journal* 81, 1933, 481–500.

Describes origins of the aborigines. Praises security, including the cessation of headhunting, imposed by the Japanese, although critical of Japanese for not permitting missionary work among these natives. In ethnographic material, stresses aboriginal marriage patterns. Some material on flora and fauna of area included. Uses itinerary format and as such includes details of mountain climbing. Conclusions regarding the positive effect of Japanese administration echoed in discussion session by E. A. de Bunsen, former British counsel in Tamshui.

0648. WARD, F. Kingdon. Across the Chung-tien Plateau, *Geographical Journal* 42, 1913, 461–66.

Goal of trip to Yunnan was to make accurate measurements of latitudes. Emphasizes hardships of travel. Comments on intrusion of Chinese military into the area. Ethnographic data include details about villages, houses, religious practices, and origins of minority peoples.

0649. WARD, F. Kingdon. Through the Lutzu Country to Meekong, *Geographical Journal* 39, 1912, 582–92.

Route of entry was through India. Lists trip participants. Uses itinerary format to describe nineteen-day trip. Comments on housing, origins of Lutzu, the Lutzu relationship with the Tibetans, and Lutzu interactions with Chinese officials.

0650. WARD, F. Kingdon. Through Western Yunnan, *Geographical Journal* 60, 1922, 195–205. Map, p. 240.

Deals with parts of Yunnan that are approached via Lashio, terminus of the North Shan State Railroad in Burma, and through Muli in Sichuan. Notes in particular the Chinese influence on villages, agricultural practices, and the flora and fauna. Although the area is poor and sparsely populated, poppy cultivation is extensive. Uses secondary materials to describe the rest of Yunnan.

0651. WARD, F. Kingdon. Wanderings of a Naturalist in Tibet, *Scottish Geographical Magazine* 29, 1913, 341–50.

Describes trip of uncertain purpose starting in Bhamo, Upper Burma. Contains voluminous and pointed comments on what is seen as the positive traits and culture of the non-Han population.

0652. WARD, F. Kingdon. Yunnan and the Tai Peoples, *Journal, Royal Central Asiatic Society* 24, 1937, 624–36.

Uses itinerary format to describe a trip taken from Burma to Yunnan in April 1937. Argues that the true border between the two countries is found when tea plants appear. Describes the Tai physical, social, and economic environment, their agricultural practices involving fallow, architecture, religion, and dress. Categorizes them as lazy opium addicts of short and mean physique. Remarks on Chinese-Tai relationships and on Chinese plan to absorb, not assimilate, the Tai. Notes that more progressive Tai are being educated and that large numbers of Chinese from Yunnan who went overseas for education are returning to the area as government officials and consultants.

0653. WARWICK, Adam. A Thousand Miles along the Great Wall of China: The Mightiest Barrier Ever Built by Man Has Stood Guard over the Land of China for Thirty Centuries, *National Geographic Magazine* 43, 1923, 113–43.

Begins with the claim that astronomers feel that the Wall would be one of the few human creations visible from the moon. Provides a history of the Wall's building as well as the mythology describing the path it follows. Notes the role of the Ming dynasty in expanding the Wall and building watchtowers along it. Notes that, although the Wall was built to separate two worlds, it was never a dependable barrier for keeping nomads out or Chinese in.

0654. WATTS, Harvey Maitland. The Chinese Paradox, *National Geographic Magazine* 11, 1900, 352–58.

Article framed in context of uncertainty as to why the Chinese government permitted the Boxer attacks on westerners. The paradox is that China permitted the West to impose unequal treaties while it sought to get rid of the westerners by using imperial etiquette and displays of anti-Western feelings. Argues that in the end China has no choice but to open up to the West: it must yield to nineteenth-century science and sense.

0655. WEBSTER, Harrie. China and Her People, *National Geographic Magazine* 11, 1900, 309–19.

Describes the boundaries and main hydrological and topographical features of China. Outlines the political structure of the country, including provincial administration, the role of the emperor, and problems of succession. Discusses issues relating to commerce and open ports. Compares Chinese education to that of the West. Notes that there is a wide range of physical variation among the ethnic Chinese. Reports that Chinese antipathy to industrialization is out of fear of displacing workers. A sympathetic reading of Chinese concerns.

0656. WEBSTER, Harrie. Japan and China: Some Comparisons, *National Geographic Magazine* 12, 1901, 69–76.

Despite their apparent racial similarity, the two nations differ in terms of political attitudes, smell, architecture, historical perspective, intellect, sense of ethnicity and position, cleanliness, burial practices, nationalism, legal systems, and status of women. In all cases, finds Japan to be superior to China. Ponders how two peoples with a common origin can be so different.

0657. WHITE, Herbert Clarence, and Bao-ling DENG. China's Wonderland: Yen Tang Shan, *National Geographic Magazine* 72, 1937, 687–94.

Unstructured, unrelated photo essay inserted in article by Groff and Lau [item 0524].

0658. WIENS, H[erold]. J. The Ili Valley as a Geographic Region of Hsin Chiang (China), *Current Scene* 7:15, 1969, 1–19.

Companion article to that appearing in *Annals, Association of American Geographers* [item 0811]. Describes the administrative functions of Ili as well as details of ethnic, demographic, physical, hydrological, climatic, and floral phenomena. Despite long tradition of nomadism, sees great industrial potential for region. Notes political tensions between Chinese and Russians in area and that Ili now more oriented toward Urumqi, that is, the Chinese side. Concludes with warning that water may be limiting factor in future development.

0659. WILLIAMS, F. E. Hong Kong, *Journal of Geography* 16, 1918, 221–22.

Catalogs population groups in Hong Kong by nationality. Optimistic about the future of Hong Kong because it has large harbor with the largest docks in the East, has a government dedicated to free trade, is centrally located in the Far East, and has a cheap labor force.

0660. WILLIAMS, Maynard Owen. Britain's Far-Flung Output in China, *National Geographic Magazine* 73, 1938, 349–60.

Photographs of selected street scenes of Hong Kong.

0661. WILLIAMS, Maynard Owen. The Descendents of Confucius, *National Geographic Magazine* 36, 1919, 253–65.

Title should be read figuratively, although pictures of living relative of Confucius included. Real focus is on Qingtao and Shandong. Reviews the roles of the Huang He and coolie labor in building the economy of the area. Notes positively the efforts of the Japanese in developing the Qingtao region. Evaluates the disruptive role of bandits on the rural economy.

10. Human Geography: General

Concludes that Shandong is a vast labor reservoir for areas such as Manchuria.

0662. **WILLIAMS, Maynard Owen.** From the Mediterranean to the Yellow Sea by Motor, *National Geographic Magazine* 62, 1932, 513–67, 577–80.

Uses itinerary format to describe Citroen-Harrdt Expedition. Describes life along route of expedition, including religious practices. Comments positively on the role of missionaries. Goal of trip reported to be to establish friendships, and in this regard it can be argued that the travelers acquired "face."

0663. **WILLIAMS, Maynard Owen.** Land of Ghenghis Khan and Its True Lolos, *National Geographic Magazine* 62, 1932, 568–76.

Photographic set embedded in article by same author marking the successful completion of the Citroen-Harrdt Expedition [item 0662].

0664. **WILLIAMSON, Alexander.** Notes on Manchuria, *Journal, Royal Geographical Society* 39, 1869, 1–35.

After describing the physical and human geography of area, notes its potential for absorbing surplus Chinese population. Predicts that area will become "one of the most important districts in this quarter of the earth."

0665. **WILSON, Maj. Gen. James Harrison.** China and Its Progress, *Bulletin of the American Geographical Society* 20, 1888, 401–31.

Describes the significance of China's location in the context of accessibility, interaction, and isolation. Notes roles of sea and land in determining China's world orientation. Comments on problems of political divisions within China. Topics covered more generally include city forms and cityscapes, ethnicity, the Grand Canal, and hydrology. Sees Chinese civilization as basically democratic. Notes frequency of foreign dynasties. Sees economic and political progress since 1861–63. Sees major drawback to economic development as lack of a formal, organized, capital market. Tries to identify United States' interests in an awakening China.

0666. **WILTON, E. C.** Yunnan and the West River of China, *Geographical Journal* 49, 1917, 418–40.

Describes four possible routes to get to Yunnan from the China coast: via Hong Kong and the Xi River, via Shanghai along the Changjiang, through

French Indochina, and from Burma. Based on the experience gained as member of the Chinese Government Conservancy Board and adviser to Western governments, details the problems of navigating the Xi River resulting from population growth and deforestation. Includes materials about origins of subgroups in population and relations with the Han Chinese. Notes that agricultural practices include widespread cultivation of poppies. Concludes that any exploitation of mineral wealth of area must await investment and the construction of a railroad, which will also accelerate assimilation processes.

0667. **WINGATE, A. W. S.** Recent Journey from Shanghai to Bhamo through Hunan, *Geographical Journal* 14, 1899, 639–46.

Enumerates specific members of travel party for a 1898 journey, including a translator and a taxidermist. Describes seasonal deterioration of Tongting lakes environment due to low water-level flows. Impressed with local industries and mineral wealth, even though they are less well known than the gold mines of Yunnan.

0668. **WULSIN, Frederick R.** The Road to Wang Ye Fu: An Account of the Work of the National Geographic Society's Central-China Expedition in the Mongol Kingdom of Ala Shan, *National Geographic Magazine* 49, 1926, 195–234.

In describing encounters with Mongols, uses a modified itinerary format. Desires to present a portrait of the economic and social life in the city of Wang Ye Fu, also known as Ting Yuanying. The rationale for the city is tied to the traditional migration patterns of the Mongols. In terms of economy, apart from herding and farming, all occupations are in the hands of Chinese residents. However, Chinese migrant farmers are displacing the Mongols. Notes the only other city in region is Tongkou, a salt production and distribution center. Includes a set of fifteen unrelated pictures of life and landscape in China proper.

0669. **WYLIE, J. A.** Journey through Central Manchuria, *Geographical Journal* 2, 1893, 443–50.

Goal of 1,460-mile trip in 1892 was to expand knowledge of the size, situation, shape, structure, and relative importance of cities and towns in central Manchuria. Describes crops grown and comments on trade and religious practices. Remarks on the need for bilinguality if one expects to travel or trade in region.

0670. YATE, A. C. Peking and Back: The Journey from Shanghai to Peking, *Scottish Geographical Magazine* 14, 1898, 643–48.

Describes trials and tribulations of travel. Notes that it is no longer possible to go from Beijing to Tianjin via steamer due to the silting up of streams. Finds Beijing to be dirty and its residents "too" curious. Black and white photographs of "Mongolian" and Jesuit astronomical instruments are included.

0671. YETTS, W. Perceval. Links between Ancient China and the West, *Geographical Review* 16, 1926, 614–22.

Article is part of the debate regarding cultural origins of Chinese civilization. Reviews Zhou dynasty relations with nomads to the north as well as contacts with Central Asia. Includes descriptions of Greek fashion textiles and clothing as well as Scyto-Siberian artworks. Concludes that findings of Kozlov expedition to northern Mongolia in 1925 support the theory of an early diffusion of Western culture eastward to China.

0672. YOUNGHUSBAND, Frank. Geographical Results of the Tibet Mission, *Geographical Journal* 25, 1905, 481–98.

Admits that report contains little new in substantive findings, but reiterates that Tibet is a poor, inhospitable country. Reprinted in *Scottish Geographical Magazine* 21, 1905, 229–45.

0673. YULE, H[enry]. A Visit of Mr. F. Paderin to the Site of the Karakorum, *Geographical Magazine* 1, 1874, 137–39.

A comparison of Paderin's report, which appeared in the *Bulletin of the Imperial Geographical Society* of St. Petersburg in 1873, with those of other westerners in the area. Main focus is on toponymic problems.

11. Population

0673. ANON. Manchuria as a Demographic Frontier, *Population Index* 11, 1945, 260–74.

Reviews the history of Han and non-Han population in the area. Describes modern population movements in and out of Manchuria. Rejects the notion that Manchuria can serve as a long-term demographic safety valve for population pressure in China proper.

0674. ANON. Population of China in 1902, *Bulletin of the American Geographical Society* 34, 1902, 440–41.

Presents and analyzes data from 1902 that reported the Chinese population as 407 million. Finds data consistent with 1882 Chinese government estimate of 380 million. Tables and maps include data for eighteen provinces and "Four Dependencies," Manchuria, Mongolia, Tibet, and Turkistan (Xinjiang).

0675. ALEXANDER, J. W. Prewar Population of China: Distribution and Density, *Annals, Association of American Geographers* 38, 1948, 1–5.

Uses 1934 data, which showed the total population to be 458.9 million. Analysis of 1:5 million dot map permits five major clusters and four minor areas of population concentration to be delimited.

0676. BEAL, Edwin G., Jr. The 1940 Census of Manchuria, *Far Eastern Quarterly* 4, 1945, 243–62.

Notes that the 1940 census was one of a series conducted by the Japanese starting in 1925. Includes translations of census law and raw and adjusted data for total population, males and females. Data for Chientao and East Hsingan Provinces and Shenyang and Harbin cities included.

0677. BOWRING, Sir John. The Population of China, *Transactions, China Branch, Royal Asiatic Society*, part 5, 1855, 1–16.

Estimates population to be between 350 and 400 million. Tables include data for eighteen provinces from different censuses. Interprets data in strict Malthusian framework as food supply in China does not appear to keep up with population growth. Predicts that a demographic catastrophe can be avoided only by emigration or migration to Manchuria. Includes material on population distribution and food habits. Reprinted in *Journal, Royal Asiatic Society, Hong Kong Branch* 5, 1905, 27–45.

0678. BUCHANAN, Keith. Land and People in China: Some Recent Studies of China's Population, *Tidjschrift voor economische et sociale geografie* 53, 1962, 46–50.

Article is the product of a 1958 visit at the invitation of the Chinese Academy of Sciences. Sees China as classic case of overpopulation, yet a large population is viewed as an asset by China's leadership. Reviews literature based on the 1953 census. In discussion of birth control and family planning, sees these programs as conveniences rather than government strategies for bringing about long-term reduction of growth rates.

0679. CHANG, Chi-yun. China's Population Problem: A Chinese View, *Pacific Affairs* 22, 1949, 339–56.

Argues that overpopulation in China is due to deterioration of Chinese society under the Manchus. Therefore, China's population problem is solvable. Notes the ambiguity in the term and theories of overpopulation and sees them as providing the means for helping China. Provides detailed list of ways to improve the size and availability of food and food products. Warns against relying too heavily on population projections, especially since Chinese demographic data are so poor. Notes that the Chinese population does need to make up for war losses.

0680. CHANG, Chi-yun. Geographical Distribution of the Chinese People, *Chinese Culture* 2, 1959, 74–97.

Describes the historical changes in the numbers, distribution, and ethnicity of the Chinese population. Material presented on a regional basis for plains, hilly lands, plateaux, and mountains.

0681. CHEN, Cheng-siang. Population and Settlement in Formosa, *Tidjschrift voor economische en sociale geografie* 45, 1954, 176–80.

Uses 1905 as index year and presents data in five-year increments to describe distribution and density, population structure, and rural-urban differences. Strong comparisons of north-south differences in settlements due to water, native landscape, aboriginal defenses, and the impact of reclamation organizations. Contains frequent comparisons with both South and Southeast China and Europe.

0682. CHEN, Cheng-siang. Population Distribution and Change in Taiwan, *Proceedings, International Geographical Union Regional Conference in Japan*, 1957, 290–95.

Provides a history of the census on Taiwan. Notes the use of the *ta-tzu* as the smallest statistical unit between 1905 and 1956. Demographic variables analyzed include density, ethnicity, occupation, rate of natural increase, and doubling time.

0683. CRESSEY, G[eorge]. B. 1953 Census of China, *Far Eastern Quarterly* 14, 1955, 387–88.

Presents overview of population by sex, minority group, and locale in China. Concludes that since the census totals were more than 100 million greater than any previous estimates, the data must be regarded with considerable skepticism.

0684. DAVIS, Sydney George. Population Growth and Pressure in South China and Hong Kong, *Proceedings, International Geographical Union Conference in Japan*, 1957, 296–301; reprinted in *Economics and Finance in Indonesia Tahun* KE10, 1957, 682–95.

Prefers to see increasing population pressure in South China as the continuation of a long-term Malthusian trap, not a new phenomenon. Attributes the fourfold increase in Hong Kong's population between 1945 and the early 1970s to the return of former residents after the departure of the Japanese, legal Chinese migration, refugees fleeing the Chinese civil war, and natural increase. Argues that the Hong Kong government must enunciate policies that will ensure a standard of living in reasonable balance with that in southern China so as to avoid a flood of migrants. Similarly, it must regulate labor costs so that its exports remain competitive on world markets.

0685. DAVIS, S[yndey]. G[eorge]. The Rural-Urban Migration in Hong Kong, *Geographical Journal* 128, 1962, 328–33.

Analyzes the redistribution of the Hong Kong population in the context of the establishment of the People's Republic of China and the subsequent refugee movements to Hong Kong. Specific items covered include location, topography, rural change, old walled cities, agricultural and manufacturing patterns, and strip conurbations. Notes that population growth frequently runs ahead of the government's ability to engage in orderly planning.

0686. DWYER, D. J. Chinese Population Puzzle, *Geographical Magazine* 46, 1974, 704–8.

Despite past progress in improving the standard of living, China has not been able to escape from a population dilemma because productivity is so low. China is still an underdeveloped country and can expect only modest, if encouraging, improvement in its standard of living. The effects of China's population policies are seen as equivocal. Increased urbanization will present the Chinese Communist Party with both ideological and social challenges as it tries to provide housing, food, and employment for an increasing urban-based population. Concludes that the only way out of China's dilemma is increased productivity.

0687. FREEBERNE, Michael. Birth Control in China, *Population Studies* 18, 1964, 5–16.

Against the background of poor harvests in 1960 and 1961, China appears to have implemented a birth control policy. Reviews the debate over birth control and family planning within the Communist Party and the emergence of rationales that permit birth control within a Marxist framework. Includes verbatim excerpts from the Chinese press regarding the dedication and willingness of Chinese workers to postpone or defer marriage and childbearing for the good of the country. Notes the paradox in the apparent abandonment of birth control except for emphasizing late marriage.

0688. FREEBERNE, Michael. Changing Population Characteristics in Tibet, 1959–1965, *Population Studies* 19, 1966, 317–20.

Point of departure is report on the Tibetan population found in the 1953 census. Explores Chinese explanations for a 7.4 percent decrease in the Tibetan population between 1953 and 1959. Expresses hope that the release of Tibetan data is a prelude to more general availability of provincial-level data.

0689. FREEBERNE, M[ichael]. Demographic and Economic Changes in Sinkiang Uighur Autonomous Region, *Population Studies* 20, 1960, 103–24.

Although the Lop Nor area is the focus of increasing Western concern regarding China's nuclear programs, the Chinese see Xinjiang as a resource/development frontier. Notes the pride the Chinese take in local improvements in health, urbanization, transportation, and communications as well as self-sufficiency in agriculture. Such achievements must be viewed against the cost to the native populations resulting from Han migrations to the area and the sinification and sendentarization programs imposed by the central government.

0690. FUSON, C[hester]. G. The Peoples of Kwangtung: Their Origin, Migration, and Present Distribution, *Lingnan Science Journal* 7, 1928, 5–22.

Describes origins and distribution of non-Han groups and the timing of their integration into Chinese society. The presence of minorities was made possible by the mountains and rivers of the area, which have preserved groups from invasions. Division of Chinese population such as the Cantonese, Hakka, and Hoklo reviewed against background of general linguistic diversity in China. Includes tradition and history of overseas migrations to Southeast Asia as well.

0691. GAMMON, Charles F. China in Distress, *Bulletin, American Geographical Society* 44, 1932, 348–51.

General review of causes of Chinese famines and their demographic and social consequences, especially the spread of diseases, the creation of refugee streams, and the separation of families. Describes what items used during famines as alternatives to regular diet such as barks and grasses. Attributes famines and consequences to the failure of the Chinese government to maintain the country's infrastructure. Estimates that some 3 million people starved in 1912. Ends with a plea for contributions to the China Famine Relief Committee.

0692. HOLLAND, W. L. Mr. Chi-ming Chao's New Study of China's Rural Population and Vital Statistics, *Pacific Affairs* 7, 1934, 77–82.

Extract of study that originally appeared in *Milbank Memorial Fund Quarterly*, October 1933. Stresses north-south differences.

0693. HUNG, Fu. The Population of China and Present Means of Subsistence, *Proceedings, International Geographical Union Conference in Japan*, 1957, 332–40.

Provides a history of census taking in China. Compares the results of the 1928–30 and 1953 censuses. Argues that, assuming 2,750 calories a day is an acceptable level of nutrition, even at the peak of Chinese twentieth-century agricultural production around 1931, China could only sustain 81 percent of its population properly. Since China by the caloric standard is overpopulated, a rational population policy aimed at reducing the size of the total population should be implemented. Given the long-term economic weakness China has experienced since the nineteenth century, even if agricultural efficiency is improved the size of the population should be reduced.

0694. HSU, Mei-ling. Map Supplement No. 11: Taiwan Population Distribution, 1965, *Annals, Association of American Geographers* 59, 1969, 611–13.

Describes data sources and previous attempts to produce large-scale map of population. Data are mapped at village level (*tsun* and *li*).

0695. KEYES, Fenton. Urbanization and Population Distribution in China, *American Journal of Sociology* 56, 1951, 519–27.

Observes that there is a close proximity between urbanized and advanced rural/agricultural regions. Points out that high density and congestion do not imply urbanization. Doubts that China will be able to quickly deal with urbanization and associated problems such as overcrowding and poor housing conditions. Avoids estimating rate of urbanization owing to deficiencies in available data. Expects China to emphasize rural over urban development, even though urban-based, advanced education is needed to pull China along.

0696. LATTIMORE, Owen. Chinese Colonization in Manchuria, *Geographical Review* 22, 1932, 177–95.

Sees migration to Manchuria differing from other colonial patterns because tensions in Manchuria and East Asia are higher and because the movement of people involves clashes between two highly developed civilizations—the Chinese and the Manchu. Notes that Manchuria is not a virgin territory, since earlier Manchu migrations preceded the Chinese. Furthermore, Chinese movements can be divided into an older, male-dominated, military colonization and a modern, Shandong-focused family-based, permanent movement. Mix of people further complicated by presence of refugees and frontier bandits.

0697. LEE, Hoon K. Korean Migrants in Manchuria, *Geographical Review* 22, 1932, 196–204.

Notes that Korean migration is one of the reasons for political tension in Manchuria. Does not feel that Korean migration is the vanguard of a Japanese one. Reviews notion that migrants are the result of Japanese policies aimed at displacing Koreans so that Japanese rice farmers could move to Korea. Estimates that there are 800,000 Koreans in all of Manchuria, a number much smaller than Chinese claims. Feels Changchun area was part of Korean ancestral homeland. Identifies a cluster of Koreans in Chientao District, in southeastern Kirin. Describes Korean routes of penetration into four Manchurian pioneer belts. Provides data from a 1931 field survey on Korean property ownerhsip, farm size, rents, and irrigation and drainage projects. Notes that, although the standard of living for Koreans is but two-thirds of that of the Chinese, Korean migration to Manchuria is driven by poor economic conditions at home.

0698. LIEU, D. K. Industrial Development and the Population Problem, *China Critic* 3:10, 1930, 226–28.

Argues that there are only three solutions to meeting the problems of rapid population growth and high density: mass emigration, which is not practical; development of so-called virgin lands, such as Manchuria, which are limited in area; and economic development, which is seen as the only viable alternative. Quantitative evidence for conclusions includes population data for 1928 for Hepei and Hupeh Provinces.

0699. LING, Pyau. Causes of Chinese Migration, *Annals, American Academy of Political and Social Science* 39, 1912, 74–82.

Explicit comparison and contrast of social, political, and economic factors contributing to the pressure to migrate in Europe and China. Notes that emigration from China is localized in the Southeast, where intense population pressure and primogeniture systems of land inheritance combine with early Western contacts and an independent spirit to precipitate migration. In addition to migrating due to adverse economic and climatic conditions, people migrate from southern China to escape taxes, debts, and slavery. Argues that the Chinese will continue to migrate despite U.S. restrictions on their entry.

0700. LO, C[hor].-P[ang]. Changing Population Distribution in the Hong Kong New Territories, *Annals, Association of American Geographers* 58, 1968, 273–84.

After showing that historically population in New Territories followed alluvial plains and coasts with good harbors, notes that contemporary distribution is linked to shifts in transportation systems. Uses Lorenz curves to document changes. Future changes are linked to development of new towns, such as Tsuen Wan, and spread of industry.

0701. OPPENHEIM, F. Birth and Death Ratios of the Chinese, *China Journal of Science and Arts* 2, 1924, 466–77.

Calculates sex ratio at birth to be 115.6 +/- 2.5, which is said to be the highest on record. The cause of this phenomenon is deliberate female infanticide and neglect, not poor data.

0702. ORCHARD, Dorothy J. Man Power in China, *Political Science Quarterly* 50, 1935, 561–83; 51, 1936, 1–35.

Argues that China's large population provides both an abundant labor pool and a large home market that can serve as the basis for industrialization. The market is depessed due to the pauperization of the population as a result of famine, war, floods, and cheap imports. The major challenge to any Chinese government will be how to get people off the land so that both agriculture and industry can be modernized. Touches on numerous policy issues that must be dealt with such as recruitment of civil and military labor supplies, working conditions, wages and hours, and women in the labor force.

0703. ORLEANS, Leo [A]. Recent Growth of China's Urban Population, *Geographical Review* 49, 1959, 43–57.

Assumes that it is impossible to evaluate precisely the size and rate of growth of the urban population. Seeks, then, to provide reasonable estimates based on sound judgments. Uses 1953 census data as well as Russian literature on China. Reviews issues such as the lack of a definition of urban and pre-Communist and pre-1953 estimates of the urban population. Includes the impact of industrialization and collectivization on the urbanization process. Redistribution programs such as the Virgin Lands Program contain too many deterrents, such as inadequate housing and utilities and low levels of peasant education, to be effective. Projects that urbanization will increase due to rural-urban migration, the construction of new towns, and the rate of natural increase in cities, in that order. Nevertheless, does not anticipate an acceleration in size of urban population, even if industrialization grows faster than expected.

0704. PRITCHARD, Earl H. Thoughts on the Historical Development of the Population of China, *Journal of Asian Studies* 23, 1963, 3–29.

Dynasty by dynasty survey of sources and documenation on population. Discussion of definitional and methodological problems in recording family numbers and individuals, population versus taxpayers, and the ambiguities of the concept of household. Ends with a plea for more historical population studies.

0705. ROBERTSON, R. Cecil. The Problem of Endemic Goitre in Yunnan Province, *China Journal* 21, 1940, 26–36.

Goitre is found in Yunnan since the area is deficient in iodine-rich foods and imports of iodized salt have been blocked by the Japanese control of eastern China. Provides the technical details regarding the planning and statistical results of a goitre survey, programs formulated to correct the problem, and mechanical difficulties in mixing iodine with available salt.

0706. ROCKHILL, W. W. The 1910 Census of the Population of China, *Bulletin, American Geographical Society* 44, 1912, 668–73.

Reprint of article first appearing in *T'oung Pao*, series 2, 13, 1912, 117–25. Presents in tables findings of 1910 census along with non-census estimates for Beijing. Total population given as 329.6 million, a figure the author finds smaller than he had been led to believe. Includes a history of the 1910 census in China and comments on reasons for its lack of completeness.

0707. ROXBY, Percy M[aude]. The Distribution of Population in China: Economic and Political Significance, *Geographical Review* 15, 1925, 1–24.

Begins by reviewing population estimates of China back to 1885. Provides comparison and contrast of these early data sets as compiled by institutions and groups such as the China Post Office and China Continuation Committee. Dot maps include one of all of China as well as regional maps using a division of China into fifteen regions. Includes material pertinent to the debate over whether or not China is "overpopulated." Notes limited areas available to serve as demographic safety valves. Puts population in the context of the issue of devolution versus unity and feels that the political demography of China requires that the political center be clearly established in the Yangtze area. This leads to a general discussion of the urban geography of China and an appraisal of which city would be best suited as a future capital.

0708. ROXBY, Percy M[aude]. Expansion of China, *Scottish Geographical Magazine* 46, 1930, 65–80.

Despite a social structure and philosophy of life that discourages mobility, the Chinese have been a colonizing people, even going to Southeast Asia. The importance of railroad development in the northeast in the Chinese expansion there is emphasized.

0709. SALTER, Christopher L. The Dynamics of Migration Flow to a Marginal Region, *Industry of Free China* 34:5, 1970, 15–24.

Case study of Taitong Rift Valley presented in the context of theories of frontier economies. Covers the period 1900–1963. Analysis includes environmental advantages and disadvantages of region, especially seismic activity and typhoon hazards. Despite heavy in-migration, the region is still a marginal one economically and is in need of increased public investment in transportation to attract private industrial investment. Feels process of modernization has set in.

0710. SALTER, Christopher L. *Hsia Fang:* The Use of Migration by the Chinese in Their Quest for a Classless Society, *Proceedings, Association of American Geographers* 4, 1972, 96–99.

Uses data gleaned from Chinese press. Notes antecedents to program between 1962 and 1966 in the form of the Socialist Education Movement. Identifies major population flows. Argues that the route of the Long March cannot be duplicated in *xia fang* movements, despite the assumption that *xia fang* is an experiment based on the belief that there is value in having a primary experience in rural areas.

0711. SCHWARZ, Henry G. Chinese Migration to Northwest China and Inner Mongolia, 1949–59, *China Quarterly* 16, 1963, 62–74.

Estimates that some 323,433 Han Chinese moved to these areas under various banishment, sinification, industrialization, and land reclamation projects, the goals of which were most likely not met. Han Chinese did not like their new environments, as evidenced by clashes with the non-Han populations and the return of several tens of thousands of Han migrants.

0712. SHABAD, Theodore. Counting 600 Million Chinese, *Far Eastern Survey* 25, 1956, 58–62.

There were three major doubts regarding the accuracy of the 1953 census of population: the reported population was 100 million larger than expected, data were only published in summary form, and there was no description of the methods and procedures used in the census. The last of these objections is refuted by referring to other Chinese statistical sources and by reviewing the public history of the planning and taking of the census. Issues regarding the rationale for taking a de jure census are discussed along with definitional problems regarding migrants, permanent residents, and age categories.

0713. SHABAD, Theodore. The Population of China's Cities, *Geographical Review* 49, 1959, 32–42.

Work based on data from the 1953 census, Chinese government documents, and comparative materials from Soviet censuses. After defining the term *city*, provides estimates for the percentage urban and number of cities. Provides table of fifty-three cities, with estimates of their populations and major economic activities.

0714. TAN, Jian-an. The Keshan Disease in China: A Study of Ecological Chemico-Geography, *National Geographical Journal of India* 28:1 and 2, 1982, 15–18.

Keshan disease, endemic mycocardosis, was first identified in Keshan in 1935. Subsequently it was found to be present in fourteen other areas. Based on statistical testing of seventeen nutrients, it appears that the disease is caused by a selenium deficiency, especially when this nutrient is found in soil, water, or grain at less than 0.25 ppm.

0715. TAUEBER, Irene B., and Chia-lin PAN. Expansion of the Chinese North and West, *Population Index* 18, 1952, 85–108.

Discounts the ability of peripheral areas such as Gansu, Qinghai, Inner Mongolia, Xinjiang, and Manchuria to absorb large numbers of Han Chinese migrants. Regardless of any migration, the economic transformation of these areas will cause changes in occupational structures, rural-urban distribution of population, standards of living, birth and death rates, and the rate of natural increase. Reviews late-nineteenth- and twentieth-century patterns of population movements, especially Russian impact on the areas.

0716. TEMPLE, Sir Richard. Population Studies of China, *Journal of the Statistical Society* 48, 1885, 1–20.

Text of paper read at meeting of Statistical Society. Attempts to normalize data about the size, density, distribution, and structure of the Chinese population found in several Chinese sources by assuming the 1881 Census of Population of India as a standard. Concludes that the population of China is about 297 million, or roughly 50 million less than Chinese data suggest. Last ten pages are transcript of discussion that followed presentation. The transcript indicates that the audience was highly critical of Temple's methods and his lack of attention to French estimates of the Chinese population.

0717. TORGASHEFFT, B. P. Town Population in China, *China Critic* 3, 1930, 317–22.

Notes difficulty in documenting precisely the percentage of the population that is rural or urban. Dismisses estimates of 15 percent urban as being too small. Using various lists of cities and their populations concludes that there were 467 towns with a population greater than 25,000, yielding a total urban population of 50 million, or roughly 20 percent of the total population.

0718. TORRANCE, T. The Emigration of the Jews: Israel in China, *Scottish Geographical Magazine* 56, 1940, 59–64.

Describes history and situation of ethnic Jews in Henan Province. Positive evaluation of status and future of the community from the perspective of a Scottish missionary.

0719. TREGEAR, T. R. Population Problems of China: An Optimistic View, *Contemporary China* 1, 1956, 32–36.

Reviews estimates of China's population for the period 1900 to 1954 and then provides own estimate of rates of natural increase. Describes options open to the Chinese in order to deal with a "surplus" population, including birth control, internal migration, and increased agricultural productivity achieved by flood control, irrigation, land reform, better communications, and rural industrialization. Rejects the Malthusian/capitalist view of population growth and reminds readers of the advances in England during the nineteenth century that were not anticipated or predicted by Malthusian doctrine.

0720. TREWARTHA, Glenn T. New Maps of China's Population, *Geographical Review* 47, 1957, 234–39.

Based on 1953 census. Notes that census showed a larger than expected population. Evaluates census as a source of data in comparison with earlier, post-1949, Chinese government publications and non-Chinese estimates of China's population. Includes maps showing distribution of population that show contrasts between eastern and western China and rural and urban populations. Argues that the distribution map indicates that the Chinese have failed to make effective use of pasturelands and forests.

11. *Population* 171

0721. VAUGHAN, T. D., and D. J. DWYER. Some Aspects of Postwar Population Growth in Hong Kong, *Economic Geography* 42, 1966, 37–51.

Notes that growth is due to birth rates being elevated above death rates and heavy in-migration. Analysis based on 1961 census includes details regarding population density, age structure, housing, water supply, and land use. Hong Kong's future is seen as subject to foreign government actions, especially with regard to trade and tariffs.

0722. WANG, I-shou. Mountain People in the Lowlands: A Preliminary Report on the Migration of Formosan Aborigines, *Proceedings, Association of American Geographers* 7, 1975, 264–68.

Reviews historical development of aboriginal populations. Measures changes in distribution for the time period 1967–71. Aboriginal migration streams are divided into two types: those reflecting movements to the major urban centers, or towns near them, and a rural movement to towns near the aboriginal areas.

0723. WANG, W[ei].-H[sia]. Population Movements in Manchuria, *China Critic* 3, 1930, 535–39.

Argues that the development of the railroad accelerated Chinese migration to Manchuria. Provides data for broad north-south regional destinations as well as cities. Major impact of migration is on agricultural and industrial employment. Migration is seen as a rational economic decision since land is available and industry provides better wages than are available in the rest of China.

0724. WILCOX, Walter F. China's Population: 400,000,000 or 300,000,000? *Chinese Students Monthly* 22:1, 1928, 23–29.

Argues that China's population has not increased materially since 1800 because there is no evidence of increased food production or an increase in poverty. Concludes that government estimates of population are appropriate.

0725. WILCOX, Walter F. The Population of China in 1910, *Journal, American Statistical Association*, new series 23:161, 1928, 18–30.

Until the 1910 census was taken, it was assumed that the question of actual size of population was an insoluble problem. Concurs with other Western observers, such as Rock and Roxby, that the accuracy of the 1910 census is questionable with regard to the size of population, mean family size, sex ratios, and dependency. Includes data in tables. Reviews history of census taking in China in general and 1910 census planning and execution in particular.

0726. YOUNG, C. Walter. Chinese Colonization in Manchuria, *Far Eastern Review* 24, 1928, 241–50.

Notes that Chinese migration of interest due to its sheer size, estimated at 1 million per year, and the contrasts in pre- and post-1925 forms of migration. Emphasizes that migration to Manchuria is associated with relatively peaceful conditions, rapid economic growth, and accessibility enhanced by the railroads. Potential migrants have been aided by direct recruitment as well as lower rail ticket costs and the work of private relief agencies.

0727. YOUNG, Reginald. Is Birth Control Necessary? *China Critic* 3, 1930, 347–48.

Criticizes use of birth control among rich and poor Chinese as a craze that will lead to the collapse of the Chinese population. Birth control proponents argue its use is the only way to deal with infanticide and the presence of misfits. Economic development viewed as the best means of lifting China out of poverty.

See also items 0099, 0167, 0168, 0448, 0530, 0550, 0659, 0799, 0902, 0936, 1011, 1186, 1187, 1196, 1226, 1241, 1243, and 1254.

12. Cultural and Historical Geography

0728. ARCHER, Mildred. Chinese Lanterns, *Geographical Magazine* 33, 1960, 452–57.

Describes design and use of eighteenth- and nineteenth-century lantern exports destined for use in the United Kingdom.

0729. BAILEY, F. M. The Spelling of Tibetan Place Names, *Geographical Journal* 97, 1941, 120–22.

Notes extreme difficulties of using the Tibetan language to map place names owing to the disparity between spellings, with the inclusion of silent letters, actual pronunciation, and the differences between the Lhasa and other dialects. Gives examples of each problem. Includes a history of attempts to standardize the spelling of Tibetan.

0730. BAINBRIDGE, Oliver. The Chinese Jews, *National Geographic Magazine* 18, 1907, 621–32.

Describes the location, history, and discovery of the Jewish community by the Jesuits. Provides details of a meeting held with the leaders of the Jewish and Muslim communities. Argues that the Chinese are more favorably disposed toward the Jews of China than the Muslims, presumably because Jewish customs are closer to traditional Chinese practices.

0731. BALLAS, D[onald]. J. An Introduction to the Historical Geography of Han China, *Professional Geographer* 20, 1968, 155–62.

Stresses seven major themes: development and core, expansion of the Han population, sinification using a Roman *limes* type of system, population growth, colonization and frontier settlement, floods and droughts, and river control and canal building. Attempts to estimate borders and provide a map of them.

0732. CHAO, Y[uan]-r[en]. Languages and Dialects in China, *Geographical Journal* 102, 1943, 63–71.

Provides a map of dialects and discusses the differences between Mandarin and other dialects from the perspective of linguistics. Provides information as to why literary Chinese is not dialectic. Explains the romanization of Chinese place names and is optimistic that a system that combines colloquial and phonetic elements will be adopted. Includes rules for dealing with general romanization problems.

0733. CHATLEY, Herbert. The Origin and Diffusion of Chinese Culture, *Asiatic Review*, new series 44, 1948, 417–22.

Uses a diffusionism argument that assumes that all of Chinese (and Japanese) culture is attributable to the spread of foreign, and especially Middle Eastern, ideas. Nevertheless, the development of these ideas is original and copyist, and it is possible that New World cultures resulted from a diffusion from China.

0734. CHATLEY, H[erbert]. The Yellow River as a Factor in the Development of China, *Asiatic Review*, new series 35, 1939, 134–41.

Uses a diffusionism framework to argue that the backbone of ancient China and subsequent Chinese history cannot be understood apart from understanding the Huang He. Describes the Huang He watershed characteristics, including hydrology, topography, and climate. In discussing the dike system, argues that the Huang He must be restored to its original [*sic*] course to ensure the welfare of the Huai River area and the southern part of the Grand Canal.

0735. CHENG, Sih-gung. China's Geography: Historical and Social, *Scottish Geographical Magazine* 34, 1918, 281–94.

Reviews history of geography in China using books, encyclopedias, and travel books. Special emphasis given to river conservation and the role of the railroad in opening new ports and providing new occupations, especially for women. Concerned that Chinese government must expand transportation systems if it is to exercise more effective control.

0736. CHRISTIE, Dugald. Manchuria a Half a Century Ago and Today, *Scottish Geographical Magazine* 46, 1930, 193–210.

Although much progress has been made in developing Manchuria, especially due to railroad building, the full potential of the area cannot be developed until there is peace and a secure government. Argues that there can be no permanent peace until China is in full possession of the area.

0737. CLARK, Leonard. Among the Big Knot Lois of Hainan, *National Geographic Magazine* 74, 1938, 391–418.

Report of trip started on June 26, 1937. Catalogs hazards of visit, including exposure to cholera, malaria, snakes, and war. Uses modified itinerary format. Explores migrations of Lois from Mainland China to

Hainan. Includes details regarding economy, governance, and religious and social customs of Lois.

0738. COULTER, John Wesley. Ch'ao Yang An: A Study in Human Geography, *Bulletin, Geographical Society of Philadelphia* 32, 1934, 113–20.

Tells of visit in 1932 to old Buddhist nunnery on the lower slopes of the Western Hills outside of Beijing, which served as a summer retreat for westerners living in the capital. Uses itinerary format. Describes the site and architecture of nunnery as well as Buddhist temples in vicinity. Long discussion of life at farmstead level in surrounding villages.

0739. CRESSEY, G[eorge]. B. Foundations of Chinese Life, *Economic Geography* 15, 1939, 95–104.

In essence a review of John Lossing Buck's *Land Utilization in China* (Nanking: University of Nanking, 1937) and James Thorp's *Geography of The Soils of China* (Nanking: National Geological Survey of China, 1936). Argues that geographers no longer need to tolerate unsupported generalizations regarding China now that volumes such as these provide hard data.

0740. CRESSEY, George B. Chinese Homes and Home Sites, *Home Geographic Monthly* 2:3, 1932, 31–36.

Attempts to introduce Chinese daily life by means of the literary device of an imaginary walk through a typical Chinese village. Contrasts the unattractive walls and street landscape with the pleasant interiors and courtyards of homes. Argues that the home is a mini city, self-contained and isolated from a hostile world. Describes the number, size, shape, and function of rooms in a typical house. Notes extended family living patterns and limits they impose on household compound size.

0741. CRESSEY, George B. Three Meals in China, *Home Geographic Monthly* 2:5, 1932, 31–36.

Describes meals at three different locations as device for describing regional restaurant architecture and cuisines for northern, central, and southern China.

0742. DEERING, Mabel Craft. Ho for Soochow Ho, *National Geographic Magazine* 51, 1927, 623–50.

Extols the delights of traveling on a rented houseboat from Shanghai to

Hangzhou along the Grand Canal. Adventures described include hiring the boat, purchasing food from vendors on boats, weather, traffic, and running aground. Although delighted with sights of Suzhou, disappointed that she missed the tidal bore at Hangzhou.

0743. EBERHARD, Wolfram. Chinese Regional Stereotypes, *Asian Survey* 5, 1965, 596–608.

Reports on a 1953 survey of ninety-seven students in Taiwan colleges and thirteen members of the San Francisco Chinese community. Finds that there have been few changes in regional stereotypes since 1200 C.E.

0744. EDGAR, J. Huston. The Tibetan and His Environments: An Interpretation, *Journal, Royal Asiatic Society, North China Branch* 57, 1929, 28–49.

Anti-environmental-determinist view of how Tibetan society has triumphed over environment. Describes land, isolation, and settlement history, beginning with refugees and fugitives from Chinese population pressure. Duly notes historical clash between Tibetan and Chinese cultures. Optimistic regarding Tibetan potential to develop under current conditions, that is, with pastures being improved.

0745. EITEL, Rev. Dr. [E. J.] Chinese Notions on Geography and Geomancy, *Proceedings, Royal Geographical Society of Australasia, South Australian Branch* 4, 1888–89, 53–67.

Begins with unfavorable and uncomplimentary comparison of and contrast between Chinese and Western views of nature and the role of science in understanding it. Sees geomancy as central to the core of Chinese geography and intimately tied to Chinese philosophy. While Chinese geomancy shares with "true" science the recognition of uniformity and universality of rational laws, its major failing is its lack of experimental and critical work on nature.

0746. EITEL, Rev. Dr. E. J. Social Life in China, *Proceedings, Royal Geographical Society of Australasia, South Australian Branch* 8, 1892–93, 1–20.

Starts with examples of how Chinese and European social conventions contrast. Such differences are not attributable to caprice or accident but rather are due to "constitutional peculiarities." Feels that, in contrast to Europeans, Chinese place value on centrality of family and reverence for the family, and as such they can be considered born communists.

12. Cultural and Historical Geography

Highlights what are some of the more flagrant behaviors resulting from a family orientation, especially with regard to the cruel treatment of women in the areas of education, marriage, childbearing, and foot binding. Argues that the best method for modernizing Chinese social life is within the system of Christianity.

0747. FERGUSON, John C. S. Migration of the Sung Dynasty, *Journal, Royal Asiatic Society, North China Branch*, new series 55, 1924, 14–27.

Traces origins and impact of forced flight of Sung emperor, 1086–1126, including the abandonment of the capital at Pien-lo (Kaifeng, Henan) and the establishment of a new one at Ling-an (Hangzhou, Zhejiang).

0748. FITCH, Robert F. Life Afloat in China, *National Geographic Magazine* 51, 1927, 665–86.

Describes boat life in the Zhujiang/Canton area. Estimates numbers of people living permanently on the boats and their difficulties in obtaining goods and services, participating in religious life of the region, and making a living. Includes materials on the construction and seaworthiness of boats and the cultural features in their painted designs. Provides information as to the location and capacity of ports and repair spots along the river and canals.

0749. FITCH, Robert F. Puto: The Enchanted Island, *National Geographic Magazine* 89, 1946, 73–84.

Describes pilgrimages, including three annual ones devoted to Guanyin, to Butou, home to some 140 monasteries, temples, and anchorite dwellings. Evaluates the impact of pilgrimages on the local economy and social organization.

0750. FORMAN, Harrison. China's Moslemia, *Canadian Geographical Journal* 37:3, 1948, 134–41.

Traces origins of Muslims in China and describes their general distribution. Focus of local pilgrimage is Houzhou, Gansu, which is referred to as the Chinese Muslims' Mecca. Potential for antigovernment sentiment and uprisings on part of Muslims reviewed.

0751. FULLER, Myron L., and Frederick G. CLAPP. Loess and Rock Dwellings of Shensi, China, *Geographuical Review* 14, 1924, 215–26.

Argues that the character of rural dwellings was determined by nature of materials available, their abundance, and ease of use. Also notes how absense of transportation can influence choice of building materials. Describes variety of construction possibilities in use of loess and rock caves for housing in Shaanxi and Gansu. Includes evaluation of advantages of such materials as well as dangers of such dwellings during earthquakes and other natural disasters.

0752. GOODNOW, Frank Johnson. The Geography of China: The Influence of Physical Environment on the History and Character of the Chinese People, *National Geographic Magazine* 51, 1927, 651–64.

Transcript of speech given before the society. Argues than no part of the earth demonstrates better than China the impact of geographic conditions on the history and character of a people. Divides China climatically between north and south. Notes need for vegetarian diet if population is to subsist. Given agricultural basis of society, sees no possibility of a complex industrial society developing in China. Apart from an occasional outside conquest, feels that Chinese civilization was not affected by outside cultural influences. Notes impact of Confucianism and Taoism on education, government, economy, and lack of learned professions. Sees Christian missionaries as helping China to modernize, especially once the Chinese realize the need for change.

0753. GOODWIN, Peter. Dragon Boat Festival, *Geographical Magazine* 33, 1961, 479–85.

Chronicles festivities in Hong Kong accompanying annual boat race marking the suicide of poet Chu Yuen to protest the misrule of Prince Tso and his court.

0754. GOODWIN, Peter. Orchid Islands, *Geographical Magazine* 33, 1960, 384–90.

Seven-page photo essay. Notes erosion of old customs due to feeding and other government programs implemented after 1945.

0755. GORDON, Maria M. Ogilvie. Ferdinand von Richthofen's Diaries from China, *Scottish Geographical Magazine* 24, 1908, 310–17.

Positive review of two volumes presenting the complete itinerary of von Richthofen's travels in China between 1868 and 1872. Sees von Richthofen's description of characteristics, culture, and habits of the Chinese as the main contribution of a man devoted to scientific principles and high ideals who succeeded despite overwhelming odds. Notes the disdain von Richthofen felt toward missionaries who adopted

Chinese dress and habits instead of establishing model agricultural settlements.

0756. GRIFFEN, Clarence. Skull-Collectors of Formosa, *Canadian Geographical Journal* 2:3, 1931, 224–46.

Describes trip to Paiwan areas of Taiwan where Japanese administration attempted to curtail practice of headhunting. Traces origins of aborigines and contrasts Chinese and Western views of origins of island and its inhabitants.

0757. GROOTAERS, Willem A., Shih-yu LI, and Chi-wen CHANG. Temples and History of Wanch'uan (Chahar): The Geographic Method Applied to Folklore, *Monumenta Serica* 13, 1948, 209–316.

Based on fieldwork conducted in summer 1947. Describes the number, distribution, history, architecture, and practices of some thirty-three temples and cult associations. Provides data regarding the topography and hydrology of area as well. Shows how maps can be used to classify materials in terms of setting, religions, and impact of buildings on local landscape. Concludes that there are two important implications of such studies using maps: that it is possible to synthesize knowledge of religious practices in China in an orderly manner, and that such studies can be used to restore and reconstruct old administrative boundaries.

0758. GUTTMAN, John, and Joseph PASSANTINO. Kunming Pilgrimage, *National Geographic Magazine* 97, 1950, 213–26.

Photo essay of pilgrimage to Buddhist temple outside of Kunming undertaken in celebration of the Chinese New Year.

0759. HANSFORD, S. Howard. The Stone Buddhas of Yun-kang, *Geographical Magazine* 14, 1942, 134–41.

Description of trip from Tatong to Yunkang, site of fifth- and sixth-century Buddhist sculpture caves.

0760. HAYES, James. Removal of Villages for Fung Shui Reasons: Another Example from Lantau Island, Hong Kong, *Journal, Royal Asiatic Society, Hong Kong Branch* 9, 1969, 156–60.

Describes discovery of abandoned villages unearthed in the process of moving residents from Shan Shek Wan after destruction wrought by a 1937 typhoon. Apart from poor *fengshui*, reasons and frequency for village abandonment not clear, although an epidemic of an unknown disease in 1931 and a tradition of abandoning villages are explored as possible explanations.

0761. H[INKS]. A[rthur] R. Names in Manchuria, *Geographical Journal* 52, 1918, 311–14.

Provides a list of names likely to be hard to find on maps due to different Russian, Chinese, and Manchu toponyms and transliterations.

0762. HSU, Shin-yi. The Cultural Ecology of the Locust Cult in Traditional China, *Annals, Association of American Geographers* 59, 1969, 731–52.

There is a high degree of association (r = 0.88) between the frequency and distribution of locust infestations and locust cult temples. The relationship is not stronger due to time lags in constructing temples and space constraints in locust-prone areas. Explanation of cults traced to culture as human coping process against environmental stress.

0763. HUNG, Frederick [Fu]. Notes on the Historical Geography of Taiwan, *Oriental Geographer* 2, 1958, 407–60.

Provides dates for the earliest Chinese exploration, settlement, and effective occupation. Explores the origins of the names Formosa and Taiwan. Argues that Taiwan's strategic role in the seventeenth-century Chinese civil war can be viewed as precursor to its importance in the twentieth century. As such, Taiwan is seen as defensible, self-sufficient in food and raw materials, and inhabited by people who are politically and ideologically insular. Provides evaluation of the status of the Cairo Declaration, Potsdam Proclamation, Japanese Instruments of Surrender, Truman Statement, and U.S.-China Mutual Defense Treaty as of 1958.

0765. HUTCHINSON, Paul. New China and the Printed Page, *National Geographic Magazine* 51, 1927, 687–722.

Reviews the history of papermaking in China. Covers the impact of paper production and availability of scholarship, communciations, journalism, service industries, literacy, literary movements, and evangelism. Set of unrelated photographs found on pp. 701–16.

0766. KIANG, Ying-cheng. Chinese Place Names in American Elementary Textbooks of Geography, *Journal of Geography* 64, 1963, 370–74.

Based on survey of nineteen leading textbooks used in U.S. elementary schools during the 1950s and early 1960s. In all, some fifty-one places in

12. Cultural and Historical Geography

China are included, but only twenty are mentioned more than once. Names the six provinces, four rivers, and ten cities most likely to be cited. Reviews the origins and meanings of place names and political divisions as the best pedagogical way to help students to understand Chinese place names in general.

0767. LAFUGIE. A Women Paints the Tibetans, *National Geographic Magazine* 95, 1949, 659–92.

Narrative describes arrival in Tibet from India via Ladakh and tribulations of travel. Actual paintings highlight religious and marriage practices, clothing, and folk arts. Expresses fear that the rich skills of the area are disappearing with no one to either record or learn them.

0768. LAI, [David] Chuen-yan. Chinese Written Language and Geographical Names, *Canadian Geographical Journal* 80:1, 1970, 20–25.

Written to clarify confusion resulting from inconsistent use of various transliteration systems and names found in Canadian press. Decribes structure of Chinese characters and provides a basic geographic vocabulary to aid in understanding meanings of place names.

0769. LATTIMORE, Owen. A Ruined Nestorian City in Inner Mongolia, *Geographical Journal* 84, 1934, 481–97.

Uses artifacts uncovered in an old city to describe the Nestorian Christian Ongut tribe, which was located from just northwest of Beijing to north of Guihuan, Suiyuan. Notes the general impact of Han migration and the opium trade on fate of Ongut. Argues that there was a subtle gradation of economies from nomadism to settled agriculture along the Chinese border.

0770. LATTIMORE, Owen. Inner Asian Approach to the Historical Geography of China, *Geographical Journal* 110, 1947, 180–87.

Uses an environmental determinist format and a key economic and strategic areas concept to assess the impact of the desiccation of Central Asia on the dynamic tensions between the nomads and the Chinese.

0771. LATTIMORE, Owen. Origins of the Great Wall of China: A Frontier Concept in Theory and Practice, *Geographical Review* 27, 1937, 529–49.

Intent of original walls was to keep nomadic peoples out of China. Speculates as to why this type of frontier delimitation was used, since earlier use of walls was for the purpose of separating Chinese states during the feudal period. Notes relationship between Great Wall and walls surrounding cities. Concludes that Great Wall provided stability and unification even though the Chinese had trouble holding the Ordos and frontier areas for long periods. Feels the wall symbolizes the limitations of both sides in two-way conflicts between China and its neighbors.

0772. LEUNG, C. K., and T. N. CHIU. Some Geographical Implications of the Revolution in Education in China, *Pacific Viewpoint* 15, 1974, 51–60.

Main focus is on changes since 1949 in higher education. Describes the origins and aims of education reform before and after the Cultural Revolution. Notes shifts in the mix of theoretical, applied, and field studies. The geographical implications of reforms include an improvement in efficiency and capacity in all sectors of the economy, a more uniform distribution of technical and production skills across China, and a minimalization of allocation problems, dropouts, and manpower waste. Long-term effects of changes should include a diminution in the divide between rural and urban economic functions. As such, the Chinese experience should provide a new model of development for Third World countries.

0773. LEUNG, George Kin. Peiping's Happy New Year, *National Geographic Magazine* 71, 1936, 749–92.

Review of customs, foods, and ceremonies attending the Chinese celebration of the Lunar New Year. Includes details about the Kitchen God, the Lantern Festival, the purchases of new clothes and gifts, and the flying of kites. Expresses the hope that when modernizing China will not have to give up such celebrations.

0774. LO, Jung-pang. The Controversy over Grain Conveyance during the Reign of Qubilai Qaqan, 1260–94, *Far Eastern Quarterly* 13, 1954, 263–85.

Presents the argument that the Chinese capital was moved from Shangdu to Yenching in 1264 to ease the problem of supplying the city with grain. To further ease crowding, the capital was moved to its current site in 1267, with the new city being called Tartu, "Great Capital." Food shortages forced the building of waterways to bring grain from the south. Apparent success in securing food faltered due to official abuses, inflation, inclement weather, and plunder by sea pirates. Argues that food shortages hamstrung the administration of the Yuan dynasty, especially when rebels would sever the road links bringing food north.

0775. LUNIN, B. A. The Origin and Extent of the Name Tien Shan, *Soviet Geography: Review and Translation* 1:5, 1960, 85–87.

Notes that toponym is thought to be of Chinese origin but argues that there is some evidence that in fact the name was originally foreign and taken over by the Chinese. Rules out Russian as origin of name, since name entered Russian geographical vocabulary from China. Notes that boundaries of Tien Shan system are not clearly delineated or fixed.

0776. MARCH, Andrew L. An Appreciation of Chinese Geomancy, *Journal of Asian Studies* 27, 1968, 253–68.

Sympathetic description of *fengshui* origins written in hopes of leading to a more critical understanding of practices.

0777. MARCH, Andrew L. The Winds, the Waters, and the Living Qi, *Parabola Magazine* 3:1, 1978, 32–33.

Concludes general review of theory and practice of *fengshui*, especially as it relates to burials, with cautionary note doubting whether Chinese geomancy can ever be domesticated in a U.S. setting.

0778. MARCINI, Fosco. Religion and People in Tibet, *Geographical Magazine* 25, 1951, 141–44, 241–43.

Relates the role of religion in the life of the Tibetan people in the context of environment and art. Argues that religion dominates the landscape, from roadside shrines and temples to monasteries.

0779. MASON, I. When and How Muhamadism Entered China, *Asiatic Review*, new series 29, 1933, 668–87.

Notes that work on questions is hampered by lack of old Chinese and Muslims records. Two traditions exist regarding the routes of entry: overland and by sea via Canton. Chinese records of entry in either 587 or 601 are not possible, as this predates development of Islam. Concludes that Islam most likely entered China during the Tang dynasty around 900.

0780. McCORMICK, Frederick. China's Treasures, *National Geographic Magazine* 23, 1912, 916–1040.

Survey of what the author considers to be the best of Chinese architecture. Literary device tying together discussion of pagodas, city gates, memorial arches, animal sculptures, and rock/cave houses and temples is a series of quotations from poetry of Coleridge.

0781. MOFFET, Abbot Low. The Saler Muhammadans, *Geographical Journal* 85, 1935, 525–30.

Ethnography of a group sandwiched between the Mongolians, Tibetans, Chinese, and Muslims of Gansu, located near the Tibetan spur of the Great Wall. Ritual center of life is located in Naimankung.

0782. MORRISON, Hedda M. The Man in the Street—Peking, *Canadian Geographical Journal* 36:5, 1948, 222–41.

Photo essay of daily life in city. Assumes that individuals are interested not in politics but in peace so that they can carry on their lives in security.

0783. MOSS, Laurence A. Space and Direction in the Chinese Garden, *Landscape* 14:3, 1965, 29–33.

Reviews principles and environmental orientation of Buddhism, Confucianism, and Taoism and the possible relationship between physical environment and spatial organization. Describes the functions of Chinese space. Sees gardens as an integral part of homesteads and landscapes. A home has two parts: a house and a garden. Outlines ideal structure of a Chinese garden.

0784. MULLIKIN, Mary Augusta. China's Great Wall of Sculpture, *National Geographic Magazine* 73, 1938, 313–20, 329–48.

Describes the history and significant features of the Dunhuang and Yungang Caves, often on a cave by cave and wall by wall basis.

0785. MULLIKIN, Mary Augusta. Taishan, Sacred Mountain of the East, *National Geographic Magazine* 87, 1945, 699–719.

Describes access to the mountain and provides a panoramic hand sketch of the monastery complex from the city of Taian to the tip of Taishan. Provides details regarding the architecture of the monastery, what services and accommodations are available for guests, and what ceremonies are performed.

0786. MULLIKIN, Mary Augusta, and Anna M. HOTCHKISS. Buddhist Calm Survives along China's Great Wall, *National Geographic Magazine* 73, 1938, 321–28.

12. Cultural and Historical Geography

Photo essay accompanying item 0784. Photographs taken by W. Robert Moore and Maynard Owen Williams also included.

0787. PEREIRA, George. Visit to Labrang Monastery, Southwest Kansu, *Geographical Journal* 40, 1912, 415–20.

Notes on trip begun at Lanzhou in May 1912. Remarks on the multicultural structure of population, which includes Chinese, Muslims, and Tibetans. Discusses the historical importance of Labrang Monastery. Provides information about the number of resident monks and acolytes as well as the special architectural features of the monastery. Some information about Tibet is given as well, as the trip included stops there.

0788. PHILLIPS, George. The Identity of Marco Polo's Zaitun with Changchau, *T'oung Pao*, series 1, 1, 1890, 218–38.

In evaluting place names, assumes that the port of Zhangzhou alternated with Jinzhao and Fuzhou as capital of Fujian Province during Mongol times. Compares the accuracy of different editions of Marco Polo. Based on a reconstruction of Polo's material about Hangzhau and Changzhau and old forms of Chinese pronuciation, concludes that Changzhau was Polo's Zaitun.

0789. PHILLIPS, George, and Henry YULE. Notes on South Mangi, *Journal, Royal Geographical Society* 44, 1874, 97–111.

Attempt to revisit places in South China as described by Marco Polo. Attributes differences between Polo's and their observations to changes in topography and economy. Yule comments on how accurate Polo and Phillips' interpretation of him really are.

0790. ROCK, Joseph F. Banishing the Devil of Disease among the Nashi, *National Geographic Magazine* 46, 1924, 473–99.

The Nashi, referred to as Moso by the Chinese, have a nominally independent country within Lijiang, Yunnan. Provides a history of the group and overview of their economy, their Tibetan-based writing system, and limited, two-surname social organization. Opium is grown as a cash crop. In the context of the religion of the group, describes events leading up to an exorcism ceremony. Includes brief translations of selected Nashi religious texts.

0791. ROCK, Joseph F. Life among the Lamas of Choni, *National Geographic Magazine* 54, 1928, 569–619.

Report is result of visit during spring 1925 to Choni, a Tibetan principality in Gansu Province, in order to collect plants for the Arnold

Arboretum in Boston, Massachusetts. Provides details of visit to area, the history of the principality, the origins of its names, and religious practices and customs. Of the latter, devotes considerable detail to the creation of Buddhist images from butter and their further decoration aimed at banishing bad luck.

0792. ROCK, Joseph F. Sungmas: The Living Oracles of the Tibetan Church, *National Geographic Magazine* 698, 1935, 475–86.

Report of visit to ceremony where a *sungmas*, who is compared to the Delphic Oracle, was consulted. Describes the ceremony, the actions and remarks of the *sungmas*, the final blessing, and the banishing of demons. Includes details regarding the costs involved in consulting a *sungmas*.

0793. ROCKHILL, W. W. People of Tibet, *Scottish Geographical Magazine* 11, 1895, 402–9.

Extract of 1893 report, "Notes on the Ethnology of Tibet," based on collections at the U.S. Naval Museum. Describes material and religious progress of Tibetans. Divides Tibet into three political-religious regions.

0794. SCOTT, Richard. The Formosans, *Geographical Magazine* 28, 1956, 598–602.

Historical overview and description of general economic, political, and social conditions. Notes ambiguities regarding who is a Formosan and Formosan relations with Mainland Chinese refugees, although there is no mention of the February 28 Affair. Argues that Formosans are not interested in international affairs and that these have "been left" to the mainlanders. Notes the ambiguous legal status of Formosa. Includes a description of agrarian reforms under the Land to the Tiller Program.

0795. SHARP, Keith H. Hong Kong's Boat Dwellers Insure against the Sea, *Canadian Geographical Journal* 66:3, 1966, 72–73.

Photomontage of celebrations attending Chinese sea goddess Tin Han in Hong Kong.

0796. SHELTON, Dr. A. L. Life among the People of Eastern Tibet, *National Geographic Magazine* 40, 1921, 295–326.

Notes the long-standing conflicts between the Chinese and Tibetans. Comments favorably on role of Western missionaries in the area, especially in the period after the Younghusband Expedition of 1904–5. Expresses the opinion that Tibetans are not inherently anti-Western and that they genuinely wish to know the West better. Reviews myths regarding the origins of the Tibetans. Describes the agriculture, diet, transportation, material goods, marriage and religious practices, demography, justice system, and metalwork of Tibet. Notes with concern that one-seventh of the population is confined to monasteries and nunneries.

0797. SHOR, Franc, and Jean SHOR. The Caves of the Thousand Buddhas (Tunhwang, China), *National Geographic Magazine* 99, 1951, 383–415.

Uses iternary format to describe trip to caves in summer 1948, traveling from Shanghai to Urmuqi and then on to Gansu. Pleased with their reception upon arrival but concerned about the negative impact of war on the caves and whether or not needed restoration will be carried out once the war is over.

0798. SOWERBY, Arthur de C[arle]. Some Chinese Animal Myths and Legends, *Journal, Royal Asiatic Society, North China Branch* 70, 1939, 3–20.

Argues that, although the Chinese do not have collections of myths and legends comparable to either Aesop's Fables or the Uncle Remus stories, there are animals in Chinese myths. Categorizes animals into real and imaginary/fabulous and further groups myths by their presence in religious or medical practices, pure superstition, and transformations of animals into humans and vice versa. Gives examples of all types, including the Chinese zodiac.

0799. SOWERBY, Arthur de C[arle]. The Spread of the Chinese Culture, *China Journal* 9, 1928, 211–14.

Sees the Chinese as pioneering and vigorous individuals, and therefore they have spread from the North China hearth to areas east, north, and west of the plain, including Central Asia. Notes that the conquest of areas was not racially tied, such that peoples coming in contact with the Han lost both their racial and cultural identities in the assimilation process. The only possible exception to this conclusion are the Japanese. Speculates on whether or not Han expansion has ended, with other parts of Asia as ultimate targets of Chinese assimilation.

0800. SPENCER, J[oseph]. E[arle]. Chinese Place Names and the Appreciation of Geographic Realities, *Geographical Review* 31, 1941, 79–94.

Reviews problems of transliterating Chinese place names. Postulates basic rules in the evolution and development of place names, including a single-character reference for provinces and preferences for names that express a hope for good fortune. Notes how many place names change with successive dynasties. Argues that place names provide evidence of domestic cultural and geographic background. Notes regional usages for terms associated with mountains or rivers. Includes detailed analysis, including origins and variants of names for China, the eighteen provinces, and the eighteen provincial capitals.

0801. SPENCER, J[oseph]. E[arle]. The Houses of the Chinese, *Geographical Review* 37, 1947, 254–73.

Sees report as a very preliminary exercise; a fuller treatment requires extensive fieldwork. Argues that existing publications on topic erroneously see but one pattern in Chinese houses, which is at variance with the facts. Main focus is on private homes for the middle classes found in farms, villages, and small cities. Notes regional preferences in use of building materials, patterns, and layouts. Describes contents of ideal house, including a courtyard, single story, raised foundation, walls, minor architectural decorations such as latticed windows, and, in the north, a *kang* warming system.

0802. SPENCER, J[oseph]. E[arle]. The Szechwan Village Tea House, *Journal of Geography* 41, 1942, 52–58.

Sees tea houses as a measure of regional identity and character across China. Discusses the cultural and social setting of tea houses, their preferred locations, tea house customs, and evolution of tea houses as regional symbols.

0803. STANLEY, A. Puto Shan: A Drought at the Well-Spring of Chinese Buddhist Art, *Journal, Royal Asiatic Society, North China Branch*, new series 46, 1915, 1–16.

Describes access, history, topography, geology, flora, and fauna of island eighty miles from Ningbo, which houses over one hundred monasteries and temples of Zhan Buddhism. Includes impact of religion on local industry, fine arts, craftsman, art, and textiles.

0804. STEER, J. B. On Formosa, *Bulletin, American Geographical Society* 6, 1876, 302–34.

Main focus is on the aboriginal populations. Includes materials on names, origins, distributions, languages, customs, economy, and religious practices of all tribes. Describes patterns of interaction between the tribes and Chinese and Western government officials.

0805. SULLIVAN, Linda F. Traditional Chinese Regional Architecture: Chinese Houses, *Journal, Royal Asiatic Society, Hong Kong Branch* 12, 1972, 130–49.

Fengshui-based examples of different styles of Chinese architecture, going from north as far south as Hong Kong. Includes detailed floor plans.

0806. SWANN, Peter C. Chinese Painting and the Chinese Landscape, *Geographical Magazine* 28, 1956, 603–10.

Relates landscape paintings to actual geological formations in China. Therefore concludes that themes of paintings are not all due to the fancies or whims of painters.

0807. THORNBECKE, Ellen. People in China, *Geographical Magazine* 2, 1936, 311–21.

Set of thirteen annotated pictures of ordinary Chinese people from book of same name as article.

0808. VALE, Marcia. The Bun Hills of Hong Kong, *Canadian Geographical Journal* 79:2, 1969, 142–48.

Informal report of trip from Hong Kong to Cheung Chao to participate in the Festival of Bun Hills. Uses itinerary format to provide details of walk to hills from time of debarkation to end of ceremony. Describes alternative explanations for origins of festival.

0809. VOON, Phin-keong. Origins of Chinese Places Names, *Geographica* 5, 1969, 34–47.

Argues that the lack of knowledge about the Chinese languages and the imprecision in romanization systems gives people the impression that it is difficult or impossible to learn the place name geography of China. Attempts to remedy problem by putting place names in a sixfold classification focusing on topographic features; political and administrative issues; languages or dialects of non-Han Chinese; minerals; plants and animals; and other. Shows distribution of categories in map format. Notes that further research on place names is needed, especially for fortuitous names and names whose origins and significance have been lost.

0810. WHYMANT, Neville. Chinese Music and Chinese Musical Instruments, *Geographical Magazine* 23, 1950, 189–95.

History of music and musical instruments written by former editor-in-chief of the China Ministry of Information's London office. Includes pictures of instruments.

0811. WIENS, Herold J. Changes in the Ethnography and Land Use of the Ili Valley and Region, Chinese Turkestan, *Annals, Association of American Geographers* 59, 1969, 735–75.

Describes in detail six historical stages of occupation and land use going back to prehistoric times and concluding with deliberate Han migrations and the establishment of communes after 1949. Pastoral dominance is seen as passing in part due to increased urbanization and industrialization. Sinification of area will continue due to increases in ideological indoctrination and the decrease of ethnic homogeneity.

0812. WIENS, Herold J. Geographical and Political Significance of China's Place Names, *Geographica* 1, 1965.

Article not available for annotation.

0813. WILLIAMS, S. Wells. China: The Country and People, *Journal of the American Geographical Society* 8, 1876, 269–84.

Stresses location and extent of China and its people. Compares China to Japan and remarks on parallels with a similar English-French comparison. Notes that as more Chinese are educated abroad China will be able to achieve true civilization.

See also items 0100, 0154, 0959, 1151, and 1161.

13. Political Geography

0814. ANON. Historical Variations of China's Frontiers, *Pacific Affairs* 18, 1945, 346–54.

Argues that administratively the China of 1945 was not the China of the past or of the future. Describes historical changes in the Chinese frontier and states that Chinese occupation of an area was not tantamount to full integration into the Chinese body politic. Traces history of Sino-Soviet clashes. Concludes with a description of the Manchu invasion of Tibet ca. 1720–22 and the Tibetan expulsion of Chinese troops in 1912.

0815. ANON. Patrolling the Troubled Formosan Straits, *National Geographic Magazine* 105, 1955, 573–88.

Photo essay of life in Taiwan under political uncertainty. Includes pictures and maps of Quemoy, Tazhen Archipelago, and Taizhou Bay, Zhejiang.

0816. ANON. Shifting Scenes on the Stage of New China, *National Geographic Magazine* 38, 1920, 423–26.

Attempt to assess the impact of the Boxer Rebellion on government, transportation, and daily life. Reviews the origins of disturbances in general. Notes that power is still divided between the royal family and the mandarinate but that the latter is really in control.

0817. BARRETT, R. T. Hong Kong and the New China, *Geographical Magazine* 8, 1939, 419–30.

Justifies the China policy of Great Britian in the late nineteenth and early twentieth centuries. Major concern is for long-term fate of Hong Kong and China were Japan to invade and permanently hold the colony.

0818. BRADSHAW, Eloise. Sino-Russian Relations in Sinkiang, *Journal of Geography* 31, 1932, 595–67.

Uses Xinjiang as a case study to argue that peripheral areas are likely to defect from the center, that there is no "scientific" boundary absent an ocean or impassible mountain range and that political claims to territory must be reinforced by demographic or economic exploitation on the ground. Describes history of area as a Chinese polity. Notes impact of Turksib railroad as factor in Sino-Soviet rivalry in area. To counter Russian aggression, China must colonize Xinjiang and Manchuria. Sees Russians as having a long-term advantage in influencing Xinjiang.

0819. BRISTOL, Horace, Sr. Pescadores: Wind-Swept Outposts of Formosa, *National Geographic Magazine* 109, 1956, 265–84.

Compares the Chinese and Portuguese names for the islands. While describing the climate, religious practices, and lack of basic amenities such as electricity, main emphasis is on the accessibility and strategic values the islands held and still hold.

0820. CHANG, Chi-yun. China's Ancient Military Geography: An Abstract of Ku Chi-yiu's *An Outline of Historical Geography, Chinese Culture* 2:3, 1959, 1–22.

Outlines Ku's autobiography and the historical background of his work. Describes the length, arrangement, and layout of book and its maps. Argues that Ku's work is innovative in that it goes beyond scenery and sacred places and deals with the national economy and people's livelihoods. Includes an abstract of Chinese text with commentary and explication. Traces Chiang Kai-shek's call for a psychologcial buildup and the spiritual mobilization of China to Ku's work.

0821. CHANG, Chi-yun. Prospects for Chinese Democracy, *Political Science Quarterly* 60, 1945, 377–84.

Argues that the prospects are good for democracy in China since it has had a long time to lay down the psychological and philosophical foundations for political democracy. Notes that China's cultural unity and history of self-rule, along with the existence of a middle class willing to discuss political principles, also bodes well for a democratic China.

0822. CHRISTIAN, John [L]. China's South Boundary, *Amerasia* 1, 1937, 260–62.

Argues that the reasons for lack of a clear boundary demaraction can be traced back to the history of the area during the nineteenth century. By the 1930s, it appeared that border negotiations were favoring the Chinese position, although the reasons for this trend are not clear. Expresses hope that Chinese negotiations over northern border conflicts will be as successful.

0823. CLARK, Milton I. How the Kazahs Fled to Freedom, *National Geographic Magazine* 106, 1954, 621–44.

Describes the historical distribution of Kazahs in Asia and China. Recounts how after negotiating with the Chinese over issues such as religious freedom, preserving tribal customs, and the liberty to travel at will throughout Xinjiang a group of Kazah fled China to Srinagar after a People's Liberation Army intrusion into Xinjiang to set up an atomic test site limited their mobility. Escape was eased by the tacit assistance of the Tibetans. Characterizes Kazah religious practices as including elements of Islam and traditional Kazah rituals. Argues that Chinese have had a negative impact on local population and economy.

0824. CRESSEY, George B. Hong Kong: Beach Head for Democracy, *Far Eastern Survey* 20, 1951, 153–55.

Argues that the United States should assist the government of Hong Kong lest the territory fall into the hands of the Communists, thus creating a humanitarian and political catastrophe. Hong Kong can act as a third force for democracy in East Asia and provide a listening post for news from the mainland. With proper support, area can be of strategic value given its free press, its cultural isolation from China proper, and the British tolerance of communist unions. Against any boycott of Hong Kong, as this would only hurt Hong Kong residents and not harm the People's Republic of China.

0825. CRESSEY, G[eorge]. B. New Map of China, *Geographical Review* 20, 1930, 652–56.

Reviews the political changes that have led to a modification in the number and names of the traditional eighteen provinces. Includes a table with the name, name of capital, area, and population of all provinces. Notes role of Great Wall in defining modern borders.

0826. DOUGLAS, Henry A. A New Map of China, *Asia and the Americas* 46, 1946, 304–6.

Presents map showing proposed division of China into sixty-four provinces by Hu Huan-yuan based on natural economic regions. Provides a history and rationale for such a project. Expects that proposal will be implemented within a year.

0827. EKVAL, Robert B., and Joseph F. DOWNS. Notes on Water Utilization and Rule in the Sakya Dominion, Tibet, *Journal of Asian Studies* 22, 1963, 293–304.

Written against the background of the Chinese invasion of Tibet. Describes the historical and environmental background of water use and how the water distribution system operated. Based on this institution, concludes that, contrary to Chinese claims, the Tibetan people were not serfs of feudal, insensitive rulers.

0828. EITEL, Rev. Dr. [E. J.] China and the Far Eastern Question, *Proceedings, Royal Geographical Society of Australasia, South Australian Branch* 4, 1888–89, 91–109.

Begins with a disclaimer: despite some thirty-five years' experience in China, author does not feel that he knows enough to be considered an expert! Nevertheless, assumes that Chinese culture was a product of diffusions from Central Asia and not indigenous. As background, provides a summary of China's view of its place in the world and cosmos, Chinese social structure, isolation, and recent political history of the Manchus and their handling of local rebellions, including the Taiping. Defines the "China Question" as whether or not China has a right to isolation and promptly argues that such a policy constitutes a gross violation of the primary laws of humanity. Touches on the causes of antiforeign attitudes in China, Japanese aggression in China, and the accomplishments and failings of the evangelical missions to China. Concludes that China must thoroughly reorganize its executive, administrative, and educational systems if it is to modernize.

0829. FENN, H. C. The New Map of China, *Current History* 26:5, 1927, 768–72.

Notes that the Republic of China has not yet revised the old provincial divisions of China. Describes the Manchu system of spatial administration based on ethnic areas. Notes potential impact on provincial structure of railroad building and other transportation projects, the return to Weihaiwei to Chinese rule, and communist attempts to sever Xinjiang from China.

0830. FIELD, A. R. Bhutan, Kham, and the Upper Assam Line, *Orbis* 3, 1959, 180–92.

Describes India's attempts to seal the border between China and South Asia as violating traditional patterns of open borders. The interests and practices of nomads and religious pilgrims were thus sacrificed. Reviews data on aboriginal guerrilla actions against Chinese domination. Notes India's use of Panca Silla principles in an attempt to reach a border agreement with China in 1954.

0831. FIELD, Frederick W. The Chinese Army: Political Composition and Geographical Distribution, *Amerasia* 1, 1937, 253–59.

Analysis of the military strength of China as viewed from the perspective of relations of local warlords with the Kuomintang and the geographic positioning of troops. Estimates total troop strength. Concludes that there is little relationship between Chinese invasion of strategic areas held by the Japanese and the location of troops loyal to Chiang Kai-shek.

0832. FISHER, Charles. Containing China? I: The Antecedents of Containment, *Geographical Journal* 136, 1970, 534–56.

Seeks to explain why, after several decades of Western governments holding China in esteem, China after 1949 is subject to containment policies. Flirts with environmental determinism in describing the development of culture in the eastern and western extremes of the Eurasian continent. Describes the evolution in Western views of China from Roman times on as well as Chinese views and reactions to the Western intrusion. Sees current containment as part of larger pattern of oscillating Western attitudes toward China and whether it is in any way sui generis.

0833. FISHER, Charles. Containing China? II: Concepts and Application of Containment, *Geographical Journal* 137, 1971, 281–310.

Uses 1904 McKinder idea regarding the containment of Russia as a reflective model. Notes that Japan, the United States, and the Soviet Union aim to contain China. As such the Sino-Soviet split is a new form of containment. Comments that China has declared its intention to reexamine all foreign treaties and to recognize, abrogate, revise, or renegotiate them as it wishes.

0834. FITZGERALD, C. P[atrick]. Tension on the Sino-Soviet Border, *Foreign Affairs* 45, 1967, 683–93.

Begins by comparing the Sino-Indian dispute with the Franco-German dispute over Alsace-Lorraine. In turn, compares the Sino-Indian and Sino-Russian disputes. Despite appearances that the Sino-Soviet disputes are based on ideology, in reality a real friction exists based on the Chinese claims of prior occupation of the disputed areas and their view that nineteenth-century Russian imperialists grabbed land while China was weak and defenseless. Notes that the Russians have no claims against the Chinese. Discounts the possibility of military conflict, since the Chinese claims are weak and the area not worth the risk of all-out war.

0835. FOORD, Edward. China and the Destruction of the Roman Empire, *Contemporary Review* 94:207, 1908, 201–15.

Compares how Rome and China dealt with threats from nomadic groups. Argues that China was more successful because the Great Wall was completed, although nomads did intrude into China if and when the wall was not properly maintained. Concludes that eastern peoples are capable of learning from the West.

0836. FRANK, V. S. Territorial Terms of the Sino-Soviet Treaty of Nerchinsk, 1689, *Pacific History Review* 16, 1947, 265–70.

Seeks to ascertain the precise meaning of article 1 of the treaty that defined the northern frontier. Quotes all language versions of the treaty and notes the differences resulting from the ambiguity of the territorial terms. Remarks that the Chinese pressed the Russians to demarcate the border in the eighteenth century but the Russians did not see that as being in their best interests.

0837. FREEBERNE, Michael. Racial Issues and the Sino-Soviet Dispute, *Asian Survey* 5, 1965, 408–16.

Racism is an important part of the dispute, not least because of a historical tradition of racial superiority and arrogance found in certain sectors of Chinese society. Dispute must also be viewed in context of varying Chinese positions regarding socialist solidarity.

0838. GATZLAFF, Charles. Frontiers of China toward Birmah, *Journal, Royal Geographical Society* 19, 1849, 42–48.

Area is dominated by non-Han peoples whose only connection to China is an annual tribute sent from Ming times on. Attempts by China in 1767–87 to colonize the area failed due to harsh conditions. Notes east-west differences in hydrology, climate, and economy.

0839. GINSBURG, Norton S. China's Changing Political Geography, *Geographical Review* 42, 1952, 102–17.

Notes that the Chinese Communist Party is concerned with three problems in formulating its approaches to international issues: Sino-Soviet relations, the occupied Korean Peninsula, and South and Southeast Asia. Reviews changes in internal political structure of China, including establishment of autonomous regions and changes in provincial borders. Notes that the Chinese are not consistent in making these changes, and thus it is hard to identify precisely which principles of political philosophy are being applied. Provides a table of internal administrative structure. Notes that the hierarchical arrangement corresponds closely to a military chain of command. Feels that under such a system the Chinese have achieved a degree of organization well in excess of anything in their history.

0840. GRANT, Charles Mitchell. Route from Pekin to St. Petersburg via Mongolia, *Proceedings, Royal Geographical Society* 7, 1862–63, 27–34.

Bulk of report deals with the non-Chinese leg of the trip across the Gobi to St. Petersburg. However, includes a discussion of the Taiping Rebellion and its impact on trade and government revenues.

0841. GREEN, L. C. Legal Aspects of the Sino-Indian Border Dispute, *China Quarterly* 3, 1960, 42–58.

Surveys entire border area and concludes that geographic considerations tend to support Indian claims. But both sides have exercised jurisdiction, levied taxes, controlled wayfarers, and otherwise fulfilled government activities in disputed regions. Since these governmental activities do not appear to be continually carried out, disputes are possible.

0842. GREEN, O. M. China and the Rise of the Kuomintang, *Geographical Magazine* 14, 1942, 271–81.

Political history of China's first real revolution, as contrasted with earlier attempts at rebellion.

0843. GREEN, O. M. Chungking Invictus, *Geographical Magazine* 17, 1944, 235–45.

Describes how Chongqing coped with air raids. Notes impact of war on transportation systems, especially the river. Sees war as having a positive impact on city, providing for its rebirth.

0844. GREEN, O. M. Macao, *Geographical Magazine* 25, 1953, 591–97.

Observes that China has never challenged the existence of Macao as a colonial possession. Provides a history of the colony.

0845. HARRER, Heinrich. My Life in Forbidden Lhasa, *National Geographic Magazine* 108, 1955, 1–48.

Reminiscences of Austrian tutor to the current Dalai Lama. Describes arrival in India, subsequent arrest and imprisonment, and details of escape and illegal entry into Tibet in 1939. Provides impressions of Tibetan religious practices, political situation and mobility, and daily life. Traces history of Potala Palace starting in 1641. Evaluates government's effectiveness in dealing with chaotic natural events such as floods. Outlines Chinese invasion in October 1950. Narrative ends with author's escape to India in 1951.

0846. HAYES, L. Newton. The Great Wall of China, *Journal, Royal Asiatic Society, North China Branch* 59, 1928, 59–77.

Describes the construction and subsequent history of the five sections of wall known collectively as the Great Wall. Feels that the wall served its purpose but that China can no longer live or afford to live in isolation. The wall is seen as a metaphor for Chinese political thinking and behavior.

0847. HERMAN, Theodore. Group Values toward National Space: The Case of China, *Geographical Review* 49, 1959, 164–82.

Argues that the Chinese demonstrate three values: pride in old China; a strong defensiveness against inroads on Chinese areal control; and a demand for political, economic, and social improvements. These values are contrasted with four factors influencing their realization: relations with neighboring states, techniques of resource use, the system of political organization, and government plans for the future. Defines the core of China as the seven coastal provinces. Includes a discussion of the growth of Chinese nationalism, the history of fixed borders such as the Great Wall, and plans to shift industry inland.

0848. HUNG, Frederick [Fu]. Causes of China's Disintegration, *China Critic* 3:19, 1930, 439–43.

There are two sets of causes, long standing and recent, associated with China's disintegration. The long-standing factors include lack of ethnic homogeneity, lack of social harmony, and great linguistic differences that lead to geographic isolation and provincialism. These factors will be ameliorated once modern transportation, which shrinks distances, is developed. In contrast, the abolition of literary exams is a recent factor that has led to intellectual confusion.

0849. HUNG, Fu. A New Plan for the Division of Chinese Provinces, *Far Eastern Review* 43:6, 1947, 1–23.

Not available for annotation.

0850. INLOW, E. Burke. The McMahon Line, *Journal of Geography* 63, 1964, 261–70.

Begins with a basic history of the line, including the Simla Conference and the contrasting Chinese and Indian legal positions toward this boundary. Explicates the use of cartography and physical aggression by the People's Republic of China as a means of settling the dispute.

0851. JENKINS, Alan. Territorial Issues and Sino-Soviet Conflicts, *Tidschrift voor economische en social geografie* 65, 1974, 35–47.

The Sino-Soviet conflict does not merely deal with ideological issues but involves nearly every aspect of state to state relations. Includes a chronology of territorial disputes, the role of irredentism in the conflict, methodological issues, and differences in negotiating practices. Predicts that territorial conflicts will play a subsidiary role in future Sino-Soviet relations.

0852. JOHNSON, Nelson T., and W. Robert MOORE. Power Comes Back to Peiping, *National Geographic Magazine* 96, 1949, 337–68.

Despite the shift in power from the Kuomintang to the Chinese Communist Party, Beijing remains structurally and socially the same, with the sole exception of the loss of a sense of the luxurious. Provides a history of the city, evaluates the impact of the Japanese on the urban landscape, and describes rural-urban relations.

0853. KARAN, Pardyumna Prasad. The India-China Boundary Dispute, *Journal of Geography* 61, 1960, 16–20.

Main focus is on the changing role of the Himalayan frontier in the context of Tibet and Tibetan nationalism within the People's Republic of China. Describes the origins and nature of the boundary conflict by sector. Minimizes impact of territorial dispute on future Sino-Indian relations due to the inaccessibility of the terrain and the Indian government's desire for a peaceful resolution of the conflict.

0854. KARAN, Pradyumna P[rasad]. The Sino-Soviet Border Dispute, *Journal of Geography* 63, 1964, 216–21.

Argues that one's view of the border conflict is a function of which view of Sino-Soviet relations one holds. If relations are perceived to be good, the border is a zone of stabilization, if poor, a zone of conflict. Feels it is naive to think that border conflicts would not develop between members of the Second World. Relates history of Far Eastern and Central Asian borders. Emphasizes how undemarcated borders are an advantage to a strong aggressive state, especially in the Pamir and Himalayan areas. Argues that China will wait to press claims against both the Soviet Union and India until it is politically stronger.

0855. KIRK, William. Sino-Indian Frontier Dispute: A Geographical Review, *Scottish Geographical Magazine* 76, 1960, 3–13.

Sees India's claims as strongest for eastern part of border. Does not feel that China's cartographic evidence supports claim to any part of disputed territory.

0856. KOZICKI, Richard J. The Sino-Burmese Frontier Problem, *Far Eastern Survey* 26, 1957, 33–38.

Describes the history of the problem and pre/post-1949 perspectives on a solution. Enumerates location, size, and ethnicity of all problem areas. Sees prospects for solutions fading due to continued Karen rebellions and the illegal migration of Chinese into disputed areas.

0857. LAAI, Yi-faai. River Strategy: A Phase of the Taiping's Military Development, *Oriens* 5, 1952, 302–29.

Argues that to maximize the use of available forces the Taiping had to develop a vast, varied naval fleet, which in turn required a high degree of geographical knowledge, organizational ability, and military planning. The Taiping were, however, handicapped in exploiting a naval strategy by their lack of cannons and their inability to foresee the reinvigoration of the imperial river fleet.

0858. LATTIMORE, Owen. The Chinese as a Dominant Race, *Journal of the Royal Central Asian Society* 15, 1928, 278–300.

Argues that China should not complain of the treatment it has received at the hands of the imperial powers since the country has historically been a major imperialist nation. Traces history of Chinese imperialism and notes that Chinese justice in newly acquired areas can be as harsh as the terms of extraterritoriality. In addition to outright conquest of regions and peoples, China has used the civil service, Chinese currency, and agricultural systems as mechanisms to enforce its control. Notes conflict between imperial goals of Russia and China and remarks that China does and always will harbor the desire to dominate every race with which it comes in contact. An in-text note indicates that a slightly different version of the paper appeared in the journal *Asia* in June 1928.

0859. LATTIMORE, Owen. Inner Asian Frontier: Chinese and Russian Margins of Expansion, *Journal of Economic History* 7, 1947, 24–52.

Argues that lessons learned from the study of the Chinese-Russian frontier can be applied to the northwest frontier separating India and China. Predicts that the Chinese will not succeed in Inner Asia unless they adopt an assimilationist model that stresses equality and cultural autarky for non-Han peoples.

0860. LATTIMORE, Owen. Japan Hung Up on the Hypotenuse, *Amerasia* 3, 1938, 475–80.

Argues that the entirety of China's geography can be analyzed by considering the triangular area defined by lines running from Shanhaikwan to Lanzhou to the Vietnam-China border and back to Shanhaikwan. The major question for Japan is how to conquer the rest of China. Advises to stay close to the hypotenuse. Japan must consider its ability to supply industrial manpower, the difficulty of self-defense, and how to rule and divide local leaders when contemplating further military action in China. Japan can be successfully beaten as long as Chinese forces control two legs of the triangle.

0861. LATTIMORE, Owen. The Unknown Frontier of Manchuria, *Foreign Affairs* 11, 1933, 315–30.

Sees solution to "Manchurian Problem" as prelude to struggle in Mongolia. Laments lack of concern by powers, especially Russia and China, regarding interests or desires of Mongolian and Manchurian peoples themselves, such as the Mongol fear that railroad development will lead to land alienation.

0862. LATTIMORE, Owen. Stalemate in China, *Foreign Affairs* 19, 1941, 621–32.

Views stalemate regarding control of China as best explained by dividing China into three parts: free, marginal, and invaded, with the latter being rich in agriculture but poor in industry. Sees as a strategic mistake the failure of the Japanese to send in enough troops to ensure a complete victory in 1937. Finally, the anarchy associated with a two-front war is taken into consideration.

0863. LATTIMORE, Owen. Yunnan: Pivot of Southeast Asia, *Foreign Affairs* 21, 1943, 476–93.

Asks whether Yunnan and the Burma Road will be the paths of future Chinese expansion into Southeast Asia. Reviews evidence for considering Yunnan to be a potential key economic area for China. Notes that the attitude of the central Chinese government toward Yunnan will be more positive in the future given the area's important role during World War II.

0864. LEONARD, Jane Kate. Chinese Overlordship and Western Penetration in Maritime Asia: A Late Ch'ing Reappraisal of China's Maritime Relations, *Modern Asian Studies* 6, 1972, 151–74.

Analysis of work of Wei Yuan, including methodology and content. Argues that Wei was able to correctly identify the Western source of wealth and power as well as the weaknesses of the Chinese imperial system. However, Wei did not fully appreciate the extent of Western naval power nor the geopolitical implications of China's ceding Hong Kong to Great Britain. Therefore, he discounted the nature of the British threat to coastal China.

0865. LITTLE, Archibald [J]. Hanoi and Kwang-Chow-Wan: France's Latest Acquisition in China, *Scottish Geographical Magazine* 22, 1906, 181–88.

Major focus on positive descriptions of Hanoi and Haiphong in contrast to state of Chinese cities. Expresses hope that the French will succeed in building a Yunnan railroad, for whoever builds such a railroad will open the poverty-stricken to development.

0866. LONG, George W. Eyes on the China Coast, *National Geographic Magazine* 103, 1953, 505–12.

Reports on preparations by the Republic of China and the United States to ensure that Taiwan will not be invaded by the People's Republic of China. Includes descriptions of conditions in Hong Kong and Macao, as well as specific Mainland China military targets such as railroads.

0867. LOWY, Rennold L. Adventures in Lolo Land (China), *National Geographic Magazine* 91, 1947, 105–18.

Uses itinerary format. Report of trip taken in October 1944 to investigate fate of pilots reportedly captured by Lolos and being kept as slaves. Trip had to be canceled when the Naitong Bridge collapsed, leaving no other land route into the area to be explored. Investigation did discover the remains of two downed B-29 planes.

0868. MALLORY, Walter H. The Northward Migration of the Chinese, *Foreign Affairs* 7, 1928, 72–81.

Refers to Manchuria as the Belgium of the Far East. Notes three conflicting views of Manchuria: the Chinese see it as a home for excess population from other provinces, the Japanese view it as an area for them to develop, and the Russians are preoccupied with the title to the area since they are concerned with strategic and trade issues.

0869. MARTIN, W. A. P. The Causes that Led Up to the Siege of Pekin, *National Geographic Magazine* 12, 1901, 53–62.

Contrasts the attempts at reform by the Manchu government with the growth of antiforeign feelings in China. Notes that Chinese government did not heed the warnings of Western diplomats regarding the Boxers. Describes the siege and relief manuevers. Sees Chinese reaction to the West as inhibiting China's long-term development.

0870. McCOLL, Robert W. A Political Geography of Revolution: China, Vietnam, and Thailand, *Journal of Conflict Resolution* 11, 1967, 153–67.

Uses concept of nonrandomly distributed base areas to demonstrate process by which the Chinese Communist Party established itself. The rationale for choice of base areas is applicable to Vietnam and possibly to Thailand.

0871. McCOLL, Robert W. Development of Supra-provincial Administrative Regions in Communist China, 1949–60, *Pacific Viewpoint* 4, 1963, 53–64.

Categorizes changes based on five time periods since 1949. Notes increases in the use of local and national discretion in establishing regions and in local administrative latitude. Feels that the Chinese leadership is having trouble integrating regional goals in the face of separatist tendencies and strong intraregional feelings. Predicts that supraregions, which in general create a threat to the central government, will not be continued.

0872. McCOLL, Robert W. The Oyuwan Soviet Area, 1927–32, *Journal of Asian Studies* 27, 1967, 41–60.

Deals with the Hubei-Hunan-Anhui Soviet. Despite its local and strategic advantages, it did not succeed as a guerrilla base because Mao preferred Jiangsu, which he saw as a more politically correct area.

0873. MEADOWS, T[homas]. T[aylor]. The Chinese and Their Rebellions, *Proceedings, Royal Geographical Society* 1, 1855–57, 100–104.

Abstract and summary of book of the same name. Traces history of rebellions in China against the theory of the Mandate of Heaven. Special attention given to Ming period rebellions as well as the Taiping Rebellion. Includes analysis of conditions under which Western powers might or should interfere. Concludes that Britain, France, and the United States should interfere so as to block further Russian aggression against China.

0874. MELLOR, Roy. Changing Geographical Value of Tibet, *Scottish Geographical Magazine* 75, 1959, 113–14.

Reviews nineteenth- and early-twentieth-century political geography of Tibet in context of China-Great Britian-Russia rivalries. Notes that their 1956 invasion of Tibet gave the Chinese a clear, strong military position in Asia, even though historically Tibet had been regarded as militarily negative terrain.

0875. MOJUMDAR, K. K. The Chumbi Dagger, *Geographical Observer* 2, 1966, 62–67.

Place in question is a tongue-shaped salient of Tibet between Bhutan and Sikkim. The area is now closed, since it is part of a Chinese military base. Description of area includes details about terrain, trade, religion, and its role in a potential Chinese invasion of either India or Southeast Asia.

0876. MORGAN, G. Sino-Russian Border Dispute, *Contemporary Review* 216, 1970, 231–35, 345.

After reviewing the history of Sino-Soviet encounters over Central Asian territory, concludes that China has never been an expansionist country nor has it ever fought a war to recover lost territory. Nevertheless, China has not abandoned its traditional sinocentric view of the world.

0877. MURPHEY, Rhoads. China and the Dominoes, *Asian Survey* 6, 1966, 510–15.

Discounts theory that China is an insatiable expansionist country seeking to absorb Southeast Asia based on contrast between the rationality of Communist Party leaders when it comes to perceptions and actions and their rhetoric when making public statements.

0878. NORRIS, Martin R. Tribal Boundary of the Burma-Yunnan Frontier, *Pacific Affairs* 12, 1939, 67–79.

Provides the historical (i.e., nineteenth-century) background of the disputed area that falls within the Wa state. Divides frontier into sectors based on degree of controversy over location of actual boundary. Notes the topographic and hydrologic problems involved in actually delimiting a boundary. Remarks that work toward solving disputes was intrerrupted by the June 1937 invasion of China by Japan.

0879. OSBORN, Sherard. Notes on Chinese Tartary, *Proceedings, Royal Geographical Society of London* 11, 1867, 162–66.

Divides territory along political lines based on the heavy Russian presence in the area.

0880 REITSMA, Hendrick J. China in Africa, *Focus* 26, September-October 1975, 9–14.

Comparison and contrast of diplomatic efforts of the People's Republic of China from 1956 to 1975. The years 1968–69 witnessed an important initiative, in the context of the north-south split, to gain African support for seating the People's Republic of China in the United Nations. The aid provided was tied to eight principles of mutual respect and understanding and led to important diplomatic gains at the expense of Israel, France, and the United Kingdom. In contrast, African ties to the Soviet Union and its satellite states in Eastern Europe, to the United States, and to Japan were not adversely affected.

0881. RICHARDSON, H. L. Szechuan during the War, *Geographical Journal* 106, 1945, 1–25. Map after p. 22.

The war intensified the differences between the old and new in Sichuan. Province seen as last refuge for the Chinese. China as a power has slender resources to call upon apart from manpower and the will to resist the Japanese. Describes size, hydrology, and geology of area as well as the irrigation of the Chengdu area, which provides a degree of insurance against the possibility of drought.

0882. RIGGS, Margaret. Power of Japan and China: A Study in Political Geography, *Journal of Geography* 36, 1937, 177–86.

The population-induced pressure to industrialize was greater in Japan than China. Nevertheless, China has the potential to outstrip Japan as an economic power. Predicts that neither country will ever be a world power. A stable Chinese government could act as a block to any Japanese aspirations of empire.

0883. SAMSON, Gerald L. G. Free China's New Gateway, *Geographical Magazine* 9, 1939, 312–18.

Describes Kunming as an administrative, educational, economic, and political center in the context of the ongoing war against Japan. Includes photo essay.

0884. SHAW, Earl B. The McMahon Line, *Military Review* 46:7, 1966, 61–63.

Notes pre-twentieth-century attempts to determine the Sino-Indian boundary. When setting the McMahon line, the British assumed that it was best to use the principle of a water divide. Describes Chinese reasons for rejecting McMahon line as well as extent and nature of Sino-Indian hostilities in area during the 1960s.

0885. SHOR, Franc. Life under Shell-Fire in Quemoy, *National Geographic Magazine* 115, 1959, 414–38.

Report on return trip after fifteen-year absence. Describes impact of alternate day shelling, missionaries, Republic of China officials, Joint Commission on Rural Development workers, and U.S. military advisers on standard of living. Notes changes in infrastructure such as tunnels and reinforced housing to permit survival of air raids and shelling.

0886. SOWERBY, Arthur de C[arle]. Moving the Capital, *China Journal* 9, 1928, 55–57.

Reports that Chinese reactions to the Nationalist government moving the capital from Beijing to Nanjing was generally positive. Describes logistical problems involved in the move and speculates that Shanghai would have made an even better choice since it is not as vulnerable and is also a major economic center.

0887. SPENCER, Joseph E[arle]. Kueichou: An Internal Chinese Colony, *Pacific Affairs* 13, 1940, 162–72.

Seeks to understand why Guizhou is so poor. Notes its distance from center of Chinese civilization and its late Han settlement. Economically and politically, the area has been treated as a colony. Thus, tribute has been extracted and opium has become a cash crop. Under such circumstances, it will be difficult to exploit the province's mineral resources. Development seen as possible test case for ability of central government to rule effectively.

0888. STAHNKE, Arthur A. The Place of International Law in Chinese Strategies and Tactics: The Case of the Sino-Indian Border Dispute, *Journal of Asian Studies* 30, 1970, 95–120.

While using a chronology of events, main object is to establish nature and extent of China's willingness to present and defend its case against India's border claims within a framework of international law. Although

China does not accept Western international legal principles when it comes to justifying its position on border disputes, it nevertheless has learned the principles of international law too well, as it manipulates them for its own purposes.

0889. STATEN, George L. Use and Misuse of Maps in a Boundary Dispute, *Special Libraries Association, Geography and Map Division Bulletin* 93, 1973, 18–22.

Uses Sino-Soviet and Aksai Chin border disputes to demonstrate how continuous monitoring of maps, as found in atlases, the press, and professional and popular magazines, can give insight into changing governmental attitudes toward boundary delimitation problems.

0890. STEEL, Richard. Peking under the Allies, *Scottish Geographical Magazine* 19, 1903, 147–53.

The Allies divided Beijing into sectors in order to establish a level of security for all citizens that met Western standards. The expectation was that the Chinese would regain control once the Allies reestablished transportation and communications links. Notes the run down condition of the Forbidden City.

0891. STEINER, H. Arthur. New Regional Governments in China, *Far Eastern Survey* 19, 1950, 112–16.

Describes how border regions and liberated areas come to be combined into new provinces. Such changes are traced to Communist needs to control, coordinate, and supervise the direction of change as well as interprovincial issues. Argues that such changes were made in earlier Chinese periods and do not represent a break with Chinese tradition.

0892. STEVENS, Dan. The Sino-Afghanistan Boundary, *Contemporary Review* 213, 1968, 18–23.

Describes the impact of the British-Russian rivalry in Afghanistan on treaty texts. Reviews post-World War II relations among the three parties. Notes how local peoples had rejected boundaries resulting from tripartite negotiations. Describes the Sino-Afghan boundary and the ethnic makeup of the border areas, noting the presence of true nomads who systematically ignore modern, set boundaries. Identifies the issues involved in Wakhan Corridor territorial dispute.

0893. TAYYEB, Ali. A Note on the Political Geography of the India-China Border, *Canadian Geographer* 16, 1960, 22–26.

Border conflicts arise because the line of demarcation runs through areas that lack any semblance of integration between the physical, cultural, and political aspects of the zone. Solution of the dispute is seen as necessary in order to provide other Third World countries with a viable model for conflict resolution.

0894. von RICHTHOFEN, F[rederich]. China, Japan, and Korea, *Geographical Journal* 4, 1894, 556–61.

Abstract of paper read before the Berlin Geographical Society, October 12, 1894. Seeks to provide the background of the Sino-Japanese War. Argues that the independence of the Chinese Empire is unassailable. Hypothesizes that Japan will establish its suzerainty over Korea and use the area as a base for acquiring industrial raw materials and for further expansion into Manchuria.

0895. WANG, I-shou. A Chinese Model: The "Ideal Universe" in Yukung, *Yearbook of Association of Pacific Coast Geographers* 32, 1970, 167–71.

Presents a spatial political system based on concentric rings found in a part of the *Tribute of Yu* (*Yu-kung*). Each main ring is about 500 *li* wide and thus resembles von Thunen's "Isolated State." Argues that this ideal model was ignored because it was simple and abstract. The conceptual basis of the model is based on the tension between areal differentiation and spatial interaction, as measured by tax collection, with the latter being a function of distance from the royal capital.

0896. WIENS, Herald J. China's North and Northwest Boundaries, *Contemporary China* 5, 1961–62, 33–56.

Traces the diplomatic history of the Sino-Soviet and Sino-Mongolian boundaries on a segment by segment basis. Concludes that China was not only under constant Russian pressure to cede land but could never negotiate from a position of strength. Notes the use of "creative" cartography by all sides in the disputes. When the Sino-Soviet split occurred, this gave rise to maximalist claims on both sides.

0897. WIENS, Herald J. Fundamental Aspects of China's Geography Influencing China's Political Policies, *Asian Studies* (Quezon City) 2, 1964, 409–20.

Describes ten geographic characteristics of China, such as a large

13. *Political Geography* 209

population and land area, that suggest China has the potential to engage in mischief in East, Southeast, and South Asia.

0898. YONEKURA, Jiro. The Indian Subcontinent and Mainland China, *International Geography* 1, 1972, 377–78.

A comparison and contrast of Chinese and Indian patterns of integration and isolation in the world. Focus is on two main subregions: the Ganges and Yangtze river valleys.

See also items 0101, 0157, 0165, 0384, 0495, 0707, 0934, 1116, and 1264.

14. Economic Geography: General

0899. ANON. Conditions in China, 1914–15, *Journal of Geography* 14, 1915, 20–23.

Abstracts of press reports on the fiscal and political conditions confronting the Chinese government.

0900. ANON. Formosa, *Geographical Journal* 2, 1893, 441–43.

Describes contents of "Foreign Office Report, Commercial," no. 11, 1893. Focuses on the fact that data are still missing so it is impossible to construct a complete physical geography of the island. Describes current status of island as that of "independent province of the Chinese Empire," with the governor responsible to the central government. Given exports of camphor and sugar, sees the potential for development of trade.

0901. ANON. The Geography of Mainland China: A Concise Sketch, *Current Scene* 7:17, 1969, 1–21.

After reviewing the concepts of a Greater China and describing the physical and cultural setting of China, concludes that China's situational advantages have not been sufficient for a developmental breakthrough. This is related to a general lack of economic integration, good planning, and peaceful conditions. As a result, what economic growth has occurred has been costly.

0902. APPLETON, John B. The Economic and Commerical Development of Manchuria, *Bulletin, Geographical Society of Philadelphia* 32, 1934, 75–87.

Includes data on size, location, and ethnic breakdown of the population, excluding the Japanese. Measures agricultural development in terms of total area, arable area, and cropped area. Notes that as economy has expanded with the exploitation of forest and mineral resources, both imports and exports have increased as well. As such, Manchuria is now a part of the world economy. Further economic progress requires peaceful conditions, population growth, and infrastructure construction as planned by the Japanese.

0903. CHENG, Yin-tang. Economic Development along the Yunnan-Burma Railway, *Geography* 27, 1942, 1–8.

Begins by describing the basic outlines of climate, location, hydrology, and vegetation of the area. Three routes linking Burma and China are mentioned. Provides estimates of comparative costs of transporting goods in both areas. Notes the challenge in using local, discontinuous raw materials, such as coal, to improve economy. Future economic development will be slowed by out-migration of labor and population to Burma, the lack of a lingua franca, no unified currency or weights and measures, and no cash crop, since the growing of opium has been officially banned.

0904. CHISHOLM, George G. The Resources and Means of Commercialization of China, *Geographical Journal* 12, 1898, 500–519.

Catalog of population densities, mineral regions, and transportation data showing potential of Chinese market once adequate rail transportation is constructed.

0905. COALES, Oliver. Economic Notes on Eastern Tibet, *Geographical Journal* 54, 1919, 242–47.

Supplements item 0485. Describes major items found in markets and trade between Tibet and China. Imports include tea, silk, tobacco, cotton, rice, and sundries, while exports include musk, wool, skins, gold, copper, and medicines. Tibet also produces silver, mica, and possibly iron ore. Notes that area tin and coal deposits are extensive but hard to exploit. Remarks on degree to which trade has been disrupted by war.

0906. CRESSEY, George B. Changing China, *The Progressive* 19:9, 1955, 8–11.

Describes goals and financing of the first five-year Plan. China must also deal with problems of inadequate communications, floods, drought, agriculture, and industry. Repeats doubts as to the accuracy of 1953 population census. Given the size of its population, predicts that China will remain a basically agricultural country pressed to feed and clothe its citizens. Access to Russian aid and technology will not make up for a lack of resources with which to industrialize.

0907. CRESSEY, G[eorge]. B. The Changing Map of China, *Economic Geography* 31, 1956, 1–16.

Against the background of the goals and claims of quick successes of the first five-year plan, describes the challenges the new Chinese leaders will have to meet if they are to develop China economically. These include food shortages, creating a new and accurate accounting system, boundary problems, communications, river control, the social organization of agriculture, industrial expansion, and urban growth. Acknowledges that

14. *Economic Geography: General*

there have been some accomplishments, especially in the area of electricity production. Concludes with presentation, without editorial comments, of the results of the 1953 census of population. Article critiqued in item 0911.

0908. CRESSEY, George B. China's First Five-Year Plan, *Foreign Policy Bulletin* 34:14, 1955, 109–11.

Reviews sectoral goals of plans and argues that if China has a decade of peace it can expect significant advances in industry and transportation. Expects difficulties in agricultural development since incorrect policies are being implemented, such as land reform when 74 percent of the peasants already own their land. Feels mineral resources are modest compared to vast plans and flood control works are inadequate. Describes specific cities slated for industrial development. Expresses concern over role of Soviet Union in China's development. Even though there are 141 approved projects in which the Soviet Union is assisting, it is not clear that in the long run all aid will be delivered.

0909. DUFFIELD, Minnie M. Making a Living in China, *Journal of Geography* 32, 1933, 66–77.

Lesson plan for secondary school teachers, including tests, for showing how hard life is in China, the growth of the soy industry, the positive impact of trade in tea and silk, how human activities are influenced by a poor resource base, economic and political isolation, unpredictable weather, and floods.

0910. DWYER, D. J. Economic Development in China, 1960–4, *Geography* 51, 1966, 140–42.

Uses U.S. Consulate-General in Hong Kong reports to estimate output across the economy. Notes the dual negative impacts of natural calamities and the breakdown of the commune system on output. Sees industrial capacity as underutilized. Describes trade patterns by goods and partners.

0911. FANG, Chao-ying, and Lienche FANG. Notes on "The Changing Map of China" *Far Eastern Quarterly* 15, 1956, 267–68.

Sees Cressey's work on changing China [item 0907] as generally praiseworthy but concerned with errors and degree of incompleteness. These deficiencies are corrected and missing data updated, especially for the reconfiguration of Heilongjiang area and minority groups such as the Chuang.

0912. **FETTER, Frank Whitson.** China and the Flow of Silver, *Geographical Review* 26, 1936, 32–37.

Maps and notes by Herbert M. Bratter. Notes the fact that although China always preferred silver as a currency little of the mineral was actually mined or refined there. Provides a history of monetary standards in China and describes the impact of changes in silver prices and U.S. silver policy on the Chinese economy between 1874 and 1934. Does not expect China to adopt the gold standard.

0913. **FREEBERNE, Michael.** Internal Developments in China, 1962, *Pacific Viewpoint* 4, 1963, 95–99.

Describes economic changes in China during 1962 and argues that no breakthroughs were made in the areas of agriculture, forestry, manufacturing, or population policies. Main sources include *Survey of Mainland China Press*, *Peking Review*, and the *BBC Summary of World Broadcasts*.

0914. **FREEBERNE, Michael.** Progress during 1963, the First Year of China's Third Five-Year Plan, *Tidjschrift voor economsiche en sociale geografie* 55, 1964, 196–201.

Analysis of April 23, 1963, *Beijing Review* article by Fang Chung. Argues that much of the Chinese information regarding their economy is for internal consumption, reflecting the need to overcome a Western anti-China campaign. Concludes that China has the potential to be a great power and therefore should be taken seriously.

0915. **FUNNELL, W. C.** Hong Kong Revisited, *Australian Outlook* 23, 1969, 279–93.

Reaction to physical, economic, and social changes that have taken place over a twenty-year period. Speculates on reasons for changes. Not sure whether Hong Kong is a true microcosm of Chinese society or a unique Chinese region. Argues that it is not reasonable or realistic to expect Hong Kong to achieve political independence or true democracy.

0916. **FUSON, Chester G.** Geography of Kwangtung, *Lingnan Science Journal* 6:3, 1928, 244–56.

Provides an outline geography. Argues that the prosperity of the province is due to its abundant communications lines, water, and good transportation. Notes that fully one-half of the province is forested, an unappreciated resource.

0917. GUTMAN, John. Market Day in Cheng-Kiang {Yunnan}, *Geographical Magazine* 19, 1947, 508–12.

Photos of market and goods offered in specific stalls.

0918. HERMAN, Theodore. The Economic Development of China; Studies Reviewed in Tranquility, *Geographical Review* 51, 1961, 114–20.

Classifies available studies on Chinese economy into three broad categories: descriptive, interpretative owing to an author's biases, and biased due to heavy reliance on Chinese and Soviet sources. Collectively, the studies show that China has achieved impressive economic growth, that there is neither population nor long-range planning, and that Chinese economic programs are to a large measure based on trial and error procedures. Reflections include the notion that most studies of the Chinese economy are aspatial and premature in that they ignore whether or not the Chinese have learned from mistakes such as the Great Leap Forward.

0919. HORSBURGH, A. J. The Cultural Revolution in China, *New Zealand Geographical Society Record* 44, 1967, 1–3.

Minimizes the violence of the Cultural Revolution. Argues that the Cultural Revolution was more than a power struggle and included the need for a continuous attack on the remnants of feudalism and capitalism. Programs such as the Cultural Revolution help peasants to develop a sense of awareness and direction about the leadership of China, which is necessary if development is to occur. In general, seeks to show the constructive aspects of the Cultural Revolution and how it is congruent with the development aims of China.

0920. JACK, R. Logan. From Shanghai to Bhamo, *Geographical Journal* 19, 1902, 249–77.

Replete with references to other trade reports about the region. Notes desire of Chinese to establish an overland railroad link to Bhamo in order to secure a land route to the sea via Burma and Tonkin. Expects an economic renaissance once the Chinese have reckoned with the Japanese. Feels that Chinese are capable people and therefore will build railroads.

0921. KING, George W. Notes on Kansu, *Journal, Royal Asiatic Society, North China Branch*, new series 50, 1919, 185–88.

Divides Gansu into three regions—central, north, and south—based on topography, hydrology, and economy. Describes industrial uses of riverbanks for gravel. Power sources include waterwheels and coal from local mines. Notes development of horticulture and pear culture, particularly within the agricultural sector.

0922. KOO, V. K. Wellington. Reconstruction in War-Time China, *Scottish Geographical Magazine* 57, 1941, 97–102.

Emphasizes challenges of simultaneously fighting a war and developing a country. Focuses on major developments in transportation, especially railroad, road, bridge, and airport construction.

0923. LINDGREN, Miss E. J. Northwestern Manchuria and the Reindeer Tungus, *Geographical Journal* 75, 1930, 518–36.

Reviews and contrasts the history of Chinese knowledge of the area and Western exploration as demanded by railroad expansion. Describes the vegetation and hydrology of the area along with the basics of the economy of the Tungus. Special attention is given to demographic issues, including the shortage of women.

0924. MAINPRISE, B. W. Reminiscences of China after the Recent Trouble, *Scottish Geographical Magazine* 19, 1903, 480–83.

Concludes that once transportation and communications networks are built China can become developed, given the mineral wealth available for exploitation.

0925. KNAPP, Ronald G. Itinerant Merchants in Taiwan, *Journal of Geography* 69, 1970, 344–47.

Report based on fieldwork undertaken in 1966–67. Shows how the reach of periodic markets is extended by itinerant merchants who travel around by bicycle or foot. Describes range of goods and services provided, mostly food and nonedible household goods. Notes that, as in fixed markets, haggling is expected.

0926. KNAPP, Ronald G. Marketing and Social Patterns in Rural Taiwan, *Annals, Association of American Geographers* 61, 1971, 131–55.

Based on fieldwork during 1965–66, uses four townships [Chong-li *chen* and Lungtan, Bate, and Pingchen *hsiang*] in Taoyuan *hsien* to test the hypothesis that marketing systems have important social, as well as economic, dimensions. Describes and maps locations of market centers and marketing patterns at wholesale and retail levels for selected commodities. Notes tie between marketing patterns and journey to work, religious activities, and marriage patterns. Concludes that even as modernization processes operate marketing patterns are still determined or influenced by site, communal cooperation, social connections, transportation connectivity, inertia, and the place of settlements in the administrative hierarchy.

0927. MAGEE, Guy, Jr. "The Man in the Street" in China: Some Characteristics of the Greatest Undeveloped Market in the World Today, *National Geographic Magazine* 38, 1920, 406–22.

Notes the potential of the Chinese market, including its large size, cheap labor, love of money, and lack of a developed sense of economic nationalism. Describes ethnic diversity of China. Attempts to define, and transmit through photographs, a sense of the "man in the street" in Beijing. Comments on reasons for poverty in China, including lack of transportation; the high costs of weddings, funerals, and burials; and the lack of knowledge regarding local markets.

0928. MILLER, Henry B. Russian Development of Manchuria, *National Geographic Magazine* 15, 1904, 113–27.

Main focus is on Russia's role in creating the city of Harbin and building its infrastructure. Specific topics reviewed include administration, population, transportation, land use, banking and finance, agriculture, and the development of an industrial economy. Major industrial products include flour, bricks, and Russian liquors. Concludes with speculations on the impact of Russia acting alone in the development of Manchuria.

0929. "Old Cathay." Formosa, *Journal, Royal Asiatic Society, North China Branch*, new series 50, 1919, 158–61.

Anonymous report based on brief visit. Under Japanese administration, trading interests of Europeans have declined. Reports on how lack of deep water ports inhibits growth of exports, especially of agricultural goods and minerals. Classifies four major population groups and correctly identifies origins of aborigines.

0930. ORCHARD, John E. American Economic Policy and China's Reconstruction, *Proceedings, Academy of Political Science* 22:4, 1948, 14–24.

Assumes that the basic tenets of U.S. foreign policy will include an open door policy and an emphasis on encouraging world economic expansion through substantial assistance to wartorn and underdeveloped areas. Comments on the negative impact of the Chinese civil war on U.S.

policies and programs for China. Optimistic that China has sufficient resources to industrialize, given the successful examples of development in Manchuria and Taiwan. However, does not expect China to be self-sufficient in raw materials in the short run.

0931. ORCHARD, John E. Japan's Economic Invasion of China, *Foreign Affairs* 18, 1940, 464–76.

Seeks to assess what impact Japan's occupation of Manchuria and China will have on U.S. economic and financial interests in China. An accurate assessment requires clear answers to whether Japan can take and hold substantial areas of China; whether signs of stress are appearing in Japan's economy; whether Japan is successful in obtaining wool and cotton from China; and the amounts of iron ore, coal, and salt Japan is transporting from China to Japan.

0932. PORTER, Catherine. Korea and Formosa as Colonies of Japan, *Far Eastern Survey* 5, 1936, 81–88.

Questions the economic importance of Japan's colonies in the overall budgetary planning for Japanese development. Doubts whether the colonies are actually good for the Japanese economy. Similarly, sees little benefit to colonial peoples from Japanese overlordship.

0933. PRICE, Willard. Japan Faces Russia in Manchuria, *National Geographic Magazine* 82, 1942, 603–34.

Describes the impact of the war on the Manchurian economy. Argues that Japan saw the area as a "first essential" in its plan to rule an empire and that the loss of Manchuria would be the loss of the foundation of its ideal world. Sees potential damage to Japan if it were try to conquer Russian territory.

0934. ROORBACK, G. B. China: Geography and Region, *Annals, American Academy of Political and Social Science* 39, 1912, 130–53.

Explores the hypothesis that the ultimate test of a nation and its political power is grounded in its geographical position and physical resources. Wonders whether China, with its dependencies of Tibet, East Turkestan [Xinjiang], Manchuria, and Mongolia, can become a first-class world power. Concludes that despite isolation and lack of accessibility should China even minimally develop its resources it could be a world power.

0935. ROXBY, Percy M[aude]. Wu-Kan: The Heart of China, *Scottish Geographical Magazine* 32, 1916, 266–79.

Describes the importance of Wuhan (Hankou, Hanyang, and Wuchang) in the context of site and nodality. Enumerates extent of specific industries and optimistically concludes that tri-city region has great potential to foster economic development of China.

0936. SHABAD, Theodore. China's "Leap Forward" Reconsidered, *Far Eastern Survey* 28:6, 1959, 156–58.

Despite overpopulation, China is advancing, in part because higher than expected population growth, as anticipated by planners, did not occur. Describes programs to expand agricultural production by all means.

0937. SHABAD, Theodore. China's Year of the Great Leap Forward, *Far Eastern Survey* 28:10, 1959, 89–96, 105–9.

Evaluates key Chinese economic reports published in 1959. Inclined to accept data at face value and sees economic progress except in agriculture, where droughts, floods, and other natural disasters cut into production. Expects pace of growth in 1957 to continue into 1958, except for agriculture.

0938. SHABAD, Theodore. Communist China's Five-Year Plan, *Far Eastern Survey* 24, 1955, 189–91.

Favorable evaluation of accomplishments of first five-year plan, which ran from 1953 to 1957. Major achievements include elimination of the private sector, progress toward collectivization, restructuring of industry, and especially the production of capital goods. Data presented in analysis are actual production figures, not indices. The single most impressive development was in the area of transportation, especially improvements to the railroads, which carry some 90 percent of all freight traffic.

0939. SHABAD, Theodore. Communist China's Production Statistics, *Far Eastern Survey* 24, 1955, 102–8.

Uses data from September 1954 to access the accomplishments of the first stage of the 1953–57 five-year plan. Describes sources of data and the difficulties of using production indices. Argues that Chinese economic statistics have come of age, since they are internally consistent.

0940. SHEN, Y. S. Industrial and Agricultural Development of Kweichow Province, *China Journal* 33, 1940, 339–42.

Reviews programs and progress of the Kweichow Development Corporation and Agricultural Improvement Board. Notes how both have cooperated with the provincial government and the Industrial and Mining Administration, especially in the building of infrastructure and importing raw materials. Major constraint to further development is the poor transportation system of province.

0941. SIMPICH, Frederick. Manchuria, Promised Land of Asia, *National Geographic Magazine* 56, 1929, 379–428.

Describes economic and social transition of area as a result of railroad building. Argues that three decades of railroad building have advanced the area one hundred years economically. Reviews history of migration and ethnic conflicts among Russians, Chinese, Japanese, and Koreans. Analyzes impact of Japanese investment in railroads on Japanese home economy.

0942. SKINNER, G. William. Marketing and Social Structure in Rural China, *Journal of Asian Studies* 24, 1964, 3–44; 24, 1965, 195–228, 363–400.

Classic study using Christaller's model of central place theory to analyze marketing structure in southwest China. Notes the longevity of the system is such that the policies of the Chinese Communist Party must take the imperfections and misalignment of the trade systems into account when establishing its commune structure.

0943. SOWERBY, Arthur de C[arle]. Through the Silk Producing Districts of Central China, *China Journal* 8, 1928, 248–50.

Study region also included Jiangsu, Zhejiang, and parts of Anhui. Notes major features are waterways and transformed swamps. Describes agricultural practices by season and notes differences between natural flora and domesticated plants. Describes the location of mulberry cultivation on dikes and between fields. Notes that region is autarkic, with its main export being silk. Remarks on degree of Western impact on area in terms of mechanization of silk production but feels the railroad will not displace water traffic.

0944. STEWART, John R. Foreign Investment in Manchuria, *Far Eastern Survey* 4:11, 1935, 81–85.

Begins by elucidating the apparent logic behind the "Open Door Policy," which forced the the withdrawal of foreign companies from oil distribution in Manchuria. Notes protest by Great Powers. Describes nexus of Japanese monopolies, Russian investments, railroad development, and loans to Chinese government. Sees opportunities for investment as overrated.

0945. STEWART, John R. Is Manchuria Vital to Japan? *Bulletin, Geographical Society of Philadelphia* 30, 1932, 88–108.

Attempts to go beyond narrow conception of Japan's interests as driven by population pressure on resources. Reviews data on Manchuria as a source of food, raw materials, and fuels for Japan as well as a market for Japanese raw silk, silk tissue, and cotton piece goods. Concludes that imports into Guandong from Japan are a small percentage of total Japanese exports. Conversely, Manchuria's exports to Japan—soybeans, bean cake, and coal—are of increasingly less use to the Japanese economy. Net conclusion, then, is that Manchuria is not vital to Japanese economic interests.

0946. STEWART, John R. Manchuria: The Land and Its Economy, *Economic Geography* 8, 1932, 134–60.

Uses regional, descriptive method. Topics include physical conditions, geographic and geological resources, and wide range of economic activities. Remarks on Chinese, Korean, and foreign migrants and the conflicts that have resulted. Concludes that Manchuria can comfortably support between 50 and 75 million people, especially if fertility is reduced and migration is selective. A larger population will result in a deterioration in the standard of living.

0947. STEWART, Rosemary. Inside China's Factories and Communes, *Geographical Magazine* 39, 1967, 967–76.

Report by an industrial sociologist who visited Beijing, Wuhan, Nanjing, Wuxi, Suzhow, Shanghai, Hanzhou, and Canton. Compares work situation for factory workers and commune members. Feels that factory workers are more secure due to benefits. Sees China as not different in kind in its approach to economic and social welfare, just taking a different approach.

0948. TURLEY, Robert T. Climatic and Economic Conditions of North Manchuria, *Geographical Journal* 40, 1912, 57–59.

Impressed with richness of rivers and forests. Reports that since its opening area has been attractive to Chinese immigrants despite its dryness. Describes which crops, including wheat and soy, can be grown successfully. Notes the decline in poppy cultivation. Argues that future development requires the expansion of railroad facilities by either the Russians or the Chinese.

0949. TURLEY, Robert T. A Visit to Yalu Region and South Manchuria, *Geographical Journal* 23, 1904, 473–81.

Emphasizes geology and agriculture of region. Indicates that Manchurian trade is underdeveloped but that under "a good government" its great potential could be realized.

0950. TURLEY, Robert T. Through the Hun Kiang Gorges [Manchuria], or Notes of a Tour in "No Man's Land," Manchuria, *Geographical Journal* 14, 1899, 292–302.

Trip to former neutral zone once conquered by Koreans. Describes the history of ethnic succession and consequent economy of region. Notes that the food surplus there acts as an inhibiting factor in adopting new, commerical crops. Posits that there is no relationship between commercial activity of the region and the needs of ordinary people.

0951. von LINDHOLM, K. H. Notes on the Kirin Province, Manchuria, *Geographical Journal* 49, 1917, 56–58.

Describes history of trade for area in context of the provisions of the Manchurian Convention of 1905. Assumes that China is open to foreign trade but is handicapped by lack of adequate transportation.

0952. VOSBURGH, Frederick. Poor Little Rich Land: Formosa, Hot Spot of the East, *National Geographic Magazine* 99, 1950, 139–76.

Describes the impact of the retrocession from Japan and subsequent retreat there from the mainland by the Kuomintang on the economy and demography of the island. Reviews the legal basis for the retrocession to Chinese control. Concerned with the decline of transportaion and the development of a black market. Major focus is on changing status and role of aboriginal populations under the Japanese and Kuomintang administrations.

0953. WARD, Barbara E. A Hong Kong Fishing Village, *Geographical Magazine* 31, 1958, 300–303.

Reports on fieldwork done in Kau Sai village during the period 1951–53. Describes fishing techniques. Notes that language is different from that found in land-based villages.

0954. YEH, George K. C. Builders of a New China, *Geographical Magazine* 18, 1945, 179–89.

Describes the traditional social structure of China and how it is being transformed. Emphasis is on social mobility. Concludes that modernization will be a gradual thing, achieved by means of social and economic progress for workers. Progress is not best measured by the number of students returning to China from the United Kingdom and the United States.

See also items 0183, 0206, 0384, 1195, and 1242.

15. Agriculture

0955. ANDERSON, Eugene N., Jr. Changing Patterns of Land Use in Rural Hong Kong, *Pacific Viewpoint* 9, 1968, 33–50.

Traces shift from traditional rural land use to modern urban structure in the New Territories. Reinterates the relatively late settlement of area even before arrival of the British. Describes the traditional resource management style, including peasant farming villages, boat-dwelling fisherman, (walled) market towns, and associated levels of agricultural production, marriage patterns, administration, and use of *fengshui*. Notes impact of modernization under pressure from post-World War II refugees. Market conditions have driven out rice production in favor of vegetables. Concludes that ecology is related to social patterns and human behavior and that planners can learn much from the traditional resource system, including *fengshui* principles.

0956. ANDERSON, E[ugene]. N., Jr. Traditional Aquaculture in Hong Kong, *Journal of Tropical Geography* 30, 1970, 11–16.

Reviews the general locations of aquaculture and the impact of vegetation, water temperature, and water pollution on output. Case studies include oyster culture in Lau Fau San and pond fish in the New Territories, especially northwest of Yuen Long.

0957. BAKER, O. E. Agriculture and the Future of China, *Foreign Affairs* 6, 1928, 483–97.

Doubts that China can rely on as small a percentage of its population in agriculture as the United States does to produce its food. Chinese agricultural development will require the expansion of use of inanimate power sources; mineral fertilizers; improved farm animals, plants, and crops; and means to control pests and diseases of both plants and animals. Not sure China has the will to use large amounts of inanimate energy on farms out of fear of what to do with displaced rural populations.

0958. BAKER, O. E. Land and Food in China, *Far Eastern Review* 24, 1928, 121–25.

Article is based on secondary sources for period 1918–22. Sees China as being in a Malthusian trap and wonders whether modern technology can improve or save the situation. Describes constraints to increased agricultural production, including limited arable land, topography, soil conditions, and climatic limitations. Compares China's resources to those of the United States.

0959. BALLAS, Donald J. Some Notes on Agriculture in Han China, *Professional Geographer* 17, 1965, 13–14.

Describes work on topic by non-geographers. Major topics reviewed include principle crops, drought, amount of arable and non-arable land, irrigation, craft industries, and the role of religion and tax structure on agriculture. Notes new farming practices introduced under Han, including drought-resistant rice, improved crop rotation, intercropping, multiple cropping, slope utilization, reclamation, and new crops.

0960. BERGER, Roland. Profile of a Chinese County: Agriculture Blooms in Tsun Hua, *Geographical Magazine* 44, 1972, 481–86.

After describing the location of the commune and its administrative structure, uses development measures to demonstrate the application of the planning principle used in five-year development plans of "taking agriculture as the foundation with industry as the leading factor."

0961. BERGER, Roland. Reality on the Chinese Communes, *Geographical Magazine* 43, 1971, 326–32.

Retells history of agrarian reform in China by referring to Sun Yat-sen's theories and post-1950 Communist policies. Describes the economic advantages of communes but notes that managerial errors occurred when implementing government policies. Over-exuberance and poor judgment, combined with floods, droughts, and typhoons during 1959–61, severely weakened communes. Sees communes as one of the most remarkable chapters in history of human endeavor.

0962. BUCHANAN, Keith. The Changing Landscape of Rural China, *Pacific Viewpoint* 1, 1960, 11–38.

Favorably impressed with changes in social conditions brought about by post-1949 change in government. Especially open to the scale of economic and social changes that contrast with past local and regional agricultural revolutions. Feels that transition through collectives to communes has had a positive impact on reforestation, flood control, expanded cultivation, and rural industrialization. Urges that the Chinese model be used in all developing countries.

0963. BUCHANAN, Keith. The People's Communes after Six Years, *Pacific Viewpoint* 6, 1965, 52–64.

Report based on 1958 visit to four communes in Guangdong Province: Chang-cha, Xinjiao, Fatung, and Sha-chiao. Describes location, land use, size, degree of urbanization, sources of income, and population for each place. Notes improvements in water control, availability of adequate fertilizers, and improvements in services and infrastructure. Argues further progress will require adoption of appropriate technologies. Not able to estimate incomes, especially in light of grinding poverty of past.

0964. BUCK, John Loessing. Agriculture and the Future of China, *Annals, American Academy of Political and Social Science* 152, 1930, 109–15.

Argues that China will remain a country dominated by small-scale farming. Feels that the physical basis for agriculture is as good in China as anywhere else. Notes impact of population pressure on land use and mean size of farms. Expresses belief that rural areas cannot react rapidly to changes in either the economy or the physical environment in part due to low levels of education, government assistance, and transportation. The future of the Chinese farm economy will be tied to the ability of the overall economy to make effective use of human labor and the availability of small-scale off-farm economic opportunities.

0965. CAMERON, Nigel. Tibetan Herdsman in China, *Geographical Magazine* 33, 1961, 692–705.

Describes life in Anyang, administrative hub of the Tibetan Autonomous County, one hundred miles northwest of Lanzhou. Argues that life is better under Communist rule, especially since the commune government provides services and insurance.

0966. CHANG, Jen-hu. Sugar Cane in Hawaii and Taiwan: Contrasts in Ecology, Technology, and Economics, *Economic Geography* 46, 1970, 39–52.

Argues, based on analysis of area under cultivation, farm size and type, quantity of chemical inputs, climate, soil and soil management, cultivation practices, tasseling, and plant breeding, that Hawaii has a natural comparative advantage over Taiwan in sugar production. In addition, Taiwan is particularly handicapped in the areas of mechanization, fertilization, irrigation, and pest and damage control.

0967. CHANG, Sen-dou. Agricultural Regions of China, *Geographical Review* 61, 1971, 600–602.

Reviews work of Cheng-siang Chen on topic based on climatic criteria. Sees Chen's work as a good quantitative supplement to Cressey's earlier work [item 0977], especially with regard to the north-south differences in China's agriculture.

0968. CHANG, Sen-dou. China's Crop Land Use, 1957, *Pacific Viewpoint* 12, 1971, 75–87.

Notes that quantitative data on subject is scarce and conflicting. Nevertheless, favorably reports on expansion in cultivated area, increases in multiple cropping, and changes in the relative output of major crops. Concludes that in the post-Great Leap Forward period China has been able to make more effective use of its best land.

0969. CHANG Sen-dou. Role of the Agricultural Geographer in Communist China, *Professional Geographer* 18, 1966, 125–28.

Reports that professional geographers, termed geographic workers, have been directed to agricultural projects at various scales. Examples of specific problems they are solving include the selection and definition of commune borders, the planning for the rational distribution of functional commune centers, compiling large-scale maps and data bases for agricultural regionalization, intensifying land use and soil conservation, tracking the rhythms of floods and droughts, and planning model farms.

0970. CHANG, Tao-shing. The Food Situation in China, *Asiatic Review*, new series 41, 1948, 196–200.

Argues that China is self-sufficient in food. Imports are necessary, however, due to inadequate inland transportation and the variable quality of rice and wheat produced in interior provinces in contrast to imports. Alludes to the possibility that rice and wheat are dumped in China since foreign producers are exempt from tariffs.

0971. CHAO, Kuo-chun. China's Agriculture, *Focus* 10:8, 1960, 1–6.

Characterizes pre-1949 rural China as experiencing poverty and hopelessness due to abuses of landlords. Post-1949 increases in output and yield subject to limits due to climatic and water constraints. Lists possible ways to increase output with focus on role of communes.

0972. CHEN, Cheng-siang. The Banana Industry in Taiwan, *Journal of Tropical Geography* 2, 1954, 48–55.

Main focus is on the status of banana production during the period 1936–45. Provides five reasons for the success of banana plantations in Taiwan:

good natural conditions; monopoly markets in Japan, Korea, and Manchuria; twentieth-century improvements in transportation, permitting exports; the ease of cultivation and resistance to diseases; and an efficient cooperative system for the production and distribution of the final product. Classifies locations of production by land type. Includes technical details regarding cultivation, yields, and value of crop.

0973. CHEN, Cheng-siang. Land Utilization in Formosa, *Geographical Review* 41, 1951, 438–56.

Uses data from 1920–30, 1940, and 1947. Focus is on farm size, rents, cropping systems, and extent of irrigation. Emphasizes the topographic constraints on land use of all types: only 30 percent of land is used and only 24 percent is under cultivation. Includes thirty-three maps.

0974. CHEN, Cheng-siang. The Length of the Growing Season in China, *Australian Geographer* 7, 1959, 59–61.

Uses Prescott's 1948 method, described in *Proceedings, Royal Geographical Society of Australasia, South Australian Branch* 5, 1948–49, with data from samples of 148 sites. Compares his results to those of Thornthwaite and concludes that temperature is as important as precipitation in analyzing agricultural patterns in China.

0975. CHEN, Cheng-siang. The Sugar Industry of China, *Geographical Journal* 137, 1971, 29–40.

Surveys sugar production from pre-World War II period through the 1968–69 crop season. Increases in output were related to a 1958 decentralization policy, the northern expansion of the traditional production area of Guangdong-Fujian to Guangxi and Yunnan, and the southern extension of sugar beet production of Heilongjiang to the Karin and Mongolian border regions.

0976. CHUNG, Yuet-ping. Geography and Agricultural Development in China, *Professional Geographer* 20, 1968, 163–66.

Seeks to establish the extent to which geographic techniques were used to develop agriculture in China, especially after the droughts of 1959–61. Identifies the main agricultural problems requiring research as regional imbalances in water and soil and the resulting need to expand arable land. Relies on materials from *Survey of Mainland Press*. Concludes that geographic contributions to agricultural progress are indirect and hard to specify but nevertheless real and have brought about improvements in the agricultural production indices.

0977. CRESSEY, G[eorge]. B. Agricultural Regions of Asia, Part VI: China, *Economic Geography* 10, 1934, 109–42.

Digest of material found in author's *China's Geographic Foundations: A Survey of the Land and Its People* (New York: McGraw-Hill, 1934). Includes both topical and regional coverage. Concludes that since China is a nation of farmers the country will prosper only if farmers do.

0978. DAVIDSON, Owen L. China's Food Problem, *Foreign Agriculture* 8, 1944, 99–109.

Estimates food production and consumption for free and occupied China for major crops. Includes data on imports of food. Notes the impact of drought and crop failure on food balance sheet. Urges the use of dietary supplements to ensure a balance of nutrients. Describes how parboiling of grains preserves nutritional value. Impediments to improving the diets of all Chinese include an inadequate transportation system, hoarding, speculation, and the lack of new crops.

0979. DAVIS, Ira C. Agriculture in China, *Journal of Geography* 17, 1918, 129–36.

Uses technique of comparing China to the United States in terms of per capita land availability, land use intensiveness, and climate. The major challenge facing Chinese agriculture is the need to support a large, densely packed population. China can meet this challenge based on its superior use of all types of fertilizers, its method of social organization, and the fact that the Chinese have a vegetarian diet. Describes rice cultivation in detail.

0980. DEASY, George F. The Future of Manchurian Agriculture, *Journal of Geography* 37, 1938, 20–27.

Seeks to establish how Manchurian agriculture will adapt to changes in the economic structure of the province. Although land will become available for farming in areas such as the Sungari region, expects that any increases in output or yield will be at decreasing rates, since most new lands have poor soil and scanty rainfall. Therefore, expects agriculture to be of less significance in total economy.

0981. DEASY, G[eorge]. F. Soya Beans in Manchuria, *Economic Geography* 15, 1939, 303–10.

Although soy was first cultivated and used in China around 7000 [*sic*] B.C., it is actually the latest of a series of seed crops to be grown commercially in China. Analysis uses 1930 data and reports that Manchuria is the world's major soy producer, with China proper as the only serious competitor. Manchuria's comparative advantages in soy are related to the fact that this is where the crop was domesticated and Manchuria possesses an appropriate climate, has land available, has relative peace, and features a better railroad system to transport the crop to ports.

0982. DEASY, George F. Tung Oil Production and Trade, *Economic Geography* 16, 1940, 260–74.

Looks at worldwide production and notes that China is the world's largest producer. Main ports for exports are Hong Kong, Shanghai, Canton, and Hankou.

0983. FANG, Fu-an. Notes on the Problem of Food, *China Critic* 3, 1930, 128–32.

The Chinese do not have an adequate diet due to a relative lack of arable land, heavy taxation, and low productivity. Although heavily statistical in nature, main argument is that optimists regarding China's ability to feed itself use data that in fact over-estimate both China's actual and potential output.

0984. FREEBERNE, Michael. Lonely Taiwan Sows for the Future, *Geographical Magazine* 44, 1972, 268–64.

Population growth is seen as the major challenge facing Taiwanese farmers, who can now use the most modern of growing techniques thanks to the work of the United States-Chinese Joint Commission on Rural Reconstruction, land reform, land consolidation, and farmers' associations. The implications and applications of the Taiwan model are constrained by world politics.

0985. GOLAB, L. Wawrzyn. A Study of Irrigation in East Turkistan, *Anthropos* 46, 1951, 187–99.

Main focus is on the "cultivation" strip of loess some six to thirteen miles wide along the base of the Tian Shan. Main concern is for oasis agriculture and how water is delivered for irrigation. Includes details regarding types of irrigation systems, local water law and rights, and religious practices.

0986. GOUROU, Pierre. Notes on China's Unused Uplands, *Pacific Affairs* 21, 1948, 227–38.

Argues that, despite a seemingly high population density, in fact Chinese peasants cultivate very little of the country. They especially avoid hills and mountains, except in Sichuan, Zhejiang, Shandong, and Shaanxi, where terraces are used. Feels that hills and mountains are not used because they do not fit into the vegetable basis of Chinese civilization and not because of unfavorable climatic conditions. Urges exploitation of hills, especially by planting fruit trees, since Chinese consume very little fruit per capita.

0987. GROVE, Robert G., and Robert R. WALKER. Rice Farming in Hong Kong, *Geographical Magazine* 39, 1967, 750–63.

Describes visit to Tung Chung valley on Lantau Island. Major concern is with landscape, accessibility, climate, and water allocation. Fully describes rice cultivation from field preparation through harvesting and marketing. Rice yields are similar to those found in the People's Republic of China in the 1950s.

0988. HALL, Robert Burnett. Agricultural Regions of Asia, Part VII: The Japanese Empire, *Economic Geography* 11, 1935, 33–52.

Taiwan discussed on pp. 36–40. Conditions in the western and eastern parts of the island are contrasted in terms of crops, output, animals, irrigation, and ethnic populations. Role of Japanese colonial government in agricultural development emphasized.

0989. HU, Huan-yong. A New Cotton Belt in China, *Economic Geography* 23, 1948, 60–66.

Focus is on the northern Jiangsu coastal plain. The area was previously used to collect salt, but as soil deposition occurred salt was replaced as the land was reclaimed. Cotton, often grown as the sole crop, is the major use of the land. Both plantations and small proprietors grow the crop. The future of the new industry will depend on political stability and the improvement of dikes and canals.

0990. JEN, Mei-ngo. Agricultural Landscape of Southwest China: A Study of Land Utilization, *Economic Geography* 24, 1948, 157–69.

Deals with Sichuan, Guizhou, and Yunnan as the backbone of free China. Topics descriptively covered include surface features, climate, and land use by topographical region. Estimates a cultivation index of 75 percent.

Main limitations to expanding cultivation are degree of slope in mountains, climate, and soils. Rather than opening new areas to cultivation, urges that existing land be used more efficiently.

0991. LaFLEUR, Albert, and Edwin J. FOSCUE. Agricultural Production in China, *Economic Geography* 3, 1927, 297–308.

Uses 1918 data and makes frequent comparisons with the United States. Dot maps of rice, wheat, sorghum, millet, and cotton included. Concludes that with proper use of scientific methods China can expand agricultural production capacity but only if a strong, peaceful, central government can be established.

0992. LAMPREY, Charles. Notes of a Journey in the North-West Neighborhood of Peking, *Journal, Royal Geographical Society* 37, 1867, 235–68.

Emphasizes Manchuria's dependence on cotton production and processing. Yields have been improved by use of a cotton-millet crop rotation cycle.

0993. LEE, Frank C. Land Redistribution in Communist China, *Pacific Affairs* 21, 1948, 20–32.

Outlines salient points of Basic Agrarian Law. Since in 1948 it is too early to conduct quantitative studies of the impact of implementing the law, the pre-1948 programs undertaken by the Chinese Communist Party are described and analyzed. Includes actual text of law and compares its provisions to laws and programs of the Kuomintang for the territory under its control as well as Japanese agrarian programs in Manchuria. Optimistic about success of law.

0994. LEE, Shu-ching. Pattern of Land Utilization and Possible Expansion of Cultivated Land in China, *Journal of Land and Public Utility Economics* 23, 1947, 142–52.

Provides estimates of total and cultivated land areas in China. Enumerates topographic and climatic constraints to expanding agriculture. Describes patterns of land use in the context of George Perkins Marsh's concept of land as modified by human action and Confucian "this worldliness," with its emphasis on savings, landholding, and preferences for human over material resources.

0995. LIANG, C[hi].-S[en]. Three Types of Agricultural Water Use in the Yangtze Basin, *Chung Chi Journal* 5, 1965, 40–59.

Provides a comparison and contrast of water use in the Tongting Basin, Taihu Basin, and Chengdu Plain. Includes details regarding dams, dikes, and canals. Background material includes information about hydrology, geomorphology, topography, and agricultural potential of all three areas and their subdivisions.

0996. LIU, Jung-chao. Fertilizer Supply and Grain Production in Communist China, *Journal of Farm Economics* 47, 1965, 915–32.

Chinese planners recognize the limits on agricultural production imposed by lack of appropriate fertilizers. Therefore, the government has emphasized the need to increase fertilizer supply by increasing domestic production and imports. Describes the composition of fertilizers, yield responses, and the ability of fertilizers to help China meet its food needs. Concludes that fertilizer alone can only provide enough food to meet 1957 levels of nutrition. Therefore, fertilizer availability will have to increase at rates greater than 2 percent a year. No opinion expressed as to whether China will or should meet this goal via greater domestic production or increased imports.

0997. LOWDERMILK, W. C., and D. R. WICKES. Ancient Irrigation in China Brought Up to Date, *Scientific Monthly* 55, 1942, 209–25.

Retelling of the history of the Wei River canal. Details of modern canal construction and maintenance are also described.

0998. MURAKOSHI, Nobuo, and Glenn T. TREWARTHA. Land Utilization Maps of Manchuria, *Geographical Review* 20, 1930, 480–95.

Includes some twenty maps of population, physical variables, and crop production. Notes that there was no clear boundary between Mongolia and Manchuria. As such, the focus is on the so-called three eastern provinces and part of Mongolia. Reviews agricultural development and extent of cash crop production. Notes limited rice cultivation. Contrasts recent Chinese and Japanese migration to area.

0999. MURPHEY, Rhoads. The Food Supply of Shanghai, *Far Eastern Survey* 17, 1948, 133–35.

Describes how food is supplied for what was the world's fifth-largest city in 1948. Divides rural hinterland of city based on physical environment and accessibility. Notes that rice can be profitably shipped no further than 75 miles and thus foreign sources for this staple are common. Categorizes foods and delivery by transportation type. Notes the need for an expanded railroad system if internal Chinese markets are to be fully exploited.

1000. NEEDHAM, Joseph. China: The Land and the People, *Pacific Affairs* 22, 1949, 282–90.

Extended review of book that appeared in 1948 by Gerald F. Winfield with same title as article. Argues that the greatest challenge to developing China's agriculture is getting farmers to adopt a composting method that will kill all the pathogens in night soil. Describes the pathogens present in soil and their public health consequences. Disagrees with Winfield's assessment of the efficacy of traditional Chinese medicine and his discounting of Chinese technology. Nevertheless, feels Winfield's book can play a positive role in correcting stereotypes of China.

1001. OUTERBRIDGE, Rev. Leonard M. Seeds of China's Arid Areas, *Annals, American Academy of Political and Social Science* 192, 1930, 99–104.

Sees new and improved seeds as a short-term solution to the problem of aridity in China. Urges that long-term solutions based on improved irrigation be undertaken as new seeds are adopted. Describes experiments at the agricultural station in Fenzhou, Shanxi, where over one hundred new varieties of seeds were tested and some twenty-seven actually introduced for widespread cultivation. Most promising crops are milo and the *feterita* and *hegira* varieties of duct corn.

1002. ROBINSON, H. The Chinese Fishing Industry, *Geography* 41, 1956, 158–66.

Starts with assumption that fish is an important part of the Chinese diet. Describes the financial and organizational status of the industry, the types of fish caught, the location of major fishing ports, fishing techniques, and production levels. Improvements in the industry will require the adoption of modern vessels and technology and better means of either transporting or preserving fish so that they arrive at market in the best saleable condition. Expects the government to play a major role in developing the industry, especially as standards of living increase.

1003. ROSE, John. Sinjao: A Chinese Commune, *Geography* 51, 1966, 379–83.

Xinzao is located southeast of Canton. A map of land use supplements the description of size of commune and extent of cultivated land. Provides a history of commune's founding and administrative structure. The commune's success stems from its specialization in vegetables, fruits, and fish; the inclusion of food processing, machinery repairs, and embroidery as industrial activities; and its proximity to Canton. Sees commune members as healthy, well fed, and happy, despite their shabby appearance.

1004. SALTER, C[hristopher]. L. Changing Role of Sugar in the Taiwan Economy, *Tunghai Journal* [*Tunghai Hsuehpao*] 4, 1962, 1–20.

Analysis divided into three parts: factors contributing to Taiwan's comparative advantage in sugar such as climate, topography, soil, and proximity to market; the role of sugar in Taiwan's early, pre-Japanese history; and internal demand, production, and pressures to plant other crops.

1005. SALTER, C[hristopher]. L. The Litany of Tachai and the Foolish Old Man: Agricultural Landscape Modification in Mainland China, *Professional Geographer* 24, 1972, 113–17.

Seeks to explicate the facts behind the 1964 exhortation "In Agriculture, Learn from Dazhai." Describes the size, location, economy, and physical constraints of Dazhai. Recounts the "Fable of the Foolish Old Man" and how he modified the landscape by hard work. Sees slogans used in agricultural development as part of the local-scale emphasis of the Great Leap Forward.

1006. SHAW, Earl B. Swine Industry in China, *Economic Geography* 14, 1938, 381–97.

Pig breeding goes back to 3000 B.C.E. in China. Pork is seen as preferred meat for Chinese Buddhists. Comments that feeding practices rely on the pig as scavenger. Notes close relationship between distribution of pigs and people in China. Reviews housing, breeding, marketing, and health of pigs. Describes in detail pork products exported. Sees improvements in quality and quantity of production restricted by lack of government funding and political instability.

1007. SOWERBY, Arthur de C[arle]. The Domestic Animals of Ancient China, *China Journal* 23, 1935, 233–43.

Uses literary, artistic, and historical evidence to compile a list of domestic animals in the Zhou and Han periods.

1008. SPENCER, J[ospeh]. E[arle]. Agriculture and Population in Relation to Economic Planning, *Annals, American Academy of Political and Social Science* 321, 1959, 62–70.

Reviews post-1949 phases of land reform, cooperatization, and collectivization. Notes need to improve technology. Argues that government's ability to feed the population is better than it was before, despite planning mistakes. Optimistic regarding the future since food production is increasing faster than population growth. Concludes that to be truly successful agricultural reforms must take into account the needs and desires of the poor peasants.

1009. STEWARD, John R. The Soya Bean and Manchuria, *Far Eastern Survey* 5, 1936, 221–26.

Analyzes the comparative advantage of Manchuria in the world soy market. Wonders what impact the expansion of soy production in the United States will have on Manchurian production and sales.

1010. THOMPSON, J. Charles. Trawling the China Seas, *National Geographic Magazine* 97, 1950, 381–95.

Photo essay of life on traditional Chinese fishing boats as they search for fish off China's coasts. Touches on boat construction and modernization as well as the life and work routines of sailors when they are at sea.

1011. TORRANCE, T. Origin and History of the Irrigation Works of the Chengtu Plain, *Journal, Royal Asiatic Society, North China Branch*, new series 55, 1924, 60–65.

Literary analysis of Chinese historical documents aimed at establishing who built the irrigation works. Concludes that the preponderance of evidence favors Li Ping.

1012. TREWARTHA, Glenn T. Ration Maps of China's Farms and Crops, *Geographical Review* 28, 1938, 102–11.

Uses 1932 data to map at provincial level sixteen agricultural variables, including specific crops such as rice and topics such as cultivated and irrigated areas. Most of text consists of descriptive notes accompanying the maps.

1013. TREWARTHA, Glenn T., and Sheu-jen YANG. Notes on Rice Growing in China, *Annals, Association of American Geographers* 38, 1948, 277–81.

Authors challenge Chang Chi-yun's 1946 article [item 0211] on two points: Chang's contentions that triple cropping is found in most of southern China and that double cropping is found in most of China north of the Changjiang.

1014. TSCHUDI, Aadel Brun. People's Communes in China, *Norsk Geografisk Tidsskrift* 27:1, 1973, 5–34.

Based on fieldwork in 1957 and 1971, provides a basically optimistic evaluation of agricultural policies of the People's Republic as implemented through the commune program. Sees Chinese emphasis on regional autarky as logical goal in a country with a large population and poor transportation system. Concludes that China's experience with communes is relevant to that of other developing countries.

1015. TWITCHETT, Denis. Some Remarks on Irrigation under the T'ang, *T'oung Pao*, series 2, 48, 1960, 175–94.

Basically a refutation of Wittvogel's hydrologic society, as expressed in *Oriental Despotism*, as it would have applied to China. Focuses on who in the Chinese government was actually responsible for water and irrigation. Reviews the structure of government offices, water and irrigation regulations issued, and the role of local authorities and individual initiatives in local situations. Concludes that in contrast to what Wittvogel's hypothesis would predict the central Chinese government had a minimum role in ensuring water and irrigation to local users.

1016. TUNG, Shih-tsin. Food Supply of China, *Scientific Monthly* 23, 1926, 454–61.

Despite appearances, China is not an overcrowded country. Readers reminded that each province of China is about the size of an average European country but that the provinces are hampered by inadequate transportation, which limits the ability to readily move food to where it is needed. Argues that it must be remembered that data on cultivated areas and output are either inaccurate or inadequate. In normal years, sufficient amounts of food are produced. Increased production is possible because there are large tracts of land that can be either reclaimed or put under cultivation for the first time. If China's agricultural resources were fully developed, there is a possibility that it could be a net food exporter, which would enable it to industrialize.

1017. VALE, J. Irrigation of the Chengtu Plain and Beyond, *Journal, Royal Asiatic Society, North China Branch* 33, 1899–1900, 22–36; 36, 1905, 36–50.

Describes the four main dams (Capital River, General Relief, Frog's Chin, and Great Transformation) that make up the irrigation system in study area. In addition to technical and engineering details, provides a description of the administration, inspection, and repair of the system. Sees further economic potential of irrigation system once area has access to new markets, which a railroad would provide.

1018. VanderMEER, Canute. Changing Water Control in a Taiwanese Rice Field Irrigation System, *Annals, Association of American Geographers* 58, 1968, 720–47.

Study of how farmers along the Nan-hung Canal, adjacent to Puli City, adapted after 1959–60 field studies showed that rice production could be maximized with less, not more, water.

1019. VanderMEER, Canute. Water Thievery in a Rice Irrigation System in Taiwan, *Annals, Association of American Geographers* 61, 1971, 156–79.

Investigates the operation of the Nan-hung gravity canal near Puli City during the 1930s and 1960s to see if there are any temporal or spatial patterns of water thievery. Thefts were expected since farmers could not always get the amount of water they wanted to cultivate rice. Describes the types of thefts against the background of water rights and customs. Over time, thievery became less of a problem as cropping systems and canals were improved. Provides a series of thirteen conclusions regarding general principles of thievery in water systems and how such behavior can be avoided and eliminated.

1020. WARD, F. Langdon. Tibet as Grazing Land, *Geographical Journal* 110, 1947, 60–75.

Argues that the main economic activity of Tibetans, grazing, has been overlooked by geographers and explorers. Notes sharp contrast between land use in deserts and grazing areas. Includes mention of flora and fauna of areas and potential for upgrading of flocks and grasslands. Attributes political problems to lack of clearly defined borders or boundaries.

1021. WARWICK, Adam. Farmers since the Days of Noah: China's Remarkable System of Agriculture Has Kept Alive the Densest Population in the World, *National Geographic Magazine* 51, 1927, 469–500.

Discusses the Chinese mythical traditions regarding the origins of agriculture. Traces development of cultivation from loess areas along Huang Ho. Sees the greatest triumph of Chinese farming as the ability to maintain soil fertility. Describes population densities supported, mean farm size, types of rice farming, and the lack of modern tools. Catalogs cash and imported crops grown alongside rice. Despite the frugality, industriousness, and endurance of Chinese farmers, without better sources of fuel and transportation it will be hard to increase marketing of products. Includes twenty-one pictures of rice culture.

1022. WASHENKO, Steve. Improved Drainage in China's Hai Ho Valley Increases Farm Output, *Foreign Agriculture* 10:9, 1972, 5, 16.

As a result of a program of building dikes between 1949 and 1971, the Hai Ho Valley now has 8.2 million acres freed from periodic flooding and waterlogging. Protection is year round.

1023. YAO, Augustine Y. M. Estimated Trends of Land Use in China, *Professional Geographer* 20, 1968, 149–54.

Reviews previous estimates going as far back as 1918. Concludes past data inflated but nevertheless argues that there is no indication that crop land expanded after 1949. Urbanization, in the form of new roads, airports, factories, and homes, in fact is contributing to a net loss of agricultural land, especially in places such as Zhejiang, Fujian, Jiangxi, and Kirin. Classifies land use and attempts to identify types and locations of areas for agricultural expansion.

1024. YEN, Chiang-kwoh. The Tung Region of China, *Economic Geography* 19, 1943, 418–27.

The production of tung oil is determined as much by the transportation system as by the type of climate and soils that the tung tree prefers. The tree thrives best at elevations ranging from two hundred to two thousand meters above sea level. Describes cultivation, distribution, and exports for 1913–41.

See also items 0202, 0226, 0237, 0246, 0455, 0457, 0543, 0679, 0943, and 0953.

16. Industry

1025. ANON. Salt for China's Daily Rice, *National Geographic Magazine* 86, 1944, 329–36.

Photo essay showing production and distribution of salt in Sichuan.

1026. BALLAS, Donald J. Development of China's Iron and Steel Industry through the Ch'ing Period, *Virginia Geographer* 9:1, 1974, 13–19.

Starts with Zhou period. Describes objects made. Doubts that the technology for producing cast iron was imported. Notes role of coal outcrops in determining location of iron and steel industry. Includes a table with estimates of output for period 1806–1928. Provides estimates of Western explorers regarding the quality and quantity of ores.

1027. BENHAM, F. C. Growth of Manufacturing in Hong Kong, *International Affairs* 32, 1956, 456–63.

Begins by lamenting the lack of hard data due to difficulties in estimating the number of refugees in the colony. Notes shift in entrepôt function and trade. Traces impact of World War II on trade patterns and how after the war, with the shift in Chinese policy toward the Soviet Union, Hong Kong's trade with China declined. Describes changes in type and organization of manufacturing before and after 1956. Sees Hong Kong's greatest deficits for industrialization in its population and lack of land; conversely, its greatest assets are its good government, good services, and a trained labor force. Hong Kong should prove to be a good model for other Asian areas seeking to develop manufacturing.

1028. BURTON, Wilbur. The Natural Resources of the Far East: A Qualitative Survey, *Asiatic Review*, new series 33, 1937, 787–95.

Argues that, except for Manchuria, China is extraordinarily poor in minerals, with the exception of tungsten and antimony. Admits that there has never been a complete quantitative survey of China's subsurface resources; what surveys have been conducted have been disappointing, as hopes of large mineral findings were not realized, especially for Sichuan, Yunnan, and Xinjiang. What resources were found are inadequate for long-run development. Quotes heavily from the works of Cressey.

1029. CHANG, Kuei-shang. Fertilizer Manufacturing in Mainland China, *Proceedings, Association of American Geographers* 4, 1972, 28–32.

Focuses on the quality of the technical base for fertilizer production. Emphasizes the need for spatial planning of fertilizer production within the context of regional specialization of provinces. Evaluates the resource base for fertilizer production. Although the expansion of the railroad network and upgrading of fertilizer factories are factors favoring the expansion of production, imports of foreign fertilizers are expected to continue for foreseeable future.

1030. CHANG, Kuei-shang. Geographical Basis for Industrial Development in Northwest China, *Economic Geography* 39, 1963, 341–50.

Begins essay with a comparison of the fate and direction of industrialization under free enterprise and communist systems. Argues that the main raw material advantage of northwest is its energy riches, especially oil and coal. Mentions the availability of other raw materials, including hydropower, iron ore, ferro-minerals, and salt beds. Lists advantages and disadvantages of area in context of Chinese economic development. Feels greatest challenges to development in area are creating transportation links to the coast, building and maintaining urban centers, and feeding the population working in planned industrial centers.

1031. CHANG, Kuei-sheng. Nuclei Formation of Communist China's Iron and Steel Industry, *Annals, Association of American Geographers* 60, 1970, 257–85.

Sees the pre-1949 location of iron and steel industry as a function of transportation, capital, and (international) market conditions. Post-1949 distribution is related to the development of new raw material sources, especially for coal and iron ore. Important centers of Anshan, Wuhan, and Baotou treated separately.

1032 CHIU, Yan-tsz. Chemical Industry in Kwangtung Province, *Journal, Royal Asiatic Society, North China Branch*, new series 50, 1919, 133–43.

Development of the chemical industry in China is inhibited due to the fact that chemistry was not in the educational curriculum and therefore there is no link between industry and centers of learning. Lack of modern, up-to-date equipment also hurts an industry still using techniques that are basically four thousand years old. The Guangdong industry got its major start only in reaction to the availability of Western products. Lists factories, their locations, and sources of raw materials.

1033. DRAPER, Marshall D. Tin Industry of Yunnan, China, *Mining and Metallurgy* 12, 1931, 178–86, 242–47.

Notes that China is the world's largest tin producer and exporter, using shipping facilities in Haiphong. Describes distribution of mining towns, accommodations available for foreigners, technology in mining, and role of politics in production and distribution of products. Expresses concern for conditions under which the laborers must work. Native industry hampered by paucity of surveys and restrictive regulations. If Western mining methods were adopted, output could be increased rapidly. However, if traditional methods are used, continued slow growth is to be expected.

1034. ERROLL, F. J. Industrial Progress in China, *Geographical Magazine* 31, 1958, 265–76.

Describes a 1957 visit to Canton, Shanghai, Beijing, and Shenyang. Concedes that fieldwork raised more questions than there are answers for, such as what the harvest is like and whether Chinese workers desire freedom.

1035. ErSELCUK, Muzaffa. The Iron and Steel Industry in China, *Economic Geography* 32, 1956, 347–71.

Analysis of steel output in the context of the first five-year plan. Notes a shortage of geological, technical, and statistical data needed for a full investigation of steel and iron in China. Especially dubious as to whether the Soviet Union will prove to be a reliable source of funding and technical assistance. Describes distribution and estimates of raw material reserves. Provides a description, with historical background, of thirteen major steel and iron centers, including Anshan, Baotou, Tianjin, Hankou, and Chongqing. Despite the fund of knowledge China can drawn on, does not expect the same returns to capital investment found in Western Europe and United States. Transportation is seen as the major long-term bottleneck.

1036. FIELD, Robert Michael, Nicholas R. LARDY, and John Philip MERSON. Industrial Output by Province in China, 1947–73, *China Quarterly* 63, 1975, 409–34.

Compares different measures of output using linked indices. Data included in tables. Concludes that provincial and national data are in close agreement and therefore the product of a unified accounting and reporting system.

1037. FONG, H. D. Prospects for China's Industrialization, *Pacific Affairs* 15, 1942, 44–62.

Sees China as being a member of the class of countries that can industrialize. Reviews history of industry from early-nineteenth-century crafts production through 1937. Recounts challenges of moving and relocating manufacturing capacity from areas occupied by the Japanese. Notes impact of Japanese on economy of Manchuria. Argues that China's greatest need is for capital investment and as such the small-scale cooperative movement is not an appropriate model to meet China's needs. Urges overseas Chinese to provide investment funds. Describes advantages and disadvantages of China in terms of resources, markets, skilled labor, and transportation. Optimistic that once peace is restored the government will implement appropriate policies to promote industrialization.

1038. FREEBERNE, Michael. China Promotes Local Industries, *Geographical Magazine* 43, 1971, 505–7, 509, 511.

Describes distribution of small-scale industry around 1970 at provincial level. Sees the development of small-scale industry as part of plan to both decentralize manufacturing and achieve regional and national autarky. Small-scale industries can help redress the irrational regional imbalance in manufacturing China inherited in 1949 and permit China to exploit all available technologies under the "Walking on Two Legs" principle. Notes the strategic value of decentralization, given the 1969 Sino-Soviet border clashes. Argues that implementation of small-scale industries is proceeding more slowly than the Great Leap Forward, thus ensuring a greater chance of success. Concludes that local impact of small-scale industry will be evident before its impact at the national level. Provides case studies for iron and coal, machinery, and hydropower.

1039. GAGE, Eugenia. Industrial Development in Formosa, *Economic Geography* 26, 1950, 214–22.

Although industrialization came to Taiwan late in the Japanese period, by the end of 1945 the island had credible power, sugar, paper, cement, petroleum, fertilizer, aluminum, and caustic goods production capacity and production. Sees Taiwan's proximity to other Asian markets, its tropical and subtropical climates, hydropower, and literate population as major advantages favoring further industrialization. The major drawbacks to rapid growth are a lack of native capital for investment, a lack of raw materials for heavy industry, and an unclear set of government development policies. Once these obstacles are overcome, war damage and the ill effects of the repatriation of Japanese technical and managerial workers can easily be overcome.

1040. GRADZDANZEV, Andrew J. Manchuria: An Industrial Survey, *Pacific Affairs* 18, 1945, 321–39.

Defines study area by comparing Manchuria's size and population to those of the United States and Europe. Notes that despite Japanese, Chinese, and Korean immigration the economy is hampered by the lack of skilled workers. Estimates reserves of raw materials. Despite being basically an agricultural economy, there are reasons to be optimistic that Manchuria will play a major role in the world economy since its communications, especially railroads, are well developed. Discusses Japanese role and rationale in developing industry.

1041. HARTWELL, Robert. Market, Technology, and the Structure of Enterprise in the Development of the Eleventh Century Chinese Iron and Steel Industry, *Journal of Economic History* 26, 1966, 29–58.

Sees eleventh-century China as experiencing an early industrial revolution similar to the one enjoyed in Europe between the Crusades and the French Revolution. In general, processing of minerals such as alum, salt, and mercury and the creation of consumer products such as ships, paper, and books were associated with a growing economy. The extraction and refining of ferrous ores was especially important to this process. Describes the geographic distribution of the industry and the financial and ownership structure of all phases of steel making and compares the industrial organization to the European *arbeitsgenossenschaften*. Remarks on mining technology and general problems of supply. Industry was centered in triangle defined by lines connecting southern Hebei, northern Jiangsu, and Henan. Kaifeng was at the center of the industry.

1042. HERMAN, Theodore. Cultural Factors in the Location of the Swatow Lace and Needlework Industry, *Annals, Association of American Geographers* 46, 1956, 122–28.

Five factors account for the location of the industry in Shantou: prior existence of a similar craft in nearby Chaoyang, dynastic decline necessitating a means of supplementing household incomes, arrival of missionaries who taught lace making and needlework, the preference of Chinese women to work part time at home, and both Chinese and Western entrepreneurs expanding lace trade by strengthening of the raw materials distribution and product collection systems.

1043. HSIA, Ronald. Changes in the Location of China's Steel Industry, *China Quarterly* 17, 1964, 125–33.

Article is a chapter from author's book on steel in Communist China. Location measured by distribution in capacity and output. Employs sevenfold regional division of China as defined in 1958 by the Chinese Communist Central Committee. Since industrial dispersion is subservient to the objective of maximizing capital-output ratios, the distribution of capacity has become more concentrated over time, while output has become more dispersed.

1044. HSIAO, Ch'ien. China's Industrial Cooperatives, *Geographical Magazine* 15, 1942, 126–31.

History of INDUSCO movement in China, which started as an answer to the refugee problem created by the war with Japan. Cooperative activities focus on a desire to be self-sufficient in civilian goods.

1045. JAMES, H. F. Industrial China, *Economic Geography* 5, 1929, 1–21.

Notes that more people in China are engaged in manufacturing than in the United States but that they are found in rural areas. Manufacturing in China, then, is not of the modern type. Dates industrial revolution in China to 1890. Assumes that given its size and history, China should be a greater economic power, especially since it has sufficient coal to modernize. Doubts China will accomplish this due to its geographic isolation, its lack of efficient transportation, and the power of custom and tradition.

1046. LACY, Walter N. Crude Sugar Making in China, *Journal of Geography* 16, 1917, 15–16.

Brief description of machinery and buildings involved in small-scale production of sugar. A typical small-scale factory can produce between sixty and one hundred pounds of sugar a day. Notes heavy reliance on bamboo as fuel.

1047. LAI, [David] Chuen-yan. Small Industries in Hong Kong, *Town Planning Review* 44, 1973, 135–46.

Based on a 1970 survey of some 188 firms, describes the distribution, structure, and locational and economic behavior of small manufacturing establishments in a blighted 280-acre part of Hong Kong Island known as the 1964 Urban Renewal District. Sees medium-scale manufacturing as the future of a prosperous manufacturing sector. Provides list of the intraurban locational factors about which entrepreneurs are most concerned. Notes that entrepreneurs would prefer to remain in the district, close to their residences, rather than relocating to a new site.

1048. LAI, David C[huen]. Y[an]., and D. J. DWYER. Tsuen Wan: A New Industrial Town in Hong Kong, *Geographical Review* 54, 1964, 151–69.

Despite a lack of raw materials, Hong Kong industry developed as a result of investments from China proper, the influx of refugees, and government policies that favored free enterprise and free trade. Provides information regarding the rationale for government developing a new town, the town's plan, fast pace of growth, and industrial structure. The major problem confronting planners involved the assimilation of farmers displaced when the town was built.

1049. LEE, T. S. Coal Resources of China, *Asiatic Review*, new series 31, 1935, 571–85.

Region by region survey of resources and production. Remarks that large regional variations in methods and costs of production exist. The key to the future of coal production will be the expansion of modern transportation. Coal seen as an example of how wealth in China does not always live up to promises.

1050. LEITH, C. K. The Mineral Resources of the Far East, *Foreign Affairs* 4, 1926, 433–42.

Feels that enough exploration has been completed to disclose the main outlines of future potential production. This is especially important because other writers tend to explain the low levels of production by referring to the lack of exploration. Not optimistic that sufficient reserves have been discovered to offer hope of an industrialized China. Sees promise of future finds as a myth.

1051. LENZ, Frank B. The World's Ancient Porcelain Center, *National Geographic Magazine* 38, 1920, 391–406.

Focus is on the town of Qingdezhen, Jiangxi. Notes that lack of a wall means settlement is not legally a city. Uses itinerary format and covers the topics of site, location, accessibility, history, population, raw materials, and production of porcelain. Notes technology for making and firing the dishes. Reports that the classification of products is a function of shape, design, and color.

1052. LIANG, C[hi].-S[en]. New Locational Patterns of Industries in the Middle Yangtze Provinces, *Chung Chi Journal* 5, 1966, 167–94.

Main focus on reasons why Sichuan can be considered unique. Includes details regarding location of raw materials and industrial sites. Describes projects for redistribution of manufacturing in Hubei, Hunan, and Jiangsu Provinces.

1053. LIEU, O. S. Vital Problems in China's Industry, *Annals, American Academy of Political and Social Science* 152, 1930, 181–83.

Chinese industries suffer from labor unrest, foreign competition, continuous civil war, irregular taxation, and lack of trained and experienced management personnel. China's greatest industrial asset is its plentiful supply of labor.

1054. LIN, Shu-yen. Salt Manufacture in Hong Kong, *Journal, Royal Asiatic Society, Hong Kong Branch* 7, 1967, 138–51.

Reprint of article that appeared in *Hong Kong Naturalist* 10:1, 1940. Main areas for extracting salt from seawater are in Tai-O on Lantau Island, Shataukok in Starling Inlet, and Sam Hsin in Castle Peak Bay. Describes sites and techniques used to extract salt including leaching and ordinary solar evaporation. Estimates of output included.

1055. McCLURE, F. A. The Native Paper Industry in Kwangtung, *Lingnan Science Journal* 3, 1927, 255–68.

The best Chinese paper is produced in an area northeast of Shuizhou, where the local industry is based on *phyllostachys edulis*. Describes production, working conditions, distribution of raw materials, and ancillary supplies.

1056. MORRISON, Hedda M. Making Books in China, *Canadian Geographical Journal* 39:6, 1949, 232–41.

Brief history of bookmaking in China illustrated by processes involved, from papermaking through sales.

16. *Industry* 249

1057. MYERS, Ramon H. Cotton Textile Handicrafts and the Development of the Cotton Textile Industry in Modern China, *Economic History Review* 18, 1965, 614–32.

Provides history of pre-Qing raw cotton and cotton textile production. Notes changes in regional and structural patterns of modernizing production and trade after Opium War. Sees cotton as an example of trend in China toward specialization in use of both land and labor.

1058. NIKOLUEV, S. A., and R. I. MOLODTSOVA. Present Status of the Chinese Iron and Steel Industry, *Soviet Geography: Review and Translation* 1, 1960, 55–71.

Uses mostly Chinese sources. Concerned with size of reserves and output. Notes that the Great Leap Forward had a positive impact on production of pig iron but not on output of steel. Includes a map showing the number of plants by city.

1059. ORCHARD, John E. Industrialization in Japan, China Mainland, and India: Some World Implications, *Annals, Association of American Geographers* 50, 1960, 193–215.

In this Association of American Geographers presidential address, the commonalities of the three countries, an agricultural sector plagued by low productivity in all sectors, and the need to create more jobs for those released from agriculture as productivity there rises are highlighted. Argues that industrialization will lead to increased world trade competition. In China section, there is a discussion of the progress China has made toward recovery under the first two five-year plans. Questions whether industrialization has not already absorbed surplus rural labor, which will result in overall labor shortages in the near future.

1060. OVDIYENKO, I. Kh. Basic Shifts in the Structure and Distribution of China's Industry, *Soviet Geography: Review and Translation* 2:1, 1961, 47–53.

Begins by noting the post-1949 emphasis on heavy industry as an appropriate base for all future industrial developments. Provides details regarding five-year plans. Notes role of military viewpoint in the development of new industrial regions, especially in the northeastern, northwestern, Central Wuhan, and western regions. Industrialization emphasizes dual development—rehabilitation of the old and establishment of the new. The overall goals of industrial planning are to diminish regional disparities and strengthen regional autarky.

1061. OVDIYENKO, I. Kh. The New Geography of Industry of China, *Soviet Geography: Review and Translation* 1:4, 1960, 63–77.

A catalog of the accomplishments of the Communist goverment and Party in restoring industry. Emphasis on restructuring and relocating what had been built by Western entrepreneurs. Expresses admiration for Chinese use of multiple levels of technology and handicrafts. Notes use of socialist locational principles, including the bringing of industry to both the sources of raw materials and markets. Details for specific industries such as coal, iron, petroleum, hydropower, chemicals, and textiles included.

1062. PRICE, Dalias A. China's Coking Coal, *Illinois Bulletin of Geography* 10, 1947, 9–12.

Not available for annotation.

1063. PRUITT, Ida. Small-Scale Cooperative Industry in China, *Journal of Geography* 41, 1942, 161–68.

Begins with a brief history of Western exports to China. Notes impact of the Japanese invasion on growth and distribution of Chinese industry. Small-scale workshops are seen as a means of increasing output and providing jobs for refugees fleeing Japanese occupied areas. Attributes idea of adopting small-scale industries to Rewi Alley, a New Zealander who supports the Chinese Communist Party. Generally the advantages of small-scale industries include the supply of war materials, the development of raw materials, the provision of a social life for workers, and the establishment of democracy.

1064. PRYOR, E. G. Workshops in Domestic Premises: A Hong Kong Case Study, *Pacific Viewpoint* 13, 1972, 169–86.

Report based on surveys conducted in western district of Hong Kong and Shau Shui Po, Kowloon. Describes number, size, distribution, employment patterns, years of operation, and site satisfaction levels of entrepreneurs for broad types of industries. Contrasts the economic benefits of workshops with their fire and safety hazards. Notes that without an improved legal framework government's control of these workshops will be restricted, as seen by their diffusion to the new towns of Kwun Tong and Tsuen Wan, where theoretically they should not be permitted. Such workshops will be hard to eliminate since they are an integral part of the small- and medium-sized business structure of the economic life of Hong Kong.

16. *Industry* 251

1065. READ, Thomas T. Chinese Iron: A Puzzle, *Harvard Journal of Asiatic Studies* 2, 1937, 398–407.

Argues that the art of iron smelting and working did not arrive in China from India via Sichuan but developed indigenously. Sichuan was not the historical center of the iron industry, despite mention of it in the classic *Yu-kung*. Rather, the birthplace of iron technology will be found in southern and southeastern Shanxi.

1066. READ, Thomas T. Economic Geography: Aspects of China's Iron Industry, *Geographical Review* 33, 1943, 42–55.

Notes that modern interest in the topic can be traced to von Richthofen's 1870–72 letters to the Shanghai Chamber of Commerce. Argues that iron use in premodern China was mainly confined to cutting tools. The major impetus for a modern industry was the demand for rails needed to build railroads. Describes individual plants built by European and Japanese investors by location. Notes impact of Japanese invasion on distribution of industry. Feels that Xigang Province has necessary raw materials to be a center of any future iron industry. Based on Japanese experiences in Manchuria, concludes that the international trade in iron and steel will be more important in developing a Chinese iron industry than location of raw materials or internal markets.

1067. ROBINSON, H. W. The Hairnet Industry in Northern China, *National Geographic Magazine* 44, 1923, 327–36.

Sees production of hair nets as an example of both a new industry and the changes in domestic demand fostered by exposure to the West. The industry developed to replace imports. It was centered in North China, as this area had a good supply of human hair, cheap labor, and a history of cottage industry. The raw material was collected by barbers. The major disadvantages of the production in a cottage industry format includes the physical strains on workers producing a product in unheated, poorly lit rooms and the lack of standards, resulting in imperfect products. However, such cottage industries provided an income to sustain the rural poor during the 1920–21 famine.

1068. RODGERS, Allan. The Manchurian Iron and Steel Industry and Its Resource Base, *Geographical Review* 38, 1948, 41–54.

Uses wartime data to evaluate whether a resurgence in industry in Manchuria after the war will be the basis for any future Chinese industrialization. Notes how the Japanese from 1930 to 1944 drove all foreign competition out of Manchuria. Describes resource base, iron production districts, and actual production. Notes wartime shortages of both raw materials and final products in Manchuria. Postwar production was down due to war damage and deterioration in the quality of ores mined. Concludes that Manchuria has the resources available to help China rebuild but expresses concern regarding Soviet role in any joint development schemes.

1069. SHABAD, Theodore. China's Resources for Heavy Industry, *Focus* 9:3, 1958, 1–6.

Answers positively the query regarding whether or not China has adequate resources to industrialize on a large scale due to the systematic efforts of geologists, which has resulted in the discovery of new mineral deposits. Expresses concern, however, regarding whether China will have sufficient numbers of trained technicians to run its mines and factories. Concludes with note that the contending approaches to industrialization found in China and India need to be continually contrasted.

1070. SMITH, F. P. Chinese Chemical Manufacturers, *Journal, Royal Asiatic Society, North China Branch*, new series 6, 1869–70, 139–48.

Argues that, contrary to other reports, an indigenous Chinese chemical industry does exist, albeit one that meets the needs of a Chinese educational and social setting. Cites specific minerals, locations of processing, and finished or final products available.

1071. SOWERBY, Arthur de C[arle]. China's Resources Worth Having, *China Journal* 27, 1937, 146–48.

Provides a catalog of the valuable resources of North China, including coal, iron, salt, mineral oils, livestock, hemp, ramie, cotton, and wool. Unfavorably compares Japanese resource takings to those of German treaty ports.

1072. SOWERBY, Arthur de C[arle]. Shanghai Industrially Considered, *China Journal* 12, 1930, 233–47.

Despite a general lack of availability of statistics for industrial production in Shanghai, there is no question that the city is a major center for both family-based craft and modern industrial production. Essay divided into distinct occupational categories. Describes precisely concentrations of industry. Sees Shanghai's chief asset as its large population, which provides both cheap labor and a market. Concludes with synopsis of labor situation in all major industrial branches.

16. Industry

1073. SPENCER, Joseph E[arle]. Gypsum and Salt Mining in Central Hupeh, China, *Economic Geography* 14, 1938, 282–86.

The history of gypsum production is related to that of salt since the two are associated geologically. Production is restricted to small mines, using little machine power. The main mining techinque involves flooding a mine for ten to fifteen months and then pumping the brine to the surface, where it is boiled. Locationally, gypsum is processed in Yingcheng and then shipped to coastal cities, while salt is sold locally. Includes description of daily lives of miners. Refers reader to item 1074.

1074. SPENCER, Joseph Earle. Salt in China, *Geographical Review* 15, 1935, 353–66.

Describes the raw materials of salt production, the technology used in exploiting the raw materials, the marketing and transportation of the finished product, and the role of salt in the tax system. Maps of areas of production, consumption, and both production and retail costs included in analysis.

1075. STEWARD, John R. Japan and the Manchurian Iron Industry, *Journal of Geography* 32, 1933, 181–90.

Goal of article is to assess the value of Manchurian iron resources in relation to Japan's desire to free its iron and steel industry from dependence on foreign sources of raw materials. Describes the extent of dependence. Concludes that given the unprofitable operation history of iron production in Manchuria, due in part to poor ores, that absent massive Japanese investments there, Manchuria will not reduce Japanese dependence on ore or scrap imports.

1076. VINACKE, Harold M. Obstacles to Industrial Development in China, *Annals, American Academy of Political and Social Science* 152, 1930, 173–80.

Chinese industry suffers from primitive economic organization, an imbalance in natural resource availability, a lack of new cotton and silk strains, an inability to produce its own machinery, a poor fiscal system, a lack of capital, and an unskilled, immobile labor force torn between meeting family demands and the need to acquire technical training.

1077. VOSKUIL, Walter. The Iron and Steel Industry of China, *Annals, American Academy of Political and Social Science* 152, 1930, 191–95.

Although coal is available in every province, iron ore is more widely scattered and of low grade in about 35 percent of the mines; hence, there are few large-scale mining operations for iron ore. China cannot support an iron industry without imports, railroad development, and foreign capital.

1078. WIENS, H{erold}. J. The Japanese Role of in China's Industrialization, *Asian Studies* (Hawaii) 3, 1969, 1–50.

Basic premise is that both Japan and China played roles in the industrialization of China, but each in its own self-interest. In this regard, one of Japan's main goals was to make China dependent upon Japanese investment and technology. Points out geographic areas, such as Taiwan, Manchuria, and North China, where the Japanese were most effective in fostering industrialization. Roles of treaty ports, Japanese geological surveys, and Chinese boycotts of Japanese goods are also included in analysis. Concludes that Japan's major contributions were building infrastructure and providing models of investment, which the Chinese copied.

See also item 1228.

17. Transportation and Communications

1079. ANDERSON, George E. The Wonderful Canals of China, *National Geographic Magazine* 16, 1905, 68–69.

Curious about what the United States could learn from China's use of canals. In addition to their use as part of the transportation system, canals are a source of mud for fertilizer and of food. Does not approve of Chinese use of canals to do laundry, prepare food, or wash dishes. Urges further Chinese investment in construction and rehabilitation of canals.

1080. ANON. A Year's Progress in Transportation and Commercial Services, *Far Eastern Review* 30, 1934, 417–22.

Reprint of article that originally appeared in *Chinese Economic Journal* 15, 1934, 44–66. Laudatory review of government programs undertaken in 1933–34. Touches on railroad construction and rate restructuring as well as road building, the expansion of shipping, aviation, telegraph service, radio, and postal services. Laments the lack of coordination among local, provincial, and central government plans and projects.

1081. ANON. The Peking-Hankow Railway, *Bulletin, American Geographical Society* 38, 1906, 554–56.

Summary of material appearing in *le mouvement geographique*, November 28, 1906, upon the departure of Jean Jadot, who was in charge of constructing the Beijing-Hankou railroad. Includes details regarding the route, mileage, number of bridges, and branches of the railroad as well as data on the importation of raw materials and cars needed to complete the project. The impact of political unrest on the construction schedule is described. Extension of the railroad to Canton must await Chinese capital and entrepreneurs.

1082. ANON. Transportation Facilities of Manchuria, *Journal of Geography* 8, 1910, 167–68.

Argues that given China's size and high population density its transportation infrastructure is inadequate. Describes specific, traditional Chinese transportation technologies such as wheeled carts, their cost, and their carrying capacities. Notes that transportation needs have not been properly surveyed and that the system is not legally controlled.

1083. ARNOLD, Julean. New Transportation for China, *Asia and the Americas* 34, 1934, 664–71.

Reviews U.S. aid to mitigate farmers' inefficiencies due to lack of modern transportation. Provides a catalog of traditional transportation types and their costs. Notes how an improved and modernized transportation system could enhance resource exploitation, international trade, public safety, and political unification. Describes progress made during World War II in developing railroads, aviation, and communications.

1084. BAKER, John Earl. Transportation in China, *Annals, American Academy of Political and Social Science* 152, 1930, 160–72.

Detailed catalog of components of China's transportation system with emphasis on man, canals, highways and road construction, motor trucks, and railroads.

1085. BLACKWELDER, Eliot. Transportation in Interior China, *Journal of Geography* 10, 1911, 89–93.

Due to China's distance from the Industrial Revolution, it still relies on means of transportation used by previous generations. These old methods, such as coolies, pack animals, wheelbarrows, boats, and canals, are all primitive, slow, and tedious and subject to handicap by climate and topography. Expects the railroad to extend the range of movement and radically change the transportation mix.

1086. CAMERON, Nigel. The Burma Road, *Geographical Magazine* 33, 1960, 73–87.

Argues that, although the road was built for war purposes, in the long run it has increased accessibility and permitted remote areas to be studied.

1087. CANCELLARE, Frank. China's Hand-Built Air Bases, *National Geographic Magazine* 88, 1945, 231–36.

Photo essay showing the use of traditional Chinese building techniques to finish air bases capable of use by B-29s.

1088. CARDWELL. Robert. Pirate Fights of the South China Sea, *National Geographic Magazine* 89, 1946, 787–96.

Photo essay about the proliferation of pirates and the efforts taken by owners of large junks to increase the safety of boats, crews, and cargoes.

1089. CHANG, Kia-nga. China's Need for Transport, *Foreign Affairs* 23, 1945, 464–75.

Sees choice of transportation investment as maximizing available funds so that both the low standard of living and political stability can be improved. On a sector by sector basis, recounts the history of transportation in China and the challenges of modernization.

1090. CHANG, Kuei-sheng. The Changing Railroad Pattern in Mainland China, *Geographical Review* 51, 1961, 534–48.

Argues that much publicity has been given to the planning and achievements of railroad development since railroads are good indicators of the growth of the Chinese economy and progress toward economic development. Analyzes map of pre-Communist railroad patterns to show how uneven railroad development was. Expresses concern that although additional kilometers of line have been laid down, they were all completed ahead of schedule with a resulting waste of labor and resources since much of the track had to be relaid. Notes impact of Soviet planning on Chinese rail development as well as Chinese economic objectives associated with rail expansion. Sees railroads as a visible sign of vitality and solidarity of Sino-Soviet relationship.

1091. CHEN, Cheng-siang. Port of Keelung, *Tijdschrift voor economische en sociale geografie* 48, 1957, 142–48.

For the period 1897 to 1940, outlines the development and freight-handling capacity of Keelung as a part of the Taiwan transportation system. Describes the internal organization of the port and city, their site characteristics, and the services available once a boat has docked. Sketches the advantages and disadvantages of Keelung as a port. The fishing port and its functions are described separately.

1092. CHEN, Han-seng, and Miriam S. FARLEY. Railroad Strategy in China, New Style, *Far Eastern Survey* 6, 1937, 165–73.

Argues that railroads have the potential for fostering economic development in China but only if new construction is financed so as to avoid putting China at the mercy of foreign interests, as was the case with nineteenth-century railroad building.

1093. CHOU, Shun-hsin. Railway Development and Economic Growth in Manchuria, *China Quarterly* 45, 1971, 57–84.

Focuses on four questions: What factors made possible the rapid development of the railway system in Manchuria? What was the timing of development? What are the characteristics of freight patterns? And how do capital costs and the structure of the Manchurian railway system compare to those of the United States and China proper?

1094. CHRISTIAN, John L. Trans-Burma Trade Routes to China, *Pacific Affairs* 13, 1940, 173–91.

Describes the range of Burmese railroad links to the rest of Asia and especially the importance of the link to China. Records the history of China-Burma trade before and after the coming of the British to India. Notes impact of local uprisings on trade.

1095. COLQUHOUN, A. R. The Railway Connection of Burmah with China, *Journal of the Manchester Geographical Society* 3, 1887, 141–54.

Concerned with identifying new markets for British goods given the depression of trade during the 1880s. Sketches the history of British interest in Burma-China trade. Proposes and evaluates possible alternative rail links between Chittagong and Yunnan. Estimates markets in Yunnan and Southwest China. Expresses concern for competition from French.

1096. COLQUHOUN, A. R. South China Borderlands, Exploration from the mouth of the Sikiang to the Irrawadi, *Proceedings, Royal Geographical Society of London* 4, 1882, 713–30.

Report of 1881 trip designed to establish trade potential and routes. Reviews previous European trips to Canton and Yunnan regions. Includes timetables of travel in area. Notes that no one route will permit tapping the entire Yunnan area.

1097. COTTON, Arthur. On a Communication between India and China by the Line of the Burhampooter [*sic*] and Yangtze, *Journal, Royal Geographical Society* 37, 1867, 231–38.

In the debate over whether or not the availability of a land link between Southwest China and Burma will enhance trade for Britain, the building of a narrow gauge railroad is favored.

1098. CRAW, Henry. The Burma Road, *Geographical Journal* 99, 1942, 238–48.

Main focus is the efficiency of the Burma Road as a supply route. Describes the background of the building of the road and problems in its construction. Notes that Chinese engineers did not choose the shortest route when laying out the road, but followed settlement patterns so that a supply of labor would be ensured. Describes the technical and engineering reasons for deterioration of the road after 1940. Urges that a railroad be built to connect China and Burma. Argues that after the war China will seek an additional outlet to the sea, this time via India.

1099. CREAGH, E. Fitzgerald. A Journey Overland from Amoy to Hankow in 1879, *Journal, Royal Geographical Society* 50, 1880, 275–306.

Informal report of 1,446-mile journey to areas rarely seen by visiting Westerners. Complains of difficulties in walking, yet details revolution in inland transportation brought about by the introduction of steamers. Advises Western traders to be prepared to control tempers if they wish to succeed.

1100. CRESSEY, George B. How the Chinese Travel, *Home Geographic Monthly* 2:6, 1932, 31–36.

Describes means of transportation using the literary device of an imaginary trip by a young boy and his uncle. Provides a catalog of both inter- and intra-urban means of movement. Notes that there are no standard axle gauges, requiring a change of axles as one passes from one area to another. Estimates that goods can travel about fifteen miles a day using traditional transportation means.

1101. DENG, Ling Hau. Methods of Transportation in Fukien Province, China, *Journal of Geography* 13, 1914, 91–93.

Since isolation is a major factor inhibiting the development of China, there is a need to focus on how to improve transportation. Describes coolie/porter, chair, horse, junk, and canal transportation by location and site. In addition to the extension of railroads, the province needs the dredging of ports and upgrading of roads to fully make use of any railroad developments.

1102. DWYER, D. J. The Development of China's Inland Waterways, *Geography* 46, 1961, 65–67.

Since there is a shortage of steel for railroad expansion, China should more fully exploit its waterways. However, river transportation is handicapped by a lack of boats. Assumes many of these were taken by the Kuomintang in its 1949 retreat to Taiwan. Reports on improvements on selected rivers, including the Heilong Jiang and Wu Jiang, a tributary of the Changjiang, and the dredging of the Grand Canal. Sees improvements as progressing piecemeal. Questions what he reads as Murphey's skepticism [item 1127] regarding rapid expansion of the railroads.

1103. FISCHER, Emil S. Modern Travel from Tai Yuan Fu via Mount Wu Tai to the Mongolian Frontier, *Journal, Royal Asiatic Society, North China Branch*, new series 54, 1923, 81–113.

Notes efforts of the Royal Asiatic Society to ascertain conditions of travel and how they were improved by both Catholic and Protestant missionaries. Describes a trip and emphasizes the degree of improvement in transportation accompanying the building of railroads.

1104. FREEBERNE, Michael. Bridge across the Yangtze Barrier, *Geographical Magazine* 41, 1969, 586–91.

Notes that since 1949 three bridges have been built across the river that had divided China culturally and politically. Describes the local impact of bridges. Contrasts the engineering challenges in building bridges after the withdrawal of Russian engineers as a result of the Sino-Soviet split with the impact of the Great Leap Forward.

1105. GINSBURG, Norton S. China's Railroad Network, *Geographical Review* 41, 1951 470–74.

Describes state of the railroad system in 1950 by broad region. In reviewing construction projects, notes the concentration of rail lines and track in the northern and northeastern parts of China. Feels railroad is administered as a well-integrated unit, in contrast to operations during the warlord period. Doubts whether there will be a rapid expansion of track into inaccessible areas due to the difficulty of terrain. Provides a map of track circa 1950.

1106. GINSBURG, Norton S. Manchurian Railway Development, *Far Eastern Quarterly* 8, 1949, 398–411.

Three maps of railroad development are the heart of the article. The working hypothesis is that "civilizing rails" are the key to the development of Manchuria and that this development occurred under the Japanese. Notes that agriculture did not benefit as much as industry from the expansion of the railroads. Sees a danger in belittling Japanese contribution to what should evolve into the industrial heart of China.

17. Transportation and Communications 261

1107. GROSVENOR, Gilbert H. Railways, Rivers, and Strategic Towns in Manchuria, *National Geographic Magazine* 11, 1900, 326–28.

Descibes the progress made in completing the Trans-Siberian Railroad and its potential impact on Manchuria. Notes territorial conflicts between China and Russia.

1108. HALL, Russell E. China's Domestic Transport System, *Far Eastern Survey* 6, 1937, 253–57.

Survey of major sectors of transportation and who controls them by region. Notes that there is a long lag between the time transportation projects are completed and the ability of the Chinese to make full use of them.

1109. HALLET, Holt S. Exploration Survey for a Railroad between India, Siam, and China, *Scottish Geographical Magazine* 2, 1886, 78–92.

Mentions 1882 work of Colquhoun (item 1095). Notes the importance of geographical knowledge in evaluating proposals for improving trade in Southwest China. Outlines proposal for a railroad line, including estimated costs. Emphatic that private enterprise must carry on after the government has concluded the basic survey work.

1110. HOCKLY, J. Minett. Notes on Yang-tse-kiang, Together with Corrections of Existing Charts, *Proceedings, Royal Geographcial Society of London* 11, 1867, 261–69.

Describes problems of civilian access to region. Very specific about individual ports and what type of trade is available at each of them.

1111 HOYANAGI, Mutsumi. Geography [*sic*] Problems Concerning the Old Silk Road Region in the Tarim Basin, *Geographical Reports of Tokyo Metropolitan University* 1, 1966, 1–32.

Seeks to identify the route of the Silk Road, especially in the eastern portion of the Tarim Basin. Since oases there are rare, there are no natural routes, and the Chinese sources give no exact route, evidence from sand dune excavation, river shrinkage patterns, fluctuations in snow lines, and old maps must be used. Despite the use of these new materials, the route still cannot be identified definitively.

1112. HUNTER, Holland. Transportation in Soviet and Chinese Development, *Economic Development and Cultural Change* 14, 1965, 71–84.

Sees improved transportation as a precondition for development. Notes

Communist approach to transportation planning and construction in which transportation is seen as a means to an end and thus must compete for scarce resources. As such, rejects Communist model of transportation development for Third World countries. Recounts history of railroad building in China, the Soviet Union, and the United States.

1113. KING, W. H. The Telegraph to Lhasa, *Geographical Journal* 63, 1924, 527–31.

Describes the construction of a 144-mile telegraph line built from Gyantze to Lhasa at the expense of the Tibetan government. Corvée labor was able to install four miles of wire a day. Finds that Tibetan workers perform best despite their reputation as slow, stupid, and indolent. Numerous offhand remarks about the privileged classes of Tibet and role of lamas in daily life. Surprised at keen interest of the general population, and especially the Dalai Lama, in the telegraph.

1114. KINGSMILL, T. W., ed. Inland Communications in China, *Journal, Royal Asiatic Society, North China Branch*, new series 28, 1893–94, 1–213.

Monograph-length survey, based on contributions from forty-four individuals, which describes on a region by region basis the following transportation-related topics: ancient and modern transportation and trade routes, safety of roads, accommodations available for travelers, status of bridges, and the nature and extent of intra- and interurban transportation systems.

1115. KOESTER, Capt. Hans. Four Thousand Hours over China, *National Geographic Magazine* 73, 1938, 571–93.

Enumerates physical and logistical challenges of flying over China in order to develop airline routes. Flights were especially hampered by lack of accurate large-scale maps. Describes trips over Changjiang from Shanghai to Hankou undertaken for the Curtiss-Wright Exploration Group and from Hankou to Canton. Sees air travel as the most practical way for China to overcome the vast distances and geographic boundaries that inhibit effective communications. Includes large selection of air photographs.

1116. LACY, Walter N. Road Improvements in Foochow, China, *Journal of Geography* 19, 1920, 343–48.

Uses Fuzhou as an example to argue that as transportaion changes the habits and lives of the population shift. Describes Fuzhou as a dual city made of up of an old and new section. Notes changes when new city developed, especially when a bridge was built over the Min River and roads were paved. Although may people still walked, they went further than before and the use of rickshaws and horse-drawn carriages increased markedly, as did that of two-wheeled vehicles, including bicycles. The extension of roads beyond the city has hastened the growth of suburbs.

1117. LATTIMORE, Owen. The Desert Road to Turkestan, *National Geographic Magazine* 55, 1929, 661–702.

Traces route taken instead of two customary roads that were made impassible due to the presence of banditry and anti-foreign feelings. Route went from Tianjin to Guchengzi via Guihuading and on to Urumali (Dihuadu). Recounts customs of caravan men, tribulations of fording streams, contacts with nomads, weather conditions, and state of desert communications. Remarks on how few Chinese were encountered, even though the territory crossed was nominally under Chinese control.

1118. LATTIMORE, Owen. China's Turkestan-Siberia Supply Road, *Pacific Affairs* 13, 1949, 393–412.

Argues that knowledge of Soviet routes important since the Japanese cut off China's access to Indochina. Describes the four main rail links between Soviet Union and China as well as their ancient desert track counterparts. Provides data on length of track, freight shipments, and challenges of maintaining the railroads, especially with regard to repairs, providing labor, and dealing with terrain. Feels that there are no technical problems in maintaining the rail links but is pessimistic about whether political problems can be resolved.

1119. LI, Chang. Railway Construction in China, *Far Eastern Survey* 22, 1953, 37–42.

Describes plans for rehabilitating railroads after 1949 and projects completed during 1951–52. Analyzes new routes, especially the ones for Sichuan. Concludes that China has made a good start in major construction projects despite a shortage of raw materials and the distraction of the Korean War.

1120. LING, Han-deng. Methods of Transportation in Fukkien [*sic*] Province, China, *Journal of Geography* 13, 1914, 91–93.

Although westerners see China's transportation system in negative terms, that is, as primitive, slow, and tedious, the Chinese see it as a suitable adaptation to the climatic and topographic features of China. Uses Fujian

Province as an example to show how and why traditional modes of transportation such as coolie, porter chairs, horses, and canals are suited to an area with poor roads. To improve the system and usher in a new era of prosperity, roads will need to be rebuilt, rivers dredged, and railroads built. Once this has been done, automobiles, bicycles, and larger boats can be introduced.

1121. LIPPITT, Victor D. Development of Transportation in Communist China, *China Quarterly* 27, 1966, 101–19.

Development of transportation reflects changing economic policies, but it is possible to see how national integration and development of the interior has been fostered. By 1966, emphasis was on development of short-distance transportation, an indication of a shift in emphasis from industry to agriculture. In the long run, even this type of transportation should assist in furthering overall economic development at a more sustained rate.

1122. LLOYD, W. V. Notes on the Russian Harbours on the Coast of Manchuria, *Journal, Royal Geographical Society* 37, 1867, 212–30.

Although focus is on Russian ports, since the territory was formerly Chinese it is possible to note the enduring presence and impact of Chinese law and customs on trade among China, Korea, and Russia.

1123. LOWE, Chuan-hua. The Yunnan-Burma Highway in Its Second Year, *Amerasia* 4, 1940, 331–35.

Article written before the British road was closed at the insistence of the Japanese. Recounts the history of the road in the context of general British road building. Includes data on terrain coverage and length of road. Discusses railroad building as well. Provides typical trip itinerary. Sees bright future for the road.

1124. MANIFOLD, C. C. Recent Exploration and Economic Development in Central and Western China, *Geographical Journal* 23, 1904, 281–315.

Main focus is on difficulties in maintaining steamboat traffic due to low water levels and the presence of rapids. The presence of great raw material and mineral wealth (including silk and hemp), abundant agricultural surpluses, and cheap skilled and industrial workers bodes well for the development of the area as a major center of manufacturing.

1125. M'COSH, Dr. On the Various Lines of Overland Communication between India and China, *Proceedings, Royal Geographical Society of London* 5:2, 1860, 47–54.

Posthumous report on five possible routes from Tibet to India. Notes importance of opening practicable road between the two areas as part of an oversall British strategy to limit Russian influence in the region.

1126. MOORE, W. Robert. Raft Life on the Huang Ho, *National Geographic Magazine* 61, 1932, 743–52.

Describes the physical features of the river and manner of regional traffic control by ethnic minorities. Provides technical details regarding the assembly, maintenance, and use of rafts as shipping craft. Includes eight pages of photographs.

1127. MURPHEY, Rhoads. China's Transport Problems and Communist Planning, *Economic Geography* 32, 1956, 17–28.

Working hypothesis is that China's economic development is best served by the extension of low-cost, high-volume transportation. By extension, transportation is seen as the main bottleneck in any attempt at economic development. Urges revival of all types of systems in use, including water, modern truck, and traditional carts and human carriers, as well as railroads. Comments on the fact that local needs tend to foster north-south or east-west networks of transportation, while a national view requires a more diverse and complicated set of routes. Points out that not all transportation development projects are carried out for economic reasons. For example, railroad development also involves issues relating to national prestige. Urges that the quickest way to promote industrialization and commercialization would be to expand water transportation.

1128. ORCHARD, John E. Overland Routes into China: Transport Facilities in China's Defense, *Far Eastern Survey* 6, 1937, 251–53.

Describes the routes of land lines between the Soviet Union and China and their potential for assisting China to win the war against the Japanese. Notes importance of northern railroad links given Japanese aggression in the Hong Kong-Macao area.

1129. OUTRAM, Frank, and G. E. FANE. Burma Road, Back Door to China, *National Geographic Magazine* 78, 1940, 629–58.

Report of trip along road. Goal of trip is to verify the Chinese claim that the Burma Road is an all-weather road, passable even during monsoons.

Describes construction of the road. Concludes that despite hard work much remains to be done to complete the road and that the Chinese claims must be discounted.

1130. PETROV, Victor P. New Railway Links between China and the Soviet Union, *Geographical Journal* 122, 1956, 471–77.

Describes routes of new rail links between Xinjiang, Manchuria, and the Soviet Union. Provides dates when links were completed. Notes both advantages and disadvantages of links through prism of China's participation in or withdrawl from Soviet sphere of influence.

1131. PRYBYLA, Jan S. Transportation in Communist China, *Land Economics* 42, 1966, 268–81.

Outlines the economic, political, and military reasons why China wants to modernize its transportation networks. After describing the spatial distribution of pre-1949 transportation elements, including railroads, shipping, and civil aviation, modernization needs are enumerated. Notes reliance on the Soviet Union for blueprints and models as well as the high human cost of improving transportation. This cost is seen as part of a purposeful totalitarian effort to alleviate poverty and thus as justifiable in the eyes of the Chinese.

1132. ROSS, John. Trade Routes in Manchuria, *Scottish Geographical Magazine* 17, 1901, 303–10.

Impressed with extent of trade routes in Northeast China. Enumerates major roads, railroads, and rivers used in trade of wood and grain. No map included.

1133. ROXBY, P[ercival]. M[aude]. The Burma Road, *Geography* 25, 1940, 170–71, plus map.

Sees Burma Road, the Chinese portion of the Sino-Burmese Road, as a good example of how war can provide a stimulus to regional development. Includes a brief history of trade among Burma, China, and Central Asia. Traces route of road and links to major cities in China and Burma. Describes what commodities were transported over road, enabling China to continue to export. Mentions that motor transport was less affected by monsoons than expected. Cites Chinese sources to point to the higher commercial value of the road contrasted with the Haiphong railroad.

1134. SPENCER, Jospeh Earle. The Junks on the Yangtze, *Asia and the Americas* 38, 1938, 466–70.

Differentiates between river- and ocean-going junks in terms of construction, design, and size. Notes changes in junk technology, especially the abandonment of sails, and the resulting decline in the number of junks as steam power was adopted. Describes sail making. Enumerates the special equipment found on river junks such as a balanced rudder, long booms, sculls, and oars. Includes two pages of pictures of scale models of junks and information about the manufacture and purchase of such models.

1135. TAYMAN, Nelson Grant. Stilwell Road: Land Route to China, *National Geographic Magazine* 87, 1945, 681–98.

Concerned with the Ledo-Burma Road linking North India to Yunnan. Describes the costs and topographic constraints that made air transport from India to China unfeasible. Describes the building of the road, bridges, and pipelines. Notes the help given to the Negro Army Brigades working on the road by non-Han minorities along the route.

1136. TODD, O[liver]. J[ulian]. Modern Highways in China: Five Years' Progress in Transportation Cheaper than Railways, *Far Eastern Review* 22, 1926, 526–29.

Argues that China is in no position to finance railroads and that more progress in providing modern transportation would be made if roads were built. Describes the work of the Red Cross in building some one thousand miles of roads in Shandong, Shanxi, and Henan. Argues that building roads is very cost effective but that there are major problems involving upkeep, and especially repairing war damage, once they are built.

1137. von RICHTHOFEN, Baron Ferdinand. Land Communication between Europe and China, *Geographical Magazine* 1, 1874, 144–46.

Compares the Trans-Siberian Railroad to the American Transcontinental Railroad. Describes Asian sections of the Trans-Siberian Railroad in terms of topographic constraints and location of passes and oases. Not sure of best route to use if a railroad going west from Kuldja were to be constructed. Not optimistic about the role of the railroad in expanding Chinese trade.

1138. WATT, John. The Effect of Transportation on Famine Prevention, *China Quarterly* 6, 1961, 76–80.

Argues that should famine result from floods or drought blame cannot be assigned to lack of adequate means of moving available foodstuffs from grain surplus to deficit areas. Compares the 1960 famine, said to be "the worst in 100 years," to that of 1877–78.

1139. WHEELER, James O., and Clifton W. PANNELL. A Teaching Model of Network Diffusion: The Taiwan Example, *Journal of Geography* 72:5, 1973, 21–31.

Uses Taiwan as an example of how to introduce students to the literature on transportation development and network diffusion. Suggests a six-step transportation-development model and applies it to Taiwan. Provides maps of theoretical road building and actual settlements and roads circa 1972.

1140. WIENS, Harold. The Shu Tao or Road to Szechuan, *Geographical Review* 39, 1949, 584–604.

Begins by noting how transportation is a major bottleneck in attempts to develop China. Uses Chi's concept (and 1936 book published in London) of key economic regions as a device for describing Sichuan and its importance to China. Describes the historical roles of western Qinling mountain roads. The road network in China and Sichuan must be expanded to ensure the political unity and economic development of China. Also urges building and upgrading railroads.

1141. WILLIAMS, E. T. Open Ports of China, *Geographical Review* 9, 1920, 306–34.

Notes the anomaly of using the term *inland port*. Traces the history of Western opening of Chinese cities to trade. Remarks on the fact that not all "openings" were forced upon the Chinese. Surveys the impact of trade on provinces with open ports. Classifies ports by degree of control, including extraterritoriality, which westerners enjoyed.

1142. YETTS, W. Perceval. Links between Ancient China and the West, *Geographical Review* 16, 1926, 614–22.

Material presented in the context of the debate regarding whether Chinese culture was the product of spontaneous, indigenous developments or imported. Describes Zhou dynasty relations with the Hsiung-nu and visits of Qin dynasty officials to Central Asia. Includes comparative textile analysis. In the end concludes that the Kozlov expedition of 1925–26 to northern Mongolia supports diffusionism and the assumption that much of Chinese culture derived from the diffusion of Western cultural elements to China.

1143. **YULE, H[enry]**. Notes on the Oldest Records of the Sea Route to China from Western Asia, *Proceedings, Royal Geographical Society, and Monthly Record of Geography*, new series 4, 1882, 649–60.

Goal of report is to show the persistence of a maritime tradition connecting Western Asia to China. Draws heavily on Greek, Arab, and Christian sources and devotes considerable attention to toponymic problems.

See also items 0168, 0453, and 1152.

18. Trade

1144. AGASSIZ, A. R. Our Commercial Relations with Chinese Manchuria, *Geographical Journal* 4, 1894, 534–56.

Recommends use of an atlas before exploring the history, politics, or commerce of a country. First describes economic, political, and physical geography of Manchuria. Then provides lists of amounts and values of imports. Notes great potential for trade with Britain. Area can be repopulated but prefers free migration to settlement of demobilized soldiers. Sees strong link between population growth and trade.

1145 BOURNE, F. S. A. Trade of Central and South China, *Scottish Geographical Magazine* 15, 1899, 13–28.

Summary of report number 458 to Foreign Office with same title. Great potential of trade inhibited by *likin* duties imposed by the Beijing government after Taiping Rebellion. Native industry has been hurt by imports, but investment after 1895 shows that native enterprises can compete.

1146. COLQUHOUN, A. R. Physical Geography and Trade of Formosa, *Scottish Geographical Magazine* 3, 1887, 567–77.

Printed version of paper read before the British Asociation in 1887. Notes specific advantages of Taiwan in agriculture and raw materials. Trade prospects have much improved with the decline in piracy in area.

1147. DEASY, George F. Recent Trends in Manchoukuoan Trade, *Economic Geography* 16, 1940, 162–70.

Trade trends feature pronounced declines in the value of exports and pronounced increases in imports. Old exports include food and industrial raw materials, while new imports include industrial equipment, luxury goods, and processed materials for mass consumption. Germany has been replaced by India, Japan, and the United States as the main trading partner(s). These changes are attributed to the world economic depression.

1148. DOUGLAS, Robert K. Our Commercial Relations with China, *Scottish Geographical Magazine* 7, 1891, 11–26.

Covers three main topics: history of United Kingdom's trade with China, current relations, and prospects for future trade. Argues that China progresses and prospers in spite of a corrupt government. China-United

Kingdom trade has suffered as other European countries, especially Germany, have intruded into Chinese markets. Nevertheless, sees great potential in Chinese market once western areas, especially Yunnan with its mineral wealth, are opened and improved transportation developed through either public or private investment.

1149. FIELD, Frederick V. China's Foreign Trade, *Far Eastern Survey* 4, 1935, 33–40.

Concerned with 1934 trade patterns. Notes the negative impact of depression and use of the gold standard on China's trade. Provides data and analysis of types and value of Chinese goods in the context of total world trade. Describes the role of Hong Kong, Japan, the United Kingdom, and the United States in China's trade patterns.

1150. FUNG, K. I. China's Grain Trade: Explanation and Prospects, *Canadian Geographer* 16, spring 1972, 15–28.

Explains reasons why China went from net grain exporter to net grain importer in early 1960s. Although drought accounted for some of the shift, imports will continue due to strains on the transportation system, differences in world prices for wheat and rice, and the Chinese view that trade is as much a political issue as an economic one.

1151. JAN, G. P. Japan's Trade with Communist China, *Asian Survey* 12, 1969, 900–918.

Traces ebb and flow of trade. Outlines the differences in assumptions and rules used by the two parties when engaging in trade. Concludes that the prospects for improved trade relations are poor given the incompatibility of trade politics. The Japanese want to separate politics and trade, while the Chinese see the two issues as linked. Were Japan to extend diplomatic recognition to China, predicts two-way trade would improve.

1152. KUO, Tsung-fei. A Brief History of the Trade Routes between Burma, Indochina, and Yunnan, *T'ien Hsia Monthly* 12, 1940–41, 9–32.

Chinese trade was sustained during World War II by use of ancient land-based trade routes to Burma and Southeast Asia. Describes the development of these routes in the context of Chinese expansion south of the Changjiang and the tribute system. Includes details of ethnic groups, their origins, and their struggles for survival. Notes the decline of the traditional trade routes as the railroad developed. Reports with pleasure the successful resurrection of trade routes under necessities of war.

18. Trade

1153. LITTLE, Archibald J. Geography of Trade of Western China, *Journal, Manchester Geographical Society* 3, 1887, 1–13.

Really a summary of a trip along the Yangtze. Describes the basic topographic and hydrologic features of the river, as well as the traffic encountered. Touches on impact of floods and droughts on traffic and notes the high cost of Chinese administration of ports in contrast to Europe. Speculates on what other routes there might be to open Chinese markets. Urges attention be paid to a Burmese route and moving farther up the Yangtze, which is preferred. In terms of trade, argues that the Chinese need an infusion of "Western brains" to give them a proper idea of the value of their possessions. Hopes the current generation of westerners in China will assist in this task.

1154. PARKES, Harry. Report on the Russian Caravan Trade with China, *Journal, Royal Geographical Society* 24, 1854, 306–12.

Trade takes place in Kiakhta and Maimaizhen. Describes the rules and regulations surrounding the trade, including barter and the prohibition of traders bringing their families with them. Seasonal trading is initiated when Chinese traders appear. The Chinese import furs and woolen and leather goods and export tea, manufactered goods such as silk, and rhubarb. Typical prices for full range of goods traded included. Notes that if the Chinese were to begin trading at other centers new rules for a nonbarter system would have to be implemented.

1155. PHILLIPS, Geo[rge]. The Mediaeval Fuh-Kien Trading Ports, Chuan-chow and Chang-chao, *T'oung Pao*, series 1, 6, 1895, 449–63; 7, 1896, 223–40.

Describes the history of foreign trade passing through Changzhou and Quanzhou. Questions the reliability of the medieval texts of Marco Polo and Ibn Batuta and their modern translators. Uses inscriptions in mosques and temples to verify medieval claims.

1156. ROCKWELL, W. W. Notes on the Relations and Trade of China with the Eastern Archipelago and the Coasts of the Indian Ocean during the 14th Century, *T'oung Pao*, series 2, 15, 1914, 119–47; 16, 1916, 61–159, 236–71, 437–67.

Provides a history of Chinese trading relations with study area. Text consists of a place by place listing of goods traded along with a description of the climate, economy, and production levels of source areas.

1157. SOWERBY, A[rthur]. [de Carle]. China's Trade with Malaysia, *China Journal* 25, 1936, 32-36.

Notes the longevity of the trade and its impact on the landscape and society of Malaysia. Provides lists of goods traded between the two countries and argues that the trade patterns shown in the data are similar to those between China and the Philippines and India. Urges the Chinese government to develop the Malaysia trade connection further.

1158. SPENCER, J[oseph]. E[arle]. The Szechuan Village Fair, *Economic Geography* 16, 1940, 48-58.

Points out the local economic and social importance of village fairs. Reviews distances traveled to fairs and the times and management of fairs. Describes a division of labor wherein the sales staff is made up of elderly fathers whose sons concentrate on production.

1159. SPENCER, Joseph Earle. Trade and Transshipment in the Yangtze Valley, *Geographical Review* 28, 1938, 112-23.

Sees Changjiang as main avenue for Chinese trade. Reviews changes in volume, commodities, and ship technology involved in trade over time. Reports on the impact of treaty ports and maritime customs on trade. Provides details of status of thirteen newer river ports such as Wan Xian. Questions in whose hands the river trade really is.

1160. STOUT, Arthur Purdy. The Penetration of Yun-nan, *Bulletin, Geographical Society of Philadelphia* 10, 1912, 1-35.

Sees history of exploration of Yunnan as inspired by the competition between Great Britain and France over trade in Southwest China. Provides a description of the physical characteristics of Yunnan as well as a history of Western interest in the region going back as far as Marco Polo. Includes an extensive bibliography covering the period 1890 to 1911, with strong emphasis on French sources. Main rivalry focuses on city of Tali. Concludes that in the competition between the two colonial powers "the light of western civilization has fallen again on a dark corner of the world."

1161. SWINHOE, R. Special Mission up the Yang-tsze-kiang, *Journal, Royal Geographical Society* 40, 1870, 268-87.

Report of 1869 mission of inquiry designed to assess trade potential along river. Recommends specific places as possible ports for British trade. Notes that tribute from Tibet sent along via river every three years. Includes secondhand reports of westerners regarding city life along stream.

1162. TWITCHETT, Denis. The T'ang Market System, *Asia Major* 12, 1966, 202–48.

Assumes that despite a large body of data on markets, it is still difficult to relate the data to the economic life of markets. Describes the origins, administration, expansion, and regulations of official as well as unregulated rural and local markets and fairs. Appendix contains translations of major Tang laws and regulations regarding all aspects of market activities.

1163. WIENS, Herold [J]. Riverine and Coastal Junks in China's Commerce, *Economic Geography* 31, 1955, 248–64.

Absent other forms, junk traffic is the most common form of transportation. Fortunately, it is also highly mechanized. Uses data from 1902 and 1922–30. Describes early history of trade with particular focus on Changjiang as well as Tianjin and Shanghai. Details include size and capacity of junks as well as crew size and function. Includes maps of inland routes as well as detailed city maps. Notes that China is highly dependent upon foreign bottoms to transship even inland trade.

1164. WHEATLEY, Paul. Geographical Notes on Some Commodities Involved in the Sung Maritime Trade, *Journal, Royal Asiatic Society, Malaysian Branch* 32:2, 1959, 5–140.

Evaluates sources of data. Notes that materials covering the history of the trade in the Chinese sources are tenuous and erratic. Reviews the reaction of the Chinese government to trade and its social impact on Chinese society. Majority of the article devoted to a catalog-like description of specific spices, textiles, metals, minerals, and porcelains involved in the trade.

See also items 0169, 0905, 0925, 1188, 1203, 1205, and 1221.

19. Urban Geography

1165. ALEXANDER, Grant. Housing Hong Kong's 600,000 Homeless, *Geographical Magazine* 31, 1959, 573–86.

Describes relief efforts and long-term housing and education plans after the fire at Shek Kip Mei, a sixty-five-acre squatter housing area that was home to some 600,000 residents. Origins of the squatter settlement included.

1166. AYSCOUGH, Florence W. Symbolism of the Forbidden City, Peking, *Journal, Royal Asiatic Society, North China Branch*, new series 61, 1930, 111–26.

Detailed description of Forbidden City and many of its objects, their placement, and colors.

1167. BOYDEN, Amanda. Changing Shanghai, *National Geographic Magazine* 72, 1937, 485–508.

Impressions of city from time of entrance to Whangpoo [*sic*] River to berthing of ship. Describes governance, commerce, use of servants, changes in clothing standards, role of Chinese women, and available amusements and diversions for westerners on a street by street basis.

1168. BRAKE, Brian. Peking: A Pictoral Record, *National Geographic Magazine* 118, 1960, 194–97.

Photo essay embedded in article by Shor [item 1249]. Most pictures show propaganda posters and transportation in the city.

1169. BUCK, David D. Urban Development: Beyond the Ta-ch'ing Model, *Contemporary China* 1, 1977, 43–50.

Not available for annotation.

1170. BUXTON, L. H. Dudley. The Historical Geography of Peking, *Geographical Teacher* 12:5, 1924, 42–49.

Summary of Beijing's development under the Mongol, Ming, Qing, and Republican governments. Development continued even when city was not the capital of China. Main topics surveyed include location, site, how Beijing was chosen to be a capital, transportation, and public buildings.

1171. **CHANG, Sen-dou.** The Historical Trend of Chinese Urbanization, *Annals, Association of American Geographers* 53, 1963, 109–43.

Uses walled *hsien* capitals as an example. Starts with pre-1111 B.C.E. sites and progresses historically. Concludes that each dynasty had its own region of urban development within China that was related to the geographic region of dynastic origins, population, and the state of the national economy.

1172. **CHANG, Sen-dou.** Land Use and Intra-urban Travel in Taipei, *Proceedings, Association of American Geographers* 2, 1970, 40–45.

Traces transformation of land use patterns from a traditional Chinese walled city to a modern, urban-industrial center. The central business district has expanded along the major traffic routes. Regarding intra-urban trips, the distances traveled to work and school are correlated with income levels. Traffic congestion is attributed to journey to school, which makes up 45.9 percent of all trips, and the journey to work, which constitutes 24.5 percent of all trips. Concludes that continued horizontal development of the city is not viable, that apartments are symbols of modernity and privilege and will increase rapidly in number, and that the transportation system is clogged by school trips.

1173. **CHANG, Sen-dou.** Peking: The Growing Metropolis of Communist China, *Geographical Review* 55, 1965, 312–27.

Reviews the historical roles of the two capitals, Beijing and Nanjing. Explains choice of Beijing as capital of People's Republic of China in terms of historical sentiment, with Beijing representing a powerful dynasty with a strategically forward capital, and geomancy. Describes the morphology of the older and newer parts of the city. Traces historical development of city since 1421. The functions of Beijing include educational, cultural, industrial, and communications ones. Notes city's main problem will be securing an adeqaute water supply. Expects Beijing to overtake Shanghai in size and influence.

1174. **CHANG, Sen-dou.** Some Aspects on the Urban Geography of the Chinese Hsien Capital, *Annals, Association of American Geographers* 51, 1961, 23–45.

Focuses on four aspects of *hsien* capitals: historical development, sites and distribution, internal spatial structure, and major urban functions.

1175. CHANG, Sen-dou. Some Observations of the Morphology of Chinese Walled Cities, *Annals, Association of American Geographers* 60, 1970, 63–91.

Discusses changes in preferred building materials, shapes, and orientations of cities. Details how population growth and economic expansion were spatially accommodated via extension of walls. Notes that historically Chinese cities did not have tall buildings and that internal layouts were flexible.

1176. CHANG, Sen-dou. The Million City of Mainland China, *Pacific Viewpoint* 9, 1968, 128–53.

Traces urbanization patterns from 1950 through mid-1960s. Identifies seventeen cities with a minimum population of one million. Argues that million cities have increased in number due to deliberate planned growth of provincial capitals, the building of strategically placed new cities, the economic goal of regional autarky, and the deliberate overbounding of cities. Major challenges facing the central and local governments is how to provide adequate housing, land, utilities, and transportation to maintain economically and socially viable large cities.

1177. CHEN, Cheng-siang. Population Growth and Urbanization in China, 1952–1970, *Geographical Review* 63, 1973, 55–72.

Based on 1953 census and annual updates by the State Statistical Bureau. Describes population increases and regional patterns of growth. Notes negative impact of Cultural Revolution of 1966–68 on urban growth. Expects urban population to grow only moderately despite industrialization.

1178. CHEN, Cheng-siang. Population Growth and Urbanization in China, 1953–70, *Ekistics* 38:226, 1974, 192–98.

Describes the political issues related to the taking of the 1953 census and the resulting answers as to the true definition of a city and the nature of the spatial distribution of urban places. Outlines a framework of stages of post-1949 urban development starting with recovery and ending with industrialization. Economic development has resulted in the building of new cities, especially in areas of resource frontiers. Anticipates only modest increases in urban population in the future.

1179. CHEN, C. Z. Some Ancient Chinese Concepts of Town and Country, *Town Planning Review* 19, 1943, 160–63.

Uses the etymology of the Chinese characters for *city* to describe the essential elements and characteristics of a traditional Chinese city. Cities, in contrast to market towns, were walled, with subdivisions into quarters, and included agricultural land and designated public buildings. Cites classical Chinese texts to provide details and sources of urban units.

1180. CHUAN, Shao-ching. The Most Extraordinary City in the World: Notes on Lhasa, the Mecca of the Buddhist Faith, *National Geographic Magazine* 12, 1912, 959–95.

Report based on a 1906–07 Chinese mission to Tibet. Describes the location, morphology, government, and religious practices of Lhasa. Detailed information on the Polata as well as the Dupon, Sera, and Gandan monasteries.

1181. COLLIE, George L. The Port of Shangai, *Journal of Geography* 12, 1913–14, 51–55.

Describes the site, situation, and surroundings of Shanghai. Assesses its economic significance. Provides a list of eight port regulations. Sees Shanghai as major economic center but plagued by physical problems such as silting of the river and competition from other ports, especially along the Yangtze River.

1182. COULTER, John Wesley. Harbin: Strategic City on the "Pioneer Fringe," *Pacific Affairs* 5, 1932, 967–72.

Deals mainly with Russian sector of city from its founding in 1896. Although the primary economic activities derive from the city's location in Manchuria, dumping of Russian goods inhibits further economic expansion.

1183. COULTER, John Wesley. Peiping, *Journal of Geography* 33, 1934, 161–71.

Sees city as a link between past and present for those wishing to understand China. Sketches out his impressions of street scenes, places, temples, alleys, industries, and educational institutions. Expresses hope that even as the city grows its walls will be preserved.

1184. DRAKAKIS-SMITH, D. W. Housing Needs and Planning Policies for the Asian City: The Lessons from Hong Kong, *International Journal of Environmental Studies* 1, 1971, 115–28.

Despite its apparent successes in providing minimal housing for residents, Hong Kong is not necessarily a model for the rest of Asia in meeting housing needs. This is so because slum removal did not lead to new housing that improved the urban landscape, no legislative framework was established to guide the rehousing process, and the needs of slum dwellers were not considered when new housing was constructed. Prefers Singapore's housing schemes. Includes data from a 1969 survey of rehoused citizens.

1185. DRAKAKIS-SMITH, D. W. Tenement Slum Renewal: Hong Kong, *Pacific Viewpoint* 13, 1972, 155–68.

Argues that, in contrast to other Third World areas, Hong Kong's housing crisis is not one of an absolute shortage of housing but rather one in which the existing stock needs improvement. The Hong Kong government's attempt to house squatters does not provide a model for fully solving that housing problem since the squatter resettlement schemes did not consider illegal migration, rates of natural increase, or displacement due to urban renewal. Questions assumption that the best way to house a population is in government-owned rental facilities. Urges government to use free market to get the proper balance in size and quality of housing units. Provides indices and maps of variations in housing quality.

1186. DRAKAKIS-SMITH, D. W. Traditional and Modern Aspects of Urban Systems in the Third World: A Case Study in Hong Kong, *Pacific Viewpoint* 12, 1971, 21–40.

A quantitative analysis of market areas for towns in the New Territories. Sees urban and market development as following four stages: attraction, equilibrium, attraction and equilibrium, and dispersal. As these stages progress, permanent shops assume a more important economic role while itinerant merchants lose ground. Notes role of tradition and loyalties in residents' use of purchasing power.

1187. DWYER, D. J. The Problem of In-Migration and Squatter Settlement in Asian Cities: Two Case Studies, Manila and Victoria, Kowloon, *Asian Studies* [Quezon City] 2, 1964–65, 145–69.

Argues that Asian squatter settlements differ from those in other parts of the world because Asian cities have high-density agricultural settlements on their peripheries. Therefore, in Asian cities squatters must occupy urban sites such as lofts, staircases, passageways, tunnels, and even sewers. Sees squatters as the result of pull factors. For the Hong Kong case, describes the evolution of government policies and programs in the resettlement process. Provides architectural drawings of typical Hong Kong resettlement flats and seven-story blocks. Sees Hong Kong as a model for the rest of Asia when dealing with squatters.

1188. DWYER, D. J. The Recent Development of the Port of Hong Kong, *Geography* 48, 1963, 317–20.

Notes that given the rise of the People's Republic of China the historic China-Hong Kong trade patterns have changed. Describes these patterns as far back as 1936. Changes in trade have resulted from changes in People's Republic trade policies, the 1951 United Nations embargo, and the U.S. ban on all Chinese commodities. Nevertheless, expects Hong Kong to prosper as it develops its industrial base. Enumerates the infrastructure problems that will have to be addressed if Hong Kong is to become a major economic center and government programs designed to meet these problems.

1189. DWYER, D. J. Urban Squatters: The Relevence of the Hong Kong Experience, *Asian Survey* 10, 1970, 607–13.

Since Hong Kong's policy toward settling squatters is an integral part of the overall background of Hong Kong's economic success, other Southeast Asian countries are urged to employ similar policies.

1190. EBERHARD, Wolfram. Data on the Structure of the Chinese City in the Pre-Industrial Period, *Economic Development and Cultural Change* 4, 1956, 253–68.

Laments general lack of studies by historians on Chinese cities and is disturbed that the 1948 hypothesis by Li Chi regarding the origins and spread of Chinese civilization has not led to either measuring or mapping the process of new city building in premodern China. Describes the origins of Chinese cities and urban populations, the size of early cities, urban forms and structures, the nature of the urban hierarchy, and the administration and provision of public services in early cities.

1191. EDGAR, J. H. The Great Weal, or a Christmas Journey to the Huangho Mouth, *Journal, Royal Asiatic Society, North China Branch*, new series 45, 1914, 46–56.

Describes towns, their ecology, and their layout along the lower reaches of the Huang He. Reports on unsafe travel conditions. Notes the lack of accurate maps and surveys of river and coastline.

19. *Urban Geography*

1192. EIGNER, Julius. Rise and Fall of Nanking, *National Geographic Magazine* 73, 1938, 189–234.

Describes how Nanjing was modernized during the period 1928–38, especially with regard to infrastructure such as water supply and transportation and the taxation system. As such, Nanjing was a symbol of the new China. Provides sketches of how the traditional economic sector functioned in the streets. Laments the halt to progress that resulted from the Japanese invasion in December 1937.

1193. EYRE, Alan L. Shanghai: World's Second City, *Professional Geographer* 23, 1971, 28–30. Comments, pp. 237–38.

Describes the spread of Shanghai under the Nationalist government and deliberate overbounding by the Communist one. Growth has continued despite the negative attitude of Communists toward this capitalist center. As such, it stands as a rival to Beijing. Using satellite imagery, divides the city into historic, periurban, urban, and rural hinterland zones.

1194. FAULKNER, H. E. Peking, *Journal, Manchester Geographical Society* 52, 1942, 18–26.

Based on author's experiences as a resident of city between 1925 and 1937. Major concerns are with the geography, climate, and flora of city. Describes what was considered to be the "spirit" of the city. Provides some historical information about city. Favorably impressed by the design, architecture, urban forms, and housing of traditional city. Expresses great nostalgia about old way of life. Sees Western influence on city as basically disruptive of the way of life and the man-nature relationship about which westerners could be learning.

1195. FORBES, Edgar Allen. Macau (China), "Land of Sweet Sadness," *National Geographic Magazine* 62, 1932, 336.

Uses poetry of Luis de Camoens to extol the virtues of Macao over Hong Kong. Describes role of Macao in Portuguese trade. Touches on local economy and describes fishing and gambling industries. Recounts the best things to see in Macao and how to see them.

1196. FRASER, J. M. Choi Hung Housing Estate, Hong Kong, *Ekistics* 20:119, 1965, 194–98.

Begins with the history and financial and legal framework of the Hong Kong Housing Authority. Choi Hung is the fifth housing scheme to be completed. Describes the projected population and number and mix of shops as well as amenities included to make the area more appealing. Touches on role of full-time staff in each estate to deal with health and sanitation problems as well as vandalism.

1197. GINSBURG, Norton [S]. Ch'ang-ch'un, *Economic Geography* 23, 1947, 290–307.

Seeks to discover the reasons why the Japanese made the city, which they renamed Hsin-king (New Capital), the center of the administration of Manchuria. Tests hypothesis that Zhangzhun was chosen because it was located on a well-integrated transportation system featuring the railroad. Describes the character of the city, land use, postwar changes, the deterioration of infrastructure due to abandonment, and early history as far back as 1791. Concludes that under Chinese administration the city will still be an important center since it retains the advantages that the Japanese found attractive.

1198. GINSBURG, Norton [S]. Ch'ing-tao: Development and Land Utilization, *Economic Geography* 24, 1948, 181–200.

Covers the site and position, historical setting and modern development, economic activities, landscape, daily life, land use, and water supply of this important port and transportation link. Points out that rebuilding of the city will require a stable political environment.

1199. GOLGER, Otto J. Hong Kong: A Problem of Housing the Masses, *Ekistics* 33:196, 1972, 173–7.

Argues that resettlement of squatters is necessary in order to reduce densities, crime, and fire hazards and improve sanitary conditions. Remarks that fully one-half of squatters do not want to be resettled. Nevertheless, resettlement will provide a better quality of life, as resettlement flats are larger than existing housing units. Provides technical details regarding resettlement estates as well as the social aspects of resettlement as a process. Notes the government responded to the crisis in housing that precipitated the 1966–67 riots.

1200. GUINNES, Walter. China; A Young Man's First Encounter, *Geographical Magazine* 23, 1950, 41–48.

Extracts of letters written by Lord Moyne to his wife in 1902 describing life in Beijing.

19. Urban Geography

1201. HARRIS, Nigel. China's Cities, *Economy and Society* 1, 1972, 106–15.

Review article focusing on two works: Lewis's *The City in Communist China* (Stanford University Press, 1971) and Howe's *Employment and Economic Growth in Urban China, 1949–1957* (Columbia University Press, 1971). Traces Chinese approach to the tensions resulting from urbanization and economic development. Concludes that China has provided no cures for urban ailments but has had some successes in stabilizing urban conditions. Questions whether the cost of such stability was worth the effort.

1202. HAYES, Helen. Life on the Hutungs of Peking, *Geographical Magazine* 10, 1940, 258–71.

Describes daily life in the alleys and side streets of Beijing, with special emphasis on Chinese New Year celebrations in 1936 in the alley where the author lived.

1203. HITCH, Margaret A. Port of Tientsin and Its Problems, *Geographical Review* 25, 1935, 367–81.

Reports, using data from 1898 through 1910, that Tianjin is the third-largest port in China. Its growth is directly related to its location. Notes decline in port activity due to diversion of trade resulting from the Chinese civil and world wars. Principle goods shipped through Tianjin are textiles, especially cottons and woolens. Main problems in maintaining port are floods and siltation. Describes plans of government agencies, including Hai Ho Conservancy Board, to solve these problems. Sees only permanent solution as involving upstream reclamation and reforestation.

1204. HO, Ping-ti. Lo-yang: A.D. 495–534, *Harvard Journal of Asiatic Studies* 26, 1966, 52–101.

A study of the physical and socioeconomic planning of a metropolitan area. Describes the location of the city, its walls and land use, and its social structure. Includes maps showing location of gates as well as economic, governmental, and religious institutions.

1205. HUBBARD, George D. Geographic Setting of Chengtu, *Bulletin, Geographical Society of Philadelphia* 21, 1923, 109–39.

Argues that Chengdu has the potential to be a great trade center once a stable Chinese government can be established. Specific topics covered include history of city, location and situation, urban land use, resources, water, agriculture, industry, and defenses. Compares the older imperial part of city to modern section.

1206. HUBBARD, James Mascarene. Singan: The Present Capital of the Chinese Empire, *National Geographic Magazine* 12, 1901, 63–66.

Reviews the site and situational advantages of Xian that have enabled it to remain a capital for a long time. Describes the city form. Comments on the presence and impact of the Syrian Christian Church and Muslims.

1207. HUGHES, R. H. Hong Kong: An Urban Study, *Geographical Journal* 117, 1951, 1–31.

Provides an outline history of the colony. Describes topography, relief, and climate. Section on urban development focuses on site problems and the need for land reclamation and local architecture.

1208. IMPEY, Lawrence. Shangtu: The Summer Capital of Kublai Khan, *Geographical Review* 15, 1925, 584–604.

Begins by reviewing European literary and scientific sources about Shangdu. Rich in detail about the road from China proper to the capital. Actual site described, starting with suburban defenses and moving into the old outer and inner city centers. Provides details regarding size and materials of walls, land use patterns, and urban layout. Points out urgent need for scientific examination of remaining materials of archaeological interest.

1209. JOHNSTON, Sir Reginald. Peking, *Geographical Magazine* 1, 1935, 185–97, with photogravure supplement.

Explanation by former tutor to Emperor Pu-yi and the last British commissioner in Weihaiwei of the reasons for Beijing remaining the Chinese capital for such a long time as well as its demoted status in 1935. Includes a comparison between Beijing and Nanjing.

1210. KEITH, Ronald A. Tsinan: A Chinese City, *Canadian Geographical Journal* 12:3, 1936, 153–60.

Describes historical development, location, site, daily life, and modernization of city, which was still walled in 1935.

1211. LACY, Walter N. The Approach to Shanghai, *Journal of Geography* 21, 1922, 276–81.

Colorful description of the shifting urban scenes as a passenger ship enters port and docks at assigned berth.

1212. **LACY, Walter N.** Fires in Chinese Cities, *Journal of Geography* 16, 1917, 67–69.

Although fire is commonly associated with Japanese cities, it is a problem for Chinese cities as well. The threat of fires derives from the type of building materials used, the close proximity of one building to another, and methods of firefighting that emphasize tearing down adjacent buildings to stop the spread of a fire and in reality helping it spread. Although cities have grown in size, there has not been a comparable increase in the size of firefighting forces or resources.

1213. **LANNING, George.** Names and Nicknames of the Shanghai Settlements, *Journal, Royal Asiatic Society, North China Branch*, new series 51, 1920, 84–98.

Traces history and development of Shanghai using native and Western names of areas. Argues that use of individual and family names to designate streets is a Western practice.

1214. **LEEMING, Frank.** Reconstructing Late Ch'ing Fengt'ien, *Modern Asian Studies* 4, 1970, 305–24.

Uses memoirs of European residents, Imperial Maritime Customs trade reports, and Japanese sources to describe Shenyang between 1906 and 1909. Decribes changes in economy, morphology, population, social structure, and urban functions. Sees it as an atypical Chinese city and urges more studies of such cities, including Xiangtan in Hunan.

1215. **LIANG, Chi-sen.** Urban Land Use in Hong Kong and Kowloon, Part 1: Tsim-sha-Tsui District, *Chung Chi Journal* 6, 1966, 1–24.

Report based on a 1966 survey at the block level. Uses a number of indices, such as the height index, to identify and classify different types of urban-economic land use. Creates a fourfold division of land use in the Hong Kong central area.

1216. **LIANG, Chi-sen.** Urban Land Use in Hong Kong and Kowloon, Part 2: Central Business District, *Chung Chi Journal* 8, 1968, 107–35.

Defines limits of the Central Business District (CBD) on Hong Kong Island using the theoretical geographical literature. Describes the location and functions of the retail, services, administrative, residential, and wholesale sectors. The expansion of the CBD will involve both urban renewal of the older sections of the current CBD as well as new sections built on land released by various government agencies, such as the War

Department, and land reclamation. Describes plans for expansion of CBD and the probable future of CBD functions on both the Hong Kong and Kowloon sides of the harbor.

1217. LO, C[hor]. P[ang]. A Typology of Hong Kong Census Districts: A Study in Urban Structure, *Journal of Tropical Geography* 34, 1972, 34–43.

Applies cluster analysis to 1966 census data and creates a sevenfold classification of combinations of ten demographic measures. Hong Kong shows evidence of both axial development and a concentric ring land use pattern. Concludes that despite the general nonapplicability of Western urban models to Asian situations they are useful in creating an idealized model of Hong Kong.

1218. LOCKHART, W[illiam]. Notes on Peking and Its Neighborhoods, *Proceedings, Royal Geographical Society of London* 10, 1869, 154–58; *Journal, Royal Geographical Society* 36, 1866, 128–56.

Impressions of city by surgeon who worked for a missionary society in Beijing for many years. Describes tribute retinues, climate, and urban structures and forms such as walls and temples. Estimates population to be around 1 to 1.5 million, which, it is claimed, is close to other estimates.

1219. LONG, George W. Hong Kong Hangs On, *National Geographic Magazine* 105, 1954, 239–72.

Touches on history of port and its functions, the impact of refugees, government programs for dealing with piracy and smuggling, growth of new manufacturing, social customs and practices, land reclamation, and improvements in health. Notes that private investors are optimistic regarding the colony's prospects.

1220. McCUNE, Shannon. Harbin, Manchoukuo, *Journal of Geography* 39, 1940, 187–96.

Describes location, site, and climate of city. Traces development of city, especially the Russian role in its founding and expansion. Sketches land use areas. Most quantitative part of material involves city circa 1937 and deals with population, ethnicity, and economic strengths related to imports and exports. Expects city to expand to a radius of about fifteen miles with a population of one million by 1970. Feels city will remain predominantly Chinese, despite the heavy Russian and Japanese influences.

19. Urban Geography

1221. MOORE, W. Robert. Coastal Cities of China, *National Geographic Magazine* 66, 1934, 601–43.

Vignettes of thirteen coastal cities (Macao, Hong Kong, Canton, Swatow, Fuzhou, Amoy, Hangzhou, Ningbo, Shanghai, Zhingdao, Chefoo, Tianjin, and Dalian). Describes U.S.-China trade. Includes impressions of dangers of traveling along the coast as well as adventures of city life.

1222. MOORE, W. Robert. Cosmopolitan Shanghai: Key Seaport of China, *National Geographic Magazine* 62, 1932, 310–35.

Traces history of function of port. Decries the negative impact modernization has had on the old city landscape. Describes means of transportation within the city and along the river. Concerned with how and where non-Chinese spend their leisure hours. Considers entire population to be international and cosmopolitan. Impressed with the accessibility of city to other parts of China and the world. Amazed that a letter can go from Shanghai to Paris in only sixteen days.

1223. MOORE, W. Robert. Glory That Was Imperial Peking, *National Geographic Magazine* 63, 1933, 745–80.

Provides sketch of daily life in capital and especially the difficulty of coping with winter. Compares urban morphology of city with special focus on the Forbidden City and its political and tourist role.

1224. MOORE, W. Robert. Miniatures of Macao (China), *National Geographic Magazine* 62, 1932, 340–48.

Eleven pictures of local economy with no comments or notes.

1225. MORRISON, Hedda [M]. Colors of Peking, *Geographical Magazine* 23, 1950, 49–53.

Four color pages of pictures of scenes of Beijing with no text or comments.

1226. MULLER, James Arthur. Peking, the City of the Unexpected, *National Geographic Magazine* 38, 1920, 335–55.

Describes a city with no skyline but a colorful cityscape. Reviews architecture, religion, role of women in Chinese society, and transportation. Mentions Western Hills and Beacon Towers. Notes approvingly that U.S. Boxer Indemnity funds were used to further Chinese education.

1227. **MURPHEY, Rhoads.** Aspects of Urbanization in Contemporary China: A Revolutionary Model, *Proceedings, Association of American Geographers* 7, 1975, 165–68.

Sees the Chinese plans for new cities and the diffusion of industry from old centers as a model for Asia that can help prevent or avoid the negative aspects of urban concentrations.

1228. **MURPHEY, Rhoads.** City and Countryside as Ideological Issues: India and China, *Comparative Studies in Society and History* 14, 1972, 250–67.

Argues that India and China are skeptical regarding the industrialization-urbanization link because rising expectations have not been fulfilled, cities are not attractive places to live, the model is based on colonial experiences, and there was no traditional rural-urban dichotomy in Asia. Notes nevertheless the role that cities can play in modernizing the population as well as providing the goods and services needed to improve the standard of living for all citizens. Urges investment in both rural and urban areas as a development strategy.

1229. **MURPHEY, Rhoads.** City as a Center of Change: Western Europe and China, *Annals, Association of American Geographers* 44, 1954, 349–62.

Uses three variables, education and its sociopolitical function, urbanization and politics, and urban-rural links, to examine different roles that cities have played in the economic development of China and Western Europe. Concludes that the study of cities and their roles provides a useful indicator of the nature and dynamics of societies.

1230. **O'HARA, Albert R.** Development of Urbanization in Asia and Taiwan, *Journal of the China Society* 7, 1970, 38–52.

Summarizes differences between Asian and Western cities. Sees Asia as overurbanized, with rural-based poverty push factors contributing to city growth. Notes difficulty of deriving definitions of urban and urbanization. Recounts history of Taiwanese urbanization in the context of political changes since the early nineteenth century. Argues that Taiwan's urban hierarchy is dominated by Taipei as a primate city. Concludes that Taiwanese cities do not fit the pattern of Asian cities. Since they are similar to Western cities, urbanization should be a slow process.

1231. ONOYE, Etsuzo. Regional Distribution of Urban Population in China, *Developing Economies* 8, 1970, 93–127.

Study covers the periods 1953–57 and 1964–67. Goal is to clarify the regional distribution of urban population and to trace its changes since 1949 in the context of the regional division of labor. Postulates four models of Chinese cities' ability to absorb surplus rural labor and the subsequent impact on urban growth. Notes impact on analysis of deliberate overbounding cities. Data on a province by province basis are presented in graph form. Concludes that shifts in urbanization were tied to progress toward industrialization.

1232. ORCHARD, John E. Shanghai, *Geographical Review* 26, 1936, 1–31.

Describes how Shanghai holds the commercial, financial, and industrial leadership of China and the lower reaches of the Yangtze. Includes a discussion of the pre-Western origins and growth of settlements in the general area. In noting how Shanghai has come to eclipse Canton, compares and contrasts the advantages and disadvantages of the two cities, especially with regard to security, location, and accessibility to railroads and raw materials for industry. Separate section devoted to industrial development and location of manufacturing. Sees the question of the future of Shanghai as a center as being more political than economic in nature.

1233. PANNELL, Clifton W. Changing Space Use and the Retail Market in Taichung's Urban Structure, *Proceedings, Association of American Geographers* 6, 1974, 153–57.

Focus is on the First Market of Taizhong City. Describes its location, structure, operations, and supply and demand functions. Argues that the First Market is still viable and dynamic despite the growth of the modern urban economy. Expects that as Taiwanese cities expand they will follow a Chinese rather than a Western model of development, especially with regard to location of services and land use patterns.

1234. PANNELL, C[lifton]. W. City and Regional Growth in Taiwan, *Journal of the China Society* [*Taipei*] 7, 1970, 1–17.

Purpose of article is to "consider" the demographic aspects of urbanization in Taiwan and to analyze the spatial/locational aspects of cities. Provides history of Taiwanese cities since the seventeenth century, compares population densities of cities, reviews urbanization plans, and evaluates the hierarchy regarding primacy and the rank-size rule.

1235. PANNELL, Clifton W. City Morphology in T'ai-wan: A Variation on a Chinese Theme, *Proceedings, Association of American Geographers* 5, 1973, 210–16.

Uses Taizhong City as an example of how urban development in Taiwan can be seen as a combination of both Chinese and Western urban models. Includes maps of land use. Argues that future expansion of an urban economy is not an exclusively Chinese, Japanese, or Western question.

1236. PANNELL, C[lifton]. W. Outlanders on the Island: Some Historic Notes on Form and Function in the Taiwanese City, *Journal of the China Society [Taipei]* 6, 1969, 61–78.

Divides Taiwanese urban history into four stages. Describes which economic, political, and social processes have affected urban form and morphology on a city by city basis. Notes use of the shop house as a distinctive urban form. Evaluates impact of Japanese planning on degree of urban orderliness, infrastructure, and social differentiation. Comments on role of military in land use development after 1945.

1237. PANNELL, Clifton W. Urbanization and City Growth in T'ai-wan, *Journal of Geography* 72, 1973, 11–21.

Against the background of the United States recognizing the People's Republic of China, a review of Taiwan's urbanization is viewed against progress toward industrialization. Explores issues such as problems of defining an urban area, place hierarchy, overbounding, and patterns of settlement. Argues that Taiwan's level of urbanization is within a range normally associated with developing countries but that the spatial distribution of cities is bipolar, focusing on the north and south and connected by an urban corridor along the west coast.

1238. PASSANTINO, Jospeh E. Kunming, Southwest Gateway to China, *National Geographic Magazine* 90, 1946, 137–68.

Describes how the mixed populations share space and create a series of changing economic and transportation functions with rural areas. Notes importance of city given its distance from other places.

1239. PENG, George T. C. Philosophy of City Design of Peking, *Ekistics* 33:195, 1972, 124–29.

Relates design of Beijing to yin/yang and *fengshui* principles. Recounts the history of the city and the growth and function of its concentric wall systems. Sees Beijing as a harmoniously unified place, an ideal expression of the Chinese city.

1240. PRYOR, E. G. A Historical Review of Housing Conditions in Hong Kong, *Journal, Royal Asiatic Society, Hong Kong Branch* 12, 1972, 89–129.

Reviews 130 years of housing problems and the various government schemes designed to correct them.

1241. PRYOR, E. G. Private Housing in Hong Kong, *Planner* 59, 1973, 455–58.

Marvels at the rapid rate of increase in the built environment in Hong Kong between 1965 and 1971. Notes older environment was more horizontal in character, while new areas are vertical. Relates building to impact of World War II and subsequent influx of refugees. Describes the positive impact of imposing in 1956 building regulations that permitted a private housing sector to develop. Notes impact of economic and political events on boom and bust cycles. Provides a positive evaluation of private housing in the future, while noting that the government will still have a role in determining total supply and demand for housing.

1242. RAWLINSON, H. C. On the Recent Journey of Mr. W. H. Johnson from Leh in Ladakh to Ilchi in Chinese Turkistan, *Proceedings, Royal Geographical Society of London* 11, 1866, 6–14.

Describes major cities of areas such as Kashgar, Yarkand, Aksu, Yenghiseher, Ilchi, and Oosh-Turfan. Compares political and physical characteristics of area with other parts of Asia.

1243. REED, Andrew. Hong Kong: The Water Problem Solved? *Geography* 52, 1967, 418–20.

Focus is on Plover Cove Reservoir System and related tunnels. Predicts that this set of projects, by doubling Hong Kong's water storage capacity, will lead to water self-sufficiency. Once the reservoir is completed, water will be available on a year-round basis, thus eliminating the need for periodic water use restrictions.

1244. ROSE, John. Hong Kong's Water Supply Problem and China's Contribution to Its Solution, *Geographical Review* 56, 1966, 432–37.

Water has been a problem for Hong Kong since the area became a British Crown colony. This is due to its location: the climate is monsoonal and rainfall is therefore highly seasonal and dependent upon typhoons. Describes how the colonial government has extended the water supply through projects such as those in Plover's Cove and the Tolo Channel. Sees major problems with a Chinese solution to the water problem given the need to develop reservoirs, pipelines, and pumping stations. Sees desalinization as a possible solution to water shortages.

1245. SALTER, Cristopher L. Chinese Experiments in Urban Space, *Habitat* 4, 1976, 19–35.

Uses Dazhing as an example of China's quest for an agropolitan form of urban development. Describes the micro- and macro-innovations Chinese planners have developed in order to implement the concept.

1246. SCHENK, H[ans]. Concepts behind Urban and Regional Planning in China, *Tijdschrift voor economische en sociale geografie* 65, 1974, 381–88.

Chinese cities were ordinarily not merely consumer centers but also production bases. Seeks to find explanations for the shift to a greater emphasis on production. Ideas explored include pre-1958 patterns of urban development, changing concepts of economic organization, and development of urban communes and their restructuring. The social transformation of the means of production and increased political consciousness of the population have enabled China to reduce regional disparities in wealth and opportunity and as such have solved the contradiction between town and countryside.

1247. SCHENK, Hans. Notes on Urban Spatial Planning and Development in China, *Eastern Horizon* 11, 1972, 34–41.

Based on visits to the construction departments of urban revolutionary committees in Shanghai, Xian, and Beijing in 1971. Main focus is on housing, location of living quarters, care for the environment and pollution, and traffic. Although at the city level urban places are separate from rural ones, in the political and social context of China there is a growing convergence of the two locational types that will result in new urban forms.

1248. SCOFIELD, John. Hong Kong's Many Faces, *National Geographic Magazine* 121, 1962, 1–41.

Discusses changes in industry, housing, and recreation in the context of refugees' stories and the impact of British life in Hong Kong on government and social life. Describes the spread of industrialization and urbanization into the New Territories.

1249. SHOR, Franc. The City They Call Red China's Showcase, *National Geographic Magazine* 118, 1960, 193–223.

Despite the return to Beijing of the United Nations' relief and rehabilitation staff, the economy has worsened, especially with the decline and disappearance of local markets and itinerant merchants and the banning of rickshaws, requiring one to now leave the house in order to shop daily. Does acknowledge new buildings but concerned that progress is being made at the expense of old sites.

1250. SILVER, Sylvia A. Tienstin: Treaty Port, *Canadian Geographical Journal* 4:6, 1932, 381–92.

Describes daily life of a coolie and his reaction to Westernization. Pays special attention to concession area and administrative and police issues.

1251. SIMPICH, Frederick. 1940 Paradox in Hong Kong, *National Geographic Magazine* 77, 1940, 531–38.

Despite the influx of refugees, Hong Kong continues showing signs of ability to rebound and progress. Describes history of area, the government and defense establishments, housing, general and street economies, amusements, health, and education. Contrasts life in Kowloon and Hong Kong.

1252. SMITH, Helen L. Shanghai and Its Hinterland, *Journal of Geography* 38, 1939, 173–80.

Argues that, in the long run, the climate, agriculture, and transportation facilities of the city are the facts of life that must be adjusted to. Notes the limits that silting and gorges may place on future expansion of port. Characterizes harbor as far from ideal owing to the lack of bedrock and the resulting difficulty of building large structures. City is superficially Western in that neither the Chinese nor the Western race or culture dominates.

1253. SPENCER, J[oseph]. E[arle]. Changing Chungking: The Rebuilding of an Old Chinese City, *Geographical Review* 29, 1939, 46–60.

Notes that city was opened to foreigners in 1891. Assesses impact of being selected as new seat for the central Chinese government. Describes the streets, walls, and site of old city and growth of overbounded new city. Reviews demographic characteristics of city, especially overcrowding and high sex ratios.

1254. **THOMASON, Major John W.** Approaches to Peiping, *National Geographic Magazine* 69, 1936, 275–308.

Assumes that to know Beijing, one needs to know the roads and footpaths that connect the city and its inhabitants. Topics covered using this viewpoint include architecture, construction, urban structure, food, and shopping. A second context for describing the city is its situation within China and its latitude, which, it is noted, is the same as Washington, D.C.

1255. **TISDALE, Alice.** The Enchantment of the Old Order, *Geographical Review* 12, 1919, 11–23.

Focuses on the sights and sounds of urban life in China, such as itinerant peddlers and their calls as well as the sounds of harvesting and threshing rice and *kaoliang*. Laments the passing of the old order and the appearance of a new society dominated by the monotonous clicking of clocks and steam engines.

1256. **TOWERS, Graham.** City Planning in China, *Journal of the Royal Town Planning Institute* 59, 1973, 125–27.

Uses Shanghai and Xian to demonstrate how planners in China seek to avoid the negative externalities associated with Western cities, especially overconcentration of industry and the growth of regional imbalances. Describes the history of origins and structures of Chinese cities. Notes how planning falls to local authorities of the City Construction Bureau and District Street Committees, while the central government provides only macroeconomic planning guidelines and standards. Main planning challenges are urban renewal of old, overcrowded residential areas and developing new industrial areas. Contrasts the use of stereotypic socialist housing blocks with a trend toward preservation and rehabilitation.

1257. **TREGEAR, T. R.** Shih Hui Yao: A Chinese River Port with a Future, *Geography* 39, 1954, 113–17.

Port is located some fifty miles beyond Hankou on the right bank of the Changjiang. Describes topography and population of area. Relic landscape indicates past prosperity based on exploitation of local raw materials such as coal, iron, and lumber. Provides details on origins, types, and quality of local industrial raw materials. Expects the return of peace will usher in a new era of prosperity, too, especially if Chinese planners include the city among those slated to foster regional autarky.

19. Urban Geography

1258. TREWARTHA, Glenn T. Chinese Cities: Numbers and Distribution, *Annals, Association of American Geographers* 41, 1951, 331–47.

Maps data for 1930s, although data for period 1922–49 are discussed. Cities are classified and then mapped by size, location, and proximity to major transportation systems.

1259. TREWARTHA, Glenn T. Chinese Cities: Origins and Functions, *Annals, Association of American Geographers* 42, 1952, 67–93.

Classifies number and functions of cities by broad historical periods. Modern Chinese cities function as administrative or economic centers, depending on scale of analysis. Asserts that it is not clear what the raison d'être for more contemporary cities in China may be.

1260. TYRWHIFF, Jaqueline. The City of Ch'ang-an, *Town Planning Review* 39, 1968, 21–37.

Traces the history of the city from 583 to 904. Special attention devoted to site characteristics and the layout and design of the city. Specific topics reviewed include walls, water supply, architecture and building materials, religion and festivals, and land use. Provides an evaluation of historical records available for study.

1261. WANG, I-shou. Urbanization in Manchuria, 1907–40, *International Geography* 2, 1972, 850–52.

Devotes considerable space to the history of databases used in past analyses and issues relating to definitions of urban places in China. Relates increases in the number and size of urban places to establishment of Manchukuo and Japanese investments. Notes that after World War II, urban growth was concentrated in large cities, with low or declining rates of change in towns. Predicts the eventual filling in of an urban hierarchy, especially in the north and northeastern parts of Manchuria.

1262. WHITE, John Claude. The World's Strangest Capital, *National Geographic Magazine* 29, 1916, 273–95.

Describes Lhasa by focusing on the Potala as part monastery, part citadel, part administrative center. Surveys land use in Lhasa using different perspectives of the Potala. Is disappointed by the interior architecture and decoration of Potala. In discussing the religious functions of monks and monasteries, provides a crude, Western-oriented comparison and contrast of religion and magic.

1263. WIENS, Harold J. Historical and Geographical Role of Urumchi, Capital of Chinese Central Asia, *Annals, Association of American Geographers* 53, 1963, 441–64.

Seeks to establish the signature of the city and oasis by exploring their evolution, including situation in the 1960s. Includes information on physical setting, climate, vegetation, political history, population, and ethnicity. Concludes that Urumchi has been the center of political storms for well over a thousand years and will continue to be due to its strategic location. Notes potential of region to be a major economic and industrial base once railroads connecting eastern China and the Soviet Union are completed. Interprets the development of new towns as part of the sinicization and communization of the Chinese colonial realm in Central Asia.

1264. WRIGHT, Arthur F. Symbolism and Function: Reflections on Changan and Other Great Cities, *Journal of Asian Studies* 24, 1965, 667–69.

Main focus is on city during the Sui-Tang period. Concerned for how site of city was selected and then how design and construction proceeded. Compares process and architecture of Chinese cities with those of the Roman Empire. Argues that the Chinese city is a microcosm of Chinese cosmology and reflects the values of all Chinese philosophies, including Buddhism, in its design and buildings.

See also items 0118, 0132, 0382, 0703, and 0717.

20. Regional Development and Planning

1265. BOOTH, Alfred W. Hainan: Stepping Stone of Japanese, *Journal of Geography* 40, 1941, 231–34.

Postulates that Japan's objectives in taking over Indochina require a base for aggression and commerical expansion and that Hainan is that base, given its location only fifteen miles off the China shore. Describes economic, especially agricultural, advantages of Hainan as well as the history and ethnic development of the island. Argues that Japanese undertakings in Hainan should be viewed as a direct threat to both Southeast Asia and the United States.

1266. CHANG, Chih-yi. Land Utilization and Settlement Possibilities in Sinkiang, *Geographical Review* 39, 1949, 53–75.

Report based on 1943 expedition by members of Academia Sinica. Includes evaluation of landscape, climate, soils, agricultural regions, farming practices, food production and yields, and land ownership. Points with concern to inter-ethnic disputes and massacres that have occurred as the population has grown in size and ethnic diversity. Takes Schomberg (item 0258) to task for his evaluation of water resources in Taklamakan. In the end, not very optimistic that area has much economic potential for Han colonization given the problems of irrigation, transportation, lack of improved livestock, and current use of even wild growth areas by oasis residents.

1267. CLYDE, Paul Hibbert. Japan's Investment in Manchuria, *Geographical Magazine* 10, 1939, 25–42.

After Japan's takeover, investment undertaken in an semi-socialist framework under army guidance. Private capitalists were not welcome until after 1937, when Manchuria was opened to all types of investment. Questions whether Japan's investment will ever pay off.

1268. CRESSEY, George B. The Geographic Regions of China, *Annals, American Academy of Political and Social Science* 152, 1930, 1–9.

Describes fifteen Chinese regions based on a physical condition/human adaption framework. In addition, divides China into a north/south contrast and then into an agricultural and political China. Tables of data accompany text.

1269. FREEBERNE, Michael. China Promotes Local Industries Both for National and Regional Self-Sufficiency, *Geographical Magazine* 43, 1971, 505–7, 509, 511.

War preparedness and equalization of living standards are the rationales for emphasizing regional autarky. It is assumed that it will take several years for the results of this new, small-scale approach to be seen. Planners in the People's Republic of China are now more cautious than they were under the Great Leap Forward scheme. The results should be more lasting. Provides several examples of policy implementation of investment policy such as Yenti City, Shandong; Feng-cheng County, Kiangsi; and Chiyuan County, Henan.

1270. GARRELS, Agnes T. Regional Contrasts in China, *Journal of Geography* 40, 1941, 181–84.

Model of how a college-level course focusing on the environment and man-environment interactions could be taught. Although the basic division of China is into a north-south dichotomy, includes seven subregions. Even provides model essay examinations.

1271. HALL, Robert Burnett. The Geography of Manchuria, *Annals, American Academy of Political and Social Science* 152, 1930, 278–92.

Refers to Manchuria by alternative names, Land of Beans or Bread Basket of Asia. Topically deals with climate, surface geology, topography, agriculture, population and ethnicity, urban settlements, transportation, trade, and industry. Separate regional discussions of the Manchurian, Sungari, and Liao Plains, with special emphasis on their industrial potential and Chinese-Japanese-Russian settlement and rivalry.

1272. HUNG, Fu. The Geographic Regions of China and Their Subdivision: A Study in Methodology, *Proceedings, 8th General Assembly amd 17th International Congress, International Geographic Union*, 1972, 578–90.

Describes the history of traditional and modern Chinese thinking regarding regions against the background of contemporary geographic theory regarding regional systems. Proposes a five-level division of China. Includes an extended table that contains the labels and characteristics for each level in the proposed regional hierarchy.

1273. PANNELL, Clifton W. Recent Changes and Stagnation in the Pescadores Islands, Taiwan, *Philippine Geographical Journal* 17:2, 1973, 31–45.

After a general description of climate and human geography of Penghu, it is noted that the islands are not formally a part of the economic planning process in place in the Republic of China and as such are not keeping pace with economic advances in the rest of Taiwan. Tourism is seen as major economic promise.

1274. ROXBY Percy M[aude]. The Major Regions of China, *Geography* 22, 1938, 9–14.

Report is part of a larger project undertaken by the Geographical Asssociation on the issue of classifying the regions of the world. After dividing China into five basic regions (North, lower Yangtze, Red River Basin, Southwest, and Southwest), relates information in determinist format. For each region, the time of acquisition and incorporation into China is also discussed.

1275. SPENCER, J[oseph]. E[arle]. On Regionalism in China, *Journal of Geography* 46, 1947, 123–35.

Uses diet, clothing, provincialism, and temperament/disposition to divide China. Concludes that there are not enough data available to support further regional breakdowns, although some broad patterns are obvious. Uses frequent North American/United States analogues to explain use of Chinese materials. Warns that too much official emphasis on regionalism in China could subvert political unity.

1276. STEWARD, John R. Recent Development in Manchuria, *Journal of Geography* 34, 1935, 217–28.

Argues that Manchuria's rapid progress since 1910 is related to railroad development and an era of comparative peace. Nevertheless, sees a positive role for foreign rivalry in development in general. Notes need to upgrade grazing lands and to protect them from Chinese intrusion as well as the potential conflict between urban-industrial and agricultural development.

1277. WARD, F. Kingdon. The Broken Land between India and China, *Journal, Royal Central Asiatic Society* 24, 1937, 482–86.

Analyzes shift in perception regarding Yunnan from that of a potential link between China and India to that of a broken land. Describes the Ango-French railroad rivalries in Southeast Asia and their impacts on local economic development. Comments on railroad routes, trade patterns, and alternative trade flows from Burma and Thailand into

Yunnan. Doubts whether aviation will provide an additional means of transporting goods. Notes how topography favors a north-south flow of goods in Yunnan. Favorably impressed with Chinese entrepreneurial spirit. Speculates on impact of split of British India into three states on future development of Yunnan.

1278. **WIENS, Herold J.** Continuity in Development and Expansion in China's Colonial Realm in Central Asia, *Journal of Asian Studies* 26, 1966, 67–88.

Although China has been involved in Xinjiang for some two hundred years, full control was blocked by nomads until the twentieth century. Relates stages of Chinese control to four major land use changes.

See also items 0640, 0736, 0902, and 1228.

21. Tourism

1279. HARRINGTON, Lyn. Land beyond the Great Wall: Inner Mongolia, *Geographical Magazine* 40, 1967, 560–69.

Report describes the rebuilding that has taken place since 1949. Author senses continuity among all the changes.

1280. LIU, En-lan. Pootu: A Lost Island, *Economic Geography* 13, 1937, 132–38.

Island, whose economy is based on the tourist industry, is a part of the Zhushan cluster of islands off the Zhejiang coast. Describes settlement history, population, geological features, climate, and religious practices.

See also items 0450, and 1274.

Part II

Author Index

Author Index

ABRAMOT, M. A. 0086
AGASSIZ, A. R. 0436, 1144
AIMORE, Prince, of Savio-Aosta, Duke of Spoleto. 0087
ALEXANDER, Grant. 1165
ALEXANDER, J. W. 0675
ALLEN, Nellie B. 0437
AMUNDSEN, Edward E. 0438
ANDERSON, Eugene N., Jr. 0955, 0956
ANDERSON, George E. 1079
ANDERSON, J. 0350
ANDREWS, Roy Chapin. 0088, 0308, 0309
ANON. 0001, 0002, 0003, 0004, 0089, 0090, 0091, 0092, 0093, 0094, 0095, 0096, 0351, 0439, 0440, 0441, 0442, 0443, 0444, 0445, 0673, 0674, 0814, 0815, 0816, 0899, 0990, 0901, 1025, 1080, 1081, 1082
ANTE, Robert. 0004
APPLETON, John B. 0902
ARCHER, Mildred. 0728
ARNOLD, Julean. 1083
ATWOOD Wallace W. 0446
AU, Kam-nin. 0414
AUROUSSEAU, M. 0005
AYSCOUGH, Florence W. 1166
BABER, E. Colborne. 0097, 0447
BADDELEY, J. F. 0006
BAILEY. F. M. 0098, 0099, 0100, 0352, 0353, 0354, 0448, 0729
BAIN, H. Foster. 0409
BAINBRIDGE, Oliver. 0730
BAKER, John Earl. 1084
BAKER, O. E. 0957, 0958
BALLANTINE, Joseph W. 0449
BALLAS, Donald J. 0731, 0959, 1026
BANGS, N. H. 0243
BANKS, Mike. 0450
BARBOUR, George B. 0197, 0310, 0311, 0355, 0410
BARRETT, John. 0451
BARRETT, R. T. 0817

BARTON, A. 0101, 0452
BEAL, Edwin G., Jr. 0676
BEECH, Joseph. 0453
BELDEN, W. 0411, 0412
BELL, Sir Charles. 0454
BELL, G. J. 0007
BENETT, Adrian. 0102
BENHAM, F. C. 1027
BENZELEY, M. 0103
BERGER, Roland. 0960, 0961
BERRY, L. 0278
BICKMORE, Albert S. 0455
BILLARD, Jules B. 0456
BISCH, Jorgen. 0457
BISHOP, Carl Whiting. 0458, 0459, 0460
BISHOP, Mrs. [J. F.] Isabella L. 0461
BLACKNEY, William. 0356
BLACKWELDER, Eliot. 0357, 1085
BLUE, A. D. 0104
BLUMEN, William. 0208
BOOTH, Alfred W. 1265
BORCHERT, John R. 0209
BORRADAILE, A. A. 0105
BOURNE, F. S. A. 0279, 0462, 1145
BOWRING, Sir John. 0677
BOYDEN, Amanda. 1167
BRADSHAW, Eloise. 0818
BRAKE, Brian. 1168
BRATTER, Herbert M. 0912
BRINE, Lindsey. 0106
BRISTOL, Horace, Sr. 0819
BROCK, R. W. 0413
BROOKS, C. E. P. 0210
BROWN, Josephine A. 0463
BROWN, T. Graham. 0107
BRUCE, C. D. 0108

BRYCE, E. J. 0464
BUCHANAN, Keith. 0678, 0962, 0963
BUCHANAN, Sir Walter. 0465
BUCK, David D. 1169
BUCK, John Loessing. 0964
BURDSALL, Richard L. 0109, 0280
BURKI, H. K. 0466
BURRARD, S. G. 0281
BURRILL, Meredith F. 0008
BURTON, Wilbur. 1028
BUSHELL, S. W. 0467
BUXTON, B. F. 0278,
BUXTON, L. H. Dudley. 0468, 1170
CAMERON, Nigel. 0358, 0965, 1086
CAMPBELL, W[illiam]. 0469, 0470
CANCELLARE, Frank. 1087
CARDWELL, Robert. 1088
CAREY, A. D. 0471
CARLES, W. R. 0009, 0010, 0198
CARR, William K. 0011
CASELLA, Alexandro. 0472
CHAMBERLIN, Rollin T. 0473
CHAN, Gershom. 0501
CHANG, Chi-wen. 0757
CHANG, Chi-yun. 0012, 0211, 0474, 0679, 0680, 0820, 0821
CHANG, Chih-yi. 1266
CHANG, Jen-hu. 0212, 0213, 0214, 0966
CHANG, Kia-nga. 1089
CHANG, Kuei-sheng. 0013, 0014, 1029, 1030, 1031, 1090
CHANG, Sen-dou. 0015, 0967, 0968, 0969, 1171, 1172, 1173, 1174, 1175, 1176
CHANG, Tao-shing. 0970
CHAO, Kuo-chun. 0971
CHAO, Y[uan]-r[en]. 0732
CHAPIN, William W. 0475
CHAPMAN, Frederick G. 0359

CHAPMAN, F. Spencer. 0476
CHAPMAN, Herman H. 0360
CHARLES, W. R. 0361
CHATLEY, Herbert. 0215, 0362, 0363, 0477, 0733, 0734
CHEN, C. Z. 1179
CHEN, Cheng-siang. 0016, 0216, 0414, 0478, 0479, 0480, 0681, 0682, 0972, 0973, 0974, 0975, 1091, 1177, 1178
CHEN, Han-seng. 1092
CH'EN, Kenneth. 0017, 0018, 0019
CHENG, Sih-gung. 0735
CHENG, Tso-hsin. 0312
CHENG, Yin-tang. 0903
CHENGTUNG, Liang-cheng. 0481
CHEO, Shu-yuen. 0335
CHIN, P. C. 0217
CHISHOLM, George G. 0904
CHIU, T. N. 0772
CHIU, Yan-tsz. 1032
CHOU, Shun-hsin. 1093
CHRISTIAN, John L. 0822, 1094
CHRISTIE, Dugald. 0736
CHU, Co-ching. 0218, 0219, 0220, 0221, 0222, 0223, 0234
CHUAN, Shao-ching. 1180
CHUNG, Yuet-ping. 0976
CLAPP, F. G. 0482, 0751
CLARK, F. R. H. 0483
CLARK, Leonard. 0737
CLARK, Milton I. 0823
CLARKE, F. C. M. 0484
CLEMENTI, Cecil. 0110
CLOSE, Upton. 0282
CLUBB, Edmund. 0364
CLYDE, Paul Hibbert. 1267
COALES, Oliver. 0485, 0905
COBB, Collier. 0313
COLCHESTER, Lord. 0365

COLLIE, George L. 1181
COLLINGWOOD, Dr. A. 0486
COLLINSON, Capt. 0365
COLQUHOUN, A. R. 0111, 1095, 1096, 1146
COOPER, J. J. 0020
COTTON, Arthur. 1097
COULTER, John Wesley. 0738, 1182, 1183
COVILLE, Lilian Grosvenor. 0366
CRAW, Henry. 1098
CREAGH, E. Fitzgerald. 1099
CRESSEY, George B. 0021, 0022, 0199, 0283, 0487, 0488, 0489, 0490, 0492, 0683, 0739, 0740, 0741, 0824, 0825, 0906, 0907, 0908, 0977, 1100, 1268
CROSBY, Oscar T. 0492, 0493
CUTSHALL, Alden. 0494
DARLEY, James M. 0023
DAVIDSON, Basil. 0495
DAVIDSON, Owen L. 0978
DAVIES, Llewellyn James. 0496
DAVIS, Ira C. 0979
DAVIS, John Francis. 0497, 0498
DAVIS, Sydney George. 0684, 0685
DAVIS, William Morrison. 0284
DEASY, George F. 0980, 0981, 0982, 1147
DeBEER, Dora H. 0112
deBUNSEN, E. H. 0499
DEERING, Mabel Craft. 0742
D'ELLA, Pasquale M., S.J. 0024.
DENG, Bao-ling. 0657
DENG, Ling Hau. 1101
deTERRA, H. 0225
DODD, John. 0500
DOERR, Arthur H. 0501
DORESETT, J. H. 0314
DORESETT, P. H. 0314
DOUGLAS, Henry A. 0826

DOUGLAS, Robert K. 1148
DOWNS, Joseph F. 0827
DRAKAKIS-SMITH, D. W. 0502, 1184, 1185, 1186
DRAKE, Fred W. 0025
DRAPER, Marshall D. 1033
DUFFIELD, Minnie M. 0909
DUNCAN, Marion H. 0503
DWYER, D. J. 0226, 0415, 0686, 0721, 0910, 1048, 1102, 1187, 1188, 1189
EBDON, R. A. 0227
EBERHARD, Wolfram. 0026, 0743, 1190
EDGAR, J. H. 0285, 0504, 0744, 1191
EDKINS, Joseph. 0367
EDMUNDS, Charles Keyser. 0113, 0368, 0505
EIGNER, Julius. 1192
EITEL, Rev. Dr. E. J. 0745, 0746, 0828
EKVAL, Robert B. 0827
ELGAR, J. Huston. 0228
ELIAS, Ney. 0369, 0370, 0506
ELIASSEN, Sig. 0371, 0372
ENGLANDER, A. L. 0229
ERROLL, F. J. 1034
ErSELCUIK, Muzaffer. 0416, 1035
EYRE, Alan L. 1193
FAIRCHILD, David. 0315
FANE, G. E. 1129
FANG, Chao-ying. 0911
FANG, Fu-an. 0983
FANG, Lienche. 0911
FARLEY, Miriam S. 1092
FARQUHARSON, R. D. 0027
FARRER, Reginald. 0114 , 0115
FAULKNER, H. E. 1194
FENN, H. C. 0829
FENNENMAN, N[eville]. M. 0507
FERGUSON, John C. S. 0747

FETTER, Frank Whitson. 0912
FIELD, A. R. 0830
FIELD, Frederick W. 0831, 1149
FIELD, Robert Michael. 1036
FISCHER, Emil S. 0509, 1103
FISHER, Charles. 0832, 0833
FITCH, Robert F. 0748, 0749
FITZGERALD, C. Patrick. 0116, 0117, 0118, 0508, 0834
FOLDI, Ervin. 0028
FONG, H. D. 1037
FOORD, Edward. 0835
FORBES, Edgar Allen. 1195
FORMAN, Harrison. 0750
FORREST, George. 0119, 0510
FOSCUE, Edwin J. 0991
FOSTER, John W. 0511, 0512
FOUNTAINE, Capt. Eadric Clifford. 0120
FRANK, V. S. 0836
FRANZ, Michael. 0048
FRASER, J. M. 1196
FREEBERNE, J. D. M. 0373
FREEBERNE, Michael. 0230, 0374, 0687, 0688, 0689, 0837, 0913, 0914, 0984, 1038, 1104, 1269
FRESHFIELD, Douglas W. 0513, 0514
FREY, John W. 0417
FRIEDERISCHEN, Max. 0286
FUCHS, Walter. 0029, 0030, 0031
FULLER, Myron L. 0287, 0751
FULORD, H. 0135
FUNG, K. I. 1150
FUNNELL, W. C. 0915
FUSON, Chester G. 0515, 0690, 0916
GAGE, Eugenia. 1039
GAMMON, Charles F. 0691
GARDNER, Chr. T. 0516
GARRELS, Agnes T. 1270

GATZLAFF, Charles. 0517, 0838
GHERZI, Rev. W., S.J. 0231
GILES, L. 0032
GILL, W. J. 0518
GINSBURG, Norton S. 0033, 0034, 0418, 0519, 0839, 1105, 1106, 1197, 1198
GODWIN, Austen H. H. 0200
GOFORTH, W. W. 0520
GOLAB, L. Wawrzyn. 0985
GOLGER, Otto J. 1199
GOODCHILD, Thomas. 0521
GOODNOW, Frank Johnson. 0752
GOODRICH, L. Carrington. 0035
GOODWIN, Peter. 0753, 0754
GORDON, Maria M. Ogilvie. 0755
GOUROU, Pierre. 0986
GRADZDANZEV, Andrew J. 1040
GRANT, Charles Mitchell. 0840
GREEN, L. C. 0841
GREEN, O. M. 0842, 0843, 0844
GREGORY, C. J. 0036, 0201, 0288
GREGORY, J. W. 0036, 0201, 0288
GRIEG, James A. 0522
GRIFFEN, Clarence. 0756
GRINNELL, Walton. 0523
GROFF, G. Weidman. 0524
GROOTAERS, Willem A. 0757
GROSVENOR, Gilbert H. 0525, 1107
GROSVENOR, W. Clayton. 0526
GROVE, Robert G. 0987
GUIBAUT, Andre. 0121
GUINNES, Walter. 1200
GUTMAN, John. 0917
GUTTMAN, John. 0758
GUTZTAFF, Charles. 0122
HALL, Robert Burnett. 0988, 1274

HALL, Russell E. 1108
HALLET, Holt S. 1109
HAMILTON, A. B. 0123
HAMMOND, C[aptain]. Robert. 0124
HANBURY-TENISON, Euphan. 0527
HANSFORD, S. Howard. 0759
HANSON-LOWE, J. 0125, 0232, 0289, 0290
HARRER, Heinrich. 0126, 0845
HARRINGTON, Lyn. 0528, 0529, 1279
HARRIS, Nigel. 1201
HARTWELL, Robert. 1041
HAYDEN, H. H. 0281
HAYES, Helen. 1202
HAYES, James. 0760
HAYES, L. Newton. 0846
HEAWOOD, E. 0037
HEDIN, Sven. 0128, 0129, 0130, 0291
HEDLEY, John. 0127, 0131
HEENAN, L. D. B. 0419
HEIDENSTANN, H. von. 0375
HEIM, Arnold. 0292
HENRY, Alfred J. 0233
HERMAN, Theodore. 0847, 0918, 1042
HEYWOOD, G. S. P. 0234
HINKS, Arthur R. 0038, 0761
HIRTH, Frederick. 0039, 0235
HITCH, Margaret A. 1203
HO, Ping-ti. 1204
HOCKLY, J. Minett. 1110
HOLLAND, W. L. 0692
HORSBURGH, A. J. 0919
HOSIE, Alexander. 0236, 0376, 0530
HOSIE, Lady. 0040, 0041
HOTCHKISS, Anna M. 0786
HOU, Jen-chih. 0132
HOWARTH, H. H. 0316

HOYANAGI, Mutsumi. 1111
HSIA, Ronald. 1043
HSIAO, Ch'ien. 1044
HSIEH, Chiao-min. 0042, 0043, 0237, 0531, 0532, 0533
HSU, Ginn-Tze. 0044, 0238
HSU, Jen. 0239
HSU, Mei-ling. 0694
HSU, Shin-yi. 0762
HU, Huan-yong. 0202, 0240, 0989
HUBBARD, George D. 0377, 0378, 0534, 1205
HUBBARD, James Mascarene. 0379, 0535, 1206
HUGHES, R. H. 0536, 1207
HUNG, Fu [Frederick]. 0693, 0763, 0848, 0849, 1272
HUNTER, Holland. 1112
HUNTINGTON, Ellsworth. 0133, 0241, 0293, 0294, 0537
HUTCHINSON, G. Evelyn. 0225
HUTCHINSON, Paul. 0765
HUTTMAN, William. 0045
HWANG, Sze-sung. 0270
IMANISHI, Kinji. 0134
IMPEY, Lawrence. 1208
INLOW, E. Burke. 0850
JACK, R. Logan. 0920
JACOT, Arthur Paul. 0242
JAMES, H. E. 0135
JAMES, H. F. 1045
JAN, G. P. 1151
JEN, Mei-ngo. 0046, 0990
JENKINS, Alan. 0851
JIRO, Yonekura. 0381
JOHNSON, Nelson T. 0852
JOHNSON, Ray G. 0317
JOHNSTON, A. R. 0538
JOHNSTON, Sir Reginald. 1209
JONES, Fred O. 0380
JUAN, V[ei]. C[how]. 0420

JUDGE, Joseph. 0539
JUNOR, Kenneth F. 0540
KAMBARA, Tatsu. 0421
KARAN, Pardyumna Prasad. 0853, 0854
KAULBACK, Ronald. 0136, 0137
KEENLEYSIDE, Hugh. 0541
KEENLEYSIDE, Katherine. 0541
KEITH, Ronald A. 1210
KELBURN, Viscount. 0138, 0139
KEMP, Emily G. 0542
KEYES, Fenton. 0695
KIANG, Ying-cheng. 0766
KIKOLSKI, Bohdan. 0203
KING, F. H. 0543
KING, George W. 0921
KING, W. H. 1113
KINGSMILL, T. W. 1114
KIRBY, E. Stuart. 0544, 0545
KIRBY, John. 0382
KIRJASSOFF, Alice Ballantine. 0546
KIRK, William. 0855
KNAPP. Ronald G. 0925, 0926
KNIGHT, Thomas. 0047
KOEPPE, C. E. 0243
KOESTER, Capt. Hans. 1115
KOO, V. K. Wellington. 0922
KORKER, Bruno. 0549
KOWALSKI, K. 0295
KOZICKI, Richard J. 0856
KOZLOFF, P. K. 0547, 0548
KROPOTKIN, P. 0140
KUO, Tsung-fei. 1152
LAAI, Yi-faai. 0048, 0857
LACY, Walter N. 0550, 1046, 1116, 1211, 1212
LaFLEUR, Albert. 0991
LAFUGIE. 0767

LAI, David Chuen-yan. 0768, 1047, 1048
LAMPREY, Charles. 0992
LANNING, George. 1213
LARDY, Nicholas R. 1036
LATTIMORE, Owen. 0551, 0552, 0553, 0554, 0555, 0556, 0696, 0769, 0770, 0771, 0858, 0859, 0860, 0861, 0862, 0863, 1117, 1118
LAU, T. C. 0524
LEE, A. O. 0049
LEE, Frank C. 0993
LEE, Hoon K. 0697
LEE, John. 0244
LEE, Shu-ching. 0994
LEE, Shu-tan. 0557
LEE, T. S. 1049
LEEMING, Frank. 1214
LEITH, C. K. 1050
LENZ, Frank B. 1051
LEONARD, Jane Kate. 0864
LEPPIK, E. E. 0318
LESLIE, L. A. D. 0558
LESZCZYCKI, S. 0050
LEUNG, C. K. 0772
LEUNG, George Kin. 0773
LI, Chang. 1119
LI, Hui-lin. 0319
LI, Shih-yu. 0757
LIANG, Chi-sen. 0995, 1052, 1215, 1216
LIEU, D. K. 0698
LIEU, O. S. 1053
LIN, Gong-yuh. 0245
LIN, Shu-yen. 1054
LINDGREN, Miss E. J. 0923
LING, Han-deng. 1120
LING, Pyau. 0699
LIPPITT, Victor D. 1121
LITTLE, Archibald J. 0383, 0865, 1153

LITTLE, Mrs. Archibald. 0141
LIU, En-lan. 0204, 0246, 0247, 0559, 0560, 1280
LIU, Jung-chao. 0996
LLEWELLYN, Bernard. 0561
LLOYD, W. V. 1122
LO, C[hor]. P[ang]. 0700, 1217
LO, Jung-pang. 0774
LOCKHART, Jack. 0422
LOCKHART, William. 0384, 1218
LOCKWOOD, Edward T. 0385
LONG, George W. 0562, 0866, 1219
LONGSTAFF, T. G. 0296
LOWDERMILK, W. C. 0248, 0320, 0321, 0322, 0323, 0997
LOWE, Chuan-hua. 1123
LOWY, Rennold L. 0867
LU, Alfred. 0249, 0250, 0251
LUNIN, B. A. 0775
MA, L. J. C. 0051
MAGEE, Guy, Jr. 0927
MAINPRISE, B. W. 0924
MALLORY, Walter H. 0868
MANIFOLD, C. C. 0142, 1124
MARCH, Andrew L. 0776, 0777
MARCINI, Fosco. 0778
MARGARY, Augustus Raymond. 0143
MARKHAM, C. R. 0052
MARKHAM, J. 0563
MARTIN, W. A. P. 0869
MASON, I. 0779
MASON, Kenneth. 0053
McCARTHY, J. 0564
McCLURE, F. A. 1055
McCOLL, Robert W. 0054, 0870, 0871, 0872
McCORMICK, Elsie. 0282
McCORMICK, Frederic. 0565
McCORMICK, Frederick. 0780

M'COSH, Dr. 1125
McCUNE, Shannon. 1220
MEAD, Daniel W. 0386
MEADOWS, T. T. 0873
MEARES, C. H. 0144
MEIJER, M. J. 0055
MELLOR, Roy. 0874
MENG, C. Y. W. 0566
MERSON, John Philip. 1036
MERZBACHER, Gottfried. 0145
METCALF, Franklin P. 0567
MICHIE, A. 0568, 0569
MILLER, Henry B. 0928
MILLS, J. W. 0056
MOFFET, Abbot Low. 0781
MOJUMDAR, K. K. 0875
MOLODTSOVA, R. I. 1058
MONTGOMERIE, T. G. 0146, 0147, 0570, 0571
MOORE, Terris. 0109
MOORE, W. Robert. 0572, 0573, 0574, 0852, 1126, 1221, 1222, 1223, 1224
MORGAN, E. Delmar. 0148, 0575
MORGAN, G. 0876
MORRISON, G. J. 0576
MORRISON, Hedda. M. 0577, 0578, 0579, 0580, 0782, 1056, 1225
MORRISON, Ian. 0581
MORSE, H. B. 0057
MOSS, Laurence A. 0783
MOSSMAN, Samuel. 0387
MOULE, A. C. 0388
MOYER, Raymond T. 0252, 0324
MU, Tsung-ju. 0340
MULLER, James Arthur. 1226
MULLIKIN, Mary Augusta. 0784, 0785, 0786
MURAKOSHI, Nobuo. 0998
MURPHEY, Rhoads. 0431, 0877, 0999, 1127, 1227, 1228, 1229

MYERS, Ramon H. 1057
NAKAMURA, Hirosi. 0058
NEEDHAM, Joseph. 1000
NELSON, Howard. 0059, 0060
NG, Ronald C. Y. 0061
NIKOLUEV, S. A. 1058
NORIN, Erik. 0253, 0423
NORRIS, Martin R. 0878
NYSTROM, Erik T. 0424
O'CONNOR, Sir Frederick. 0582
ODELL, N. E. 0583
O'HARA, Albert R. 1230
"OLD CATHAY." 0929
OLIPHANT, Laurence. 0389, 0584
OLIVER, Lieutenent. 0149
ONOYE, Etsuzo. 1231
OPPENHEIM, F. 0701
ORCHARD, Dorothy J. 0702
ORCHARD, John E. 0930, 0931, 1059, 1128, 1232
ORLEANS, Leo A. 0432, 0703
OSBORN, Sherard. 0585, 0879
OUTERBRIDGE, Rev. Leonard M. 1001
OUTHWAITE, Alison. 0586
OUTRAM, Frank. 1129
OVDIYENKO, I. Kh. 1060, 1061
OXENHAM, E. L. 0390
PAN, Chia-lin. 0715
PANFILOV, D. V. 0325
PANNELL, Clifton W. 0586, 1139, 1233, 1234, 1235, 1236, 1237, 1273
PARKES, Harry. 1154
PARSONS, William Barclay. 0587, 0588
PASSANTINO, Joseph E. 0758, 1238
PEARCY, G. Etzel. 0589
PELLER, C. S. du Richi. 0150
PENG, George T. C. 1239
PENNELL, W. V. 0590

PENNINSTON, John B. 0326
PEREIRA, Cecil. 0151
PEREIRA, George. 0591, 0787
PETROV, Victor P. 1130
PHILLIPS, George. 0788, 0789, 1155
PORTER, Catherine. 0932
POTANIN, M. 0575
POWELL, John B. 0592
PRATT, A. E. 0593
PRATT, Sir John. 0391
PRICE, Dalias A. 1062
PRICE, M. Philips. 0594
PRICE, Willard. 0595, 0933
PRITCHARD, Earl H. 0704
PRUITT, Ida. 1063
PRYBYLA, Jan S. 1131
PRYOR, E. G. 1064, 1240, 1241
QUIRINO, Carlos. 0062
RAISZ, Erwin. 0063
RAMAGE, C. S. 0254, 0255, 0256
RAVENSTEIN, E[rnst]. G. 0596
RAWDEN, Fisk N. 0597
RAWLING, C. C. 0152
RAWLINSON, H. C. 1242
READ, Thomas T. 1065, 1066
REED, Andrew. 1243
REITLINGER, Gerald. 0598
REITSMA, Hendrick J. 0880
REYNOLDS, J. H. 0064
RHYNSBURGER, Willert. 0392
RICHARDSON, H. L. 0881
RICHARDSON, Ralph. 0599
RIGGS, Margaret. 0882
ROBERTSON, R. Cecil. 0705
ROBINSON, H. 1002
ROBINSON, H. W. 1067

ROCK, Joseph F. 0153, 0154, 0393, 0600, 0601, 0602, 0790, 0791, 0792
ROCKHILL, W. W. 0603, 0706, 0793, 1156
RODGERS, Allan. 1068
ROLLERSTON, George. 0433
ROORBACK, G. B. 0604, 0934
ROOSEVELT, Theodore. 0327
ROSE, John. 1003, 1244
ROSS, E. A. 0605
ROSS, John. 0606, 1132
ROXBY, Percy Maude. 0607, 0608, 0609, 0707, 0708, 0935, 1133, 1274
RUDNEV, Andrej. 0065
RUSSELL, Claude. 0610
RUTTER, Owen. 0611
RUTTLEDGE, Hugh. 0612
RYDER, C. H. D. 0155, 0156, 0394
SALTER, Christopher L. 0066, 0709, 0710, 1004, 1005, 1245
SALTER, M. 0411, 0412
SAMSON, Gerald L. G. 0883
SANDER, E. M. 0257
SAREL, Lt.-Col. Henry Andrew. 0157, 0613
SARGENT, R. H. 0067
SCHENK, Hans. 1246, 1247
SCHOMBERG, R[eginald]. C. F. 0158, 0258, 0259, 0260, 0614, 0615
SCHREIDER, Frank. 0616
SCHREIDER, Helen. 0616
SCHWARZ, Henry G. 0711
SCHWEINFURTH, Ulrich. 0328
SCIDMORE, Eliza R. 0617
SCOFIELD, John. 1248
SCOTT, Richard. 0794
SEMENOFF, P. P. 0159
SHABAD, Theodore. 0068, 0069, 0712, 0713, 0936, 0937, 0938, 0939, 1069
SHALLEY, I. J. 0329
SHARP, Keith H. 0795

SHAW, Earl B. 0160, 0884, 1006
SHELTON, Dr. A. L. 0796
SHEN, Y. S. 0940
SHERMAN, J. C. 0048
SHIELDS, E. T. 0618
SHIH, Chan-chun. 0161, 0162
SHIH, Ya-feng. 0395
SHIMAN, Russell G. 0425
SHIPTON, Eric. 0163, 0164
SHOR, Franc. 0797, 0885, 1249
SHOR, Jean. 0797
SHOVE, D. Justin. 0261
SILVER, Sylvia A. 1250
SIMPICH, Frederick, Jr. 0619, 0941, 1251
SKINNER, G. William. 0942
SLADEN, E. B. 0620
SMITH, A. Donaldson. 0165
SMITH, F. P. 1070
SMITH, H. U. 0166
SMITH, Helen L. 1252
SMYTH, Helen. 0426
SO, Chak-Lam. 0297
SOLTAU, Henry. 0167
SOOTHILL, W. E. 0070
SOWERBY, Arthur de Carle. 0262, 0263, 0330, 0331, 0332, 0333, 0334, 0396, 0621, 0622, 0798, 0799, 0886, 0943, 1007, 1071, 1072, 1157
SPENCER, Joseph E. 0623, 0624, 0625, 0626, 0800, 0801, 0802, 0887, 1008, 1073, 1074, 1134, 1158, 1159, 1253, 1275
SPICER, Eva D. 0168
SPRYE, R. H. F. 0169
STAHNKE, Arthur A. 0888
STANLEY, A. 0803
STATEN, George L. 0889
STEEL, Richard. 0890
STEER, J. B. 0804
STEIN, Sir M. Auriel. 0071, 0072, 0170, 0171, 0172

STEINER, H. Arthur. 0891
STEVENS, Dan. 0892
STEVENS, H. 0073, 0173
STEVENSON, Paul Huston. 0627
STEWARD, Albert N. 0335
STEWARD, John R. 1009, 1075, 1276.
STEWART, John R. 0427, 0944, 0945, 0946,
STEWART, Rosemary. 0947
STONE, John. 0628
STOUT, Arthur Purdy. 0629, 1160
STRAHEY, H. 0205
SULLIVAN, Linda F. 0805
SUTTMEIER, Richard. 0432
SUTULOV, Alexander. 0428
SWANN, Peter C. 0806
SWINHOE, Robert. 0174, 0630, 1161
SZCZESNIAK, Boleslaw. 0074, 0075, 0076, 0077
TAN, Jian-an. 0714
TATOR, Benjamin A. 0206
TAUEBER, Irene B. 0715
TAYLOR, Alice. 0533
TAYLOR, Annie R. 0631
TAYLOR, George. 0632
TAYMAN, Nelson Grant. 1135
TAYYEB, Ali. 0893
TEICHMAN, Eric. 0175, 0176, 0633
TEMPLE, Sir Richard. 0716
THOMASON, Maj. John W. 1254
THOMPSON, H. Gordon. 0634
THOMPSON, J. 0635
THOMPSON, J. Charles. 1010
THORNBECKE, Ellen. 0807
THORP, James. 0336
TIEH, T. Min. 0337
TIPTON, C. E. 0636
TISDALE, Alice. 1255

TODD, Oliver. J[ulian]. 0264, 0372, 0397, 0398, 0399, 0400, 0401, 1136
TOLSTOY, Lt. Col. Ilin. 0637
TOPPING, Audrey. 0638
TORGASHEFFT, B. P. 0717
TORRANCE, T. 0718, 1011
TOURS, B. G. 0639
TOWERS, Graham. 1256
TREAGAR, T. R. 0402, 0719, 1257
TREWARTHA, Glenn T. 0640, 0720, 0998, 1012, 1013, 1258, 1259
TRINKLER, Emil. 0177, 0265
TROTTER, H. 0641
TSCHUDI, Aadel Brun. 1014
TSOU, Pao-chun. 0207
TSUKADA, Matsuo. 0266
TSYBIKOFF, G. G. 0642
TU, Chang-wang. 0267, 0268, 0269, 0270
T'U, Chang-wang. *See* TU, Chang-wang.
TUAN, Yi-fu. 0434
TUNG, Shih-tsin. 1016
TURLEY, Robert T. 0403, 0948, 0949, 0950
TURNER, F. B. 0271
TWITCHETT, Denis. 1015, 1162
TYRWHIFF, Jaqueline. 1260
VALE, J. 1017
VALE, Marcia. 0808
VandorMEER, Canute. 1018, 1019.
VAUGHAN, T. D. 0721
VENBT, Herbert J. 0643
VENIUKOF, M. 0404
VINACKE, Harold M. 1076
VISSER, Ph. C. 0191
VITA-FINZI, C. 0329
von ENGELN, O. D. 0644
von LINDHOLM, K. H. 0951
von RICHTHOFEN, Baron F. 0338, 0894, 1137

VOON, Phin-keong. 0809
VOSBURGH, Frederick. 0952
VOSKUIL, Walter. 1077
WALKER, Egbert H. 0339
WALKER, Gen. J. T. 0178, 0405, 0645, 0646
WALKER, Robert R. 0987
WALLIS, Helen M. 0080, 0081
WALTON, W. H. Murray. 0647
WANG, Ch'ien, 0082
WANG, Chih-cho. 0083
WANG, I-shou. 0722, 0895, 1261
WANG, Kung-ping. 0429
WANG, Shou-chun. 0340
WANG, W[ei]-H[sia]. 0723
WARD, Barbara E. 0953
WARD, F. Kingdon. 0179, 0180, 0181, 0182, 0183, 0184, 0185, 0186, 0298, 0299, 0300, 0301, 0302, 0303, 0341, 0342, 0343, 0344, 0345, 0346, 0347, 0406, 0648, 0649, 0650, 0651, 0652, 1020, 1277
WARWICK, Adam. 0653, 1021
WASHENKO, Steve. 1022
WASHINGTON, Warren M. 0208
WATT, John. 1138
WATTS, Harvey Maitland. 0654
WEBSTER, Harrie. 0655, 0656
WELLBY, M. S. 0187
WESTOBY, Jack C. 0348
WHEATLEY, Paul. 1166
WHEELER, James O. 1139
WHITE, Herbert Clarence. 0657
WHITE, John Claude. 1262
WHITNEY, J. B. R. 0435
WHYMANT, Neville. 0810
WICKES, D. R. 0323, 0997
WIENS, Herold J. 0084, 0407, 0658, 0811, 0812, 0896, 0897, 1078, 1140, 1164, 1263, 1278
WILCOX, Walter F. 0724, 0725

WILLIAMS, A. T. 0304, 0305, 0306
WILLIAMS, E. T. 1141
WILLIAMS, F. E. 0659
WILLIAMS, Jack F. 0082
WILLIAMS, John. 0272
WILLIAMS, Maynard Owen. 0660, 0661, 0662, 0663
WILLIAMS, S. Wells. 0813
WILLIAMSON, Alexander. 0664
WILLIS, Bailey. 0188, 0430
WILSON, Maj. Gen. James Harrison. 0665
WILSON, R. C. 0307
WILTON, E. C. 0666
WINGATE, A. W. S. 0189, 0408, 0667
WITTVOGEL, Karl. 0273
WOLLASTAN, A. F. R. 0190
WRIGHT, Arthur F. 1264
WULSIN, Frederick R. 0668
WYLIE, J. A. 0669
YANG, Han-yung. 0349
YANG, Sheu-jen. 1013
YAO, Augustine Y. M. 0274, 1023
YAO, C. S. 0275
YAO, Shan-yu. 0276, 0277
YATE, A. C. 0192, 0670
YEH, George K. C. 0954
YEN, Chiang-kwoh. 1024
YETTS, W. Perceval. 0671, 1142
YONEKURA, Jiro. 0898
YOUNG, C. Walter. 0726
YOUNG, E. C. 0193, 0194
YOUNG, Reginald. 0727
YOUNGHUSBAND, Sir Francis E. 0135, 0195, 0672
YULE, Henry. 0085, 0196, 0673, 0789, 1143

Part III

Place Name Index

Afghanistan 0892
Africa 0014, 0880
Aghil Range 0163
Agias River 0145
Aksai chin 0889
Aksu 1242
Ala Shan 0668
A-Li So area 0152
Amnyi Machen 0154
Amoy 0497, 1099
Amu-Daria River 0404
Amur River. *See* Heilong Jiang
Anhui 0215, 0943
Anshan 1031, 1035
Anyang, Gansu 0965
Aomen. *See* Macao
Aotou 0057
Bai Hua River
Baltoro Glacier 0087
Baotou 1031, 1035
Batang 0503, 0564
Bate 0926
Beijing 0031, 0108, 0132, 0151, 0165, 0239, 0314, 0462, 0577, 0610, 0634, 0670, 0763, 0773, 0774, 0782, 0852, 0869, 0886, 0890, 0927, 0947, 1034, 1166, 1168, 1170, 1173, 1183, 1194, 1200, 1202, 1209, 1218, 1223, 1225, 1226, 1239, 1247, 1249, 1254
Beijing-Hankou Railroad 1081
Beiking. *See* Beijing
Beishan 0135
Bohai 0122, 0569, 0585, 0662
Brahmaputra River. *See* Yarlung Zangbo Jiang
Bun Hills, Hong Kong 0808
Burma 0119, 0557, 0838, 0856, 0878, 1094, 1095, 1097, 1152
Burma Road 0168, 0508, 1086, 1098, 1123, 1129, 1133
Burma-Yunnan frontier 0878
Burma-Yunnan Railroad 0903, 1095

Butou 749, 0803, 1280
Canton 0111, 0436, 0455, 0497, 0524, 0568, 0576, 0748, 0779, 0947, 0982, 1034, 1115, 1221, 1232
Canton Delta 0640, 0748
Castle Peak Bay 1054
Central Asia 0090, 0146, 0170, 0171, 0281, 0338, 0778, 0879
Chahar 0425, 0467, 0757
Chang'an 1260
Chang cha 0963
Changchao. *See* Changjou
Changchau. *See* Changjou
Chang chun 1197
Chang Jiang and Delta 0050, 0101, 0104, 0112, 0138, 0139, 0141, 0142, 0157, 0175, 0182, 0197, 0199, 0248, 0264, 0268, 0279, 0290, 0303, 0346, 0356, 0357, 0361, 0364, 0365, 0367, 0375, 0381, 0383, 0384, 0389, 0390, 0393, 0452, 0453, 0477, 0498, 0504, 0549, 0572, 0584, 0587, 0612, 0666, 0898, 0995, 1097, 1102, 1104, 1110, 1134, 1159, 1161, 1163
Changjou 0788, 1155
Chanhua 0232
Chaoch'ing. *See* Chaojing
Chaojing 0019
Chaoyang 1042
Ch'ao Yang An. *See* Chaoyang An
Chaoyang An 0738
Chefoo 0592, 1221
Chekiang. *See* Zhejiang
Chengdu 0144, 0153, 0422, 0473, 0633, 1011, 1017, 1205
Chengdu Plain and Plateau 0473, 0995
Cheng-jiang 0917
Cheng-kiang. *See* Cheng-jiang
Chengtu. *See* Chengdu
Chengtu Plateau. *See* Chengdu Plain and Plateau
Cheung Chao 0808
Ch'ien-tang River. *See* Qiantang Jiang
Chigla Range 0114

Chihli. *See* Hebei
Chihli River 0371
Chilian Range 0395
Chin-kiang. *See* Jinjiang
China, Central 0189, 0943, 1085, 1124, 1145
China, coastal 0244, 0574, 0592, 0866, 1141, 1163, 1221
China, eastern 0223, 0231, 0244, 0497
China, far interior 0067
China, general 0003, 0004, 0005, 0006, 0008, 0011, 0012, 0013, 0015, 0016, 0017, 0018, 0020, 0021, 0022, 0023, 0024, 0025, 0028, 0029, 0030, 0032, 0033, 0034, 0035, 0037, 0038, 0039, 0040, 0041, 0042, 0043, 0044, 0045, 0046, 0047, 0049, 0050, 0051, 0054, 0056, 0058, 0059, 0060, 0061, 0062, 0063, 0066, 0068, 0069, 0071, 0074, 0075, 0076, 0077, 0078, 0080, 0081, 0082, 0083, 0084, 0085, 0196, 0198, 0203, 0204, 0208, 0209, 0211, 0212, 0213, 0214, 0219, 0220, 0221, 0222, 0224, 0226, 0227, 0230, 0233, 0235, 0243, 0246, 0247, 0251, 0261, 0262, 0267, 0268, 0269, 0270, 0273, 0276, 0277, 0312, 0315, 0316, 0318, 0319, 0321, 0323, 0325, 0327, 0329, 0331, 0332, 0333, 0334, 0336, 0337, 0339, 0341, 0345, 0360, 0374, 0376, 0409, 0412, 0413, 0415, 0417, 0419, 0420, 0421, 0424, 0426, 0428, 0429, 0430, 0431, 0432, 0433, 0434, 0435, 0440, 0443, 0446, 0447, 0451, 0457, 0458, 0459, 0460, 0463, 0475, 0481, 0483, 0487, 0488, 0489, 0491, 0496, 0511, 0512, 0528, 0535, 0540, 0541, 0550, 0551, 0554, 0555, 0557, 0561, 0565, 0578, 0579, 0580, 0586, 0587, 0589, 0597, 0604, 0605, 0607, 0608, 0609, 0623, 0625, 0626, 0638, 0654, 0655, 0656, 0665, 0671, 0674, 0675, 0677, 0678, 0679, 0680, 0683, 0686, 0687, 0691, 0692, 0693, 0695, 0698, 0699, 0701, 0702, 0703, 0704, 0706, 0707, 0708, 0710, 0712, 0713, 0716, 0717, 0719, 0720, 0724, 0725, 0727, 0728, 0730, 0731, 0732, 0733, 0735, 0739, 0740, 0741, 0743, 0745, 0746, 0752, 0755, 0765, 0766, 0768, 0772, 0776, 0777, 0779, 0780, 0783, 0798, 0799, 0800, 0801, 0805, 0806, 0807, 0809, 0810, 0812 0813 0814, 0816, 0817, 0820, 0821, 0825, 0826, 0828, 0829, 0831, 0832, 0833, 0839, 0840, 0842, 0847, 0848, 0849, 0857, 0858, 0859, 0860, 0862, 0864, 0870, 0871, 0873, 0877, 0882, 0891, 0894, 0895, 0897, 0899, 0901, 0904, 0906, 0907, 0908, 0909, 0910, 0911, 0912, 0913, 0914, 0918, 0919, 0920, 0922, 0924, 0930, 0931, 0934, 0936, 0937, 0938, 0939, 0942, 0954, 0957, 0958, 0959, 0961, 0962, 0963, 0964, 0967, 0968, 0969, 0970, 0971, 0974, 0975, 0976, 0977, 0978, 0979, 0982, 0983, 0986, 0991, 0993, 0994, 0996, 1000, 1001, 1002, 1006, 1007, 1008, 1012, 1013, 1014, 1015, 1016, 1021, 1023,

1024, 1026, 1028, 1029, 1031, 1035, 1036, 1037, 1038, 1041, 1043, 1044, 1045, 1046, 1049, 1050, 1053, 1056, 1057, 1058, 1059, 1060, 1061, 1062, 1063, 1065, 1066, 1069, 1070, 1071, 1074, 1076, 1077, 1078, 1079, 1080, 1083, 1084, 1085, 1087, 1089, 1090, 1092, 1100, 1102, 1105, 1108, 1109, 1112, 1114, 1115, 1119, 1121, 1127, 1128, 1131, 1136 1138, 1142, 1143, 1148, 1149, 1150, 1151, 1156, 1162, 1163, 1164, 1171, 1174, 1175, 1176, 1177, 1178, 1179, 1190, 1191, 1201, 1212, 1227, 1228, 1229, 1231, 1245, 1246, 1247, 1255, 1258, 1259, 1264, 1268, 1269, 1270, 1272, 1274, 1275

China, North 0189, 0218, 0229, 0248, 0252, 0263, 0268, 0271, 0274, 0287, 0310, 0311, 0320, 0324, 0326, 0338, 0371, 0390, 0398, 0416, 0458, 0555, 0556, 0609, 0762, 0896, 1067, 1078, 1105

China, Northeast 0349, 1060

China, Northwest 0374, 0575, 0636, 0711, 0896, 1030, 1060, 1105

China, Sea(s) 0255, 1010

China, South 0010, 0048, 0095, 0111, 0254, 0256, 0275, 0289, 0308, 0458, 0684, 0789, 0822, 1096, 1145

China, Southwest 0097, 0620, 0942, 0990, 1037, 1109

China, western 0101, 0167, 0210, 0317, 0343, 0345, 0394, 0518, 0581, 1060, 1124, 1153

Chindru 0137

Chinese Tartary. *See* Central Asia

Chinese Turkestan. *See* Xinjiang

Ching-an Mountains. *See* Hing-an Ling

Ch'ing-tao. *See* Qingdao

Ching-ter-chen. *See* Qingdezhen

Chinghai. *See* Jinghai

Chiyuan hsien 1269

Chochau. *See* Chozhau

Choi Hung Housing Estate, Hong Kong 1196

Chongli 0926

Chongqing 0157, 0639, 0843, 1034, 1253

Choni 0791

Choukoutien 0209, 0295

Chozhau 0194

Chuanchow. *See* Quanzhou

Chu-ma River 0194

Chumbi Valley, Tibet 0465, 0875
Chungking. *See* Jongqing
Chung-tien. *See* Zhongdian
Cunhua Commune 0960
Daba 0102
Dali, Yunnan 0116, 0117, 0143, 0308, 1160
Dalian 1221
Danshui 0486
Daofu 0232
Daxian 0073, 0153, 0285, 0317, 0593, 0627
Daxian Shan 0173, 0183
Daxue Shan 0113, 0186, 0289, 0598
Dazhai 1005
Dazhing 1169, 1245
Dekho 0121
Dibang 0352
Dihang 0136, 0302
Dihuadu 1117
Dongguan 0633
Dongting Lake 0526
Duliu 0271
Dunhuang 0026, 0784, 0786, 0797
Fanshan 0248
Fatong 0963
Fen River 0397, 0399
Fencheng *hsien* 1269
Fenghsien. *See* Fengxian
Fengt'ien. *See* Shenyang
Fengxian 0199
Fenzhou 1001
Foochow. *See* Fuzhou
Formosa. *See* Taiwan
Fuchau. *See* Fuzhou
Fujian 0975, 1023, 1101, 1120, 1155
Fuk'ien. *See* Fujian
Fushin. *See* Fuxin

Fuxin 0411
Fuzhou 0123, 0788, 1116, 1221
Ganges River 0898
Gansu 0026, 0072, 0114, 0115, 0282, 0347, 0591, 0601, 0636, 0715, 0750, 0781, 0787, 0791, 0797, 0921
Ganzi 0289
Gaoxiong 0103, 0174, 0632, 0635
Gartok 0155, 0503
Garze Tibetan Autonomous Zhou, Sichuan 0161
Gobi Desert 0088
Grand Canal 0368, 0524, 0543, 0576, 0595, 0734, 0742
Great Wall of China 0055, 0194, 0441, 0467, 0475, 0482, 0595, 0653, 0771, 0786, 0825, 0835, 0846, 1279
Guan Xian 0377
Guandong 0945
Guangdong 0048, 0515, 0690, 0916, 0975, 1032, 1055
Guangxi 0048, 0335, 0524, 0975
Guangzhou. *See* Canton
Guangzhouwan 0865
Guchengzi 1117
Guihuading 1117
Guihuan 0769
Guilin 0524
Guiyang 0524
Guizhou 0542, 0639, 0887, 0940, 0990
Guling 0094
Gyala Peri 0098
Gyangste 0155
Haei lar 0134
Hai River 0363, 0371, 0373, 1022
Hainan 0113, 0122, 0737, 1265
Hangchow. *See* Hangzhou
Hangzhau 0788
Hangzhou 0362, 0568, 0742, 0747, 0947, 1221
Hanjow. *See* Hangzhou
Hankou 0141, 0143, 0295, 0385, 0389, 0390, 0455, 0564, 0576, 0584, 0588, 0613, 0935, 0982, 1035, 1099, 1115

Hanyang 0935
Haramosh Pass 0120
Harbin 0366, 0676, 0928, 1182, 1220
Hebei 0026, 0131, 0194, 0215, 0236 0295, 0410, 0416, 0467, 0698, 1041
Heilong Jiang 0911, 0975, 1102
Henan 0026, 0233, 0320, 0340, 0416, 0718, 1041, 1136
Hexi Corridor 0560
Himalayan Mountains 0185, 0281, 0302, 0342, 0345
Hingan Ling 0134, 0165, 0185
Honan. *See* Henan
Hong Jiang Gorges 0950
Hong Kong 0020, 0051, 0061, 0110, 0217, 0234, 0278, 0297, 0304, 0305, 0351, 0442, 0497, 0501, 0519, 0529, 0536, 0538, 0539, 0544, 0545, 0590, 0644, 0659, 0660, 0684, 0685, 0700, 0721, 0753, 0795, 0808, 0817, 0824, 0866, 0915, 0953, 0955, 0956, 0982, 0987, 1027, 1047, 1048, 1054, 1064, 1128, 1165, 1184, 1185, 1186, 1187, 1188, 1189, 1196, 1199, 1207, 1215, 1216, 1217, 1219, 1221, 1240, 1241, 1243, 1244, 1245, 1248, 1251
Hong River 0363
Hongzi Lake 0386
Hopei. *See* Hebei
Ho-shi Corridor. *See* Hexi Corridor
Houzhou 0750
Hsian. *See* Xian
Hsun-chou-fu. *See* Xunzhou
Hu Diaoqing, Yunnan 0118
Hu River 0397
Huai He 0202, 0364, 0386, 0734
Huang Hai 0387
Huang He 0022, 0050, 0202, 0264, 0313, 0358, 0359, 0367, 0368, 0370, 0384, 0387, 0391, 0400, 0401, 0477, 0549, 0576, 0734, 1126
Hubei 0295, 1052, 1073
Hubei-Hunan Anhui Soviet 0872
Hunan 0348, 0526, 0588, 0667, 1052
Hung Kiang Gorges. *See* Hong Jiang Gorges
Hung River. *See* Hong River

Hungmen Commune 0340
Hunza 0164
Hupei. *See* Hubei
Hwai River. *See* Huai River
Ichang 0141, 0197, 0290
Ilchi 1242
Ili Valley 0658, 0811
India 0834, 0841, 0853, 0855, 0888, 0893, 0898, 1059, 1125, 1277
Ining. *See* Yining
Inner Mongolia. *See* Nei Mongol Zizhiqu
Irrawaddy River 0111, 0119, 0182, 0303, 0350, 0354, 0393, 0405, 0620, 1096
Jang River, Shanxi 0397
Japan 0882, 0894, 0931, 0932, 0933, 1151, 1267
Jaxarites River. *See* Syr-Daru River
Jehol 0467, 0520, 0610
Jianchang 0530
Jiangnan 0509
Jiangsu 0202, 0215, 0943, 0989, 1041, 1052
Jiangxi 0094, 1023
Jilong 0486, 1091
Jinan 0355, 0505, 1210
Jinghai 0636
Jinjiang 0397, 0564
Jinsha River 0250
Jinyuan 0248
Jinzhao 0788
Juding 0348
Kaifeng 0320, 0747
Kailan coal fields 0411
Kakarpo Ranges 0186
Kam 0175, 0301, 0303, 0830
Kangding 0289, 0317
Kansu. *See* Gansu
Kantze. *See* Ganzi
Kanzi 0232

Kaohsiung. *See* Gaoxiong
Karakorum 0002, 0053, 0087, 0150, 0158, 0163, 0177, 0191, 0265, 0296, 0673
Kashgar 0110, 0495, 1242
Kau Sai, Hong Kong 0953
Keelung. *See* Jilong
Keriya River 0258, 0260
Keshan 0714
Kham. *See* Kam
Khiangan Mountains. *See* Hingan Ling
Kiakhta 1154
Kiangshi. *See* Jiangxi
Kiangsu. *See* Jiangsu
Kiaotou Valley 0112
Kirin 0522, 0951, 1023
Kok-su River 0145
Koko Mountains 0154
Koko Nor 0547
Konka Risumgoghba. *See* Konkaling
Konkaling 0600
Kowloon 1064, 1187, 1215, 1216, 1251
Kuan-hsien. *See* Guan Xian
Kuangsi. *See* Guangxi
Kuangtung. *See* Guangdong
Kuldja. *See* Yining
Kuling. *See* Guling
Kulu Valley 0471
Kun-lotu Nor 0086
Kunlun Mountains 0154, 0177, 0265
Kunming 0168, 0463, 0758, 0883, 1238
Kunming Basin 0206
Kwangshi. *See* Guangxi
Kwangtung. *See* Guangdong
Kweichow. *See* Guizhou
Kwun Tong 1064
Labrang Monastery 0787

Ladakh 0164, 0466, 0641, 1242
Lahoul Valley 0471
Lampacao. *See* Langbeizhao
Lampienchau. *See* Langbeizhao
Lan Yu 0754
Lancang River 0250
Landak Tso. *See* Rakhas Landal Tso
Langbeizhao 0057
Lantau Island, Hong Kong 0760
Lantsang River. *See* Mekong River
Lanzhou 0414, 0463, 0787
Lao He 0127
Lao Ho. *See* Lao He
Lau Fau Son 0956
Leh 0108, 0641, 1242
Leotung. *See* Liaodong
Lhasa 0126, 0147, 0151, 0195, 0238, 0240, 0249, 0454, 0476, 0513, 0599, 0641, 0642, 0646, 0845, 1113, 1180, 1262
Liandong 0568
Liao River 0363, 0403, 0408, 1271
Lidang 0232, 0289
Lifan Zidu 0559
Lihua 0289
Lijiang, Yunnan 0112, 0116, 0118, 0153, 0790
Lijiang Mountains 0186
Likiang. *See* Lijiang
Ling-an. *See* Hangzhou
Lingyuin 0338
Lob Nor 0148, 0160, 0172, 0258, 0260, 0293
Lohit River 0136, 0298
Lolo area 0001, 0144, 0602, 0867
Lou-an 0172
Loyang 1204
Lu River 0178, 0408
Lu Shan 0094
Lungtan 0926

Place Name Index   341

Macao 0030, 0318, 0450, 0456, 0502, 0562, 0590, 0844, 0866, 1128, 1195, 1221, 1224
Macau. *See* Macao
Mae-mae-chin. *See* Mai-mai zhen
Mai-mai zhen 1154
Malaysia 1157
Mali-pa 0308
Manasarowar 0166, 0307
Manchuria 0096, 0135, 0140, 0212, 0318, 0366, 0403, 0413, 0416, 0427, 0507, 0522, 0523, 0552, 0568, 0573, 0606, 0617, 0621, 0622, 0628, 0664, 0669, 0673, 0674, 0676, 0696, 0697, 0715, 0723, 0726, 0736, 0761, 0861, 0868, 0902, 0923, 0928, 0931, 0933, 0934, 0941, 0944, 0945, 0946, 0948, 0949, 0950, 0951, 0980, 0981, 0992, 0998, 1009, 1028, 1037, 1040, 1068, 1075, 1078, 1082, 1093, 1106, 1107, 1122, 1130, 1132, 1144, 1147, 1261, 1267, 1271, 1276
Mangka. *See* Taibei
Manila 1187
Mansurwur. *See* Manasarowar
Maowuse Desert 0349
Masherbrum 0107
McMahon Line 0850, 0884
Mekong River 0175, 0182, 0185, 0193, 0250, 0303, 0346, 0393, 0504
Min River, Fujian 0123, 0330, 0363
Min River, Sichuan 0001, 0250, 0377, 0380, 0402, 0445, 0534
Minshan 0601
Minya Konka 0109, 0153, 0161, 0162, 0280, 0292
Mishimi Hills 0099, 0448
Moho 0134
Mongolia 0091, 0105, 0165, 0336, 0506, 0523, 0547, 0663, 0674, 0896, 0934
Mukden. *See* Shenyang
Muli 0600, 0602, 0650
Muztagh-shaksgam 0158
Naimankung 0781
Naitong Bridge 0867
Nam Tami Valley 0180
Namcho. *See* Tengri Nor

Nangong River 0098, 0352
Nanhung Canal, Puli, Taiwan 1018, 1019
Nanjing 0886, 0947, 1173, 1192
Nanking. *See* Nanjing
Nei Mongol Zizhiqu 0113, 0349, 0468, 0472, 0480, 0711, 0715, 0769, 1279
New Territories, Hong Kong 1248
Ngagong 0137
Ning District 0566
Ningbo 0497, 0516, 0574, 0592, 1221
Ningpo. *See* Ningbo
Ningwu 0248
North China Plain. *See* China, North
Omei Mountains 0240, 0618
Oosh-Turfan 1242
Orchid Islands. *See* Lan Yu
Ordos 0009, 0490, 0591
Outau. *See* Aotou
Oyuwan Soviet Area. *See* Hubei-Hunan-Anhui Soviet
Pai Hua River. *See* Bai Hua River
Pangong Lake 0200, 0294
Patang. *See* Batang
Pearl River. *See* Zhujiang
Peiho. *See* Bohai
Peiping. *See* Beijing
Peishan. *See* Beishan
Peking. *See* Beijing
Penghu 0479, 0819, 1273
Pescadores. *See* Penghu
Pien-lo. *See* Kaifeng
Pingchen 0926
Pingshan 010, 0157, 0613
Pingshui 0509
Plover Cove, Hong Kong 0351, 1243, 1244
Pooto. *See* Butou
Potala 1262

Puli City 1018, 1019
Puto. *See* Buto
Qara Shahr 0615
Quanzhou 1115
Quemoy 0815, 0885
Qiantang Jiang 0388
Qinfang River 0388
Qingdao 0661, 1198
Qingdezhan 1051
Qinghai 0636, 0715
Qinling Mountains 0010
Rakhas Landak Tso 0166, 0307
Red River 0363
Repulse Bay, Hong Kong 0305
Rome 0835
Rong Thu River 0298
Rudock 0152
Salween River 0119, 0137, 0193, 0303, 0346, 0393, 0504, 0510
Sam Hsin 1054
San Min 0358
Sang-san 0397
Sanjiang 0335, 0367
Segy-kol 0291
Shaanxi 0026, 0320, 0322, 0349, 0372, 0411, 0421, 0426, 0591, 0633, 0636, 0751, 0986
Sha-chiao 0963
Shaksgam 0164
Shan Shek Wan, Hong Kong 0760
Shandong 0026, 0207, 0242, 0355, 0387, 0410, 0444, 0505, 0563, 0661, 0696, 0986, 1132, 1136
Shangdu 0467
Shanghai 0007, 0167, 0497, 0516, 0666, 0667, 0670, 0742, 0920, 0947, 0982, 0999, 1034, 1072, 1115, 1163, 1167, 1181, 1193, 1211, 1213, 1221, 1222, 1232, 1247, 1252, 1256
Shangtu. *See* Shangdu
Shanhaikwan 0860
Shanshi. *See* Shanxi

Shantou 1042
Shantung. See Shandong
Shanxi 0026, 0070, 0188, 0236, 0248, 0320, 0324, 0397, 0411, 0423, 0591, 0633, 1065, 1136
Shataukon 1054
Shau Shui Lo, Kowloon 1064
Shegatze. See Xigaze
Shek Kip Mei 1165
Shek O Bay, Hong Kong 0306
Shensi. See Shaanxi
Shenyang 0065, 0568, 0617, 0628, 0676, 1034, 1214
Shihuiyao 1257
Shimshal Pass 0163
Shopawdo 0137
Shor Kul 0537
Shudao 1140
Shuizhou 1055
Shuli 0369
Shutao. See Shudao
Sichuan 0001, 0144, 0169, 0173, 0342, 0345, 0347, 0357, 0438, 0421, 0445, 0453, 0461, 0473, 0530, 0547, 0559, 0593, 0802, 0867, 0881, 0986, 0990, 1025, 1028, 1052, 1065, 1119, 1140, 1158
Simla 0850
Si-jiang. See Xijiang
Si-kang. See Xigang
Singan. See Xian
Sining. See Xining
Sinkiang. See Xinjiang
Sino-Afghan border 0892
Sino-Burmese border 0836, 0856
Sino-Indian border 0834, 0841, 0850, 0853, 0855, 0884, 0888, 0889, 0893
Sino-Mongolian border 0896
Sino-Soviet border 0834, 0836, 0837
Snow Mountains. See Da Xue Shan
Songhua River 0135, 1271
Soochow Ho. See Suzhou He

South China Sea 1088
Southeast Asia 1156, 1164
Soviet Union 0834, 0836, 0837, 0851, 0854, 0859, 0876, 0889, 0896, 1112, 1118, 1128, 1130, 1137
Stanley Bay, Hong Kong 0306
Starling Inlet 1054
Stilwell Road 1135
Subansir River 0098
Suiyuan 0636
Su-lo River 0172
Sungari River. *See* Songhua River
Sungpan Mountains 0240
Sungpan Pass 0113
Suzhou 0157, 0568, 0742, 0947
Suzhou He 0742
Swatow 1042, 1221
Syr-Daru River 0159
Ta-chien lu. *See* Daxian
Taching. *See* Dazhing
Ta-ch'ing. *See* Dazhing
Tai O 1054
Tai-an 0785
Taibei 0382, 0486, 1172
Taichu City. *See* Tainan City
Taichung City. *See* Taizhong City
Taidong Rift Valley, Taiwan 0709
Taihofu Fields 0416
Taihu Basin 0995
Tainan City, Taiwan 0469
Taipei. *See* Taibei
Taishan 0785
Taitung Rift Valley. *See* Taidong Rift Valley
Taiwan 0103, 0174, 0216, 0237, 0245, 0257, 0266, 0272, 0392, 0416, 0418, 0449, 0469, 0470, 0474, 0478, 0480, 0486, 0494, 0499, 0500, 0531, 0532, 0533, 0546, 0567, 0596, 0611, 0616, 0619, 0630, 0632, 0635, 0643, 0647, 0681, 0682, 0694, 0722, 0756, 0763, 0794, 0804, 0815, 0900, 0924, 0925, 0926, 0929, 0932, 0952, 0966, 0972, 0973,

0974, 0984, 0988, 1004, 1018, 1019, 1039, 1078, 1139, 1146, 1230, 1234, 1235, 1236, 1237
Taiyuan 1103
Taizhong City, Taiwan 1233, 1235
Taizhou Wan 0815
Taklamakan 0258, 1266
Takow. *See* Gaoxiong
Tali, Yunnan. *See* Dali, Yunnan
Tamshui. *See* Damshui
Taoyuan 0926
Tarim Basin 0130, 0241, 0253, 0260, 0291, 0407, 1111
Taron Valley 0303
Tatsienlu. *See* Daxian
Tazhen Archipelago 0815
Tenfoo Mountains 0149
Tengri Nor 0571
Tianjin 0122, 0371, 0396, 0568, 1035, 1117, 1163, 1203, 1221, 1250
Tianshan 0145, 0159, 0286, 0537, 0615, 0775, 0988
Tianshan Oasis 0148
Tibet 0027, 0052, 0079, 0089, 0091, 0092, 0093, 0099, 0102, 0114, 0115, 0124, 0125, 0126, 0128, 0129, 0136, 0151, 0155, 0156, 0166, 0175, 0179, 0180, 0181, 0183, 0187, 0190, 0192, 0201, 0205, 0206, 0225, 0228, 0232, 0250, 0265, 0281, 0284, 0288, 0289, 0298, 0299, 0300, 0301, 0336, 0344, 0345, 0405, 0406, 0437, 0448, 0471, 0485, 0492, 0493, 0503, 0504, 0513, 0514, 0517, 0518, 0548, 0570, 0571, 0575, 0582, 0583, 0603, 0612, 0627, 0631, 0634, 0637, 0646, 0649, 0651, 0672, 0674, 0688, 0729, 0744, 0767, 0778, 0787, 0792, 0793, 0796, 0814, 0827, 0874, 0875, 0905, 0934, 1020, 1125
Tienshan. *See* Tianshan
Tienshan Oasis. *See* Tianshan Oasis
Tientsin. *See* Tianjin
Tiger's Leap. *See* Hu Daoqing
Tinghao 0497
Tingyuanying 0668
Tinpak 0349
Tolo Channel 1244
Tong River 0001, 0121

Tongchuan 0210
Tongkou 0668
Tongkow. *See* Tongkou
Tongting Lakes 0588, 0667, 0995
Trans-Siberian Railroad 1137
Tsangpo. *See* Yarlung Zangbo Jiang
Tsa-rung 0183
Tsian San Nor. *See* Kun-lotu Nor
Tsinan. *See* Jinan
Tsitsihar 0610
Tso-no-gua-lapi. *See* Pangong Lake
Tsuenwan, Hong Kong 1048, 1064
Tsun-hua. *See* Cunhua
Tukiangyien 0380
Tung River. *See* Tong River
Tunhuang. *See* Dunhuang
Turfan Depression 0133, 0259
Turkestan 0171, 0191
Turkestan, East 0985
Turkestan, South 0258
Tus-alghutch-kol 0291
Urumali 1117
Urumchi. *See* Urumqi
Urumqi 0658, 0797, 1263
Victoria, Hong Kong 1117
Wakhan Corridor 0892
Wanch'uan. *See* Wanquan
Wangye 0668
Wanhsien. *See* Wanxian
Wanquan 0757
Wanxian 1159
Wei River 0188, 0372, 0997
Wei-chou. *See* Weizhou
Weihaiwei 0829
Weizhou 0377
Wu Jiang 0624, 1102

Wuchang 0935
Wuhan 0935, 0947, 1031, 1060
Wushan 0598
Wusong 0389, 0584
Wusung. *See* Wusong
Wutai Shan 1103
Wuxi 0947
Wuzhou 0524
Xian 0070, 0188, 0240, 0527, 1206, 1247, 1256
Xiangtan 1214
Xigang 0317, 0503, 0566, 1066
Xigaze 0570
Xijiang 0106, 0111, 0363, 0477, 0549, 0666, 1096
Xining, Gansu 0115
Xinjiang 0064, 0072, 0146, 0149, 0150, 0164, 0165, 0241, 0439, 0471, 0594, 0614, 0615, 0636, 0645, 0674, 0689, 0715, 0811, 0818, 0823, 1028, 1117, 1118, 1130, 1266, 1278
Xinjiao 0963
Xinxiang 0340
Xinzao Commune 1003
Xizang. *See* Tibet
Xuanhua 0410
Xunzhou 0095
Yalong Basin 0175, 0250
Yalu River 0949
Yalung Basin. *See* Yalong Basin
Yandang Shan 0657
Yangtze Gorges 0141, 0572
Yangtze River. *See* Changjiang
Yarkund 0146, 1242
Yarlung Zangbo Jiang 0098, 0100, 0136, 0137, 0147, 0156, 0184, 0298, 0328, 0352, 0353, 0379, 1097
Yaro-stampo River 0178
Yellow River. *See* Huang He
Yen Tang Shan. *See* Yandang Shan
Yenchang 0421

Place Name Index 349

Yenching. *See* Beijing
Yenti 1269
Yingcheng 1073
Yining 0145, 0484
Yu Chiang. *See* Yu Jiang
Yu Jiang 0095
Yuen Long 0956
Yumen 0414
Yung 0335
Yungang 0759, 0784, 0786
Yun-kang. *See* Yungang
Yunnan 0036, 0111, 0113, 0116, 0117, 0119, 0142, 0169, 0173, 0183, 0193, 0206, 0284, 0288, 0300, 0309, 0344, 0346, 0347, 0368, 0394, 0406, 0464, 0525, 0530, 0553, 0558, 0629, 0634, 0639, 0648, 0650, 0652, 0666, 0705, 0863, 0865, 0878, 0917, 0975, 0990, 1028, 1033, 1095, 1096, 1135, 1152, 1160, 1277
Yunnan-Burma Railroad. *See* Burma-Yunnan Railroad
Zhangzhau 1197
Zhangzhou 0788
Zhejiang 0283, 0509, 0521, 0543, 0815, 0943, 0986, 1023
Zhingdao 1221
Zhongdian 0648
Zhujiang 0378, 0748
Zhushan Islands 1280
Zikewai Observatory 0007